Tl [barcode] D1629616 ore

- 7 IIII 2015

FOOD ACCEPTABILITY

Proceedings of the University of Reading—Society of Chemical Industry Symposium on Food Acceptability, University of Reading, 14–18 September 1987 (to honour the work of Dr Roland Harper).

FOOD ACCEPTABILITY

Edited by

DAVID M. H. THOMSON

Department of Food Science and Technology, University of Reading, UK

ELSEVIER APPLIED SCIENCE
LONDON and NEW YORK

02OL89

ELSEVIER SCIENCE PUBLISHERS LTD
Crown House, Linton Road, Barking, Essex IG11 8JU, England

Sole Distributor in the USA and Canada
ELSEVIER SCIENCE PUBLISHING CO., INC,
52 Vanderbilt Avenue, New York, NY 10017, USA

WITH 97 TABLES AND 90 ILLUSTRATIONS

© 1988 ELSEVIER SCIENCE PUBLISHERS LTD

British Library Cataloguing in Publication Data
Symposium on Food Acceptability (1987):
University of Reading.
Food acceptability
1. Food. Preferences of man. Psychobiological
aspects
I. Title II. Society of Chemical Industry.
Food Group III. University of Reading,
Department of Food Science and Technology
IV. Thomson, David M. H. V. Harper, Roland
641'.01'9

Library of Congress Cataloging-in-Publication Data
Food acceptability
Bibliography: p.
Includes index.
1. Food—Sensory evaluation. 2. Food—Psychological
aspects. I. Thomson, David M. H.
TX546.F65 1989   664'.07   88-21187

ISBN 1-85166-256-1

Typeset and printed in Northern Ireland by The Universities Press (Belfast) Ltd.

Preface

Food acceptability, as a scientific discipline, is the study of human food selection. In essence, this means the study of context dependent behaviours which occur when food and consumer interact, in particular circumstances and at a particular moment in time. All possible combinations of food, consumer, circumstance and moment, would yield an extensive catalogue of behaviours, but a few obvious examples might include; selection of retail outlet (corner shop, supermarket, etc.), selection of restaurant, cafe, pub, etc., purchase decision in retail outlet, menu selection in restaurant, selection of food for preparation in the home, decision not to consume food purchased (waste), acceptance/rejection at point of consumption, acceptance/ rejection during consumption (plate waste), quantity consumed, frequency of consumption of a particular food, speed of consumption of a food, spontaneous verbal expressions of liking or disliking, spontaneous facial expressions indicating liking or disliking, to name but a few.

From the foregoing, it is readily apparent that food acceptability is a marriage, albeit an uncomfortable one, between food science and behavioural psychology. I describe the marriage as uncomfortable because these two disciplines are not, at first sight, very obvious partners; there are few food scientists who are expert in psychology and vice versa. Regrettably, there have been relatively few food professionals who have even recognised the need for input from behavioural psychology, perhaps due to incorrect interpretation of food acceptability in terms of the physico-chemical properties of foods rather than as a behavioural phenomenon.

Thankfully, the situation is now changing. In the United Kingdom, at least, government agencies and industry have declared their intention to invest in food acceptability. Our obligation is to develop the underlying sciences and the methods, which will allow us to accurately answer the necessarily practical questions posed by industry. Perhaps the most obvious of these might be phrased as follows: What are the attributes that consumers perceive in a particular new food product and in what ways will these combine to determine future purchase decisions? To answer this question is a tall order, but if we fall short of this, our theories and methods will be of little practical value to industry. The fact that so very few new products are ultimately successful in the market place is an indictment of the methods used and the answers supplied, so far. Clearly there is much to be done!

As far back as the late 1940s, there was a lone but persistent voice in the UK, proclaiming the importance of fundamental psychological principles in the study of food acceptability and in the sensory evaluation of foods. That voice belonged to Roland Harper. It was to honour this pioneering food psychologist that the University of Reading (Department of Food Science and Technology) and the Society of Chemical Industry (Food Group—Sensory Panel) held the International Symposium on Food Acceptability, from 14th to 18th September, 1987, in Reading, UK. The speaker and delegate lists constituted a veritable 'Who's Who' of the subject and this was indeed a most fitting tribute to the enormous contribution made by Harper over almost four decades .

The ensuing chapters are the proceedings of this symposium and include contributions from food scientists, psychologists, statisticians, consumer scientists, nutritionists and social scientists, reflecting the diversity and multidisciplinary nature of the subject; something which Dr Harper has consistently emphasised. In the first section of the book ('A Tribute to Roland Harper') Dr Derek Land gives an account of Harper's long and varied career (Chapter 1), and Professor Jan Frijters reviews his work (Chapter 2). Chapter 3, by Dr Harry Lawless, revisits odour description and odour classification; a topic in which Dr Harper found international acclaim. The remaining 33 chapters are dedicated exclusively to food acceptability. In spite of this, the reader is asked not to construe this as the definitive text on food acceptability (in my opinion such a book could not and should not be written yet), but more as a snapshot in time, showing the state of the science in 1987.

Many people contributed to the success of this symposium. I greatly appreciate the efforts made by the speakers, poster presenters and delegates, who made the symposium such a stimulating, lively and happy event. Behind the scenes, many others made a tremendous contribution, particularly Nadya Antonaides, Harry Nursten, Barry Pierson and Tony Williams (all members of the Organising Committee), also Teresa Church, Neil Gains, Stephen Green, Fenneke Outen-Leeftink and Sharon Shurey. On behalf of the Organising Committee, I would also like to thank the following for assistance and support given in many and various ways: Academic Press, Agricultural and Food Research Council, Brooke Bond Oxo, Cadbury Schweppes, Dalgety, Elsevier Applied Science Publishers, Express Foods Group, Leatherhead Food Research Association, Mobile Sensory Testing Services, Nabisco, Reading Scientific Services, J. Sainsbury, Tate and Lyle, Tecator, Tesco Stores, United Biscuits and Masaaki Yoshida. Finally, on behalf of all who attended the symposium, I offer thanks to those involved in the Conference Office and St Patrick's Hall, University of Reading and the Conference Secretariat, Society of Chemical Industry.

DAVID M. H. THOMSON
University of Reading
March 1988

Contents

Topic 3 *Factors Influencing Food Choice—Food Related and Situational Factors*

Topic 4 *Factors Influencing Food Choice—Consumer Related Factors*

Topic 8 *Applications and Innovations*

Topic 9 *Overview of Food Acceptability*

List of Contributors

PAULINE D. BAIRD

School of Home Economics, Robert Gordon's Institute of Technology, Queen's Road, Aberdeen AB9 2PG, UK

RODERICK BENNETT

School of Home Economics, Robert Gordon's Institute of Technology, Queen's Road, Aberdeen AB9 2PG, UK

ALAN J. BLAIR

Food Response Research, Department of Psychology, University of Birmingham, PO Box 363, Birmingham B15 2TT, UK

JOHN E. BLUNDELL

Biopsychology Group, Department of Psychology, University of Leeds, Leeds LS2 9JT, UK

DAVID A. BOOTH

Food Response Research, Department of Psychology, University of Birmingham, PO Box 363, Birmingham B15 2TT, UK

MICHAEL M. BOYAR

Leatherhead Food RA, Randalls Road, Leatherhead, Surrey KT22 7RY, UK

JAYA CHAUHAN

Department of Hotel Catering and Management, Oxford Polytechnic, Headington, Oxford OX3 0BP, UK

NICOLE DAGET

Nestlé Research Centre, Nestec Ltd, Vers-chez-les-Blancs, CH-1000 Lausanne 26, Switzerland

SALLE E. DARE

Science Policy Research Unit, University of Sussex, Falmer, Brighton BN2 9RP, Sussex, UK

DALE A. DOOLEY

Department of Psychology, Clark University, Worcester, Massachusetts 01610, USA

JENNIFER L. DRAYTON

Department of Marketing, University of Strathclyde, Stenhouse Building, 173 Cathedral Street, Glasgow G4 0RQ, UK

ROLF DUDEN

Federal Research Centre for Nutrition, Engesserstr. 20, D-7500 Karlsruhe 1, FRG

ANITA EVES

Leatherhead Food RA, Randalls Road, Leatherhead, Surrey KT22 7RY, UK

CLAUDE FISCHLER

Chargé de Recherche au CNRS, CETSAP, 44 rue de la Tour, 75116 Paris, France

JAN E. R. FRIJTERS

Department of Food Science and Department of Marketing and Marketing Research, Wageningen Agricultural University, De Dreijen, Bomenweg 2, 6703 BC Wageningen, The Netherlands

KEITH GREENHOFF

Mobile Sensory Testing Services, 54–62 Station Road East, Oxted, Surrey RH8 0PG, UK

MORAG HAMILTON

School of Home Economics, Robert Gordon's Institute of Technology, Queen's Road, Aberdeen AB9 2PG, UK

ROLAND HARPER

29, Harrow Court, Bath Road, Reading RG1 6JF, UK

ZENIA J. HAWRYSH

Department of Foods & Nutrition, University of Alberta, Edmonton, T6G 2M8 Canada

HEIDEMARIE HEINE

Federal Office of Plant Varieties, Osterfelddamm 80, D-3000 Hannover, FRG

ANDREW J. HILL

Biopsychology Group, Department of Psychology, University of Leeds, Leeds LS2 9JT, UK

EDWARD S. HIRSCH

Behavioral Sciences Division, Science & Advanced Technology Directorate, United States Army Natick Research, Development & Engineering Center, Natick, Massachusetts 01760-5020, USA

JILL R. JOHNSON

Department of Food Science & Nutrition, University of Minnesota, 1334 Eckles Avenue, St Paul, MN 55108, USA

DAVID KILCAST

Leatherhead Food RA, Randalls Road, Leatherhead, Surrey KT22 7RY, UK

JAMES D. LAIRD

Department of Psychology, Clark University, Worcester, Massachusetts 01610, USA

DEREK G. LAND

Taint Analysis & Sensory Quality Services, 8 High Bungay Road, Loddon, Norwich, NR14 6JT, UK

HARRY T. LAWLESS

S. C. Johnson & Son Inc., Racine, Wisconsin 53403, USA

DOUGLAS B. MACDOUGALL

AFRC, Institute of Food Research, Bristol Laboratory, Langford, Bristol, BS18 7DY, UK

HALLIDAY J. H. MACFIE

AFRC, Institute of Food Research, Bristol Laboratory, Langford, Bristol BS18 7DY, UK

DAVID W. MARSHALL

Department of Agricultural & Food Marketing, University of Newcastle upon Tyne, Newcastle upon Tyne, NE1 7RU, UK

HARALD MARTENS

Norwegian Computing Center, N-0314 Oslo 3, Norway

MAGNI MARTENS

Norwegian Computing Center, N-0314 Oslo 3, Norway

NORBERT MAUS

Department of Psychiatry, University of Göttingen, von-Siebold-Str. 5, D-3400 Göttingen, Federal Republic of Germany

JEAN A. MCEWAN

Department of Food Science & Technology, University of Reading, Whiteknights, PO Box 226, Reading RG6 2AP, UK

HERBERT L. MEISELMAN

Behavioral Sciences Division, Science & Advanced Technology Directorate, United States Army Natick Research, Development & Engineering Center, Natick, Massachussetts 01760-5020, USA

CLIVE B. MONCRIEFF

AFRC, Institute of Food Research, Bristol Laboratory, Langford, Bristol BS18 7DY, UK

HOWARD R. MOSKOWITZ

Moskowitz/Jacobs Inc., Valhalla, New York 10595, USA

GEOFFREY R. NUTE

AFRC, Institute of Food Research, Bristol Laboratory, Langford, Bristol BS18 7DY, UK

PETER A. M. OUDE OPHUIS

Department of Marketing & Marketing Research, Wageningen Agricultural University, Hollandseweg 1, 6706 KN Wageningen, The Netherlands

ROSE MARIE PANGBORN

Department of Food Science and Technology, University of California, Davis, CA 95616, USA

RICHARD D. POPPER

Behavioral Sciences Division, Science & Advanced Technology Directorate, United States Army Natick Research, Development & Engineering Center, Natick, Massachusetts 01760-5020, USA

VOLKER PUDEL

Department of Psychiatry, University of Göttingen, von-Siebold-Str. 5, D-3400 Göttingen, FRG

EINAR RISVIK

Norwegian Food Research Institute, PO Box 50, N-1432 Aas/NLH, Norway

PETER J. ROGERS

Biopsychology Group, Department of Psychology, University of Leeds, Leeds LS2 9JT, UK

HOWARD G. SCHUTZ

Department of Consumer Sciences, University of California, Davis, CA 95616, USA

MARGARET R. SHEEN

Department of Marketing, University of Strathclyde, Stenhouse Building, 173 Cathedral Street, Glasgow G4 0RQ, Scotland, UK

RICHARD SHEPHERD

AFRC, Institute of Food Research, Norwich Laboratory, Colney Lane, Norwich, NR4 7UA, UK

JOEL L. SIDEL

Tragon Corporation, 365 Convention Way, Redwood City, CA 94063, USA

JAN-BENEDICT E. M. STEENKAMP

Department of Marketing and Marketing Research, Wageningen Agricultural University, Hollandseweg 1, 6706 KN Wageningen, The Netherlands

JACOB E. STEINER

Department of Oral Biology, The Hebrew University, 'Hadassah' Faculty of Dental Medicine, PO Box 1172, Jerusalem, 91-010 Israel

DAVID A. STEVENS

Department of Psychology, Clark University, Worcester, Massachusetts 01610, USA

HERBERT STONE

   Tragon Corporation, 365 Convention Way, Redwood City, CA 94063, USA

DAVID M. H. THOMSON

   Department of Food Science & Technology, University of Reading, Whiteknights, PO Box 226, Reading RG6 2AP, UK

HANS C. M. VAN TRIJP

   Department of Marketing & Marketing Research, Wageningen Agricultural University, Hollandseweg 1, 6706 KN Wageningen, The Netherlands

ANNE TUNALEY

   Department of Food Science & Technology, University of Reading, Whiteknights, PO Box 226, Reading RG6 2AP, UK

HELY TUORILA

   Department of Food Chemistry & Technology, University of Helsinki, SF-00710, Helsinki, Finland

ZATA M. VICKERS

   Department of Food Science & Nutrition, University of Minnesota, 1334 Eckles Avenue, St Paul, MN 55108, USA

ANTHONY A. WILLIAMS

   Sensory Research Laboratories Ltd, 4 High Street, Nailsea, Bristol BS19 1BW, UK

Topic 1

Tribute to Roland Harper

Chapter 1

Roland Harper—Pioneer Food Psychologist

DEREK G. LAND

Taint Analysis & Sensory Quality Services, 8 High Bungay Rd, Loddon, Norwich, NR14 6JT, UK

My job, in this opening talk, is to set the stage. I am very pleased and indeed honoured to be the one to tell you something about Roland, the man and his background, before you hear a more scientific analysis of his contribution to current knowledge of perception of food, and the resulting behaviour, from two eminent psychologists, Jan Frijters and Harry Lawless. I shall try to do this from the way my own personal contact has developed, rather than in strictly historical sequence.

CAMBRIDGE MEETING, AND EC

It has been my privilege to know him for almost 24 years as a colleague and close friend. He has also, at various times, been teacher, advisor, interpreter and entertainer. We first met near Cambridge, in the old stables of Anstey Hall, a former stately home taken over by the Ministry of Agriculture, Fisheries and Food. The stables had been adapted as soil analysis laboratories, in which a group of us, overflow from the Low Temperature Research Station (LTRS) in Cambridge, were doing research into several aspects of food quality. The Director of LTRS (E. C. Bate-Smith, now in his late 80s, and another largely unsung, but far-sighted pioneer in Food Science), had known Roland for some years, and brought him along to talk about possible collaboration in my work on flavour and off-flavour.

Many years before, EC had realised the importance of taste and flavour to the acceptance of food, and some work had been done, mainly on off-flavour, by chemists. He also realised the importance of what Roland, a psychologist, had been saying about the need for objectivity in the behavioural measurement of flavour; although the term behavioural science was almost unknown in food science in the UK in those days. I had had some experience of measuring flavour: EC saw that it was essential to have *both* the skills to manipulate and measure the chemicals which gave rise to flavour, *and* the skills to measure the behaviour which results from perception, if we were to understand food acceptance. He therefore invited Roland to come and talk about collaboration.

This was my second contact with a psychologist in relation to perception. The first, a couple of years earlier, was Jack Harries, another pioneer, although at the time I thought he was just a statistician. This meeting, backed by enthusiastic support from EC, was the start of a very stimulating and rewarding period of close collaboration, which actually started in September 1964 in Norwich.

Although this was new to me, it was a 'déjà vu' phenomenon for Roland, for earlier he had both worked in Norwich, and had been involved in multidisciplinary food perception research.

BEGINNINGS—COLOUR IN MANCHESTER AND WEATHER IN NORWICH

Roland is a physicist by original training. After taking his BSc at the University of Manchester, he took an MSc in psychology, which, even in those days, bridged the faculties of arts and sciences. His thesis already dealt with perception, in this case, colour constancy. Over 30 years later he was to return to Manchester to be honoured with a DSc. In early 1939 he joined the Meteorological Office, which depended entirely on visual perception, and was moved to Norwich. In 1943 he was mobilised into the RAFVR as part of the job.

READING—CHEESE, FEEL AND WORDS

In 1946, after demobilisation, he joined the University of Reading at Shinfield, or NIRD (National Institute for Research in Dairying) as it is still best known internationally, rather than by its current name of Institute of Food Research, Reading Laboratory. He immediately became involved in what I believe was the first example of multidisciplinary research between physicochemical and behavioural scientists on food. In 1938 another pioneer, George Scott-Blair, started what he later called psycho-rheological studies related to dairy products, by using samples of rubber and other materials to distinguish between levels of firmness, the main criterion by which the ripeness of cheeses was judged by the cheesemasters. Roland joined him, and used the techniques in extensive studies of cheese texture, which earned him his PhD.

These studies included setting up what must also have been one of the first mobile testing laboratories in the UK. This was used to take measurements where the cheeses were being made, matured and tested by the skilled cheesemakers; for this was the only practicable way to obtain relevant data from both them and from the cheeses. The data were used in the first ever food application of the now routinely used multidimensional, or multivariate statistical techniques, in the form of factor analysis. However, unlike present day applications, this pioneering work was done entirely by means of mechanical calculators, and it took about 3 months to do all the analyses.

He also made his first venture into the use of words as sensory data, but more of this anon.

INTERNATIONAL CONTACTS

This period also allowed Roland to establish international connections, an example of which is his letter of 1948 to L. L. Thurstone, who made a major contribution to perceptual scaling, and whom Roland had first met at a British Psychological Society meeting in Edinburgh Roland realised the importance of not being restricted to contacts with the very small number of people working on perception in the UK, or even in Europe. He has always seen a wide range of international contacts as essential for all who are involved in research, and this is wise counsel.

However, as frequently happens to pioneering activities, unless they produce instantly applicable results, financial support was removed and Roland had to move elsewhere.

LEEDS—WOOL, WORDS AND FOOD

He then joined the Department of Psychology at the University of Leeds in 1950. Here, with a heavy teaching load, he applied his interests to what were local perceptual problems in the wool weaving industry, where streakiness was one of the quality attributes he studied. However he maintained his interest in food related perception, as reflected by his paper to *Nature* on 'Attitudes to vegetables', and made further forays into the use of words to describe what are perceived attributes of food. In this, his wife, Anne, pursued the daunting task of extracting all the food-descriptive words from the 200 000 words in the Concise Oxford Dictionary. He was also involved in several unpublished industrial projects, including one which identified what consumers perceived as the difference between butter and the very restricted variants of margarines available at that time. That market has been revolutionised since then, and I am sure some of Roland's results have contributed to the enormous improvement in sensory quality of what we now know as 'yellow spreads'.

MORE FEEL IN THE STATES

In 1961–62, he paid a sabbatical visit to the USA, where he worked with S. S. Stevens, whose 'Power Law' for a time almost displaced the Weber–Fechner Law in psychophysics. This provided an opportunity, in a very active psychophysical environment, to use magnitude estimation to measure the firmness of rubber samples, previously used for cheese studies at Reading.

GAMBLE?

When Roland came to Cambridge to meet me he was established as a senior lecturer in Leeds. Together with EC we successfully made a case for a 3-year, extendable Civil Service Fellowship. To his great credit, and probably against his better judgement, Roland resigned his post to accept this temporary job which would allow him to carry out full-time research into the description of odour, which is of course, the major variant of flavour.

NORWICH AGAIN—MORE WORDS AND SMELLS

This was the start of what was for me, and I think also for him, a very stimulating, exciting and, for most of it, a happy 3-year collaboration between a very broadly based chemical botanist (EC, much more than a phytochemist), a physical psychologist (Roland, much more than a psychophysicist), and a bio- turned flavour chemist (me). We were joined later by a young botanist (Nerys Griffiths) in what proved to be an extensive analysis of the nature of odour classification, the development of a comprehensive and balanced set of chemically defined and stable odour stimuli, and a system of quantitatively describing them in a highly discriminating manner, which could be used by both experts or lay people. It is very similar to what was marketed some years later as QDA.

A start was made in one room in a temporary building at the fledgling University of East Anglia, for our 'new' premises in Norwich, a derelict prefabricated school, were not yet habitable; Roland's enormous collection of reprints and files had to be used from the garage of his new home. One of the early lessons we learnt was although at first we seemed to be able to communicate well, we rapidly found that we used words and language in different ways, even in a narrow specialised field. It probably took at least 6 months before we could really communicate properly. Multidisciplinary research requires much more time and tolerance to learn to work together, and this is a lesson from which I have certainly benefited.

MISTAKES AND COLLAPSE

I believe we achieved a lot over that 3-year period from 1964 to 1967, but we did make mistakes. The biggest of these was to lose sight of the need to publish as we went on, as small bites rather than the more coherent 'platefuls' which we had in mind. None of us had envisaged the radical and rapid change in environment which was to occur after EC had retired, such that all work on a very extensive and sound data-base was rapidly terminated, the extension to the fellowship was no longer possible, and Roland found himself with no means of continuing. Nerys and I also had to stop work on the data. The consequence of these changes was that sadly, much of that work has never been published properly, although some indications of what is still there have been given; these have been shown in the multivariate relationships within the set of odours, within the set of odour descriptors, and their correspondence across both experienced and lay responses.

INTERNATIONAL WANDERING

This was the start of what I think of as Roland's wilderness period. After several months he obtained an FAO assignment to Chile, where he spent 6 months teaching the application of sensory methods as part of a programme to improve food quality. I am sure he will have thrown himself into it with typical enthusiasm, and learnt a lot about the problems there, but the isolation from workers and main-stream developments in his field, and the frustration of not being able to harvest what had been so thoroughly and painstakingly sown in Norwich, must have been heartbreaking to both Roland and Anne. After another, shorter, break, he took an appointment as visiting Professor in the Psychology Department at Thessalonika, in Greece. This was headed by one of his old students from Leeds, and he was at least involved with some psychophysics. Towards the end of this period he was about to take up a lectureship in New Zealand, when the opportunity arose to return to Reading, first as a Leverhulme Senior Fellow, and eventually as Reader.

RETURN TO READING—MORE WORDS AND SMELLS

Thus the wheel turned full circle, and he was able to resume research, albeit with a heavy teaching load. In research, he again took up a number of aspects of his main interest, the qualitative and quantitative measurement of the behaviour which is the expressed response to what is perceived. The last few years of teaching and doing research through research students, and with visiting workers have been a happy return, and, although now retired, he still maintains a very active interest in all that is related to the field.

STANDARDS

This brief account would be incomplete without mention of some other points. First, his widespread international interests, where he is a compulsive communicator in writing with workers in many countries. He has also made long standing and substantial contributions to standardisation of sensory methodology in both International Standards, and in those produced by the American Society for Testing and Materials.

LESSONS

What then can we learn from him and his experiences? On the negative side, he has often said, in great frustration 'Never try to do anything for the first time'. Many people have found that being a pioneer is not easy, for those who have the power to facilitate pioneering research are usually too ready to say no, rather than take a risk. And, if you start a pioneering path, it is all too easy for administrators to change in mid-stream, and, as Roland found to his cost, the consequences to the pioneer can be disastrous. The open season, when the time is ripe for a particular piece of pioneering, often only comes when good fortune brings certain people and conditions together, often after long preparation. However, the window usually closes very rapidly, and the closed season frequently and inevitably follows. These cycles are a very disruptive element in almost all research, especially that which is long term and seen by those in power as speculative rather than as a sound investment for the future. I just wonder how far science would have advanced without these pioneers.

On the positive side, there are two pearls of wisdom from him which I would like to share. The first is perhaps rather misleadingly mundane. When we were designing experiments and procedures in Norwich we always used to pilot them on ourselves. We rapidly learnt that if there was a way of not following instructions, or misinterpreting them, Roland would use it, to our great annoyance. He is the most facile evader of instructions that I know. However, he taught us to ensure that instructions to assessors, or to anyone else, were not only clear and unambiguous, but that it is necessary to check that they are being followed as you wish them to be. It is very easy to assume that responses are what, in fact, they are not. This was a very important lesson. It is even more important now that on-line collection of sensory data is becoming commonplace.

The second is not only more general, but much more important. I was often highly amused when, on asking Roland what he thought about something, he would say: 'How do I know what I think "till I

see what I say" ', and then go off to his typewriter, returning later with
an extensive and thorough comment on the question. It was many
years before the wisdom of this dawned on me. The discipline of
putting a view, case or even a comment down in writing as a means of
clarifying it, balancing pros and cons, and finally distilling it into a
concise and unambiguous written, and then spoken, form is one from
which we can and should all benefit. The time required is not wasted,
for the contrast between that wise, civilised, and educated result, and
instant rhetoric is indeed striking.

SALUTE

Thank you Roland, for these, and all the many other things you have
taught me, and for the contributions which you have made for all. You
are indeed a wise, farsighted and courageous pioneer. We all wish
you, and Anne, your steadfast partner through all the ups and downs
of your career, a long, happy and healthy retirement.

Chapter 2

A Review of Roland Harper's Research in Psychology and Food Science

JAN E. R. FRIJTERS

*Department of Food Science & Department of Marketing and
Marketing Research, Wageningen Agricultural University, De
Dreijen, Bomenweg 2, 6703 BC Wageningen, The Netherlands*

INTRODUCTION

During the last 40 years Dr Roland Harper has devoted his energy to
the study of sensory assessment of foods and the psychology of food
acceptance. He has addressed a large number of questions related to
different issues in this field, but he has been concerned with three
areas in particular. These are: (1) policy issues and priorities in food
perception and food acceptance research, (2) the rheology of foods
and other materials, such as wool, and, (3) the classification and
description of odours. Dr Harper has authored or co-authored about
70 papers, two books and one monograph. The first book *Odour
Description and Odour Classification* (1968a), is co-authored with E.
C. Bate Smith and D. G. Land. The second book, *Human Senses in
Action* (1972) provides a concise review of the knowledge of sensory
perception. The monograph, entitled *Psychological and Psychophysical Studies of Craftmanship in Dairying* (1952), contains a review of
the psychorheological literature on foods and a report of Harper's own
experimental investigations on discriminability between objects
differing in perceived firmness.

Dr Harper is a pioneer in our field. He was the first psychologist in
Europe to transfer theoretical concepts from the study of sensory
perception to applied problems in the sensory evaluation of foods. In

11

an era in which the food industry put a heavy emphasis on the technology of food production and processing in order to increase the quantity of output and lower the costs per unit, he continuously stressed the need for the scientific study of food acceptance. Dr Harper has pointed out numerous times, that a good understanding of sensory and other factors determining food selection and eating behaviour is essential in product optimization, from both consumer and producer standpoints. Fortunately, this is now recognized by leaders in industry and policy makers at universities and research institutes. The study of the psychology of food acceptance has reached its current stage of maturity to a large extent because of the vision and perseverance of scientists like Dr Harper. His writings and research have contributed to a better understanding of the potentials of experimental psychology and psychophysics for food science and the food industry. Like leaders in other scientific disciplines, his impact can be seen by the extent to which he has inspired other scientists and students to adopt psychological methods in food research. In view of his contributions to our field, it is a privilege for me to review the work of Dr Roland Harper.

OVERVIEW

As already mentioned, Harper directed his attention to three key areas. Throughout the whole of his long career, Harper has attempted to explain the basic principles and methods of psychophysics to the non-psychology community involved in food science, food production and marketing. In his research he has shown how these can be applied fruitfully in sensory analysis and the assessment of food acceptability. In the early period, from 1946 to 1950, he and his primary co-worker, M. Baron, addressed issues related to the sensory perception of foods and other materials, including cheeses, rubber and bitumen. This work was carried out at the National Institute for Research in Dairying, University of Reading (now the Institute of Food Research, Reading Laboratory). Between 1950 and 1964 Harper was a Senior Lecturer in Industrial Psychology at the University of Leeds where he investigated taste, odour as well as touch and kinaesthesis. Since 1964 the focus of his research has been odour perception with an emphasis on description, classification and individual differences.

FOOD ACCEPTABILITY AND SENSORY ANALYSIS

Harper's interest in food applications of psychophysics dates back to 1946 when he, for several years, was engaged in the study of the skills of cheesemakers and graders (e.g. Harper, 1953, 1961). Obviously, he was fascinated by the fact that these craftsmen were apparently able to apply their senses of touch and kinaesthesis to arrive at quality judgements. The general line of work in this area had been initiated some years previously by G. W. Scott-Blair (e.g. Harper, 1953), who had himself come into contact with D. Katz, a German psychologist who studied the skills of testbakers (e.g. Katz, 1938). So, the primary angle from which Harper approached the area was a psychophysical one, which is not surprising considering that he had been trained academically both as an experimental psychologist and a physicist. Later, he gradually developed a much wider view of the scope of the psychological issues involved in food-related behaviour. One can find descriptions of the various kinds of contributions that could be made by psychology in a number of his publications. There are a number of essays on the role of psychology in the study of food acceptance, for example, in Harper (1950b, 1954, 1960 and 1963b). Another example is given in a paper entitled: *Psychological Aspects of Food Acceptance, with Special Reference to Feeding the Underprivileged.* (Harper, 1961). Because of the present relevance of the issues mentioned in that article, these are quoted here:

Problems of food acceptance can be approached from a number of different points of view involving different levels and orders of complexity. The following list indicates a few of the relevant approaches:
1. The study of human sensitivities including taste, smell and sight and their relation to food habits and preferences.
2. Establishing the main dimensions, or systematic variables affecting human food responses. These include a descriptive approach through commonly accepted language, the expert assessment of foods, physical, chemical and biochemical analyses, and the collection of systematic information about human likes and dislikes.
3. The direct survey of food habits as a source of factual information which may be used for a variety of purposes, including the delineation of individual, regional and national differences and the changes of these.

4. The study of factors underlying spontaneous changes.
5. The study of factors associated with deliberately inducing changes in food habits in the light of various pressures including the need for improvements in nutritional practice.
6. The study of interdependence of the various types of information noted above.

In 'The psychologist's role in food-acceptance research' (Harper, 1962*a*) the psychological study of food acceptance is conceptually divided into four technical areas of research: sensory-descriptive, the instrumental-objective, the affective and a category called 'contingent influences' comprising: individual differences, the effects of special knowledge and experience, serial influences and biases in judgement, sensory interactions, group differences, and social influences. This classification should be valued in hindsight, because a general adoption of this structure has proven to be beneficial in directing and designing studies and experiments.

A well-known contemporary American experimental psychologist, Francis J. Pilgrim, produced a most informative schematic treatment of the determinants of food acceptance (Pilgrim, 1957). This model clearly positions the factors to be studied by psychophysiological psychology, sensory psychology, social psychology and the psychology of learning and behaviour modification. The affective value of a particular food item is central in Pilgrim's food-acceptance model, because that is what ultimately governs approach-avoidance behaviour. Harper has given thought to the nature of the variables, and the relationships between them, which form the sensory basis of hedonic value and how this may be related to the physicochemical attributes of a food item. He developed a scheme specifying these variables and their inter-relationships (Harper, 1964, 1972, p. 40). A version modified by himself (Harper, 1981) is given in Fig. 1. In this scheme the physicochemical variables characterizing a particular food item are related to the sensory variables, not only in an orthodox psychophysical sense evolving from structuralism, but also in a functionalistic way. The latter was achieved by including the sensory pathways and central physiology involved. In addition to presenting a more dynamic outlook on stimulus–response relationships, the scheme highlights the distinction between different kinds of relationships. On the one hand these are the *psychophysical* relationships between

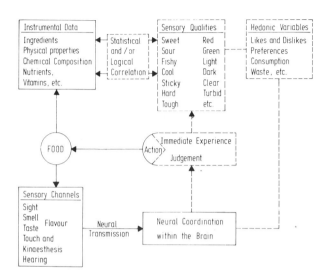

Figure 1. Harper's scheme relating physical, sensory and affective variables associated with foods (Harper, 1981).

stimulus-attributes and sensations of a complex percept. On the other, there are the relationships between those sensations and hedonic variables, such as likes and dislikes, preferences, food-waste and amount consumed. The latter can be called *psychohedonic* ones, because these contain two kinds of psychological variables. Making a formal distinction between psychophysical and psychohedonic relationships, both conceptually and experimentally, seems to be appropriate. A complete description, in terms of isolated sensations of a complex sensory percept generated by a particular stimulus (food or chemical component), is a description of a decomposed internal stimulus representation. However, a psychological model explaining the affective experience associated with such a percept must include the separate sensations as basic elements or determinants. Efforts to explain sensory preferences on the basis of physicochemically or instrumentally determined variables directly have not been very successful so far, because the sensory variables themselves are often ignored.

In addition to his efforts in defining the psychological issues of food-acceptance in a conceptual sense, Harper has always been experimentally and methodology oriented in his outlook and research. He has relentlessly tried to increase the understanding of non-psychologists of the classical psychophysical approach and the psychology of judgement. For example, in 'Psychophysical relationships and their study' (Harper, 1950a) a review of experimental methods to study sensory discriminability is given; Weber's and Fechner's laws are discussed and the 'constancy phenomena' described. This paper contains also a number of proposals as to how some of the classical psychophysical methods, well established in experimental psychology, can be applied in the area of sensory evaluation of foods. In view of the present status of the field, characterized by the heavy emphasis on statistics and statistical testing procedures, these proposals have not lost their importance. In 'Fundamental problems in the subjective appraisal of foodstuffs' (1955), Harper deals with some psychological principles of judgement in the style of Guilford's classical book *Psychometric Methods* (1954). In this paper he pointed out the extent to which judgemental factors can influence experimental results, and again indications were given for improvement of experiments in sensory analysis and evaluation. The reader's attention is focused especially on factors affecting judgements, such as training and experience, the influence of irrelevant characteristics, serial and position effects, marking labels, knowledge of results and expectation.

Although the effects of cognitions and attitudes on hedonic food-response, and the mechanisms of acquisition of food likes and dislikes, have not been the main focus of Harper's work, he has stressed the necessity for the study of food attitudes and attitude change. In 'Some attitudes to vegetables and their implications' (Harper, 1963a) a number of food-attitude surveys were reviewed in which the hedonic rating scale was used. In another review paper, the nature of monotony in food was discussed (Harper, 1966a). It was pointed out that monotony is not identical to frequent repetition, but that the monotony an individual experiences in a particular feeding regimen is determined by the state of mind of the individual and by variables related to the context in which the foods are served. It was concluded, amongst others, that frequency of serving does differentially affect the liking for food items: foods that are generally liked (e.g. sweets and desserts) will be the most resistant to the effects of monotony, whereas those that are least liked (e.g. canned meats) will be most affected.

PSYCHORHEOLOGICAL RESEARCH: THE SENSORY
PERCEPTION OF FLOW AND DEFORMATION

Many experiments in sensory analysis of foods are condemned to produce results which are difficult to interpret from a strictly theoretical point of view, even before they have been carried out. Apart from the lack of full control over the subjects' behaviour in an experimental setting, there are a number of other more important reasons why this is so. Firstly, a complete description of the physicochemical attributes of a food, to be obtained by physical and instrumental analysis, seems to be impossible in most cases because of the large number of such attributes present. Technically speaking, this means that a subject responds to an incompletely defined stimulus-object. Secondly, even if it were possible to assess all thinkable physicochemical variables of a particular foodstuff, the experimenter frequently does not know precisely which of these are active in stimulating one or more of the sensory modalities (i.e. the difference between distal and proximal stimulus has not been specified). Thirdly, even if the relevant attributes were known, prediction of the perceived sensory qualities and their intensities would require an extensive body of sensory physiological and sensory psychological knowledge. Such knowledge in the areas of visual and auditory perception is more substantive than that in the chemical senses. However, the situation in the area of what has been named 'texture perception' is even worse. Harper (1968) described this area as being still 'pre-Newtonian' in 'Texture and consistency from the standpoint of perception: some major issues'. One reason for this undesirable situation seems to be that the sensory physiology involved in the perception of touch, pressure and kinaesthesis, is, to a large extent, unknown. Another reason undoubtedly is the limited number of known psychophysical relationships between physical texture attributes of fluids or solid materials, and corresponding well-defined sensations. This is unfortunate, since the perceived textural attributes contribute substantially to the hedonic value of most foods.

With little insight into the psychophysics and with sparse understanding of the causative mechanisms of sensory texture perception, fundamental studies are almost impossible. In the ultimate hope of at least being able to make predictions about the perceived food-texture attributes, correlative studies are usually designed. In the food science literature, studies of this kind are called instrumental-subjective texture research; measurements of deformation obtained by instruments are correlated, or statistically associated in order to estimate the intensities of sensations. This may be a laborious exercise depending on the number of variables in both sets. Factor Analysis, heavily promoted in psychology by Thurstone (1947), is a technique by which the search for associative and causative relationships between the two sets of variables can be achieved. Soon after its introduction it was applied by Harper. His 1948 and 1949 studies on physical and sensory attributes of Cheshire cheese were the first applications of this technique on foods. Since then, numerous others have been published (see Martens & Russwurm, 1983 for a recent list). In 1948 a factor analysis of six instrumental variables assessed on Cheddar cheese was reported. Three factors emerged: hardness, springiness and hardening (Harper & Baron, 1948), explaining 74% of the total variance. After this encouraging result a more comprehensive study on Cheshire cheese was carried out. Originally twelve instrumental variables and six sensory attributes were assessed, but in the analysis four instrumental variables were omitted. The factor structure contained four orthogonal factors (Harper & Baron, 1950a). An almost identical repeat study carried out a year later, resulted in a five factor structure (Harper & Baron, 1951a) of which the first four were identical to the four factors from the 1948 study. This excellent agreement and other methodological issues were extensively discussed in two other papers (Harper & Baron, 1951b; Harper, 1956a). To demonstrate the use of the technique of factor analysis for other scientific disciplines, he and a number of colleagues carried out a study on a set of textural and electrical variables of plastics (Harper et al., 1950). This study, called 'The application of multiple factor analysis to industrial test data', is the first application of factor analysis in physics.

In addition to these studies, attention was paid to some issues regarding the judgemental process involved in food texture perception. Consistency and discriminative abilities of professional cheese graders in judging firmness, flavour and overall quality of cheese appeared not to be exceptional. It was shown that practice rapidly improved the judgemental consistency of lay persons (Harper & Baron, 1950b). A first effort to relate some physical measure of firmness (steel ball pressure) to firmness as perceived by pressing with the thumb, was reported in 1949. A high degree of association between these two measures was found (Harper & Baron, 1949; Harper & Baron, 1951b). In two other theoretical papers (Harper,

1947, 1949), Harper reanalysed rheological data published earlier by Scott-Blair & Coppen (1942, 1943). Two of the materials investigated in these studies were bitumen and vulcanized rubber. Using Probit Analysis, psychometric functions were fitted for discrimination of firmness as assessed by deformation between finger and thumb, so that the number of psychophysical parameters estimated for the different materials could be compared. Some of the main conclusions were:

(1) More than one form of physical parameter may be involved in the experience called 'firmness'. Both elasticity and viscosity contribute to this sensation.
(2) Points of subjective equality of the firmness of two samples defined in a physical and in a perceptual sense do differ.
(3) There is a higher sensitivity for discrimination between two soft samples than there is for discrimination of firm ones.
(4) There are pronounced differences between individuals with respect to their discriminal sensitivities of tactile firmness.

In a study similar to the early cheese studies Harper *et al.* (1958) investigated some sensory factors affecting the quality judgement of wool tops. Subjects handled the samples with and without seeing them and with and without wearing gloves. Judgements by touch alone were as good as those based on the combined use of touch and vision. It was also shown that the skill of precise tactile difference judgement can be acquired rapidly and it was found that the initial level of performance does not give reliable information about the final level that can be obtained (cf. Harper, 1962*b*).

Another theoretical article, 'Psycho-rheology of foodstuffs' (Harper, 1953) summarizes Harper's rheological studies and puts these in a wider scientific context. A less technically written article entitled, 'Texture and consistency from the standpoint of perception: some major issues' (Harper, 1968), gives a description of the state of the art in sensory assessment and psychophysics of texture related to foods. In this paper a list of 60 texture/consistency descriptors is mentioned. This list was derived by screening the Concise Oxford Dictionary for flavour terms; a tedious job that was performed by Mrs Anne Harper in 1955. To illustrate the range available, the following selection is given (see Harper, 1968, p. 16): Chalky-Crisp-Doughy-Firm-Flaky-Fleshy-Floury-Flabby-Greasy-Hard-Juicy-Lean-Limp-Lumpy-Mushy-Oily-Powdery-Ripe-Rotten-Rubbery-Sandy-Short-'Sleepy'-Slimy-Slushy-

Soft-Springy-Sticky-Syrupy-Tender-Thick-Thin-Tough-Treacly-Viscous-Watery-Waxy-Woody.
During his sabbatical leave Harper stayed at Harvard University with S. S. Stevens, where a study was undertaken to investigate the scalability of subjective hardness (Harper & Stevens, 1964; see also Harper, 1974). Because softness and hardness are the opposite in a physical and linguistic sense, an investigation was carried out to determine whether this is also the case from a perceptual point of view. The study was carried out using magnitude estimation and cross-modality matching. It was confirmed that subjects were able to judge the inverse of hardness as well as hardness itself. The scales for softness and hardness were inversely related. Differences in exponents for power functions of hardness determined with different ratio scaling procedures were reported. The exponent obtained by magnitude estimation was 0·8. For the function obtained by matching perceived hardness to force of handgrip, it was 0·42. The results showed that the exponents of the power functions obtained were different for the different estimation techniques. In discussing the results, Harper noted that multidimensionality of the rubber specimens might be the cause of this discrepancy. Matching perceived hardness to loudness, for example, may involve physical attributes other than direct estimation of sensory magnitudes.

An interesting general issue relevant in scaling sensations is the existence of an upper threshold of the dynamic range of a sensory modality. Each system must have a lower and an upper limit for its activity. In the case of the psychophysics of hardness perception, physical hardness of a certain material may further increase above an already high value, but the corresponding subjectively perceived hardness may not. Harper & Stevens (1964) proposed a modification of the power law, which was already modified before by Stevens & Stevens (1960) in order to incorporate the absolute threshold. To adjust also for the ceiling threshold, it is conceivable that the power law may take the form

$$I = k((S - S_0)/(S_\mathrm{u} - S))^b \qquad (1)$$

where I is the perceived strength, k is a constant which is specific for that system, S is the physical value of a stimulus, S_0 is the absolute threshold value, S_u is the upper threshold value and b is the exponent.

ODOUR DESCRIPTION AND CLASSIFICATION

In the structuralistic view on the nature of the contents of human consciousness, sensory percepts are thought of as being composed of sensations. Accordingly, it is supposed that percepts can be broken down into these elements when the observer takes an analytical attitude. Language is considered to be a proper vehicle for identification of these sensations, which means that the existence of a one-to-one correspondence is postulated between a certain descriptor and a certain sensation. One of the basic issues in perceptual analysis of odour percepts is the determination of the basic odour sensations and how these are verbally coded. Harper and colleagues have addressed this issue from an unorthodox viewpoint (cf. Harper, 1966b; Land et al., 1970). Traditionally odour sensation classifications such as, for example, Zwaardemaker's, Henning's, Crocker & Henderson's and Amoore's were developed with the specific aim in mind to use as few descriptors as possible (see especially Chapter 2 in Harper et al., 1968a). Classifications like these are based on the assumption that any odour percept can be reconstructed by perceptual synthesis of a number of basic odour sensations. Harper et al. took a different approach in that they started out with the list of flavour descriptors used in common language previously collected by Harper (1956a). This list, containing about 300 terms, revealed the following facts about the way odours are described by laymen (Harper et al., 1968b): (1) a complete absence of abstract terms; (2) definition primarily in terms of specific substances or process; (3) an emphasis upon undesirable or off-flavours; (4) the necessity for clarification of meaning by reference to a particular context. From these 300 terms 69 odour descriptors were selected. These were presented on a questionnaire to a number of respondents under the instructions to judge each term for its meaningfulness to describe an odour impression. This procedure ultimately resulted in the well-known list containing the 44 qualitative descriptors described in 'Odour qualities: a glossary of usage' (Harper et al., 1968b). The next step was to find a selection of single chemicals which represented certain odour qualities, i.e., certain substances which elicit odour percepts of the lowest complexity possible. An ideal reference or standard chemical is one which can be characterized by one sensory quality only. The purpose of such standards is to function like sensory anchors for the verbal descriptors.

Like Schutz (1964), (see also Harper, 1964), the approach followed was to select a number of chemicals which were subsequently rated on the intensity of each of the 44 odour attributes. In two experiments, 53 odorants were evaluated and their profiles for experienced and inexperienced subjects were given in 'A glossary of odour stimuli and their qualities' (Harper *et al.*, 1968*c*). One important fact to realize is that the odour percept for single chemicals of high purity is never simple, their profile never consists of a single attribute. Although, in this exercise the concentration-specificity of the profile was not taken into account, a list of compounds best representing a particular odour quality or odour qualities was compiled by a panel of seven experienced assessors (Harper, 1975). Although the development of the glossaries was the main aim of the experiments discussed, attention was paid to individual differences in odour description and liking/disliking of odours. These issues are extensively discussed in Harper (1979) and Harper (1981). A possible explanation is that there are systematic differences between individuals in the nature and sensitivity of peripheral coding in response to the same odorant.

It is clear from a historical perspective that these experimental studies have been a major breakthrough in the systematic study of perceptual analysis of odour percepts. These contributions have been the basis for the study of odour profiling of various kinds in a variety of investigations. Most of these studies are of an applied nature in the sense that they are directed at the odours of certain types of foods. Some early applications are by, for example, von Sydow *et al.* (1970) Clapperton (1973, 1974), and Williams (1975). A study that can be considered as a theoretical follow-up of this research was carried out by Dravnieks *et al.* (1978), who proposed an extended list of descriptors, since he felt that the original 44 terms failed to distinguish between odours which are recognizably different. Harper's later views on the status of this field can be found in Harper (1982.)

Dr Lawless will review the present status of odour description and classification in his contribution to the symposium.

ACKNOWLEDGEMENT

The author is indebted to Dr Daniel M. Ennis for reviewing an earlier version of the manuscript.

REFERENCES

Clapperton, J. F. (1973). Derivation of a profile method for sensory analysis of beer flavour. *J. Inst. Brew.*, **79**, 495–508.

Clapperton, J. F. (1974). Profile analysis and flavour discrimination. *J. Inst. Brew.*, **80**, 164–73.

Dravnieks, A., Bock, F. C., Powers, J. J., Tibbetts, M. & Ford, M. (1978). Comparison of odours directly and through profiling. *Chem. Sens. & Flav.*, **1**, 191–225.

Guilford, J. P. (1954). *Psychometric Methods*, 2nd edn. McGraw-Hill, New York.

Harper, R. (1947). On the firmness of soft materials. *Am. J. Psychol.*, **60**, 554–70.

Harper, R. (1949). On the firmness of deformable materials. *Am. J. Psychol.*, **62**, 553–9.

Harper, R. (1950a). Psychophysical relationships and their study. *Research*, **3**, 350–5.

Harper, R. (1950b). Assessments of food products. *Food*, **19**, 371–5.

Harper, R. (1952). Psychological and psychophysical studies of craftmanship in dairying. *Brit. J. Psychol.*, *Monograph Suppl. No.* 28, Cambridge University Press, Cambridge.

Harper, R. (1953). The psychorheology of foodstuffs. In: *Foodstuffs: their Plasticity, Fluidity and Consistency*, ed. G. W. Scott-Blair. North-Holland, Amsterdam, pp. 116–24.

Harper, R. (1954). The assessment of foodstuffs. *Dairy Ind.*, **19**, 307–12.

Harper, R. (1955). Fundamental problems in the subjective appraisal of foodstuffs. *Appl. Stat.*, **4**, 145–61.

Harper, R. (1956a). Factor analysis as a technique for examining complex data on foodstuffs. *Appl. Stat.*, **5**, 32–48.

Harper, R. (1956b). The language of flavour. *Symposium on Problems of Perception*, British Psychological Society, Annual Conference, Manchester.

Harper, R. (1960). Food assessment and food acceptance as a psychological theme. *Occup. Psychol.*, **34**, 233–40.

Harper, R. (1961). Psychological aspects of food acceptance, with special reference to feeding the underprivileged. *Adv. Sci., Lond.*, **17**, 568–72.

Harper, R. (1962a). The psychologist's role in food acceptance research. *Food Technol.*, **16**, 70, 72–3.

Harper, R. (1962b). The feel of things. *New Scientist*, **11**, 396–7.

Harper, R. (1963a). Some attitudes to vegetables and their implications. *Nature, Lond.*, **200**, 14–18.

Harper, R. (1963b). Contemporary psychology, food science and technology. In *Proc. 1st International Cong. Food Sci. and Tech*, Vol. 3, *Quality, Analysis and Composition of Foods*, ed. J. M. Leitch. Breach, New York, pp. 227–33.

Harper, R. (1964). The sensory evaluation of food and drink: an overview. *Lab. Pract.*, **13**, 599–604.

24   JAN E. R. FRIJTERS

Harper, R. (1966a). Monotony in food: A critical evaluation. *Royal Society for Health Congress*, Preprint. 21/66, pp. 22–6.

Harper, R. (1966b). On odour classification. *J. Food Technol.*, **1**, 167–76.

Harper, R. (1968). Texture and consistency from the standpoint of perception: some major issues. In *Rheology and Texture in Foodstuffs*, Monograph No. 27, Society of Chemical Industry, London, pp. 11–28.

Harper, R. (1972). *Human Senses in Action*. Churchill Livingstone, London.

Harper, R. (1974). On the sensory evaluation of compliant materials. In *Sensation and Measurement—Papers in honour of S. S. Stevens*, ed. H. R. Moskowitz, B. Scharf & J. C. Stevens. Reidel, Dordrecht, pp. 91–8.

Harper, R. (1975). Some chemicals representing particular odour qualities. *Chem. Sens. & Flav.*, **1**, 353–7.

Harper, R. (1979). Likes and dislikes and preferences in man: methodological and other considerations. In *Preference Behaviour and Chemoreception*, ed. J. H. A. Kroeze. Information Retrieval, London, pp. 123–30.

Harper, R. (1981). The nature and importance of individual differences. In *Criteria of Food Acceptance: How Man Chooses What He Eats*, ed. J. Solms & R. L. Hall. Forster Publishing, Zuerich, pp. 220–37.

Harper, R. (1982). Sensory methods. In *Food Flavours: Part A. Introduction*, ed. I. D. Morton & A. J. Macleod. Elsevier, Amsterdam.

Harper, R. & Baron, M. (1948). Factorial analysis of rheological measurements on cheese. *Nature, Lond.*, **162**, 821.

Harper, R. & Baron, M. (1949). Cheese grading: mechanical properties compared with quality assessed subjectively. *J. Dairy Res.*, **16**, 363–7.

Harper, R. & Baron, M. (1950a). The relationship between the mechanical properties of Cheshire cheese and grader's judgments. *Dairy Ind.*, **15**, 407–10.

Harper, R. & Baron, M. (1950b). Studies on the nature of subjective judgements in cheese grading. *J. Dairy Res.*, **17**, 329–35.

Harper, R. & Baron, M. (1951a). A further study of the relationship between the mechanical properties of Cheshire cheese and grader's judgments. *Dairy Ind.*, **16**, 45–9.

Harper, R. & Baron, M. (1951b). The application of multiple factor analysis to tests on cheese. *Brit. J. Appl. Phys.*, **2**, 35–41.

Harper, R. & Stevens, S. S. (1964). Subjective hardness of compliant materials. *Quart. J. Exp. Psychol.*, **16**, 204–15.

Harper, R., Kent, A. J. & Scott-Blair, G. W. (1950). The application of multiple factor analysis to industrial test data. *Brit. J. Appl. Phys.*, **1**, 23–9.

Harper, R., McKennell, A. C. & Onions, W. J. (1958). The subjective assessment of quality in wool tops. *J. Text. Inst.*, **49**, 126–40.

Harper, R., Bate-Smith, E. C. & Land, D. G. (1968a). *Odour Description and Odour Classification*. Churchill, London.

Harper, R., Land, D. G., Griffiths, N. M. & Bate-Smith, E. C. (1968b). Odour qualities: a glossary of usage. *Brit. J. Psychol.*, **59**, 231–52.

Harper, R., Land, D. G., Bate-Smith, E. C. & Griffiths, N. M. (1968c). A glossary of odour stimuli and their qualities. *Perf. Essent. Oil. Rec.*, **59**, 23–31.

Katz, D. (1938). The judgements of test-bakers. *Occup. Psychol.*, **12**, 138–48.

Land, D. G., Harper, R. & Griffiths, N. M. (1970). An evaluation of the odour qualities of some stimuli proposed as standards for odour research. *Flavour Ind.*, **1**, 842–6.

Martens, H. & Russwurm, H. (1983). *Food Research and Data Analysis.* Applied Science Publishers, London.

Pilgrim, F. J. (1957). The components of food acceptance and their measurement. *Am. J. Clin. Nutr.*, **5**, 171–5.

Schutz, H. G. (1964). A matching standards method for calculating odour qualities. In *Basic Odour Research Correlation*, ed. R. L. Kuehner. *Ann. N.Y. Acad. Sci.*, **116**, 517–26.

Scott-Blair, G. W. & Coppen, F. M. V. (1942). The subjective conception of the firmness of soft materials. *Am. J. Psychol.*, **55**, 215–29.

Scott-Blair, G. W. & Coppen, F. M. V. (1943). The estimation of firmness in soft materials. *Am. J. Psychol.*, **56**, 234–46.

Stevens, J. C. & Stevens, S. S. (1960). Warmth and cold: dynamics of sensory intensity. *J. Exp. Psychol.*, **60**, 183–92.

Thurstone, L. L. (1947). *Multiple Factor Analysis.* University of Chicago Press, Chicago.

Von Sydow, E., Anderson, J., Anjou, K., Land, D. G. & Griffiths, N. M. (1970). The aroma of bilberries (*Vaccinium myrtillus* L.) II. Evaluation of the pressed juice by sensory methods and by gas chromatography and mass spectrometry. *Lebensm. Wiss. Technol.*, **3**, 11–17.

Williams, A. A. (1975). The development of a vocabulary and profile assessment method for evaluating the flavour contribution of cider and perry aroma constituents. *J. Sci. Food Agric.*, **26**, 567–82.

Chapter 3

Odour Description and Odour Classification Revisited

HARRY T. LAWLESS

S. C. Johnson & Son, Inc., Racine, Wisconsin 53403, USA

ABSTRACT

*Since the publication of the now classic treatise on odour classification in 1968 (*Odour Description and Odour Classification, a Multidisciplinary Examination*) by Harper, Bate-Smith and Land, several developments in the industrial literature and in cognitive psychology have provided new perspectives on the perceptual task of describing and classifying odours. These approaches include (1) recognition of the similarities among the tasks of odour classification, concept learning and category formation; (2) recognition of the importance of hierarchical classification in the structure of any knowledge system; (3) the extraction of reasonably sized sets of general odour descriptors; and (4) the trainability and utility of general odour descriptor schemes in analytical sensory evaluation of fragrances. These approaches provide a theoretical framework for further study and for potential development of a universal system for odour description. Sub-themes of this presentation will include (1) impediments to the development of consensus odour classification schemes and (2) new questions and issues that are raised by the perspectives outlined above.*

INTRODUCTION

An enduring problem in both applied sensory evaluation and the psychology of olfaction has been the lack of consensus concerning a

scheme for classifying and describing odours. This was noted by
Harper *et al.* (1968), who stated '. . . odour classification continues to
be an intellectual challenge since for so long it has remained unsolved
and the facts disputed' (pp. 14–15). More recently, Engen (1982)
stated, 'although there has been some progress in developing a
common glossary (Harper *et al.*, 1968), no agreement has been
reached on the question of what odors are similar or how many classes
there might be among the estimated 400,000 odorous substances' (p.
8). This is still largely true today. While many practical schemes have
been worked out for the descriptive analysis of the fragrance and
volatile flavour of specific products, there still is no generally
agreed-upon system that encompasses the entire world of odours.
Such a scheme is still desirable, in that it would provide a basis for
communication among sensory evaluation professionals, perfumers,
flavourists, and product developers, it would provide an orienting
framework for the interpretation of consumer descriptions, and it
would provide a basis for advancing our understanding of the
psychological processes involved in the qualitative differentiation of
smells.

My approach to this problem, like that of Harper *et al.*, has been
multidisciplinary. I have focussed on recent contributions in two main
areas—in experimental cognitive psychology and in the industrial
practice of fragrance description. To a large extent, I have been
searching for a way to restructure our thinking about the problem, in
order to frame new questions and to suggest new experimental
approaches.

ORIENTATION AND LOGICAL DISTINCTIONS

A fundamental assumption in this paper is that olfactory perception is
inseparably linked to a process of learning. Progress can be made by
avoiding a search for structurally or physiologically determined sets of
'primary odours' and asking instead how people come to arrive at
functionally defined sets of empirically useful schemes. This is not to
suggest that functionally defined categories may not have some
physiological substrate. In studies of colour vision, for example, there
is a correspondence of colour names to a theory of unique hues which
can be related in turn to the physiological tuning of neurons in the
visual system. In olfaction, we need the intermediate theory, and such
a theory must take into account the plasticity of odour perception.

Some blurring of logical distinctions is also necessary at this point. First, a discussion of odour description invites some interchangeable references to odour attributes and odour classes. This is excusable since attributes themselves often define classes. For example, the term 'two-legged and flightless' describes primates and is roughly synonymous with a delineation of the class itself. Second, in using a scheme of odour descriptors, the *applicability* of a term to a particular stimulus is easily confused with the *perceived intensity* of that attribute in the stimulus. No attempt will be made in this paper to resolve these distinctions, although they invite further critical inquiry.

Two important sub-themes will appear throughout this discussion. First, there are certain impediments to the construction of a universal and comprehensive odour description scheme. Some of these constraining factors may be transcended; some we may just have to live with. Second, as in the case of the two logical non-distinctions outlined above, certain fundamental issues remain in need of further experimental clarification.

CATEGORY AND CONCEPT LEARNING

One approach to olfactory learning concerns the idea that learning to use an odour descriptor is like learning a category or concept. A concept learning approach has recently been applied to the study of gustatory descriptors such as 'umami', by O'Mahoney and colleagues (O'Mahoney & Ishii, 1986). Categories have several characteristics (Lakoff, 1987). First, a category represents a collection of items. Second, category membership may be established by verbalized rules for inclusion, which specify critical attributes and the logical relationships among them. Third, categories may have a prototype or best example, or may at least include items which differ in the degree to which they exemplify good members of the group. Finally, categories have boundaries or minimum requirements beyond which the probability of inclusion becomes quite low. The characteristics of prototype and boundary can also be replaced by the idea that there is a probability density function in conceptual space which delineates the category. The gradient of probability slopes away from the prototype and approaches zero at the category boundary.

In terms of understanding odour quality, a useful question then becomes, 'How do we learn categories?' In general, category learning proceeds as a function of being given examples of items which do and do not belong. Given such examples, current psychological theory proposes that people abstract the features, critical dimensions or attributes along which items are similar (within the category) and dissimilar (across category boundaries). Useful categories have some set of features or perceptual dimensions, and limits along those dimensions such that items within a category have a higher degree of homogeneity (lower variance) or more shared features within the class, than the degree of homogeneity of collections of items which cross category boundaries (Hartley & Homa, 1981; Murphy & Wright, 1984).

We can now phrase a few questions within this framework to help approach the question of how people learn odour categories. First, are odour classes specifiable as a collection of perceivable (and pre- sumably reportable) features? There may be limits to the analogy in the case of odours. Several authors have suggested that odours are processed and remembered as coherent wholes (Gestalten) with relatively few analysable features (Engen & Ross, 1973; Lawless, 1978). However, these studies have employed untrained observers. After experience or training, odours can be perceived in a more analytic fashion and rated on the intensity or applicability of a set of descriptors, as illustrated below. One characteristic of increased expertise is a change in similarity judgements from consideration of global similarity to the ability to focus on specific dimensions of stimuli (e.g. Ward, 1986).

The literature on concept learning is somewhat distinct from the category learning literature. In concept learning, emphasis has been placed on how people learn the logical rules for grouping (e.g. Bourne, 1970). A question can be raised whether there are logical rules involved in odour classification. For example, the odour class 'green' may apply to both the smell of crushed vegetation and some of the notes characteristics of unripe fruit. For the most part, however, using odour terms is more likely a case of abstracting perceptual attributes and patterns or prototypes, than it is a logical verbal process. This represents a potential limitation on the applicability of the concept learning literature.

The psychological literature has some findings of relevance to the practical question of whether we learn odour descriptors and classes more effectively by means of prototypical examples or by means of many examples, allowing the observer in the latter case to figure out what the items have in common. This is germane to the methods chosen for training in descriptive analysis. Some investigators have relied on descriptor specification by means of single, well-defined reference standards, for example, in the work of Noble in wine aroma description (Heyman & Noble, 1987; Noble & Shannon, 1987). However, using visual stimuli, Homa and colleagues have repeatedly demonstrated advantages to learning categories by means of multiple examples (the more the better) as opposed to prototypes (e.g. Homa & Vosburgh, 1976; Homa & Cultice, 1984). Whether this principle generalizes to odours remains to be seen.

Several unanswered questions remain for future research. Do we extract a set of common features when learning an odour class or are the classes coherent Gestalten without analysable components? Do we infer what a prototype would be like, even if we aren't given a prototype to learn? Finally, what is the nature of the category boundaries? Are they sharp or fuzzy? If we model categories as a probability cloud in conceptual space, we can ask whether the probability gradient near the edges of the cloud are steep or shallow. Perhaps steepened gradients or increased category homogeneity are characteristics that separate fragrance experts from naive consumers (Murphy & Wright, 1984).

HIERARCHICAL ORGANIZATION

One approach to odour description is to consider all terms to be equivalent in their degree of generality or specificity, for example, the ASTM scheme for odour description popularized by Dravnieks (1985). Odours are related for the applicability of each of 146 descriptors. However, some terms may represent superordinate categories which encompass collections of other more specific descriptors. Hierarchies are in fact implicit in the act of categorization, which necessitates at least two levels of organization.

Most of our knowledge about things in the world is organized this way. For example, as children we learn about cars versus trucks, and then go on to organize the car category into specific brands and brands into models and so on. We also extend our tree structures upward, to learn about more abstract general categories, e.g. vehicles. An example of hierarchical description is the 'wheel' for wine flavour description which is actually a tree structure with three levels (Noble, et al., 1987).

The utility of such organization is appealing. For example, descriptive panellists in training are often unable to fractionate a complex odour or flavour into very specific components, e.g. to recognize a particular variety of orange peel flavour, but they may be able to agree that there is citrus character present (recognizing the broader class). Expertise may allow the accurate use of both more specific and more general terms (may ascend or descend the hierarchy). Second, much of the debate over the number of 'basic' or 'primary' tastes (four? five? many?) could be avoided by recognizing the utility of a superordinate category like sweetness, while leaving room for subcategorization, as suggested by physiological studies (Lawless & Stevens, 1983). Another potential application of hierarchical thinking is in the current debate over the meaning of 'warmed over flavour' in meat (see for example, Johnson & Civille, 1986; Lyon, 1987). Is this term a superordinate collection of attributes (e.g. cardboard, rancid, plus others) or a flavour that can be referenced to a single prototype?

BASIC LEVELS

To construct a scheme of useful descriptors, then, we can consider parallels to category learning and the potential utility of hierarchical organization. The question then arises for any fragrance description or any panel training exercise, at what level of the hierarchy are we operating? Are all levels equally useful?

One approach, suggested by the work of Eleanor Rosch, is to recognize that different levels of an hierarchical classification scheme have different psychological properties, and that some particularly useful levels are, in her terms, 'basic' (Rosch et al., 1976; Mervis & Rosch, 1981). Basic level terms have the following characteristics, among others: basic level groupings strike a balance between within-group homogeneity and between-group differentiation. They are terms learned first by children, the first words that come to mind in spontaneous conversation by adults, and form the common coinage of everyday speech. In various cognitive tasks such as verification of category membership, terms at this level are processed most rapidly in reaction time studies.

The basic level is appealing in its trainability and communication value. The potential for identifying a basic level of odour description brings up the question of whether we can extract, from the universe of applicable terms, a reasonably sized set of simple categories. In other words, can we cut across the odour classification hierarchy at a level that would facilitate the development of a trainable consensus scheme? Unfortunately, this enterprise runs squarely into several impediments, many of which were recognized by Harper *et al.* (1968). First, we tend to name odours for unique concrete objects, places and/or situations (naming by pointing). This tends to obscure the connections and similarities of odours and works against the establishment of meaningful superordinate groupings, forcing us to work at a low and complicated level of the hierarchy. Second, odour naming tends to involve idiosyncratic experiences and recollections, which is a limitation since the communication value of descriptors depends upon shared experiences and shared points of reference.

Another limitation concerns the channel capacity for information processing (Miller, 1956) which was noted by Harper *et al.* with respect to the ability of single individuals to identify odours. However, I would also suggest that our channel capacity influences the collective behaviour of olfactory scientists, and acts to inhibit our acceptance of any classification scheme which is complex. Historically, we've preferred simple schemes for classification with about seven (plus or minus two) categories, such as those of Linnaeus, Crocker and Henderson and Henning. We don't seem to like any schemes with 20 or 30 fundamental categories, yet a scheme of this complexity may be required for odours.

SOME RECENT PRACTICAL APPROACHES

In setting up a training programme for fragrance descriptive analysis panels, a tentative classification scheme of fragrance categories was required. This scheme illustrated the similarities and nuances of consumer product fragrances and built a common language base for communication among the panellists. The classification scheme also formed the basis for general descriptor scales in actual sensory analyses. The classes/descriptors were chosen on the basis of applicability, orthogonality, simplicity, unitary-ness and other criteria (Civille & Lawless, 1986). These classes are shown in Table 1 (column 1). At about the same time, sensory scientists at Philip Morris were

Table 1
Terminology comparison

Descriptive scheme	Principal component analysis
Woody/nutty	Woody
	Nutty
Minty	Cool, minty
Floral	Floral
Fruity (not citrus)	Fruity, non-citrus
Citrus	Citrus
Sweet (vanilla, vanillin, caramel, maple, maltol)	Brown (vanilla, chocolate, molasses)
Spice (brown)	Spicy
Green	Green
Herbal	Coconut, almond
	Caraway, Anise
Other	Animal, foul
	Solvent
	Burnt
	Sulphidic
	Rubber

using the 146-item ASTM descriptor scheme to evaluate several hundred fragrance compounds (Jeltema & Southwick, 1986). They then subjected the resulting data base to principal components analysis and extracted perceptual groupings from the intercorrelations of the 146 terms (also in Table 1 (column 2)). Given their different origins and rationale, the similarity of the two schemes is noteworthy. Furthermore, apparent points of departure are explainable on the basis of (1) inclusion in the ASTM scheme of off-notes, malodours, base notes and product-specific characteristics (e.g. burnt, sulphidic), and (2) the existence of 'boundary' fragrances like coconut or almond.

Even in the realm of perfumery, we can still see some encouraging correspondences. Recently, Brud (1986) polled perfumers and other members of the fragrance industry concerning physical reference standards to exemplify major fragrance categories. The categories are shown in Table 2, along with major categories based on multivariate analyses of perfumery compounds and terms by Chastrette *et al.* (1986). Points of departure from Table 1 may be understandable. Our scheme, like the Dravnieks' list which forms the basis of the principal component analysis groups, is based on the shared and everyday

Table 2
Perfumery terms

Chastrette et al. (1986)	Brud (1986)
Miel (honey)	
Musc (musk)	Musk
Animal	Animal
Menthe (minty)	
Camphre (camphor)	
Bois (wood)	Woody
Sylvestre (forest)	
Moisi (mouldy, musty)	Fungoid
Terreux (earthy)	Earthy
Ambre (amber, ambergris)	Amber
Ethere (ethereal)	
Vineux (vinous)	
Cireux (waxy)	Aldehydic
Hesperide (citrus, orange)	
Gras (fatty)	Fatty
Buileux (oily)	
Epice (spicy)	Spicy
Herbace (herbaceous)	Herbal
Balsamique (balsamic)	Balsamic
Rose	
Vert (green, grassy)	Green
Floral	Flowery
Fruite (fruity)	Fruity
Anise	Chemical

experiences people have with odours. The perfumer's groups, however, are based on the types of raw materials which form the building blocks of their trade. Thus it is not surprising to find a category like 'balsamic' in the perfumer's scheme, which carries dimensions of both 'sweet' (e.g. vanillin) and 'woody' in our scheme.

The correspondence of the general odour classification scheme to principal component dimensions supports its validity. A second encouraging finding is the trainability of such a scheme. After training, judges show greater consensus and lower variability in their use of the terms than people who are unfamiliar with the system (see Fig. 1). In addition, trained subjects show greater selectivity in their application of the general descriptors while consumers apply just about everything to every fragrance ('if it's on the ballot, it must be there', Fig. 2).

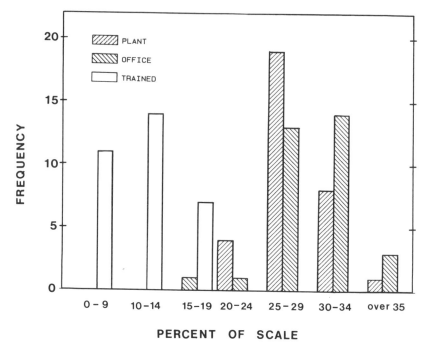

Figure 1. Standard deviations as percent of scale range are plotted in their frequency of occurrence in evaluations of ten consumer product fragrances on nine major descriptive attributes: spicy, sweet, fruity, citrus, green, woody, minty, herbal and floral. Ratings were made by three groups: a trained descriptive panel, and two groups of untrained employees used as consumer models (plant and office workers). Scales on which the trained panel had mean ratings of zero and hence zero standard deviations were omitted from the analysis.

   The general odour descriptor system has demonstrated its utility in a variety of applications, including production monitoring of fragrance quality, in selection of fragrance candidates and in surveys of competitive product fragrances. As an applied tool, questions arise as to the best methods for teaching such a system. Intuitively, it seems reasonable to build upon shared real-life experiences and to discuss the fragrance characteristics of actual product examples. Such a programme can be especially effective when paired with exposure to many examples of each major descriptive term from a reference library of fragrance materials. One goal is for panellists to transcend

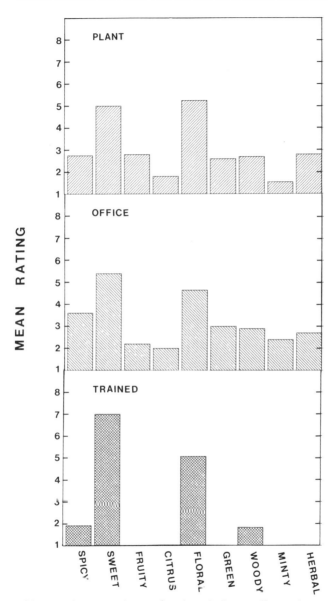

Figure 2. Mean ratings on nine major descriptive attributes (converted to nine-point scales) of the three groups on a powder-type consumer product fragrance. Trained panellists were more likely to discount an attribute as present, and give zero ratings.

their tendency to approach fragrance description as an exercise in object naming to work up the hierarchy toward the level of general descriptors. This is not to overlook, however, the advantages of also being able to work down the hierarchy, and develop expertise in the use of more specific fragrance descriptors. This is especially valuable if the panel's duties concern a delimited range of products.

SUMMARY AND FUTURE DIRECTIONS

Any attempt to produce a comprehensive consensus scheme of odour description and classification should take into account the impediments and unresolved issues discussed above. The impediments are primarily four: first, that odour naming tends to be object naming; second, odour naming tends to be idiosyncratic; third, the limits on our information processing mitigate against the acceptance of complicated schemes, and a certain level of complication may be necessary in the case of odours; fourth, in spite of the fact that much of our knowledge is organized hierarchically, a hierarchical odour classification scheme is not necessarily intuitive.

Several unresolved issues remain to be clarified by future research. First, if a classification scheme is based on culture and shared experiences, is there some large number of equally valid classification schemes based on the different experiences in different cultures or industries? Second, if there are different schemes, are they translatable? For example, a currently popular category of consumer product fragrances are the 'powdery' types, which is understandable to the consumer based on her experience with baby powders or talc. This term is nowhere explicit in our classification scheme although analytical inspection reveals that 'powders' are often combinations of sweet vanillin type odours with some lesser degree of floral, spicy and other items (see Fig. 2). Third, referring back to Rosch's definitions of basic levels, are the general odour descriptors basic levels, or perhaps one step superordinate to that? Further study may reveal psychological characteristics at each of the levels of a classification hierarchy.

Other issues deserve experimental attention. First, are judgements of 'similarity-to-prototype' (e.g. applicability scales) or are ratings of the perceived intensity, a better model? Second, what are the characteristics of odour categories with respect to the existence of prototypes, the nature of their boundaries and the degree of overlap (Lakoff, 1987)?

Finally, what are the most efficient methods of training, e.g. through the use of a single prototypical example or many examples as suggested by Homa's work? Given the psychological framework outlined in this paper, resolution of these issues may lead us to a better understanding of the nature of odour classification and description.

REFERENCES

Bourne, L. E. (1970). Knowing and using concepts. *Psychological Review*, **77**, 546–56.

Brud, W. S. (1986). Words versus odours: How perfumers communicate. *Perfumer & Flavorist*, **11**, 27–44.

Chastrette, M., Elmouaffek, A. & Zakarya, D. (1986). Etude statistique multidimensionelle des similarites entre 24 notes utilisees en parfumerie. *C. r. Acad. Sci. Paris*, **303**, (Serie II), 1209–14.

Civille, G. V. & Lawless, H. T. (1986). The importance of language in describing perceptions. *Journal of Sensory Studies*, **1**, 203–15.

Dravnieks, A. (1985). *Atlas of Odor Character Profiles*. American Society for Testing and Materials, Philadelphia. PA.

Engen, T. (1982). *The Perception of Odors*. Academic Press, New York.

Engen, T. & Ross, B. M. (1973). Long-term memory of odors with and without verbal descriptions. *Journal of Experimental Psychology*, **100**, 221–7.

Harper, R., Bate Smith, E. C. & Land, D. G. (1968). *Odour Description and Odour Classification: A Multidisciplinary Examination*. American Elsevier, New York.

Hartley, J. & Homa, D. (1981). Abstraction of stylistic concepts. *Journal of Experimental Psychology: Human Learning and Memory*, **7**, 33–46.

Heyman, H. & Noble, A. C. (1987). Descriptive analysis of commercial Cabernet Sauvignon wines from California. *American Journal of Enology and Viticulture*, **38**, 41–4.

Homa, D. & Cultice, J. (1984). Role of feedback, category size, and stimulus distortion on the acquisition and utilization of ill-defined categories. *Journal of Experimental Psychology: Learning, Memory, and Cognition*, **10**, 83–94.

Homa, D. & Vosburgh, R. (1976). Category breadth and the abstraction of prototypical information. *Journal of Experimental Psychology: Human Learning and Memory*, **2**, 322–30.

Jeltema, M. A. & Southwick, E. W. (1986). Evaluation and applications of odor profiling. *Journal of Sensory Studies*, **1**, 123–36.

Johnson, P. B. & Civille, G. V. (1986). A standardized lexicon of meat WOF descriptors. *Journal of Sensory Studies*, **1**, 99–104.

Lakoff, G. (1987). *Women, Fire and Dangerous Things. What Categories Reveal about the Mind*. University of Chicago Press, Chicago.

Lawless, H. T. (1978). Recognition of common odors, pictures and simple shapes. *Perception & Psychophysics*, **24**, 493–5.

Lawless, H. T. & Stevens, D. A. (1983). Cross adaptation of sucrose and intensive sweeteners. *Chemical Senses*, **7**, 309–15.

Lyon, B. G. (1987). Development of chicken flavor descriptive attribute terms aided by multivariate statistical procedures. *Journal of Sensory Studies*, **2**, 55–67.

Mervis, C. B. & Rosch, E. (1981). Categorization of natural objects. *Annual Review of Psychology*, **32**, 89–115.

Miller, G. A. (1956). The magical number seven plus or minus two: Some limits on our capacity for processing information. *Psychological Review*, **63**, 81–97.

Murphy, G. L. & Wright, J. C. (1984). Changes in conceptual structure with expertise: Differences between real-world experts and novices. *Journal of Experimental Psychology: Learning, Memory, and Cognition*, **10**, 144–55.

Noble, A. C. & Shannon, M. (1987). Profiling Zinfandel wines by sensory and chemical analyses. *American Journal of Enology and Viticulture*, **38**, 1–5.

Noble, A. C., Arnold, R. A., Buechsenstein, J., Leach, E. J., Schmidt, J. O. & Stern, P. M. (1987). Modification of a standardized system of wine aroma terminology. *American Journal of Enology and Viticulture*, **38**, 143-6.

O'Mahoney, M. & Ishii, R. (1986). Umami taste concept: Implications for the dogma of four basic tastes. In *Umami: A Basic Taste*, eds Y. Kawamura & M. R. Kare. Marcel Dekker, New York, pp. 75–93.

Rosch, E., Mervis, C. B., Gray, W. D., Johnson, D. M. & Boyes-Braem, P. (1976). Basic objects in natural categories. *Cognitive Psychology*, **8**, 382–439.

Ward, T. B. (1986). Classifying by learning disabled and nondisabled children: Use of overall similarity versus dimensional relations. *Bulletin of the Psychonomic Society*, **24**, 131-4.

Topic 2

Commercial Sensory Quality
and Grading

Chapter 4

Establishing a Sensory Specification

JOEL L. SIDEL

Tragon Corporation, 365 Convention Way, Redwood City, CA 94063, USA

ABSTRACT

Quality assessment of food products typically includes a combination of analytical and sensory measures. In order to establish an analytical or sensory specification it is necessary first to determine what will be measured and then how that measurement is to be achieved.

From a sensory perspective the answer to 'what should be measured' is relatively straightforward. We should measure aspects of the product which impact on that product's acceptability to the consumer. Thus, a meaningful sensory specification will identify important sensory attributes and acceptable tolerances around these attributes.

This chapter describes traditional and new alternative methods for establishing sensory specifications for foods and beverages.

INTRODUCTION

Quality, on a consistent basis and at a fair market price, is the foundation on which most manufacturers and suppliers promote their products. To achieve and maintain product quality requires a management commitment of financial and intellectual resources in the form of Quality Assurance (QA) and Quality Control (QC) functions. For many companies these are separate functions, each with a large staff of its own. Typical QA activities include development of product

43

specifications and methods for evaluating quality. QC typically concerns itself with monitoring product quality during the manufacturing process.

Of special interest to sensory evaluation is the development and evolution of methods and procedures supporting the QA and QC functions (Reece, 1979).

Sensory quality and the application of sensory principles to routine product maintenance have been discussed (Nakayama & Wessman, 1979; Wolfe, 1979; Williams & Atkin, 1983); however, the philosophical and methodological issues associated with establishing a sensory specification warrant further consideration.

HISTORICAL PERSPECTIVE

Prior to the most recent industrial revolution, product quality could be traced directly to raw ingredients and the skill of individual craftsmen. The advent of high speed machinery and mass production methods introduced additional complexities to developing and maintaining product quality. The explosive growth of consumer research has added yet another dimension; that of perceived product quality.

Industry's response to systematically measuring variables associated with processing and packaging developments was rapid and thorough. Statistical Process Control and Statistical Quality Control evolved into a major industry, with the ever present control chart as its sword and shield.

Response to incorporating consumer opinion has been less rapid, and certainly less systematic. This may be a function of the inherent difficulty of translating consumer information to useful feedback for manufacturing (Vello, 1987). Herein is the opportunity and the challenge for sensory evaluation. Harper (1983) and others (Sidel *et al.*, 1981, 1983; Sidel & Stone, 1986; Stone & Sidel, 1985) anticipated the increasing emphasis on consumer acceptability in specifying sensory quality. What is required is a more systematic approach, based on current sensory technology, which incorporates consumer information into the specification development process.

CURRENT METHODS

Traditional approaches to establishing product quality specifications that include sensory evaluation have their origin in quality grading systems. Such grading systems were usually developed cooperatively by universities, government agencies, and professional and technical organizations. Dairy products (Downs *et al.*, 1954), fermented beverages (Amerine *et al.*, 1959), fruit (Baten, 1946), and edible oil (Mosher *et al.*, 1950) are among the food categories for which standard grades and grading procedures are available. Unfortunately, as McBride (1979) demonstrated, quality grades do not always agree with consumer acceptance data.

Industrial companies developing specifications for a product rely on the technical knowledge of their product specialists. If consumer research data are available, it too may find its way into the final sensory specification; however, this is seldom done on a formal and systematic basis. A procedure utilizing consumer information was described by Vello (1987), using consumer opinion obtained from complaint letters. The letters were forwarded to the company's consumer affairs department for a reply, usually accompanied by coupons, a product replacement or a cash equivalent. If a product defect was mentioned, the information was routed to QA where the comments were tabulated. Formal analysis involved matching complaints with actual defect estimates from QC inspections and developing a complaint to defect ratio. This ratio was used as a measure of importance for the various defects. An obvious difficulty is translating consumer semantics into useful corrective action.

A CONSUMER BASED SENSORY SPECIFICATION

Consumer attitudes and perceptions are becoming increasingly important in determining sensory quality. It is appropriate that sensory evaluation, with its established body of principles and methods, contributes to the specification development process. Developments in acceptance optimization research (Horsfield & Taylor, 1976; Schutz, 1983; Sidel & Stone, 1983) and trained panel procedures (Stone *et al.*, 1974) made a significant contribution to achieving that goal (Perfetti, 1987).

Developing the Sensory Specification
Statistical Quality Control requires a product to be in conformity with a specification target and that the manufacturing process run between the lower and higher control limits (LSL and USL, respectively). Further, the limits must be reasonable in view of process capability

(Vello, 1987). This is also equally applicable to developing and monitoring a sensory specification. Process capability and its inherent variability is a critical component of product manufacture; therefore, the initial phase of sensory specification development requires an assessment of that variation.

Sensory Assessment of Manufacturing Variability

During manufacturing a variety of physical and analytical tests are routinely performed. The output of these analyses may be graphed in the form of $\bar{X}$ and R charts, representing the mean and range (respectively) for small sample sets obtained for analysis. Graphing these data over time is useful for identifying trends as well as any sudden shifts. A similar approach is possible for identifying means, ranges, variances, and trends related to sensory attributes. This phase of specification development is necessary for developing a meaningful data base that describes manufacturing trends and variability in terms of a product's sensory attributes. These data allow a sensory specification which realistically reflects manufacturing capability.

At the outset, a sample set is obtained that represents the range of normal production within and between manufacturing plants. Where seasonality is an issue, sampling is planned for different times of the year. It is important that the sample set should *not* be screened so that only the best possible product is studied; the sample set should represent a normal production range. Initially bench screening is used to select an array of products. Screening should include experienced evaluators from quality control and sensory functions. Samples representing reasonable extremes in the manufacturing process, and those representing different samples within those extremes are selected. Unusual and atypical samples, as well as those not perceptually different, are eliminated. A discrimination panel can be used to confirm sensory differences; however, it is an optional step. Typically about 8–9 different samples are selected when measuring production range. Descriptive analysis is used to characterize the products in quantitative terms (Stone *et al.*, 1974, 1980; Stone & Sidel, 1985). Judgements are of attribute intensity rather than product quality, and each attribute is scored on a graphic rating scale. The summative or quality grading scales typically identified with quality evaluations are avoided for reasons described by Sidel *et al.* (1981). No measure of attribute importance is available at this stage of specification development, as

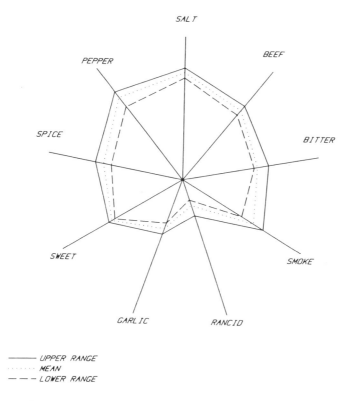

Figure 1. Example of manufacturing capability (attributes perceived on tasting).

these data are necessary only for establishing a sensory specification representing manufacturing capability.

For ease of comprehension, data are graphed on QDA plots. An illustration of a QDA plot demonstrating mean and range data is seen in Fig. 1. The test data in Fig. 1 are plotted on a circular graph. Similar graphs are prepared for all remaining sensory modalities. The graphic rating scale is analysed as a 60 point scale with the lower values occurring at the centre and higher scores toward the perimeter.

For sensory specification development, the highest and lowest mean for each attribute is graphed. This is similar in concept to the upper and lower limits seen in statistical quality control $\bar{X}$ and R charts. Some users elect to plot the mean $\pm 1 \cdot 0$–$1 \cdot 5$ standard deviations rather than the range. In either situation, samples are considered atypical of normal production if any sensory attribute is found to exceed the band around the mean. Figure 1 illustrates a number of conditions typical of specification studies. Some attributes have a small range, some exhibit a symmetrical difference around the mean and others do not. Range information will be used later with attribute importance data to develop the sensory specification. That products are different is typical and representative of normal production. Expecting no discriminable difference among samples is not realistic. A more pragmatic approach is to establish limits on production variation such that finished products are more similar to one another than they are different, and where perceived differences occur, their importance to acceptance is known.

Sensory Assessment of Attribute Importance

The information illustrated in Fig. 1 is useful for determining whether a production sample exceeds the upper and lower range limits on a sensory attribute. To stop here would imply that all attributes are equally important. Nothing could be further from the truth.

Acceptance prediction research (Schutz *et al.*, 1972) and our own client sponsored studies support the concept that sensory attributes contribute differently to acceptance scores. Therefore, the final step in establishing a sensory specification is to develop an acceptance prediction model. The model is based on ingredient and process variability and their relationship to manufacturing capability.

(a) Sample Selection

Developing a meaningful acceptance prediction model requires a diverse array of samples. A minimum of 10 different samples is recommended, but more is desirable. Samples are selected to be discriminably different and have a range of acceptance of 1·5 or more scale units (on the 9-point hedonic scale; Peryam & Pilgrim, 1957). Final hedonic scores should be reasonably distributed to avoid serious distortions of the data. The sample set also should include experimental samples that purposely exceed normal production extremes. For example, substantially reducing an ingredient may represent an extreme or unlikely occurrence; however, their implication on sensory acceptance should be studied.

(b) Sensory Analysis

Sensory descriptive analysis is used to fully characterize the entire sample set.

(c) Consumer Acceptance

Acceptance measures also are obtained for the entire sample set by a usage qualified panel of 100–150 consumers. Where a geographic difference is anticipated sufficient responses from each area are required. All consumers evaluate all samples in the study, using the 9-point hedonic scale. Samples are served in a monadic sequential order, balanced, as best as possible, for serving order and day. Seldom is the consumer given more than 4–6 samples in a session (lasting about 30 min), therefore evaluation of a sample set could take up to 4 days of testing.

(d) Sensory Acceptance Model

The data analysis is used to develop an acceptance prediction equation using consumer hedonic ratings as the dependent variable and QDA scores as the independent variable. Treatment of the data follows the recommendations published by Schutz (1983, 1987).

The first step in the analysis involves data reduction. Redundancies are expected when a comprehensive list of attributes is used to evaluate products. Multivariate techniques including Principal Components Analysis (PCA) are used to help select a smaller set of reasonably independent attributes which explain a sufficiently large portion of the descriptive differences among the products. Usually a large attribute list can be reduced by two-thirds without noticeable loss of information regarding product differences. A variety of criteria are used in final attribute selection, among them are QDA performance diagnostics, attribute factor loadings, and the univariate relationship with consumer acceptance.

The reduced attribute list represents a set of sufficiently independent variables which can be used in developing the multiple regression prediction equation. A number of equations are explored using one or more of the options available with regression procedures (e.g. Stepwise and Max R) standard to many computer programs. The multiple regression procedure results in a combination of variables and regression weights that best predict the dependent variable. We look for an equation that has a combination of highest R^2 (a measure of explained variance), smallest standard error of prediction, highest

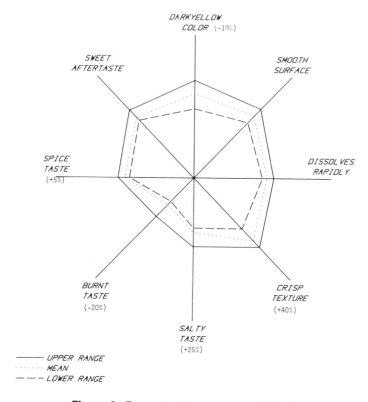

Figure 2. Example of sensory specification.

statistical significance, and exhibits no serious distortion of residuals. A variety of other standard diagnostic tests are also examined to assure results are reliable and not spurious.

Standardized regression coefficients (Beta) also are available from the analysis, and are compared to determine the relative contribution of each variable included in the prediction equation.

(e) Sensory Specification Model

Figure 2 is an illustration of a sensory specification integrating manufacturing capability data with an acceptance prediction model. Included in the sensory specification are attributes appearing in the prediction equation as well as those which we tried but did not add significantly to the model. Attributes accompanied by a percentage value are in the prediction equation. The percentage value is calculated from the standardized regression weights and represents the relative importance of the attribute to acceptance. Its sign is determined by its partial correlation. A positive sign indicates the attribute score adds to the predictive hedonic, whereas a negative one subtracts from it.

Physical and Chemical Data

The sensory specification model can be derived from sensory data alone or from a combination of sensory and analytical measures.

Analytical data are treated in the same way as the sensory. If a large number of analytical tests are used, the PCA procedure will help reduce that number. Acceptance prediction equations are developed based first on analytical variables and then on combinations of sensory and analytical variables.

In our experience models which include both sensory and analytical variables are usually statistically better than those using only sensory or analytical data. A different combination of variables, regression weights, and standardized regression weights can be expected from the combined sensory and analytical model.

APPLYING THE SENSORY SPECIFICATION

Output from the sensory specification development process includes identification of a smaller set of sensory attributes that represent the total set, definition of the normal production range for those attributes, a model describing in numerical terms the relationship between those attributes and consumer sensory acceptance, and a measure of relative importance for each attribute included in the model.

Once a sensory specification has been prepared, it is submitted to management for approval. Information from specification development is used to prepare a sensory scoresheet for QC that contains only the reduced attribute set. Fewer attributes result in a more efficient use of panel training and testing time.

The prediction equation allows for a simple computational task to determine the acceptance implication of perceptually different production samples. Attribute range data from the manufacturing capability study are tested with the model and final adjustments made to the sensory specification. These changes reflect the sensory importance of the attributes as well as production costs and capabilities. Also, they reflect an objective and systematic procedure for including consumer acceptance information in establishing the sensory specification.

Production samples exceeding the specification range are not in compliance, and are treated accordingly. Samples within the specification are used as reference standards for other QC panels and management review. Additionally, the model is used to assess the effect of ingredient and process change.

The sensory specification is used to identify important attributes which can be measured analytically, but currently are not. In some cases an analytical test is available, in others it must be developed. Finding useful sensory-instrumental relationships is not an easy task. These relationships appear to be multivariate rather than univariate. In this case a multivariate model-building approach, similar to that described above, is possible.

CONCLUSION

Sensory evaluation is a powerful resource with a variety of applications, in the commercial sector. Although its past has been dominated by product development efforts, its role in assessing product quality has been growing in recent years. Advances in sensory evaluation are changing sensory's role from that of a passive participant in the evaluation system to an active one. In the context of product quality this role change is manifested not only in its use to monitor quality, but to establish product sensory specifications as well.

ACKNOWLEDGEMENTS

The author wishes to acknowledge the contributions of Dr Herbert Stone and Professor Howard G. Schutz during the preparation of this paper.

REFERENCES

Amerine, M. A., Roessler, E. B. & Filipello, F. (1959). Modern sensory methods of evaluating wine. *Hilgardia,* **28,** 477–567.

Baten, W. D. (1946). Organoleptic tests pertaining to apples and pears. *Food Res.*, **11**, 84–94.

Downs, P. A., Anderson, E. O., Babcock, C. T., Herzer, F. H. & Trout, G. M. (1954). Evaluation of collegiate student dairy products judging since World War II. *J. Dairy Sci.*, **34**, 1021–6.

Harper, R. (1983). Future trends in the evaluation of sensory quality. In *Sensory Quality in Foods and Beverages: Definition, Measurement and Control*, eds A. A. Williams & R. K. Atkin, Ellis Horwood, Chichester, pp. 467–82.

Horsfield, S. & Taylor, L. J. (1976). Exploring the relationship between sensory data and acceptability of meat. *J. Sci. Food Agric.*, **27**, 1044–56.

McBride, R. L. (1979). Cheese grading versus consumer acceptability: an inevitable discrepancy. *Aust. J. Dairy Technol.*, **34**, 66–8.

Mosher, H. A., Dutton, H. J., Evens, C. D. & Cowan, J. C. (1950). Conducting a taste panel for the evaluation of edible oils. *Food Technol.*, **4**, 105–9.

Nakayama, M. & Wessman, C. (1979). Application of sensory evaluation to the routine maintenance of product quality. *Food Technol.*, **32**, 38–44.

Perfetti, A. (1987). Measurement of the quality of cigarette products, Presented at *41st Tobacco Chemists' Research Conference*, October 4–7, Greensboro, N.C.

Peryam, D. R. & Pilgrim, F. J. (1957). Hedonic scale method of measuring food preferences. *Food Technol.*, **11**, 9–14.

Reece, R. N. (1979). A quality assurance perspective of sensory evaluation. *Food Technol.*, **32**, 37.

Schutz, H. G. (1983). Multiple regression approach to optimization. *Food Technol.*, **37**, 46–62.

Schutz, H. G. (1987). Predicting preference from sensory and analytical data. In *Flavour Science and Technology*, eds M. Martens, G. A. Dalen & H. Russwurm. John Wiley, Chichester, pp. 399–406.

Schutz, H. G., Damrell, J. D. & Locke, B. H. (1972). Predicting hedonic ratings of raw carrot texture by sensory analysis. *J. Text. Stud.*, **3**, 227–32.

Sidel, J. L. & Stone, H. (1983). An introduction to optimization research. *Food Technol.*, **37**, 36–8.

Sidel, J. L. & Stone, H. (1986). Using panel results for management decisions. In *Proceedings, 39th Annual Reciprocal Meat Conference*. Published by National Live Stock and Meat Board, Chicago, IL, pp. 97–100.

Sidel, J. L., Stone, H. & Bloomquist, J. (1981). Use and misuse of sensory evaluation in research and quality control. *J. Dairy Sci.*, **64**, 2296–302.

Sidel, J. L., Stone, H. & Bloomquist, J. (1983). Industrial approaches to defining quality. In *Sensory Quality in Foods and Beverages: Definition Measurement and Control*, eds A. A. Williams & R. A. Atkin. Ellis Horwood, Chichester, pp. 48–57.

Stone, H. & Sidel, J. L. (1985). *Sensory Evaluation Practices*. Academic Press, Orlando, FL.

Stone, H., Sidel, J. L., Oliver, S., Woolsey, A. & Singleton, R. C. (1974). Sensory evaluation by quantitative descriptive analysis. *Food Technol.*, **28**, 24–34.

Stone, H., Sidel, J. L. & Bloomquist, J. (1980). Quantitative descriptive analysis. *Cereal Foods World*, **25**, 642–4.

Vello, N. (1987). Quality control in cigarette manufacturing. Presented at *41st Tobacco Chemists' Research Conference*, October 4–7, Greensboro, N.C.

Williams, A. A. & Atkin, R. K. (eds) (1983). *Sensory Quality in Foods and Beverages: Definition, Measurement, and Control*. Ellis Horwood, Chichester.

Wolfe, K. A. (1979). Use of reference standards for sensory evaluation of product quality. *Food Technol.*, **32**, 43–4.

Chapter 5

Commercial Sensory Quality of Food Products

NICOLE DAGET

Nestlé Research Centre, Nestec Ltd, Vers-chez-les-Blanc, CH-1000 Lausanne 26, Switzerland

ABSTRACT

The quality of food products embraces many factors of which sensory quality is only one. A definition of sensory quality is proposed, and then the relationship between quality and acceptability is discussed. From this, the idea of product 'specifications' and 'references' emerges. The role of market studies in establishing sensory specifications is discussed, as are procedures for the sensory appraisal of food quality. The application of 'profiling' as a tool to fix specifications and as a control procedure is mentioned. Finally, quality control procedures are outlined.

INTRODUCTION

In order to successfully place a product in the market, food technologists need to know what it is that makes a particular type of product acceptable. In general, a food product is at least expected to be healthy, nutritive, palatable, easy to use, it should keep for a certain period of time and should be readily available, and all for a certain price.

Kurt Kahnert of the Central Institute of Food Industries (German Democratic Republic) stated that in countries where there is high spending power and a wide choice of foodstuffs, increasing consumption of semi-luxury food is observed (Kahnert, 1985). He noted the

55

Table 1
Changes in consumption of various foods and
beverages from 1975 to 1983 (German Democratic Republic)

	1975	1983
	(kg per capita)	
Meat	77·8	92·1
Sugar + sugar products	36·8	39·2
Cocoa	3·0	3·8
Non-alcoholic drinks	70·3	91·8
Wine (litres)	7·4	11·2
Spirits	8·6	14·4
Coffee	2·4	3·3

increases in consumption from 1975 to 1983 in the German Democratic Republic given in Table 1. During the period from 1973 to 1982, the general trend in Europe, Japan and the United States, was a decrease in consumption of staple foods and an increase in meat and vegetables (OCDE, 1985).

Figure 1 shows the change of consumption for six foods, from 1973 to 1982. Parallel to this, there was, in both the European and Japanese industries, tremendous activity to educate and motivate for quality, and to manufacture products of quality.

CONCEPT OF QUALITY

Regarding quality, Webster's dictionary gives the following definition:

(a) peculiar or essential character, inherent feature;
(b) degree of excellence, superiority in kind;
(c) social status;
(d) characteristic, the attribute of an elementary sensation that makes it fundamentally unlike any other sensation.

In the Chambers' dictionary it is defined as:

(a) that which makes a thing what it is properly . . .
(b) rank; superior birth or character.

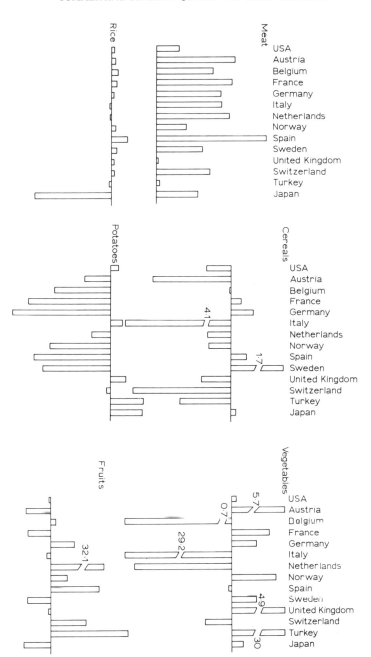

Figure 1. Difference in consumption of 6 foods, in kg/person/year between 1973 and 1982.

In the Oxford dictionary:

(a) degree of excellence relative to nature or character;
(b) faculty, skill, accomplishment, characteristic, trait, mental or moral attribute;
(c) high rank or social standing.

Interestingly, some of these definitions mix positive attributes and degree of excellence, with other descriptions. This same ambiguity exists in all European languages.

Juran (1983), the American specialist of quality management, specified that the quality of a manufactured product should be defined in pragmatic and functional terms, related to 'aptitude at use'. Thus, in Juran's terms, the quality of a food product would be defined as the sum of the utility value characteristics in relation to their suitability to meet the nutritional requirements of the consumer and the pleasure of eating.

Utility value as well as pleasure of eating depend on the consumer and the consumption environment. If a product is to fulfill consumer expectations then systematic consumer research is necessary to establish what the features of the product should ideally be.

On the basis of market research, consumer feedback, or intuition, a draft design is specified and this constitutes the 'target'. Technologists investigate feasibility and cost, and develop prototypes. The best of these are then typically submitted to consumer testing to determine the extent to which they fulfill consumer expectations. The final choice of product prototype is made in the knowledge of the consumers' responses; in essence, the chosen product will have been sanctioned by the consumer. Presumably, the selected prototype should be the optimum combination of excellence, feasibility and cost.

SPECIFICATIONS

The characteristics of the product, as identified by consumer research, should become an intrinsic part of the product definition and must be transmitted to the next link in the development chain, the manufacturing plant, along with the specification:

—ingredients,
—manufacturing procedures,
—packaging characteristics,
—and sensory characteristics.

Specifications are the means by which knowledge of the product is transmitted to all concerned in the plant. Any failure to document this will inevitably confuse those who face the problem of putting the design into production.

These specifications should be considered as 'rules' within the company and must be strictly adhered to. They should not be changed, even for what management consider to be an improvement, since the changed characteristics will not necessarily meet with the approval of the consumer.

If specifications are expressed in words there may be great uncertainty as to interpretation. To escape the description problem a reference sample has traditionally been prepared. However, problems arise with respect to the stability of the reference sample, which has to be renewed from time to time. Reference samples also have a legal facet. When dealing with expensive raw materials, such as coffee, cocoa, or tea, specimens of the reference sample are given to the seller, the buyer and a third party, and sealed. These represent a clear statement of specification which can be referred to should conflict arise. References for manufactured products are also kept in the control laboratory, as statements of specifications.

In 'fact books', references of finished products are now usually accompanied by a descriptive profile. When renewing the reference, samples are screened using descriptive profiling to identify the one which most closely matches the specification. The language used in this type of communication plays an important role and a clear definition of each term is essential (Daget, 1974). Considerable care is required when defining or translating product glossaries from one language to another: for example, tea (Indian Standards Institution, 1968) and wine (Vedel et al., 1972), also cocoa, chocolate and chocolate confectionery. Ishii and O'Mahony (1987) stated that taste description is essentially the use of labels to communicate taste concepts. Each concept should have a separate label. However, this is only one requirement for a precise taste descriptive language; another more complex requirement is that subjects should have similar boundaries to their concepts and they should interpret and label them in the same way.

Thus, specifications concerning taste, texture, aroma and appearance should be well understood and interpreted by all links in the chain, using language which will not be misinterpreted by the numerous parties involved (Fig. 2).

Figure 2. A case of language difficulty!

CONFORMANCE

Quality in production relies on conformance to specification in every respect, and by all parties. Checking is undertaken by inspectors, who examine samples collected from the production line using established sampling rules.

These inspectors, must be familiar with:

—the nature of the product;
—the specifications;
—the proper language;
—the apparatus used to measure conformity.

With repeated testing on daily production, inspectors become so familiar with the reference, that they can usually recognize 'their product' amongst a multitude of samples. Checking the conformity of a product against a sensory specification, usually involves a straightforward comparison of the product with the reference sample. This is relatively easy when the product is homogeneous and produced in bulk (e.g. a liquid). Under these circumstances paired or triangular difference tests would normally be used (Amerine *et al.*, 1965). If a product is different from the reference, the taster will usually indicate the nature of the difference using free description. When the product is made in small units, paired and triangular comparison become logistically difficult, because of the quantity of samples involved. In this situation ranking of samples according to a particular differentiating sensory characteristic would be most appropriate. Friedman has established rules for interpreting the ranked data (Friedman, 1937).

When differences from reference are detected, some form of quantification is usually required since adjustment of the production process may be necessary. In this respect, category scales are often used, either to score intensity of difference or to score quality in terms of excellence. At no time should it be permitted to use an hedonic scale in this respect, as this is a marketing tool used to monitor consumer attitude: none of the factory staff are qualified to substitute for the consumer.

The development of descriptive methods has provided a new tool for quality control (Stone *et al.*, 1974). A fixed plan for tasting and visual control, together with other controls, should be specified in the monitoring scheme. This document fixes what, where, when, who and how to control, and what to do with the information. Such monitoring schemes are tailor made for specific processes, and methods to be used are formally described in laboratory instructions or even in official standards (ASTM, 1968).

ACCEPTABILITY

From the information obtained by way of these tests, the inspector has to make a decision regarding the acceptability of the product. This could be either, release, reject, rework or regulate on line. Clearly, questions of tolerance limits arise: will a detected difference have an effect on the product's performance on the market?

Table 2
Quality conformance. Relationships between Specification and Acceptability

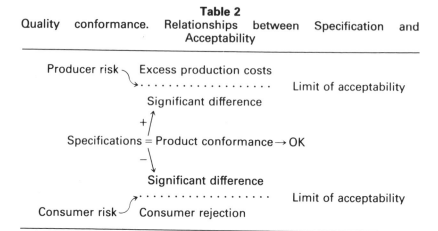

Figure 3. Monitoring scheme for set yoghurts.

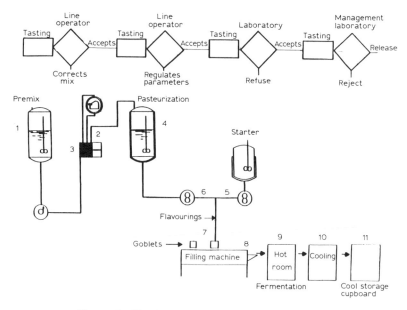

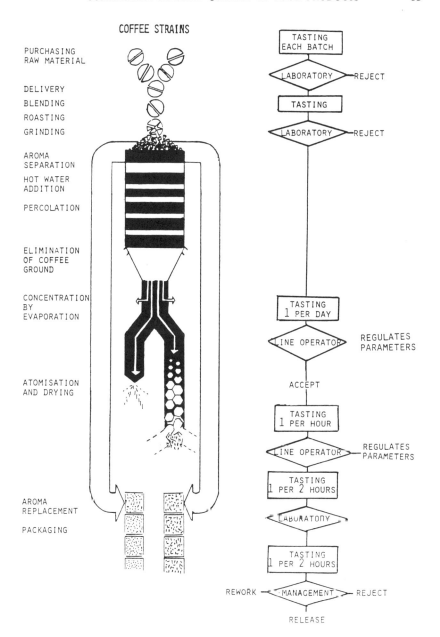

Figure 4. Monitoring scheme for instant coffee.

There are two types of risks (see Table 2):

—Consumer Risk: the product is clearly less 'good' than the reference, so the consumer might reject it.
—Producer Risk: the product is clearly 'better' than the reference. The consumer might prefer it, but it would be uneconomic for the producer to maintain such quality.

Both cases imply regulation on line.

The deviations observed can be classified according to the type or risk they represent:

—minor defects,
—critical defects,
—major defects.

Criteria of rejection are generally specified: i.e. 'rancidity' in a dairy

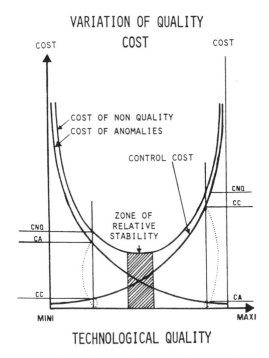

Figure 5. Variation of quality and cost. CC, control cost; CNQ, non-quality cost; CA, anomaly cost.

product is a major defect, whereas variation of sweetness level is minor. Some control checks are made on line by the operator, who immediately regulates the process. Other checks are done in the control laboratory by inspectors who, together with management, must sometimes decide whether to 'reject or rework' non-conforming samples or to down-grade the products and sell them as seconds. Examples of monitoring schemes for set yoghurts and instant coffee are shown in Figs. 3 and 4, respectively. Control data are normally recorded and, over a period of time, this will provide an important data bank on the performance of the product and the process.

In order to minimise the cost of maintaining quality, it is necessary to minimise the variability of the product's characteristics around the reference. This ultimately reduces the amount of rejected material and minimises the number of examinations required (Fig. 5). Careful choice of raw material and control of processes results in more uniform production and a consistent product of optimal acceptability (Juran and Gryna, 1985).

After a period of time, consumer attitudes may drift and so product acceptability will change. Additionally, the availability of particular raw materials may diminish, and new technologies will develop. For these reasons, it may eventually be necessary to redesign the product to re-establish the best relationship between use and cost.

REFERENCES

Amerine, M. A., Pangborn, R. M. & Roessler, E. B. (1965). *Principles of Sensory Evaluation of Food.* Academic Press, New York.

ASTM (1968). *Manual on Sensory Testing Methods.* ASTM.

Daget, N. (1974). Profile sensory evaluation of chocolate, In *1st International Congress on Cocoa and Chocolate.* Frank, OMG, Munich.

Friedman, M. (1937). The use of ranks to avoid the assumption of normality implicit in the analysis of variance. *J. Am. Stat. Assoc.,* **32,** 675.

Indian Standards Institution (1968). *Indian Glossary of Tea Terms.* Manak, Bahavan, New Dehli.

Ishii, R. & O'Mahony, M. (1987). Taste sorting and naming: can taste concepts be misrepresented by traditional psychophysical labelling system. *Chemical Senses,* **12**(1) 37–51.

Juran, J. M. (1983). *Gestion de la Qualité.* AFNOR coll. normes techniques, Paris.

Juran, J. M. & Gryna, M. (1985). *Quality Planning and Analysis,* TATA McGraw-Hill, New Dehli.

66 NICOLE DAGET

Kahnert, K. (1985). Correlations between the quality of foodstuffs and the development of the food industry in the GDR. In *Proceedings of the 29th EOQC Conference on Quality and Development.* Vol. 3. Estoril, Portugal, pp. 157–163.
OCDE (1985). *Food Consumption Statistics 1973–1982.* OCDE, Paris.
Stone, H., Sidel, J., Oliver, S., Wolley, A. & Singleton, R. (1974). Sensory evaluation by quantitative descriptive analysis. *Food Technol.,* **11,** 24–34.
Vedel, A., Charle, G., Charnay, P. & Tourneau, J. (1972). *Essai sur la Dégustation des Vins.* SEIV, Macon, France.

Chapter 6

Relation between Flavour and Instrumental Quality Parameters of Tomatoes

ROLF DUDEN

Federal Research Centre for Nutrition, Engesserstr. 20, D-7500 Karlsruhe 1, FRG

and

HEIDEMARIE HEINE

Federal Office of Plant Varieties, Osterfelddamm 80, D-3000 Hannover, FRG

ABSTRACT

Flavour tests were conducted with 11 tomato cultivars, grown under glass in the Federal Office of Plant Varieties, Hannover (FRG) over a 2-year period. Flavour scores correlated significantly with refractometer readings; in some cases there was also a significant correlation with titratable acidity. However, flavour did not correlate significantly with electrical conductivity

Refractometer readings have been found suitable for a rough estimation of tomato flavour. They may serve as a basis to classify tomatoes according to their internal quality.

INTRODUCTION

Quality is an essential prerequisite for the acceptance of a food product. High product quality therefore promotes sales and profits— provided production costs are not excessive. Sometimes, however,

Table 1
Quality attributes

External quality	Colour
	Shape
	Size
	Surface condition
Internal quality	Nutritional quality
	Flavour
	Odour
	Firmness

quality is unjustifiably claimed merely to gain more profit. It is therefore important to enable consumers to evaluate product quality. No problems exist as far as external properties are concerned. However, the so-called internal quality, i.e. flavour, odour and texture as well as physiological properties, is difficult to assess, because it is not perceived directly at the point of selection. Refer to Table 1 for the definition of terms.

In many cases a correlation exists between external and internal quality characteristics. This is one reason why so many consumers select according to the external characteristics of the commodity; they assume that size, pleasant appearance, uniformity, etc., are indicative of internal quality. Frequently also price, origin, trademark and variety suggest a certain internal quality.

In the case of tomatoes, such associations are often misleading. Consumers who pay a high price for large, smooth fruit of beautiful colour are frequently disappointed by the flavour of the produce (Miller, 1974; Gormley & Egan, 1982; Beattie *et al.*, 1983). Commercial quality classes and standards are of little help since they are based primarily on external characteristics (Duden, 1986). Where internal quality is described, this is done in rather vague terms without defining flavour standards. However, flavour standards can be established only if methods are available to quantify the characteristics concerned.

A direct quantification is possible by sensory analysis. As this is costly and time consuming, the question arises whether the flavour can be appraised from the concentrations of certain components.

The components responsible for the basic taste of tomatoes are mainly sugars and acids. They can be determined by the usual chemical methods, but also refractometer readings and electrical conductivity may be used as quality criteria (Duden & Wolf, 1987). Because of the difficult analytical procedures, volatile aroma compounds appear less suitable in this respect. pH value and acid/sugar ratio do not correlate with the fruit taste.

This chapter describes the relation between the flavour of tomatoes on the one hand and refractometer readings, titratable acidity and electrical conductivity of the fruit serum, on the other.

MATERIALS AND METHODS

Our studies were conducted over 2 years on 11 tomato cultivars, which were grown in the greenhouses of the Federal Office of Plant Varieties, Hannover, in the conventional manner. The fruit were harvested at the beginning, in the middle and at the end of the season, as soon as about 50% of the tomato surface had turned red. Half of the tomatoes were carefully packaged to prevent bruising and then sent to Karlsruhe within 1 day where the fruit was stored for 1–2 days at temperatures between 15 and 20°C, depending on the degree of ripening. The tomatoes were analysed simultaneously in Karlsruhe and Hannover using the same methods.

Sensory Analysis

The flavour of the fruit was evaluated by using a 9-point scale according to the Karlsruhe Evaluation Scheme (Duden, 1986; Table 2). This scheme includes the characteristics 'spicy', 'bodied', 'harmonious' which determine the basic taste, as well as impressions such as 'fruity' and 'typical' (tomato-like) which are caused by volatile compounds. In less perfect fruit the taste is described as 'insipid', 'watery', 'disharmonious' or 'atypical'. The first two terms of each category of the scheme refer to the basic taste, the last term denotes the aroma impression.

Seven to eight trained assessors participated in the sensory evaluation exercise. These had been selected from amongst twice as many individuals, using the following selection criteria:

—Sensitivity to the basic taste impressions sweet and sour, tested by determining the individual threshold values for sucrose and citric acid.
—The ability to recognize identical samples.

Table 2
Flavour scale (Karlsruhe evaluation scheme)

Score	Characteristics
9	Perfectly full bodied, especially spicy
	Very harmonious
	Very marked fruity-floral aroma
8	Full bodied, very spicy
	Harmonious
	Fruity-floral aroma
7	Bodied, spicy
	Harmonious
	Fruity-floral aroma
6	Somewhat flat
	Somewhat disharmonious
	(a little too sour or too sweet)
	Less fruity
5	Rather flat
	Disharmonious (too sour or too sweet)
	Not quite typical
4	Insipid, watery
	Poor or atypical—but not unpleasant aroma
1–3	Off-flavour
	(phenolic, musty, unpleasant)

In all tests, one cultivar was used as reference sample. Its taste was agreed by open discussion. Tests were carried out twice. In each repetition, samples were presented in a permuted sequence. Not more than five samples were presented per session.

One sample consisted of segments taken from about ten individual fruits. The assessors had to taste several segments of each sample in order to compensate, as far as possible, for biological variation in the material.

The test occasionally included two identical samples. Failure to identify these was regarded as being due to a temporary indisposition of the assessor. In such a case, all judgements of the assessor concerned were excluded from the test.

Refractive Value (RV)
Refractive values were measured by using a hand refractometer equipped with a built-in thermometer. It was calibrated in percentage sugar, with a reading accuracy of 0·1% sugar.

Titratable Acidity (TA)
10 ml of tomato serum, obtained by centrifugation from homogenized whole tomatoes was titrated with N/10 NaOH against cresol red.

Electrical Conductivity (EC)
Tomato serum was diluted tenfold using distilled water. Measurements were conducted using the device LF90 of Wissenschaftlich-Technische Werkstätten GmbH, FRG.

RESULTS AND DISCUSSION

Table 3 shows the correlation coefficients between flavour scores and instrumental parameters. The largest coefficients have always been found for the correlation of flavour/refractive value. In the case of the correlation of flavour/titratable acidity, considerable differences in the coefficients between the values obtained in Hannover and Karlsruhe were found. This may be due to different responses from the assessors, in Hannover and Karlsruhe, to the acid content of the samples.

Electrical conductivity was only measured in Karlsruhe. There was no significant correlation with flavour scores.

To find out to what extent flavour scores depend on the total of all three parameters, i.e. refractive value, acid content and conductivity,

Table 3
Correlation coefficients between flavour score and some instrumental parameters

		n	RV	TA	EC
HK	1985	27	0·70[a]	0·67[a]	0·41
	1986	33	0·70[a]	0·67[a]	0·13
HH	1985	27	0·79[a]	0·31	—
	1986	33	0·51[a]	0·32	—
KK	1983/84	128	0·64[a]	0·43[a]	—

[a] Significant at the 1% level.
RV, refractive value; TA, titratable acidity; EC, electrical conductivity; n, number of samples; HH, grown and analysed in Hannover; HK, grown in Hannover, analysed in Karlsruhe; for comparison: KK, market tomatoes, purchased and analysed in Karlsruhe (Duden & Wolf, 1987).

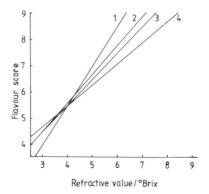

Figure 1. Tomato flavour as a function of refractive value. 1, samples grown in Hannover, analysed in Karlsruhe (1986); 2, samples grown and analysed in Hannover (1985 and 1986—nearly identical lines); 3, samples purchased in the Karlsruhe local market 1983/84 (Duden & Wolf, 1987); 4, samples grown in Hannover, analysed in Karlsruhe (1985).

coefficients of determination (squares of correlation coefficients between determined and predicted flavour values) were calculated by means of multiple linear regression.

Nearly identical determination coefficients were found for the regression models with and without inclusion of the conductivity data, i.e. these data were not relevant for the reliability of predicting flavour values. If, however, the parameter 'titratable acidity' was eliminated in the next step, the determination coefficients obtained with the Karlsruhe data sets—but not those obtained with the Hannover data sets—decreased distinctly. Taking the acidity into account (in addition to refractive values) hence may improve the reliability of the predicted flavour values. But the gain in reliability is relatively small. Moreover, it is associated with additional experimental expenditure which would reduce the possibilities of use for routine quality control. So we decided, in a first approach, to use only refractive values for prediction of flavour scores. The corresponding functions are shown in Fig. 1. The variations of the slopes and intercepts of the lines are within the range of experimental error. There seems to be no influence of the kind of sample material, harvest time and group of assessors.

To make the results of our work accessible to consumers, we propose to group tomatoes within categories (see Tables 4 and 5). The flavour and refractive values indicated in these tables are linked to

Table 4
Grouping of tomatoes according to their flavour (3 groups)

Flavour group	Fl	RV	Verbal characterization
a	>7·0	>5·5	Very good
b	6·0–7·0	4·5–5·5	Rather good–good
c	<6·0	<4·5	Satisfactory–poor

Fl, flavour score; *RV*, refractive value.

each other by the equation

$$Fl = RV + 1·5$$

which corresponds to line 3 in Fig. 1. The slope of this line is 1·0, which simplifies estimates of flavour quality.

There is no essential difference between the two tables. A grouping according to Table 4 (Duden, 1987) is less precise than a grouping according to Table 5, but the former gives a better overall view.

Gormley & Maher (1985) have proposed to categorize tomatoes on the basis of conductivity measurements. However, conductivity seems to be a less suitable quality indicator than light refraction, as has been shown above.

If commercially grown tomatoes are labelled according to flavour categories—perhaps in addition to labelling according to EC quality classes—this would be of great help for consumers in choosing the appropriate product. They could directly see whether the internal

Table 5
Grouping of tomatoes according to their flavour (5 groups)

Flavour group	Fl	RV	Verbal characterization
a_1	>7·0	>5·5	Very good
a_2	6·5–7·0	5·0–5·5	Good
b_1	6·0–6·4	4·5–4·9	Rather good
b_2	5·5–5·9	4·0–4·4	Satisfactory
c	<5·5	<4·0	Poor

Fl, flavour score; *RV*, refractive value.

quality of the fruit corresponds to the appearance and whether the product is worth its price.

Market transparence achieved by introducing internal quality criteria could lead to a higher demand for good tasting tomatoes. The higher price obtainable for such products could encourage producers to shift from a production which is essentially orientated towards high quantities, to production of high-quality fruit.

REFERENCES

Beattie, B. B. *et al.* (1983). Fresh market tomatoes—a study of consumer attitudes and quality of fruit offered for sale in Sydney 1981–1982. *Food Technology in Australia*, **35**, 450–4.

Duden, R. (1986). Die geschmackliche Qualität von Tomaten eines Lokalmarktes. *Ernährungs-Umschau*, **33**, 40–3.

Duden, R. (1987). Zur inneren Qualität von Tomaten—ein Vorschlag zur Güte. *Gordian*, **87**, 146–7.

Duden, R. & Wolf, W. (1987). Inhaltsstoffe und Geschmack von Tomaten. *Lebensm.-Wiss. u. Technol.*, **20**, 325–9.

Gormley, T. R. & Egan, S. (1982). How good are Irish tomatoes? *Farm and Food Research*, **13**, 100–2.

Gormley, T. R. & Maher (1985). Quality of intensively produced tomatoes. In *Agriculture. The Effects of Modern Production Methods on the Quality of Tomatoes and Apples*, ed. T. R. Gormley, R. O. Sharples & J. Dehandtschutter. Commission of the European Communities, Luxembourg, CEC Report EUR 9873, pp. 63–76.

Miller, J. (1974). FDA seeks to regulate genetic manipulations of crops. *Science*, **185**, 240–2.

Topic 3

Factors Influencing Food Choice—Food Related and Situational Factors

Chapter 7

Sensory, Hedonic and Situational Factors in Food Acceptance and Consumption

HERBERT L. MEISELMAN, EDWARD S. HIRSCH and RICHARD D. POPPER

Behavioral Sciences Division, Science and Advanced Technology Directorate, United States Army Natick Research, Development and Engineering Center, Natick, Massachusetts 01760, USA

ABSTRACT

Much of the research on factors affecting food acceptance has focused on sensory characteristics of foods. Another line of research has focused on hedonic measurement of different foods. A series of field and laboratory studies undertaken at Natick have provided a data base on how sensory and hedonic characteristics of foods predict acceptability (product rating) and consumption (amount consumed). Field studies have led us to conclude that important factors controlling consumption of food in natural eating situations are the situational variables which make it more or less convenient for us to eat and which signal meal times. These factors are discussed in relation to controlling food acceptance and food intake.

INTRODUCTION

Acceptance and Consumption

What is food acceptability? What is food consumption? The book by Amerine *et al.* (1965) defines acceptance as: '(1) An experience, or

77

feature of experience, characterized by a positive (approach in a pleasant) attitude. (2) Actual utilization (purchase, eating). May be measured by preference or liking for specific food item. The two definitions are often highly correlated, but they are not necessarily the same'. (p. 540)

The work by Peryam and colleagues, summarized in a 1960 report, stated: 'In fact, acceptability is defined in terms of consumption and morale—acceptable food is one that will be eaten and eaten with pleasure and satisfaction'. (p. 2)

The early view of acceptance and consumption is that they were not independent phenomena. Since that time the field has gradually come to a different view of acceptance. Stone & Sidel (1985) state: 'By acceptance testing we mean measuring liking or preference for a product. Preference is that expression of appeal of one product versus another'. (p. 227)

We have come, perhaps without realizing it, from a concept of food acceptability which intimately linked hedonic judgements and food consumption to a concept of food acceptability which is limited to the hedonic dimension. Within our recent studies at Natick we have begun to re-examine how we measure acceptance and consumption.

Situational and Sensory Factors

In considering acceptance and consumption, scientists have traditionally focused on the sensory and hedonic aspects of the food. This has led to the large number of books and conferences on sensory evaluation. Few sensory evaluation experts would disagree with a definition of sensory factors that emphasized those responses made in reaction to physical stimuli for sight, taste, smell, etc. Similarly, defining hedonic factors as the evaluative or like-dislike dimension of foods is not likely to provoke any disagreement.

Throughout the development of sensory evaluation, scientists have given lip service to the existence of another set of variables, environmental or situational variables, which are significant in food acceptability and consumption. By situational factors we mean the numerous variables in our eating environments which make it easier or harder for us to begin, continue, or complete a meal. In designing either food testing laboratories or institutional dining rooms or restaurants we are all aware of the importance of temperature (hot-cold), lighting, comfort, hours of operation, accessibility to the user, and other factors. These may be the variables which we seek to control when conducting studies in actual eating environments, or which we feel are not relevant in the laboratory where 'real meals' are not consumed. For the past several years we have had the opportunity at the United States Army Natick Research Development and Engineering Center to study eating under natural conditions for extended periods of time. The natural conditions have been either the field training conditions of the US Army or a modified cafeteria of a university. The tests have extended from 8 to 45 days. What has emerged from these studies is a developing picture of the sensory, hedonic and situational factors which control food acceptance and consumption.

Perhaps at the outset we should explain our basis of interest in this line of research. From an applied perspective, we at Natick are interested in designing a ration for our troops which is maximally consumed and minimally wasted, thus providing the maximum nutrition with the minimum logistic burden. From a basic perspective, we are also interested in a better understanding of the effects and interactions of sensory, hedonic and situational variables so we can propose better solutions to these problems in the future for some of the more unusual environments in which the military feeds troops.

THREE FIELD STUDIES

The parameters of the three studies which will be discussed are presented in Table 1. The key criteria employed in these studies were

Table 1
The three studies of food consumption

	Location	Duration	Sample	Groups
Study 1	Field	34 days	(a) 90 support soldiers	3 rations
			(b) 87 support soldiers	Ration lunch + 2 fresh meals
Study 2	University	45 days	(a) 20 students	3 rations
			(b) 20 students	3 fresh meals
Study 3	Field	8 days	(a) 31 artillery soldiers	3 fresh meals

the number of kilocalories consumed per day and the change in body weight over the course of the study. However, many other factors were measured and some will be reported below.

Study 1

In the first study (Hirsch *et al.*, 1985), two groups of combat support troops (sample sizes = 90, 87) were fed for 34 days under field conditions in a remote location with no access to other food. The first group was provided with three packaged military operational rations (hereafter called rations) totalling 3600 kcal/day. This ration (technically called the Meal Ready to Eat) is composed of 30 food items, two beverages, a cream substitute, assorted candies, condiments and a gravy base all packaged in flexible pouches. These components are divided into twelve menus with repetition of some items other than entrees across the twelve menus.

The second group was also provided with three meals per day, a ration for lunch in the field, but a breakfast and a dinner made from freshly prepared foods that were either prepared in the field or were shipped to the field.

Data on food acceptability, physical symptoms, mood, morale, perceptions of leadership, food preferences, body weight and perceptions of the rations were collected from all men in both groups prior to the test and at selected times during the test. In addition, a subsample of 30 men in each group underwent more extensive testing for body weight, height, body fat, food intake, water intake, selected nutrient intakes, urine volume and osmolality, haematocrit, and cognitive psychomotor performance.

The ration received high hedonic scores from both the group which received three rations per day (7·05 on 9 point scale) and from the group which received only one ration for lunch (6·48). The ration also rated higher than the control group's comparable hot meals. Despite the relatively high acceptability of the ration, daily caloric intake was only 2189 kcal for the three ration group and 2950 for the control group over the 34-day test. The components of the ration were not evenly consumed by the group fed three rations per day. The consumption rate for the components of the ration were: entrees 68%, starch 60%, spreads 47%, fruits 51%, desserts 50%, beverages 27% and condiments and candies 26%. Water intake for this group was somewhat lower than that of the control group (2657 ml/day versus 3132 ml/day), but was not low enough to produce increased reports of thirst or significant changes in the monitored indices of body fluid status.

The lower food intake in the three ration group appeared to result from several factors including the following: (1) The three ration group reported loss of appetite. It is uncertain whether this should be attributed to menu monotony or some other factor. (2) The most well liked and well consumed component of the ration was the main dish and it was available in relatively small portion size. (3) The ration did not contain traditional breakfast items possibly leading to reduced intake at breakfast. (4) The limited variety of beverages in the ration might have led to decreased food intake because of the reciprocal nature of food and water intake (Fitzsimons, 1972). (5) Finally, the situational factors did not support maximal eating. The ration was not served to people and therefore meal time was often self-defined; the ration is packaged in up to 8 small food packs leading to additional effort in preparing a meal; the field atmosphere without tables and chairs was not conducive to 'a meal', etc.

Study 2
In the second study (unpublished) 40 male college students (ages 18–29) were divided into two groups. One group was provided with three military rations per day, and the other group was provided with three freshly prepared meals per day, isocaloric to the rations. All 40 subjects provided daily food and fluid intakes, daily body weight, urine volume, osmolality, specific gravity, blood analyses, personal diaries, food acceptance ratings, mood evaluations, physical symptoms questionnaires, psychomotor and cognitive performance tests.

The students fed on the three ration regimen were free to go about their usual schedules with the provision that they ate breakfast (0700–0900), lunch (1130–1330), and dinner (1700–1900) at the indicated hours. The meals were eaten in a common dining room with tables and chairs to seat 40. They were provided with plates, glasses and silverware. A microwave was available to heat components of the ration, and hot and cold water were available for preparing beverages or rehydrating ration components. In short, many of the situational factors which might have reduced ration intake in the field were addressed to promote maximum ration intake in the laboratory.

Under these conditions the three ration group consumed 3149 kcal averaged over the 45 days, while the fresh food group consumed 3469 kcal per day. The average food acceptability ratings of the two groups were 6·05 and 6·27 respectively. The ration consumed by the troops in Study 1 and the students in Study 2 was identical; it is our hypothesis that the 960 kcal difference between the consumption of the rations by the two groups was largely due to the situational differences in the two eating environments. The further difference between the two student groups shows the added effect of sensory/hedonic factors. The fresh food which was more highly rated was consumed in somewhat larger quantities.

Study 3

The third study (Rose & Carlson, 1986) was conducted in an army field situation in which 31 soldiers in three artillery batteries were fed three freshly prepared meals per day for 8 days. This unusual feeding regimen was brought about by the unavailability of the military rations used in the other studies, and presented a unique situation in which to measure the consumption of a freshly prepared diet in the field. Unfortunately acceptance ratings of the food were not gathered, but the menu comprised highly preferred foods. For example, the dinner main dishes for the 8 days were steak, turkey, fried chicken, roast beef, baked chicken, roast pork, grilled steak, and pork chops. The breakfast meal contained fresh eggs daily plus fresh fruit and/or juice, grits or cereal, breakfast meat, and appropriate breakfast starch and other breakfast items. Under these conditions the men ate an average of 3713 kcal/day. The men were provided with three specific meal times per day and with sufficient time to complete their meals.

Within the context of military feeding, this study represents the ultimate combination of sensory and situational factors studied to date. The combination of preferred foods, freshly prepared, and served in an atmosphere conducive to maximize meal frequency and food consumption led to a substantial increase in consumption. Although food acceptability was not measured we assume it would have been high.

The Model of Sensory and Situational Factors

The three studies just presented are summarized in Fig. 1. Study 1 represents the lowest ration consumption measured. The increase in caloric consumption with the students eating the same ration we attribute to situational factors in that the student eating environment was more conducive to eating. The increased consumption from Study 2 to Study 3 we attribute largely to the increased sensory and hedonic aspects of the food, with the situational factors remaining relatively constant.

Figure 1. Three military feeding studies showing average energy intake and average acceptance ratings on a nine point scale (in brackets). The difference in consumption between the three ration group in Studies 1 and 2 is attributed to situational factors, whereas the difference between the three ration group in Study 2 and the three fresh meals in Study 3 to sensory/hedonic factors.

ADDITIONAL STUDIES

Further sensory improvements of the ration were tested in a field test in which four companies of Marines were fed different versions of the ration in which changes had been made after the initial finding of low consumption. The following changes produced the indicated responses:

(1) Increasing ration main dish size from 5·5 oz to 8 oz yielded a higher percentage of people saying they got enough to eat and a rating of entree portion size much closer to 'just right' than 'too small'.

(2) Fruit flavoured beverages were well liked (7·2–7·5 on 9 pt scale).

(3) Breakfast main dishes were well liked, rating over 6·2 compared with dinner main dishes rating of 5·49.

The consumption and overall acceptance rating of the ration under the different conditions are shown in Table 2. Not only were the changes rated highly by the troops, but the troops consumed more of the ration.

This study shows how product improvement can increase the acceptance and consumption of a ration for the military, or any product for an institutional or non-institutional market. As further improvements are made in products one can reach the limits of

Table 2
Average caloric intake and acceptance rating in Marine Corps troops fed three rations per day for 8 days

Condition	Calories	Acceptance
Control	2 362	5·43
Beverage	3 003	5·66
Breakfast	2 755	6·30
Large entrees (8 oz)	2 817	5·50

product improvement through changes in product design aimed at increased acceptance.

A more recent test evaluated the improvements individually tested above and now combined into a fully improved ration. Three groups, of from 117 to 129 troops each, tested three different rations including the fully improved ration and the ration tested under Study 1 reported above. Data acquired again included body weight, food and water intake, urine specific gravity, food acceptance ratings and a final questionnaire. The study lasted 12 days. The average daily caloric intake for the fully improved ration was 2842 kcal and for the older ration 2517 kcal. The higher caloric intake of the latter group resulted from new formulations of the same ration items and from the reduced duration of the test. The average acceptance ratings for all main dishes was 7·6 on the 9 point hedonic scale for the fully improved ration and 5·7 for the older ration.

The consumption ratio of the main dishes remained near 85% (consumption ratio = the ratio of the number of portions consumed to the number of portions issued). Since main dish size had been increased in the fully improved version the troops now ate 769 kcal of main dish rather than 510 kcal with the old ration.

The final questionnaire ratings indicated that the troops gave higher ratings to the taste, appearance, amount and variety of the newly improved ration.

The Model of Sensory and Situational Factors Expanded
The two studies just presented can now be added into the model (see Fig. 2). This permits a different conceptualization of how one can go from the initial low caloric consumption of Study 1 to the highest caloric consumption of Study 3. In Figure 2 the intermediate steps are

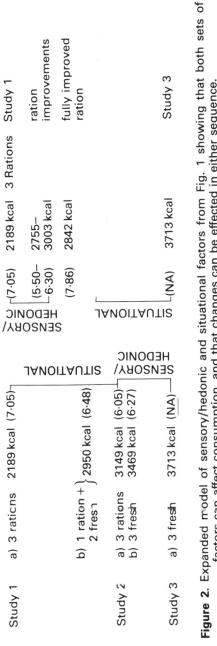

Figure 2. Expanded model of sensory/hedonic and situational factors from Fig. 1 showing that both sets of factors can affect consumption, and that changes can be effected in either sequence.

the two studies just presented. Each represents a sensory improvement from Study 1. Probably slight further improvements in the sensory hedonic dimension are possible bringing consumption to 3100–3200 kcal. The increase from that level to the level of Study 3 at 3713 kcal would be the situational factors discussed above.

DISCUSSION

The studies presented have caused us to rethink our use of the terms acceptance and consumption. They have also caused us to rethink how we measure acceptance and consumption. Many investigators in sensory evaluation and acceptance have been frustrated by the difficulty of comparing the same items in subsequent studies or in different environments. Most of us do not like to answer the question, 'How high or low should a particular product rate in a particular situation?' Also, we are comfortable with measuring the acceptability of a specific product in the laboratory or even in a food service environment. But what about the acceptability of a combination of products, or a whole meal, or a whole eating system (fast food versus institutional food service versus restaurant food service).

It is concluded that hedonic acceptability measures are appropriate for laboratory or field testing of individual items. However, we now see consumption as a better measure of the acceptance of groups of foods or of feeding systems. Acceptance measurement began as a means of predicting consumption (Pilgrim, 1957; Peryam et al., 1960). It is now concluded that consumption measures might provide a better index of acceptance.

This conclusion is not neccessarily related to the question of whether acceptance predicts consumption in a laboratory test environment. We are addressing consumption of food in a natural eating environment, and we are measuring multiple days of intake. Although more research is needed comparing laboratory models and field models for food acceptance and food intake, it is likely that the factors controlling intake in short term laboratory environments (Bobroff & Kissileff, 1986; Lucas & Bellisle, 1987) are different from those in longer term natural eating environments.

Concerning these controlling factors, our studies have forced us to focus on situational variables in food acceptance and food consumption. There are limits to how much change in eating can be brought about by product change (stimulus change). Additional change, if desired, must be brought about by changing the eating environment. Not only do situational variables have to be considered in addition to sensory and hedonic variables, but eventually economic, social and other factors need to be addressed.

REFERENCES

Amerine, M. A., Pangborn, R. M., & Roessler, E. B. (1965). *Principles of Sensory Evaluation of Food.* Academic Press, New York.

Bobroff, E. M. & Kissileff, H. R. (1986). Effects of changes in palatability on food intake and the cumulative food intake curve in man. *Appetite,* **7,** 86–96.

Fitzsimons, J. T. (1972). Thirst. *Physiol. Rev.,* **52,** 468–561.

Hirsch, E., Meiselman, H. L., Popper, R., Smits, G., Jezior, B., Lichton, I., Wenkham, N., Butr, J., Fox, M., McNutt, S., Thiele, M. N., & Dirige, O. (1985). The effects of prolonged feeding of meal ready to eat (MRE) operational rations. Technical Report NATICK/TR-85/035.

Lucas, F. & Bellisle, F. (1987). The measurement of food preferences in humans: Do taste-and-spit tests predict consumption. *Physiol. Behav.,* **39,** 739–43.

Moskowitz, H. R. (1983). *Product Testing and Sensory Evaluation of Foods.* Food and Nutrition Press, Westport.

Peryam, D. R., Polemis, B. W., Kamen, J. M., Eindhoven, J. & Pilgrim, F. J. (1960). *Food Preferences of Men in the U.S. Armed Forces.* Quartermaster Food and Container Institute for the Armed Forces Report, Chicago.

Pilgrim, F. J. (1957). The Components of Food Acceptance and their Measurement. *Amer. J. Clin. Nutrit.,* **5,** 171–5.

Popper, R., Hirsch, E., Lesher, L., Engell, D., Jezior, B., Bell, B. & Matthew, W. (1987). Field evaluation of improved MRE, MRE VII, and MRE IV. Technical Report NATICK/TR-87/027.

Rose, M. S. & Carlson, D. E. (1986). Effects of A-ration meals on body weight during sustained field operations. Technical Report T2-87. US Army Research Institute for Environmental Medicine.

Stone, H. & Sidel, J. L. (1985). *Sensory Evaluation Practices.* Academic Press, Orlando.

Chapter 8

Influence of Brand Label on Sensory Perception

MARGARET R. SHEEN and JENNIFER L. DRAYTON

Department of Marketing, University of Strathclyde, Stenhouse Building, 173 Cathedral Street, Glasgow G4 0RQ, UK

ABSTRACT

There are three sections to this paper. The first part presents an overview of the marketing objectives in branding a product. The product offering is seen by marketers to consist of more than the intrinsic properties of the product itself, it is the associated bundle of attributes of which branding is a part. Perception of a product is thus the subjective interaction with the augmented product. It is the subjective act of organising and integrating the incoming sensory stimuli which marketers aim to influence. Branding is therefore used to position the products in the mind. The application of the concepts of frame of reference and mental set are discussed.

The second part of the paper presents experimental evidence in support of these hypotheses and sets out to demonstrate the importance of the influence that branding can have on consumer preferences. The original findings, in 1964, of Allison and Uhl on the influence of beer brand identification on taste perception are acknowledged. Confirmation of this effect is presented by the authors' own results of students perceptions and preferences for branded cola drinks. Furthermore, the negative effects of generic labelling are demonstrated.

The final part of the paper returns to the theoretical domain in seeking to understand the underlying mechanism for these observed effects. The recognition that there is a parallel here with the placebo effect is drawn out. Some recent findings in the medical field which may help to explain this phenomenon are discussed.

BACKGROUND

What makes one food product more acceptable than another very similar product? How do consumers come to have preferences between food items from the same range? And why do consumers become brand loyal?

To marketers, this is a question of a sequential process, a movement from awareness and recognition of a product range, through the grouping of alternative choices within that range into a preference rating, to a belief in these preference sets and the consequent expectation of continuous satisfaction from the 'most-preferred' brand, i.e. brand loyalty.

In the food market, can this process rest solely upon intrinsic product stimuli, and in particular upon taste?

The purpose of this paper is to explore the influence of extrinsic product stimuli, the context that surrounds and extends the food product, upon the ability of the consumer to recognise a known and preferred taste.

A basic tenet of cognitive psychology lies in the nature of sensory perception—that it is humanly impossible to absorb all the stimulus objects to which an individual is exposed at any one time, in any one situation. To cope with the overload, incoming stimuli are organised into groups on the basis of perceived similarity or dissimilarity, as suggested by Gestalt theories. These groups then create the mental sets that make up a frame of reference for evaluation of future stimuli. The 'whole' may well be different from the sum of the parts.

The controlling element in the organisation of sensory stimuli is, then, the frame of reference, setting up expectations. Where the acceptability of a food product is concerned, the components of the frame of reference applied to food and drink must be identified, to recognise the nature of the extended product. Whilst evaluation of the sensory characteristics of a food item (flavour, aroma, colour, etc.), represent an obvious input, the wider aesthetic and social characteristics of the eating/drinking situation cannot be ignored. What is the contribution of the peripheral product cues of packaging, advertising, branding, etc., in the development of a mental set of positive or negative connotations?

Psychologists have long been interested in the effects of the combination of sensory stimuli, both intrinsic and extrinsic, in product evaluation, with a proliferation of studies (Pronko & Bowles, 1948a,b;

1949; Brown, 1958; Makens, 1965) showing the role of brand recognition and preference in both the ability to identify products and the rating of food products on quality and freshness.

This same area of research has, of course, been taken up by marketers, anxious to activate and assist the sequential processing of sensory stimuli from recognition to belief, thus setting up positive expectations within the frame of reference to influence future behaviour. In the marketing world, empirical evidence that brand identity can affect sensory perception has no doubt been obtained by many investigators without publishing to this effect. The original experimental findings within the marketing discipline are generally attributed to Allison & Uhl (1964), who followed up and extended the work of Pronko & Bowles in the cola market with a study of the influence of beer brand identification on taste perception. They observed that while participants in general were unable to discern differences between five brands of beer in a blind test, when these same beers were re-evaluated with their brand labels visible, brand loyal users then assigned significantly higher ratings to their preferred brands.

OBJECTIVES OF THE PRESENT STUDY

Our major objective was to re-examine these previously reported effects of brand labelling on preference-rating of products, and the ability to identify brands in a product range using only the sensory cues of the intrinsic product properties: furthermore, the study aimed to extend these findings by comparing the response of two sets of subjects, each of whom might be expected to put a different emphasis on the intrinsic and the extrinsic perceptual cues. One group of subjects had a background in science, whilst the other group was drawn from a marketing background.

METHOD

First the desired market characteristics were set, to give a realistic context:

recognisable high-consumption group;
anticipated brand loyalty;
product differentiation on ingredients;
high level of advertising support.

The market then chosen was the cola market, with its acknowledged high consumption in the 18–22 age group.

Cola is a part of the fiercely competitive £2·5 billion soft drinks market, with advertising support in the UK amongst the major brands ranging from a reported £7 million (Cadbury–Schweppes) to £25 million (Coca-Cola).

The two populations chosen as test groups were students at the University of Strathclyde—third year marketing students and final (fourth) year pharmacy students—to represent the high consumption group, or the target market segment, at which this advertising expenditure is directed.

Given the previous identification of the social context as integral in brand choice in a food or beverage market, the test was carried out under 'social' conditions. This does, of course, introduce 'noise' into the study, moving the subjects away from a focus upon any single aspect or product attribute. At the same time, it does more realistically provide the overall impression of the product as perceived in an everyday situation.

Four brands of Cola were selected:

Pepsi-Cola
Barr's Strike Cola
Fine Fare Yellow Label
Coca-Cola.

These were purchased in polycarbonate bottles identical in shape, so that when stripped of labels and the caps replaced, all the items were indistinguishable. The pairs of bottles used were purchased at the same time, and from the same retail outlet. For reference purposes, the unlabelled bottles were assigned the letters A, B, C and D.

All the drinks had been stored chilled, and students were invited to pour their own Cola into a plastic cup for tasting. Students were permitted to test in any order, and to retry if required. During the period of the test, social chat was allowed, but no discussion of the colas, or conferring on evaluations.

A first tasting was carried out using the bottles labelled A, B, C and D: simultaneously students were asked to complete the questionnaire shown as Fig. 1. After a short interval of about 10 min, the tasting was repeated using the bottles still showing the brand cues of labels and caps. A second questionnaire (Fig. 2) was distributed.

To meet the major objective of the study a null hypothesis was set

UNIVERSITY OF STRATHCLYDE

DEPARTMENT OF MARKETING

Consumer Behaviour

Cola Taste Test Questionnaire   Part 1

How often do you drink Cola?   More than once
a week
Once a week
Less than once
a week
Never

Do you have a preferred brand?

Please rate the unbranded colas
after tasting on the following scale:

	Very good	Good	Average	Poor	Very poor
A					
B					
C					
D					

Figure 1. Blind test questionnaire.

Cola Taste Test Questionnaire   Part 2

Please rate the branded colas after
tasting on the following scale:

	Very good	Good	Average	Poor	Very poor
Coca-Cola					
Fine Fare Yellow Label Cola					
Strike Cola					
Pepsi Cola					

Figure 2. Brand-labelled cola questionnaire.

up: 'that there is no difference in rating between cola drinks when presented "blind" (unlabelled) or labelled'.

RESULTS

Along the sequential process from recognition to belief, perceptions of brands within a product range can be expected to vary considerably, both positively and negatively. The extent of brand loyalty would obviously play a major part in any evaluation, and as a first step the initial questionnaire sought information on subjects' loyalty to brands in this market. As it turned out, approximately half of the pharmacy students and two-thirds of the marketing students claimed to have a preference for Coca-Cola.

A 'grey' area here was the small incidence of brand loyalty to the low calorie diet versions of Coca-Cola. As this could only tend to bias results in favour of the null hypothesis and against any effect we wished to demonstrate, these subjects were included in the Coca-Cola loyalty group.

Apart from a handful of Pepsi adherents (who were too few in number to be statistically significant) no other brand loyalty was expressed. Although too small in number, and not presented here, it is worth noting that the Pepsi-Cola loyalists demonstrated results congruent with the rest of our findings.

Results obtained are illustrated in Figs. 3 and 4. The Likert-type scale has been transferred to a rank order scale where 1 represents the 'most-liked' category and 5 represents the 'least-liked'. 'U' represents 'blind' or unlabelled, and 'L' represents labelled, i.e. branded. Each line drawn then represents one subject's response to the same product, presented first 'blind' and then branded.

A Wilcoxon's signed rank test for small samples was performed to test the significance of these results. The procedure outlined by Greensted et al. (1978) was adopted. Zero order differences were given negative rank numbers (most authors suggest ignoring zero differences) because these supported the null hypothesis, i.e., that there was no difference between unlabelled and labelled products.

Both sets of Coca-Cola taste tests were found to be significant at the $p = 0.05$ level. The null hypothesis was therefore rejected, thus confirming Allison & Uhl's findings.

The significance levels found for both the marketing and pharmacy

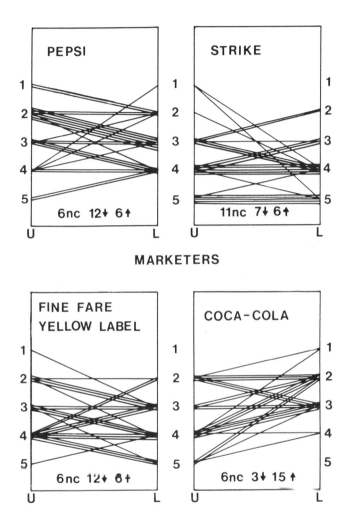

Figure 3. Response pattern of marketing students. 1, very good; 2, good; 3, average; 4, poor, 5, very poor; nc, no change; U, unlabelled (blind) test; L, brand-labelled test. Note: each line represents one student's response.

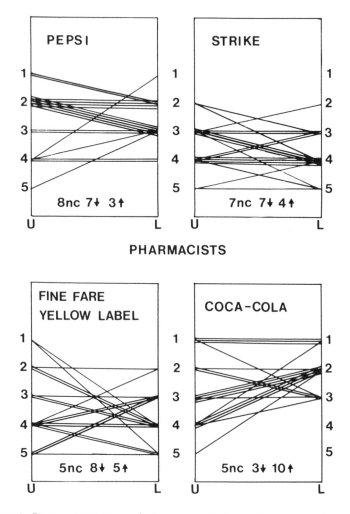

Figure 4. Response pattern of pharmacy students. 1, very good; 2, good; 3, average; 4, poor; 5, very poor; nc, no change; U, unlabelled (blind) test; L, brand-labelled test. Note: each line represents one student's response.

Table 1
Mean rating and standard deviation for labelled and un-labelled colas

	Mean	SD	Mean	SD
	PEPSI		STRIKE	
Marketers				
Unlabelled	2·8	1·1	3·7	1·2
Labelled	3·0	0·9	4·0	0·9
Pharmacists				
Unlabelled	2·6	1·1	3·5	0·9
Labelled	2·7	0·8	3·7	0·8
	FINE FARE YELLOW LABEL		COCA-COLA	
Marketers				
Unlabelled	3·2	1·0	3·5	1·1
Labelled	3·5	0·9	2·6	0·7
Pharmacists				
Unlabelled	3·4	1·2	2·8	1·3
Labelled	3·7	1·0	2·1	0·7

students, suggest similarity between the groups. This similarity is set out in Table 1, using the standard deviation as a measure of dispersion.

DISCUSSION

The results of this study suggest that for brand loyal subjects, there is an enhanced perception of the product properties of that brand, when the branding is obvious, with belief raising expectations. That similar patterns were observed with both science and business studies students indicates that, even where the frame of reference can be expected to be biased in favour of the intrinsic product features, where preference has been processed into belief, the external social context exerts an influence.

As has been discussed, marketing in practice has seen fit to utilise such effects as the enhancement of an image of a product and branding for commercial gain. Many of these techniques have been derived from the constructs of psychology. Yet telling us that sensory perception can be distorted, even how to distort it, does not bring us any closer to understanding, at a deeper and more reductionist level, the underlying mechanisms concerning perception and memory. This, of course, is one of the key issues of the age in which we live and it is unrealistic to suppose that the next few lines can provide an answer. What can be attempted is to draw some strands together from other fields of enquiry which may help to shed a little more light on the phenomenon.

Some of this evidence is now coming from the medical field. The 'placebo' effect, so widely known and utilised in ages past, is within the same domain as our current interest. Drug trials are conducted doubly blind, so as to screen out this effect. The uncritical acceptance of drug versus placebo research methodology has contributed to the neglect of the experimental examination of the psychological influences upon biological processes (White *et al.*, 1985). Nor is there any discipline where such studies readily find a home. Only recently has respectable scientific enquiry been made into this phenomenon. Ross & Buckalew (1985) have surveyed the literature and have concluded that the following dependent variables are responsive to placebo manipulation: reaction time, grip strength, pulse rate, blood pressure, pain, short-term rote memory and self perception of relaxation and activation. Here again the effects of branding have been demonstrated; brand name labelled aspirin, and an identical-appearing placebo, have been shown to give better results than either compound labelled generically (Shapiro, 1970).

Such findings, as those presented in this paper, exhibit the phenomenon of mental set. Neurophysiology is beginning to provide some anatomical evidence for these effects. Mishkin & Appenzeller (1987) have described some of the major pathways and structures in the brain which are involved when sensory information (visual) is stored in memory. What is becoming evident from these studies is that sensory information, though recorded initially as isolated aspects, is immediately reprocessed and gated through increasingly broader perceptual windows where interaction with linked pieces of information occurs. Hence before perceptual stimuli are stored there is a great potential for distortion; the human brain is much more than a recorder with sensors attached but has an extraordinary ability to integrate a multidimensional field of information.

Food acceptability in the final analysis has to be considered within the total social context. We may attempt to look at the constituent factors along the way but if the placebo effect is a model which we can follow then the sum of the parts will not be equal to the whole.

Moreover these 'social' variables, of which branding is one, can no longer be regarded as a form of magic to be manipulated only by the unscrupulous and unscientific.

REFERENCES

Allison, R. I. & Uhl, K. (1964). Influence of beer brand identification on taste perception. *J. Marketing Res.*, **1**, 36–9.

Brown, R. L. (1958). Wrapper influence on the perception of freshness in bread. *J. Appl. Psychol.*, **42**, 257–60.

Greensted, C. S., Jardine, A. K. S. & MacFarlane, J. D. (1978). In *Essentials of Statistics and Marketing*. Heinemann, London, pp. 137–8.

Makens, J. C. (1965). Effect of brand preference upon consumers' perceived taste of turkey meat. *J. Appl. Psychol.*, **49**, 261–3.

Mishkin, M. & Appenzeller, T. (1987). The anatomy of memory. *Scient. Am.*, June, 62–71.

Pronko, N. H. & Bowles, J. W. (1948a). Identification of cola beverages I: a first study. *J. Appl. Psychol.*, **32**, 304–12.

Pronko, N. H. & Bowles, J. W. (1948b). Identification of cola beverages II: a further study. *J. Appl. Psychol.*, **32**, 559–64.

Pronko, N. H. & Bowles, J. W. (1949). Identification of cola beverages III: a final study. *J. Appl. Psychol.*, **33**, 605–8.

Ross, S. & Buckalew, L. W. (1985). Placebo agentry: assessment of drug and placebo effects. In *Placebo Theory, Research and Mechanism*, eds L. White, B. Tursky & G. E. Schwarz. Guilford Press, New York, London, pp. 67–82.

Shapiro, A. K. (1970). Placebo effects in psychotherapy and psychoanalysis. *J. Clin. Pharmacol.*, **10**, 73–8.

White, L., Tursky, B. & Schwarz, G. E. (1985). Proposed synthesis of placebo models. In *Placebo Theory, Research and Mechanism*, eds L. White, B. Tursky & G. E. Schwarz. Guilford Press, New York, London, pp. 431–47.

Chapter 9

Is Sensory Evaluation of Alternatively Produced Foods Affected by Cognitive Information and Product Familiarity?

PETER A. M. OUDE OPHUIS

Department of Marketing and Marketing Research, Wageningen Agricultural University, Hollandseweg 1, 6706 KN Wageningen, The Netherlands

ABSTRACT

Taste characteristics seem to be an important motive for consumptic of alternatively produced foods like organic and natural foods. In som cases a labelling effect is supposed, while others claim experience to be the key factor to discrimination ability. In this experiment both cognitive information and product familiarity were controlled while perception and preference of alternatively and conventionally produced carrots were measured. Analysis with multidimensional scaling (MDS) and multivariate analysis of variance (MANOVA) indicates that the hypothesized effects of labelling and familiarity on sensory evaluation of foods from different origin cannot be demonstrated.

INTRODUCTION

During the past decade there has been a growing consumer demand for alternatively produced foods like *organic* and *natural* foods.

101

Somehow it is believed and claimed that these foods contain many characteristics that are superior to ordinary, conventionally produced foods. Consumer research indicates that besides health reasons and fear for chemical additives and residues, taste characteristics are an important motive for consumers to use this type of foods (Oltersdorf, 1983; Wierenga et al., 1983; Dauchez, 1985). Early studies on consumer preferences for 'health' and 'organic' foods in comparison with ordinary foods showed no significant differences for most products (Appledorf et al., 1974; Schutz & Lorenz, 1976) and there is little evidence that alternatively produced foods differ in physico-chemical characteristics from ordinary foods (Maga et al., 1976; Hansen, 1981). However, the study of Schutz & Lorenz (1976) demonstrated a 'label' effect for the word 'organic'. Deters (1983) found significantly higher preference ratings for tomatoes when they were indicated as 'biologically grown'.

The influence of labelling on taste perception was demonstrated by Allison & Uhl (1964) with their classic beer brand study. Consumers were generally not able to discern the taste differences among the various beer brands, but apparently labels and their associations did influence their evaluations. On the other hand, two studies suggest that beer consumers possess at least some ability to distinguish among different brands on the basis of taste and aroma cues alone (Jacoby et al., 1971; Mauser, 1979).

Especially in the case of fresh produce, the label (organic, biodynamic, ecological), or information about the origin, is essential in the marketing process (Oude Ophuis, 1985). Alternatively grown products are sold with this information and consumers are prepared to pay higher prices than for comparable ordinary products. Opponents of alternative agriculture frequently state that the only difference between alternative and conventional foods is the label and the price, whilst users of alternatively grown foods claim that, besides health and environmental considerations, there are genuine taste differences between alternatively and conventionally produced foods.

The research presented below, focused on the effects of labelling and familiarity, on sensory evaluation of alternatively and convention-ally grown foods. The methodology of multidimensional scaling (MDS) has been shown to be a powerful technique for the analysis of consumer perceptions (Schiffman et al., 1981). In several studies, MDS and multivariate analysis of variance (MANOVA) have been applied to investigate changes in perception and preference. Moinpour et al.

(1976) found that subjects' perceptions of cognitive stimuli in response to persuasive communications, can be monitored successfully with MDS. Information about brands in a product class, provided to consumers with the intention of altering their preference and perception, appears to affect perceptions of individual brands within the perceptual space without changing the underlying structure of the space (McCullough *et al.*, 1982). The MDS-MANOVA analysis showed encouraging results in an experiment where cognitive and sensory cues were combined in a perceptual space for coffee types (Roberts & Taylor, 1975).

In this research MDS and MANOVA techniques were applied to investigate the following questions:

1. Can consumers discriminate between samples of vegetables of different origin (alternative and conventional) on the basis of only sensory characteristics?
2. Which sensory characteristics (if any) do consumers use to distinguish among these vegetables?
3. To what extent are perception and preference for these products influenced by information about origin and familiarity with the type of product (alternative or conventional)?

EXPERIMENTAL METHOD

Carrots from six different origins were chosen as stimuli. Three varieties were alternatively grown: *biodynamic* and *ecological* which were bought in specialized stores, and *garden* which was obtained from a private gardener practising biological gardening. The three ordinary qualities were: *supermarket, market stall* and *greengrocer*. As the main objective of this experiment was to study the label effect for products under normal market conditions, there was no control for cultivar and other growing factors, like soil and climate. All stimuli were presented both blind and labelled, so there were twelve stimuli in the basic design.

Two convenience samples, each of nine consumers, were selected for participation in the experiment. One group consisted of regular consumers of alternatively grown vegetables and the other group was formed by ordinary consumers with no experience of alternatively produced vegetables. Subjects were not informed about the number and type of stimuli they had to taste. They were only advised that they were participating in a taste test of carrots from different origins. Each subject attended four sessions within 2 weeks. In the first session dissimilarity data were gathered on all possible blind pairs (21) followed by all possible labelled pairs (15) of the twelve stimuli. The second session consisted of dissimilarity ratings for all possible pairs (36) with one labelled and one blind side (randomly assigned).

Table 1 represents the design of the stimulus-presentation matrix for the first two sessions. The upper and lower triangles give the presentations for the first session, while the presentation scheme for the second session is represented by the remaining square. In the third session subjects rated all 12 stimuli on 12 attributes. In the last session preference ratings were obtained for the 12 stimuli, two for each stimulus.

Stimuli were presented in a different random order to each subject and before each session subjects could taste the 12 stimuli (blind) to get acquainted with the differences amongst stimuli.

All ratings were obtained using 150 mm graphic rating scales. For the dissimilarity ratings, the anchors of the scale were formed by *exact same* on the left side and *completely different* on the right side (Schiffman *et al.*, 1981). Scores on the scales were recorded in mm.

Table 1
Design of the stimulus-presentation matrix for pairwise comparison dissimilarity ratings

	a	b	c	d	e	f	A	B	C	D	E	F
a	aa											
b	ba	bb										
c	ca	cb	cc									
d	da	db	dc	dd								
e	ea	eb	ec	ed	ee							
f	fa	fb	fc	fd	fe	ff						
A	Aa	Ab	Ac	Ad	Ae	Af	—					
B	Ba	Bb	Bc	Bd	Be	Bf	BA	—				
C	Ca	Cb	Cc	Cd	Ce	Cf	CA	CB	—			
D	Da	Db	Dc	Dd	De	Df	DA	DB	DC	—		
E	Ea	Eb	Ec	Ed	Ee	Ef	EA	EB	EC	ED	—	
F	Fa	Fb	Fc	Fd	Fe	Ff	FA	FB	FC	FD	FE	—

a–f: unlabelled stimuli.
A–F: labelled stimuli.

For the attribute and preference ratings anchors consisted of positive/negative statements in relation to the attribute.

RESULTS

Before exploring influences of cognitive labelling and product familiarity on sensory evaluation, the basic question as to whether consumers are able to taste any differences between stimuli, has to be considered. The diagonal of the stimulus-presentation matrix for the dissimilarity ratings consists of physically equal stimulus pairs. Theoretically these comparisons should be judged exactly the same and consequently the dissimilarities should be zero. However, the overall average dissimilarity score for these comparisons appeared to be 59·33. This bias towards some degree of difference between essentially the same stimuli could be an artefact due to this type of instruction (McBride et al., 1984).

The dissimilarity data were used to calculate signal-to-noise ratios (Schiffman et al., 1981) for individual tasters by dividing the average score for different pairs by the average score for physically equal pairs. Table 2 gives these ratios for all subjects based on only the blind stimuli (the upper left triangle from the design matrix) and based on all stimuli (the complete matrix).

In the latter case also, the scores for the six physically equal pairs of the mixed labelled condition were used to calculate the average score for physically equal pairs and then the average score for each of the other 60 comparisons was divided by this score. According to Schiffman et al. (1981) one can tentatively classify subjects into three groups depending on the magnitude of the signal-to-noise ratios. Subjects with ratios greater than 1·5 can be classified as good discriminators. Those with ratios less than 1·0 are considered bad discriminators. The group with ratios lying between 1·0 and 1·5 can be considered to have intermediate discriminating ability. Closer inspection of Table 2 reveals that good, intermediate and bad discriminators are distributed more or less evenly over both types of consumers.

The pairwise dissimilarity data were first analysed using the ALSCAL program which has options for several multidimensional scaling models (Young et al., 1978). Applying both replicated and weighted multidimensional scaling models (RMDS and WMDS), under different assumptions of the scale level of the data (interval and

Table 2
Signal-to-noise ratios for individual subjects

Subject	Consumer type	Ratios	
		Blind pairs	All pairs
1	A	1·19	1·22
2	A	1·06	1·61
3	A	2·00	2·45
4	A	1·76	1·42
5	R	1·20	2·06
6	R	0·70	0·91
7	A	1·69	1·72
8	R	1·60	1·76
9	A	0·82	1·11
10	A	1·37	1·59
11	R	0·95	1·28
12	R	1·06	1·27
13	A	1·41	1·72
14	A	1·13	1·38
15	R	1·10	0·91
16	R	1·81	2·01
17	R	1·19	1·41
18	R	1·64	1·68

A = alternative; R = regular.

ordinal), resulted in low-dimensional configurations with a poor fit. Kruskal's stress values for the solutions in two dimensions varied between 0·34 and 0·38 and the explained variance for the metric solutions floated around 0·10. Because stress values did not drop considerably with more than two dimensions, only two-dimensional solutions will be considered for further analysis. Notwithstanding the high stress values, there seemed to be a consistent structure on visual inspection of the graphic plots of the various MDS-solutions. Figure 1 depicts the 12 stimuli in a two-dimensional configuration using a WMDS-model.

Despite the high stress of this common perceptual space, it is clear that except for one, all pairs of labelled and unlabelled stimuli are positioned close to each other. Typically all the stimulus pairs of alternative origin have the shortest interdistances. Only the labelled and unlabelled 'supermarket' carrots are positioned at a distance from

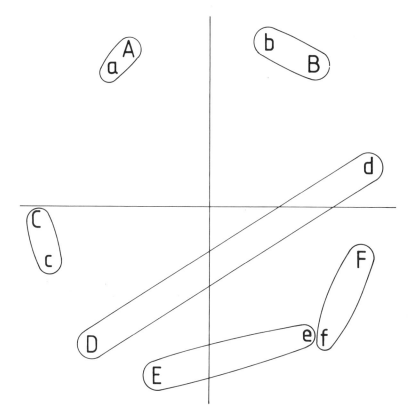

Figure 1. WMDS solution in two dimensions for the 12 stimuli (stress = 0·37). Unlabelled stimuli: a, biodynamic; b, ecological; c, garden; d, supermarket; e, market stall; f, greengrocer. Labelled stimuli: A, biodynamic; B, ecological; C, garden; D, supermarket; E, market stall; F, greengrocer.

each other. This structure was more or less the same when assumptions about scaling model and scale-level of the data were adjusted according to the previously mentioned options. Using the signal-to-noise ratios as a formal criterion for the discriminating ability of the subjects, the fit (stress) of the two-dimensional MDS solutions was investigated when the worst six subjects were dropped or when only the best six were used. The stress values were 0·35 for the best six and 0·37 when the worst six were dropped. Visual inspection of the graphic plots showed much congruence with the pattern in Fig. 1.

Further analysis of the dissimilarity data was focused on changes in the perceptual space due to the cognitive information about origin. Changes in the perceptual space can be structural or spatial (Moinpour *et al.*, 1976). Structural changes may take place when subjects alter the number or character of the dimensions used to evaluate the stimuli. Spatial changes may occur when the subjects alter the importance (salience) of one of more of the structural dimensions. Because both blind and labelled stimuli pairs were presented in one session after the other, it is very unlikely that structural changes would have occurred in this experiment. Analysis is therefore confined to spatial changes in the perceptual space. Two approaches were followed to assess and evaluate perceptual changes: C-MATCH and MANOVA.

The C-MATCH procedure (Pennell & Young, 1967) performs an orthogonal least squares rotation procedure and produces a 'best fit' matched space of two configurations. From the stimulus-presentation matrix the left upper triangle and the right lower triangle dis-similarities for all 18 subjects were used separately as input for MDS solutions of the perceptual space. Using the RMDS model of ALSCAL two common spaces in two dimensions were produced, one for unlabelled stimuli and one for labelled stimuli. Table 3 summarizes the results of the MDS procedure and C-MATCH.

Both MDS solutions showed very high stress values, indicating a poor fit of the perceptual configurations to the dissimilarity data. However, the structure of these configurations appears to be very similar for both types of stimuli. The C-MATCH index of fit between the two configurations may be considered very good (0·921). After orthogonal rotation of the configurations, the two dimensions are highly correlated with each other (0·993 and 0·956), which means that there are virtually no spatial differences between the perception of labelled and unlabelled stimuli.

Multivariate analysis of variance (MANOVA) was applied to test differences in the dissimilarity judgements that could be attributed to the experimental factors, consumer-type and label. As would be expected on the basis of the MDS analysis, no significance was demonstrated for either effect.

The number of dimensions and their interpretation is usually one of the most difficult points of MDS analysis. In the results shown so far, no attempt has been made to interpret the dimensions, and the dimensionality was restricted to two, on the basis of little stress improvement at higher dimensionalities. However, external analysis is

Table 3
Congruence between perceptual spaces for unlabelled and labelled stimuli

Stimulus	Coordinates				
	Unlabelled		Labelled		
	dim 1	dim 2	dim 1	dim 2	
A	−0·517	1·494	−0·473	−1·436	C-MATCH initial goodness of fit between configurations: 0·921
B	−1·142	−0·845	1·132	−0·317	
C	−1·301	−0·314	1·653	−0·256	
D	1·334	−0·230	−0·795	1·141	
E	0·789	1·073	−1·231	−0·496	correlation between dimensions after rotation: 1–1: 0·993 1–2: 0·000
F	0·837	−1·177	−0·258	1·365	
Kruskal's stress		0·468		0·455	2–2: 0·956 2–1: 0·000

possible using the data for the attribute scores which were gathered during the third session.

The results of a principal component analysis are summarized in Table 4. Three factors (eigenvalue >1·0) could be extracted which explained 86·8% of variance. After varimax rotation, the three dimensions could be interpreted as dim. 1: sweet-bitter, dim. 2: aromatic-watery and dim. 3: crunchy-tough. To interpret the axis of the MDS configurations the factor scores of the stimuli were rotated to the stimulus configuration of the WMDS solution, using C-MATCH. This was performed with the first two factors for the two-dimensional solution and with all three factors for the (not reported) three-dimensional configuration. The indices of fit were 0·01 and 0·16 respectively, which indicated that the perceptual dimensions based on dissimilarity could not be interpreted with the used attributes. This was not entirely surprising since attribute scores and dissimilarity judgements are two different types of data. However, the attribute data were checked to see if any experimental effects could be recovered. Table 5 summarizes the results from MANOVA for the

Table 4
Results of principal component analysis on attributes after varimax rotation

Attribute			
Bitter	0·81	−0·07	0·23
Earthy	0·81	0·23	0·04
Crunchy	0·28	0·06	0·85
Harsh	0·67	0·43	0·41
Astringent	0·38	0·06	−0·01
Vivid colour	−0·82	0·30	0·22
Aromatic	−0·61	0·72	0·18
Watery	−0·36	−0·76	0·38
Sweet	−0·77	0·42	0·35
Flat	0·16	−0·88	−0·29
Tough	0·25	−0·21	−0·92
Tasty	−0·05	0·93	0·18
Percentage variance explained	43·0	29·2	14·6

Table 5
Summary of multivariate analysis of variance for all 12 perceptual attributes

Attribute	Label ($df = 1·16$)	Label[a] consumer ($df = 1·16$)	Product ($df = 5·12$)	Product[a] consumer ($df = 5·12$)	Label[a] product ($df = 5·12$)
Bitter	4·18	0·07	13·60	1·24	3·62[a]
Earthy	11·31[b]	0·18	5·97[b]	0·46	0·87
Crunchy	3·24	1·92	4·16[b]	0·98	1·73
Harsh	3·58	1·47	7·24[b]	0·82	2·08
Astringent	2·07	0·14	4·49[b]	1·04	1·39
Vivid colour	0·60	2·20	6·56[b]	1·10	1·12
Aromatic	0·03	0·62	11·08[b]	1·88	2·80
Watery	0·75	5·17[a]	3·13[a]	1·56	1·30
Sweet	0·18	0·13	10·90[b]	0·32	2·14
Flat	0·07	0·26	11·95[b]	2·65	1·36
Cough	0·44	1·20	3·10[a]	0·57	1·51
Tasty	6·39[a]	0·33	2·93	0·81	2·14

[a] $P > 0·05$; [b] $P > 0·01$.

attribute scores with consumer type as between subjects factor and label and product as within subject factors.

From this table it can be concluded that, only for two attributes, is there a label effect; there is a difference in the mean ratings for earthy and tasty when stimuli are labelled. The effect of products is highly significant for almost all attributes. There are significant differences in the ratings of the six products on the perceptual attributes. This supports the results of the analysis of the dissimilarity judgements; consumers were able to discriminate the products on sensory cues. The F-statistics of the between-subjects effect are not included in Table 5, but for all attributes none of these was significant.

For the interactions between the main effects, only a label by consumer interaction for wateriness, and a label by product interaction for bitter are significant. Thus, the perception of bitterness differs for labelled and unlabelled stimuli. Under the influence of the label, the two consumer groups differ in their perception of wateriness.

DISCUSSION

Perceptual data collected through pairwise comparisons are usually considered to be less noisy and render a better structure than adjective data (Schiffman et al., 1981). The results of this experiment show that for this particular product class, the dissimilarity judgements contained much 'noise', as shown by the unusually high stress values for MDS solutions. Nevertheless, the derived configurations were not meaningless and showed a consistent structure. Both the configuration with 12 stimuli and the two separate configurations with six stimuli, give visual evidence of the absence of a label-effect in the perception of vegetables of different origin. Interpretation of the dimensions was difficult. Even when stimuli with known attributes are used for sensory evaluation the interpretation of dimensions of MDS configurations is impossible when stimuli with more complex sensory attributes are presented (McCullough et al., 1982).

From the present experiment it can be concluded that perceptual configurations derived from dissimilarity judgements proved to be stable and thus are powerful instruments for detecting spatial changes in sensory perceptions of complex stimuli.

The attributes used could not be related to the MDS configurations on the basis of their principal components. The relatively high percentage of explained variance for the three factors suggests less noise in this type of data than the dissimilarity scores. The preliminary analysis of the preference data did not show any significant effects for the effects of labelling and familiarity. No attempt was made to relate these data to the perception data because of the high stress values of the configurations.

In conclusion, the results of this experiment indicate that the hypothesized effects of labelling and familiarity on the sensory evaluation of carrots from different origins cannot be demonstrated. In general, consumers can discriminate between products on sensory cues alone, although the ability to discriminate is not the same for each consumer. Further research on the relation of sensory perceptual dimensions and preference in the case of alternatively produced foods, is necessary to evaluate the importance of this type of product.

REFERENCES

Allison, R. I. & Uhl, K. P. (1964). Influence of beer brand identification on taste perception. *Journal of Marketing Research,* **1,** 36–9.

Appledorf, H., Pennington, W. B. & Koburger, J. A. (1974). Sensory evaluation of health foods—a comparison with traditional foods. *J. Milk and Food Technology,* **37,** 392–4.

Dauchez, E. (1985). La consommation des produits 'bios'. *Nature et Progress,* **22,** 18–22.

Deters, S. (1983). Verbraucherpräferenzen bei Frischgemüse am Beispiel von Tomaten-Ergebnisse einer Einstellungsanalyse und eines Sensorischen Tests. In *Verhaltenswissenschaftliche Ansätze der Nachfrageanalyse,* ed. R. von Alvensleben. Beiträge auf der wissenschaftliche Arbeitstagung der Deutschen Gartenbauwissenschaftliche Gesellschaft e.V., Sektion Gartenbau-ökonomie, in Stuttgart vom 16–18 März 1983, Institut für Gartenbau-ökonomie der Universität Hannover.

Hansen, H. (1981). Comparison of chemical composition and taste of biodynamically and conventionally grown vegetables. *Qual. Plant. Foods Hum. Nutr.,* **30,** 203–11.

Jacoby, J., Olson, J. C. & Haddock, R. A. (1971). Price, brand name and product composition characteristics as determinants of perceived quality. *Journal of Applied Psychology,* **55,** 570–9.

Maga, J. A., Moore, F. D. & Oshima, N. (1976). Yield, nitrate levels and sensory properties of spinach as influenced by organic and mineral fertiliser levels. *Journal of the Science of Food and Agriculture,* **27,** 103–14.

Mauser, G. A. (1979). Allison & Uhl revisited: the effects of taste and brand name on perceptions and preferences. In *Advances in Consumer Research,* vol. **6,** ed. W. L. Wilkie, Association for Consumer Research, Ann Arbor.

McBride, R. L., Watson, A. J. & Cox. B. M. (1984). The paired-comparison method as a simple difference test. *Journal of Food Quality*, **6**, 285–90.
McCullough, J. M., Maclachlan, D. L. & Moinpour, R. (1982). Impact of information on preference and perception. In *Advances in Consumer Research*, vol. **9**, ed. A. A. Mitchell. Association for Consumer Research, Ann Arbor, pp. 402–5.
Moinpour, R., McCullough, J. M. & Maclachlan, D. L. (1976). Time changes in perception: a longitudinal application of multidimensional scaling. *Journal of Marketing Research*, **13**, 245–53.
Oltersdorf, U. (1983). Der Markt für 'gesunde Nahrungsmittel' in der Bundesrepublik Deutschland. *AID-Verbrauchersdienst*, **28**, 223–31.
Oude Ophuis, P. A. M. (1985). Consumption of alternatively produced foods. In *Consumer Behavior Research and Marketing of Agricultural Products*, ed. J. E. R. Frijters. Proceedings of the Agro-food workshop organised by the Commission of the European Communities, 13–16 November 1985 in Wageningen, The Netherlands. National Council for Agricultural Research, The Hague.
Pennell, R. J. & Young, F. W. (1967). An IBM system/360 Program for Orthogonal Least-Squares Matrix Fitting. *Behavioral Science*, **12**, 165.
Roberts, M. L. & Taylor, J. R. (1975). Analyzing proximity judgments in an experimental design. *Journal of Marketing Research*, **12**, 68–72.
Schiffman, S. S., Reynolds, M. L. & Young, F. W. (1981). *Introduction to Multidimensional Scaling*. Academic Press, New York.
Schutz, H. G. & Lorenz, O. A. (1976). Consumer preferences for vegetables grown under 'commercial' and 'organic' conditions. *Journal of Food Science*, **41**, 70–3.
Wierenga, B., Heuzen, P. S. van & Schols, D. M. M. (1983). 'Andere' voedingsmiddelen: een marktsegment met perspectief?. *Economisch Statistische Berichten*, **68**, 1028–35.
Young, F. W., Takane, Y. & Lewyckyj, R. (1978). ALSCAL: a nonmetric multidimensional scaling program with several individual differences options. *Journal of Marketing Research*, **15**, 612–15.

Chapter 10

Beyond Preference: Appropriateness as a Measure of Contextual Acceptance of Food

HOWARD G. SCHUTZ

Department of Consumer Sciences, University of California, Davis, CA 95616, USA

ABSTRACT

Acceptance for a food as represented by preference is an important factor in decisions made with regard to utilization of food products. However, simple preference may not accurately reflect the influence of different situations in which food products are used and thus weakens the external validity of preference data. A measure which can be used to overcome this problem, especially when the consumer is evaluating the names of foods, is appropriateness. Here food names are rated for degree of appropriateness for a wide variety of consumption situations and uses, including time, person, location, health factors, sensory characteristics and economic considerations. Data are presented on six studies in which this type of methodology was utilized. The product classes evaluated included a wide variety of foods; rice, wine and dairy products, for general population groups, and a smaller set of foods for a special population of hospital patients and staff. The results of these studies indicate that there is a simple cognitive structure underlying food perceptions. There are wide differences in appropriateness for foods depending on the situation/use and there are clear differences between appropriateness and general degree of liking for foods.

INTRODUCTION

There is no question that a great deal of knowledge has been gained concerning foods by studying affective or hedonic/preference attitudes towards them. This knowledge has been useful in understanding important concepts related to basic tastes and odours as well as in practical situations in which these types of judgements are used as a surrogate for actual food acceptance. The purpose of the latter is to improve the efficiency of decisions regarding the nature and types of foods which should be developed and offered, in order to increase food acceptance, both for the general consumer in the marketplace, as well as in food service situations such as in military or educational institutions.

Those who have worked in the field where preference type judgements are utilized as a proxy for acceptance have been aware that they are far from perfect predictors of actual food acceptance (Kamenetzky *et al.*, 1957; Pilgrim & Kamen, 1963; Sidel *et al.*, 1972; Lau *et al.*, 1979). By food acceptance, in this discussion I mean the actual consumption of foods or at least an estimate of consumption, such as an indication of reported frequency of consumption behaviour. If we set aside the study of food stimuli in which our interest is primarily of a theoretical nature, and/or we are willing to consider affective judgements of an integrated global nature as our primary objective, then we do not have the problem of the lack of external validity, i.e. we are not measuring something which relates to an actual eating situation. However, if our objectives are related to improving our ability to make decisions with regard to actual feeding situations in which individuals are both selecting and consuming foods it is essential that we both understand non-preference contributing factors, and develop methods by which they may be included in making our decisions. On a theoretical level, it may also be important to consider more than the pure affect dimension, in order to better understand the complex relationships among foods.

An example from a preference-consumption research study will illustrate the external validity problem. Figure 1 (Kamenetzky *et al.*, 1957) is a nomogram based on data collected on the same individuals in a military feeding situation, for mean hedonic preference judgements and actual food consumed over a 1 month period. It is obvious from examination of this nomogram that the meaning of a particular preference rating in terms of actual consumption varies widely based

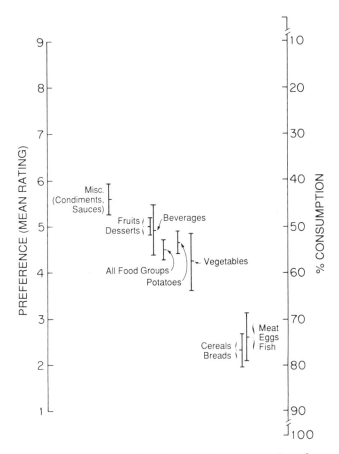

Figure 1. Nomogram for estimating food consumption from mean preference ratings. The mid-point of each bar represents the mean value and the ends are placed at one standard error from the mean. (From Kamenetzky *et al.,* 1957).

on the type of food that is considered. If one compares meats, eggs and fish with fruits and desserts, we can see that the first category may have low preference ratings and still result in relatively high consumption as compared to desserts and fruits, where a low rating leads to low consumption values. Meats, eggs and fish may be considered as necessary to the meal whereas desserts and fruits are viewed as rewards, not to be eaten unless well liked. In this case the class of foods involved clearly modifies the meaning of the preference judgement in terms of actual food acceptance and thus markedly influences the external validity of the evaluations.

FOOD ACCEPTANCE EXTERNAL VALIDITY PARADIGM

In order to better understand the factors or dimensions which influence the external validity of evaluations of food stimuli relative to food acceptance, three major dimensions are identified: (1) type of respondent, (2) type of stimuli, and (3) measurement procedure. Examination of these three dimensions in Fig. 2 shows how they relate to increasing external validity. Considering the 'type of respondent' dimension first, expert judges are placed at the lowest level of external validity (unless one is interested in predicting the food

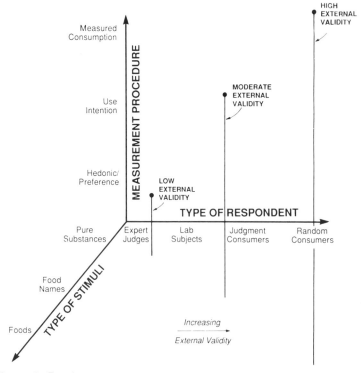

Figure 2. Food acceptance external validity evaluation dimensions.

acceptance of expert judges!) followed by laboratory trained panellists, then consumers who are selected on a judgement basis, and finally a random group of consumers chosen to be representative of a particular target population. For the 'food stimuli' dimension, the lowest level of external validity would be pure substances (or perhaps the names of pure substances might be even lower in external validity), followed by food names and the highest validity associated with food items themselves. The third dimension, 'measurement procedure', is anchored at the low level by simple affective judgements, which include measures of pleasantness and unpleasantness, hedonic measures, paired preference and so on, followed by measures of use intention, which include action-type scales and appropriateness for particular uses, and lastly, measured consumption. As a slightly less valid measure, one could have measures of consumption that are estimated, such as reported frequency of use data. In considering this paradigm, note that the distances between the various categories are ordinal, and not interval, and that the three dimensions may not combine in some simple linear additive fashion to produce external validity, but might have some nonlinear, even interactive, relationships. Examples of low, moderate and high external validity evaluations are shown by vertical lines in the three dimensional representation. Even if this paradigm has only a symbolic reality, it certainly illustrates the complexity of the external validity issue with regard to food acceptance. The simplification of such a paradigm is obvious if one just considers a few of the categories in terms of the true sources of variability that can and often do exist. For example, with food stimuli, it is known that size, temperature, menu composition (Eindhoven & Pilgrim, 1959), preceding items, number of items evaluated, etc., can influence preference scores, which may in turn strongly influence the external validity of the particular study. Considering the 'respondent dimension', factors which can influence this dimension include previous experience with the items, methods of selecting the respondent, the ambient conditions under which the respondent evaluates, physiological state, and so on. On the 'method of measurement' dimension, all of the various types of scales, ordinal, interval, ratio, as well as methods of measuring use intention and consumption, have their special measurement problems. For example, we know that data reported by individuals on their consumption of foods can suffer from systematic biases with regard to under- and over-reporting particular food categories (Krantzler *et al.*, 1982).

In the remainder of this chapter, no magical solution which results in a perfectly externally valid measure of food acceptance is offered. However an approach is described which involves measuring appropriateness for uses/situations/attributes as a use intention type of measure which can be helpful in better understanding the acceptance of food in actual consumption situations, as well as a tool for analysing and organizing the complex cognitive interrelationships and perceptual structure of foods. The importance of the cognitive aspects of food in food acceptance was discussed in detail by Olson (1981).

ITEM BY USE APPROPRIATENESS AS A USE INTENTION METHOD

The application of this technique for a wide variety of food items and uses has been investigated by the author and colleagues, over the past 16 years. It is patterned after a basic anthropological procedure (Stefflre, 1971) which has been adapted for use in a consumer marketing context. It is believed that these studies, as a group, illustrate the value of the concept of appropriateness in understanding foods and food acceptance and the cognitive structure of foods. Firstly some post hoc research hypotheses, concerning food acceptance and preference are postulated and then a summary of results of studies which directly bear on the validity of these hypotheses are presented. (1) Simple affect or preference is not the same as appropriateness for use. (2) What is appropriate to consume varies widely, depending on the nature of the consumption situation, who is consuming, occasion, cost, cultural differences, and other attributes of the item to be consumed. (3) By using a simple item by use appropriateness technique, one can find the aggregate and individual cognitive structure for a class of items. (4) Within a class of items or uses, consumers have a simple cognitive structure relative to the total number of items or uses. (5) The cognitive structure dimensions differentiate among groups and can predict consumption.

Basic Methodology
For all the studies to be reviewed, the same basic methodological procedures are involved. Where there are major variations, they will be noted in the description of that study. Food items are selected to represent a class of foods obtained through literature research and by

the use of interviews with consumers concerning what they identify as items in that class. The uses, situations or attributes to be evaluated are obtained by eliciting information on when it would be appropriate to use such items. Respondents are selected so as to produce a representative sample of a desired target population. Individuals are asked to rate the appropriateness of each food item for each of the various uses, attributes and situations in a matrix format on a self administered questionnaire. The scale generally utilized is a seven point scale ranging from 'never appropriate' (1) to 'always appropriate' (7). The uses/situations/attributes are phrased in a use intention mode, i.e. they are typically stated as 'when I want something I really like' or 'in a salad' or 'for children'. Henceforth for purposes of simplicity, uses/situations/attributes will be abbreviated simply as uses. These uses include time of day, occasion, where served, physiological states, how used, psychological characteristics, person served, physical and sensory characteristics. For analysis the mean appropriateness rating over the group or sub-group of subjects is determined for all item by use combinations. In order to determine the cognitive structure for the foods and for the uses, a principal component factor analysis is conducted among all pairs of foods and for all pairs of uses.

Study 1—General Food Perceptions

Fifty-six foods representing all classes and types of foods were selected and forty-eight uses were identified and included in a 56 × 48 matrix (Schutz et al., 1975b). Two hundred females from four different cities in the US rated the appropriateness of each of the foods for each of the uses on the seven point scale mentioned earlier. For this study, as with the others to be presented, space limitations do not allow for the details of either the entire procedure or the results (which are available in the cited publications). However, selected data will be presented which represent findings relevant to the hypotheses presented earlier.

Presented in Table 1 are the 5 highest weighted foods in rank order for each of the 5 factors that were obtained through the factor analysis of the 56 food items, where the 48 uses served as cases. The weights or factor loadings which are obtained in such an analysis can be considered like correlations with the factor; the highest weighted items having the highest correlation with that factor. The 5 factors explained 80% of the variation in the relationships among the items,

Table 1
Rank order of factor loadings for 5 highest weighted foods from
factor analysis of 56 foods (adapted from Schutz *et al.,* 1975*b*)

I 'High calorie treat'	II 'Speciality'	III 'Common main dish'
Wine	Chitterlings	Chicken
Pie	Liver	Roast beef
Cake	Chili	Steak
Dip	TV Dinner	Ham
Soft drinks	Chop suey	Hamburger
IV 'Healthy'	V 'Inexpensive-filling'	
Cottage cheese	Peanut butter	
Orange juice	Candy bars	
Milk	Potato chips	
Yogurt	Bread	
Dry cereal	Pickles	

and names were given to the factors based on examination of the
highest weighted items and their attributes. From examination of this
table it can be seen that a logical grouping of items is possible based
on common use situation characteristics. The individual cities produced essentially the same factor structure, with slightly different
items, in some instances, representing the factors. The results of
analysing the uses, with the food items as cases, is given in Table 2,
again with the 5 highest weighted items given in rank order. (In this
table and in all future factor loading results reported in this chapter
only factor weights above 0·50 are given; thus Factor III has only four
items.) Here, 4 factors explain 77% of the variance and again are
given names on the basis of particular items heavily weighted on the
factor. Table 3 presents the rank order on mean appropriateness for
selected uses. The uses selected are representative of each of the 4
'use' factors plus the affective and cost items. On examination of this
table one can see strong evidence that the affective dimension
information differs markedly from what is obtained for appropriateness for the other uses. For example, although steak ranks highest on
the affective judgement, it only appears in the top 5 rankings for the
other uses 'as a main dish'. Examining the other appropriateness
categories one can see the inherent logic in their rankings which offers
some face validity to the procedure.

Table 2
Rank order of factor loadings for 5 highest weighted
foods from factor analysis of 48 uses (adapted from
Schutz *et al.*, 1975*b*)

I 'Utilitarian'	II 'Casual'
For teenagers	When unhappy
For children	Riding in a car
Easy to prepare	For dessert
In summer	With cocktails
For men	Eat with a spoon

III 'Satiating'	IV 'Social'
As a main dish	At parties
Eat with a fork	With friends
For dinner	For guests
Really hungry	For special holidays
	Don't run out of

Table 3
Rank order of five highest appropriateness means for factor
representative uses and preference for 58 foods (adapted
from Schutz *et al.*, 1975*b*)

I 'Really like'	II 'For teenagers'	III 'Unhappy'
Steak	Ice cream	Coffee
Roast beef	Milk	Tea
Salad	Hamburger	Wine
Strawberries	Pizza	Ice cream
Spaghetti	Jello	Strawberries

IV 'As a main dish'	V 'At parties'	VI 'Inexpensive'
Roast beef	Dip	Jello
Steak	Potato chips	Hamburger
Chicken	Coffee	Spaghetti
Spaghetti	Wine	Vegetable soup
Meat loaf	Cake	Meat loaf

Table 4
Rank order of factor loadings for 5 highest weighted foods
from factor analysis of wine and wine substitutes (adapted
from Schutz & Ortega, 1974)

I 'Popular with meals'	II 'Informal entertaining'
Fifth bottle of wine	Port
Rhine wine	Sweet wine
Chardonnay	Fruit flavoured wine
Riesling	Zinfandel
Cold duck	Dry wine
III 'Special occasion'	IV 'Inexpensive'
Brut champagne	Burgundy
Extra dry champagne	
1/2 gal. wine	
Red wine	
Gamay rose	

As an example of how such data can be used to group respondents, rather than foods or uses, a random selection of respondents were chosen from the total of 200 in the study and a person factor analysis conducted with 120 representative pairs of items of the food-use ratings serving as cases. This analysis yielded five interpretable people groups (Rucker & Schutz, 1982).

Study 2—Wine
For this study there were 56 wines and wine substitutes, such as beer, hard liquor (spirits) etc., and 48 uses (Schutz & Ortega, 1974). Respondents were 50 females randomly sampled from Woodland, California, who filled out a 56 × 48 item by use matrix. In Table 4 a summary of the results of the factor analysis is shown in which 4 factors were identified, accounting for 94% of the variation. The inherent logical cognitive structure obtained is again apparent from the 5 most highly weighted wines for each of the factors. Table 5 shows selected rankings for wines and wine substitute items on an affective scale and for representative items of the 3 'use' factors that were obtained but not reported here. (Use factors will not be presented for this study or any of the subsequent studies to be reported in this chapter but are given, where conducted, in the cited publications.) It is clear that the affective dimension differs widely from the rankings on

Table 5
Rank order of 5 highest appropriateness means for factor
representative uses and preference for wine and wine
substitutes (adapted from Schutz & Ortega, 1974)

I 'Like'	II 'When I'm sad'
Fruit juice	Tea
Coffee	Coffee
Tea	Fruit juice
Sparkling wine	Rose wine
Red wine	Table wine
III 'When entertaining'	**IV** 'Goes well with meals'
Cocktails	Red wine
Coffee	Table wine
Whiskey	Chablis
Bourbon	Coffee
Vodka	White wine

the other 3 use variables. It is interesting to note the universality of
coffee; it appears on all 4 use lists among the top five in
appropriateness.

Study 3—Rice Perception
In this study there were 52 rices and substitutes (e.g. potatoes,
spaghetti) and 48 uses (Schutz *et al.*, 1975*a*). The respondents were
200 females, 100 from the Los Angeles area and 100 from the San
Francisco area, chosen by area sampling. Table 6 summarizes the
results of the factor analysis of food items, which yielded 4 factors
accounting for 89% of the variance. The 5 highest weighted items in
rank order for each factor make up a logical grouping of rice and rice
substitutes Table 7 gives mean appropriateness rankings for the
affective attribute as well as the rankings for representative uses of the
3 'use' factors that were found through the factor analysis of uses.
Here we see again the differences between preference and use
intention or appropriateness.

Study 4—Dairy Products
For this study there were 46 dairy products and dairy substitutes (e.g.
soda, fruit juice) and 45 uses generated by the experimenters from
examination of the products in the marketplace and uses from

Table 6
Rank order of factor loadings for 5 highest weighted
foods from factor analysis of rice and rice substitutes
(adapted from Schutz *et al.*, 1975*a*)

I 'Rice/starch'	II 'Cereal/grain'
Medium grain rice	Dry rice cereal
Carolina rice	Corn flakes
Golden grain rice	Cream of wheat
Townhouse rice	Barley
Uncle Ben's rice	Hominy
III 'Side dishes'	IV 'Soup'
Potato salad	Chicken rice soup
Macaroni salad	Chicken noodle soup
Baked beans	Tomato rice soup
Spaghetti	Jello
French fries	

Table 7
Rank order of 5 highest appropriateness means for factor
representative uses and preference for rice and rice substitutes (adapted from Schutz *et al.*, 1975*a*)

I 'Liked'	II 'Goes well with pork'
Baked potato	Potatoes
French fries	Baked potato
Potatoes	MJB brand rice
Spaghetti	Long grain rice
Jello	Baked beans
III 'A soggy food'	IV 'Easy to eat'
Cream of wheat	Jello
Chicken noodle soup	Potatoes
Tomato rice soup	Chicken rice soup
Chicken rice soup	Baked potato
Potato soup	French fries

previous item by use studies. The respondents were 51 randomly selected consumers from Woodland, California. Table 8 gives the rank order summary of results for the factor analysis of the food items, which resulted in 7 factors accounting for 91·4% of the variance. Examination of Table 8 again illustrates the simple yet logical cognitive structure for a particular class of foods. Table 9 gives selected use mean appropriateness rankings representing the major 'use' factors. In this case, no affect dimension was obtained for comparison; however, it is clear that there is a wide variation in what is considered appropriate for these different situations.

Study 5—Hospital Patients' and Employees' Food Perceptions
This study, rather than dealing with a general consumer population and a large number of foods and uses, targetted hospital patients and employees of the hospital, and selected foods and uses. These foods and uses were of interest to the dietitian in the hospital with the objective of improving the diet of hospital patients by obtaining their perception of appropriate use. There were 12 foods and 12 uses, rated by 26 hospital employees and 30 patients from Woodland Hospital, on a 5 point appropriateness scale. This simplified matrix yielded 3 factors (accounting for 98% of the variance) for both groups, with the top 5 weighted foods shown for each group in Table 10. The results indicate the basic comparability of both the patients and staff in terms of the cognitive structure for these particular items. In Table 11, the rank order of mean appropriateness for the top 5 rated foods for each of the 12 uses is given. ('Use' factor analysis was not conducted for this study.) The results show the now familiar pattern of high variability in appropriateness depending on use.

Study 6—Predicting Food Purchase and Use
The objective of this study was to attempt to predict food purchase and reported frequency of use, from appropriateness cognitive structure information, general good attitude data and from demographic variables, for 100 females from the Los Angeles area. The item by use matrix utilized had 10 foods and 12 uses which were selected to be representative of the 5 food and 4 use factors found in Study 1. The respondents rated appropriateness using the 10×12 matrix and also rated the frequency of purchase for 6 foods and frequency of use for 18 common food products. To obtain independent predictor variables for the respondents, a factor analysis of the 10×12 matrix was

Table 8
Rank order of factor loadings for 5 highest weighted foods from factor analysis of dairy and dairy substitutes (adapted from Bruhn & Schutz, 1986)

I 'Treats'	II 'Cheese'	III 'Non-dairy beverages'	IV 'Speciality'
Imitation ice cream	Cheddar cheese	Tea	Imitation milk
Imitation ice milk	Jack cheese	Sugar free soda	Non-fat dry milk
Ice milk	American cheese	Coffee	Buttermilk
Sherbert	Cheese food	Regular soda	Imitation sour cream
Whipped topping	Whole milk	Beer	Evaporated milk

V 'Chocolate drinks'	VI 'Cream products'	VII 'Tea and coffee'	
Chocolate milk	Whipped cream	Tea	
Hot chocolate/milk	Half and half	Coffee	
Cold chocolate drink	Canned real whip		
Hot chocolate/water	Sour cream		

Table 9
Rank order of 5 highest appropriateness means for factor representative uses for dairy and dairy substitutes (adapted from Bruhn & Schutz, 1986)

I	II	III
'Inexpensive'	'High protein'	'For guests'
Non-fat dry milk	Cheddar cheese	Ice cream
Tea	Whole milk	Jack cheese
Non-fat milk	Jack cheese	Fruit juice
Low-fat milk	American cheese	Coffee
Low-fat cottage cheese	Low-fat milk	
IV	**V**	**VI**
'When on diet'	'To help me sleep'	'When feeling ill'
Non-fat milk	Hot chocolate	Fruit juice
Fruit juice	Cold chocolate milk	Regular soda pop
Low-fat milk	Beer	Fruit drinks
Tea	Soda pop	Whole milk
Sugar free soda	Canned real whipped cream	Sugar free soda pop
VII	**VIII**	
'On a picnic'	'Eat with a spoon'	
Cheddar cheese	Ice cream	
Chocolate milk drink	Yogurt	
Jack cheese	Imitation ice cream	
American cheese	Low-fat cottage cheese	
Fruit drink	Creamed cottage cheese	

conducted with the food items as variables, as in previous studies (accounting for 74% of the variance) and then factor scores were computed for each person for each of the 4 resulting dimensions. The factor scores were used as independent variables along with demographic and general attitude variables in a step-wise multiple regression to predict frequency of use and purchase for each of the food items that were measured. Statistically significant multiple correlations were obtained between the independent variables and all of the food purchases and use items, with the item by use factor scores in general playing a larger role than demographic data. Since the main interest is in learning about the value of appropriateness data in understanding acceptance, only selected results which relate to this objective are presented. Table 12 shows an example of the significant correlation relationships between frequency of use data on 4 items and

Table 10
Rank order of factor loadings for 5 highest weighted foods from factor analysis of 12 foods for hospital patients and staff (adapted from Schutz *et al.*, 1971)

'Healthy dinner group'		'Seldom appropriate in given situations group'	
Staff	*Patients*	*Staff*	*Patients*
Spinach salad	Spinach salad	Fried eggs	Fried eggs
Popeye salad	Popeye salad	Wine	Tacos
Vegetables	Roast beef	Hamburger	Hamburger
Roast beef	Vegetables	Tacos	Popeye salad
Tacos	Tacos	Potatoes	Wine

'Treat group'	
Staff	*Patients*
Wine	Wine
Ice cream	Tacos
Tacos	Hamburger
Hamburger	Ice cream
Potatoes	Potatoes

the 4 item by use factor scores. Only the sign of the correlation coefficient is given. The face validity of this particular type of analysis can be seen in the positive relationship between the 'reward' factor scores and the frequency of use of pie and candy bars, and the negative relationship between 'nutrition' and pie.

DISCUSSION

The 6 studies reported herein and four others reported elsewhere (Baird & Schutz, 1976, 1980; Resurreccion, 1986; Martens *et al.*, 1988), all attest to the value and versatility of the appropriateness procedure.

Another practical way in which appropriateness data can be used is for determining the substitutability of one food for another, for a particular target population. This can be accomplished by selecting foods which weight in a similar fashion on the food factors or by simply using the measure of relationship between 2 specific foods calculated in producing the factor analysis (either the correlation coefficient or a similarity measure such as scaled distance).

Table 11

Rank order of 5 highest appropriateness means for 12 uses for hospital patients (adapted from Schutz *et al.*, 1971)

'For lunch'	'For special holiday'	'Not very hungry'	'Evening snack'	'For dinner'	'Nutritious'
Canned fruit	Vegetables	Soup	Ice cream	Roast beef	Vegetables
Vegetables	Potato	Canned fruit	Canned fruit	Vegetables	Roast beef
Roast beef	Ice cream	Ice cream	Hamburger	Potato	Canned fruit
Hamburger	Roast beef	Vegetables	Soup	Soup	Spinach salad
Soup	Wine	Hamburger	Tacos	Canned fruit	Fried eggs

'Not feeling well'	'Lose weight'	'Going to sleep'	'For breakfast'	'When unhappy'	'Food value = milk'
Soup	Vegetables	Ice cream	Fried eggs	Ice cream	Ice cream
Ice cream	Spinach salad	Canned fruit	Canned fruit	Canned fruit	Vegetables
Canned fruit	Roast beef	Wine	Potato	Soup	Fried eggs
Vegetables	Canned fruit	Soup	Vegetables	Vegetables	Soup
Roast beef	Soup	Hamburger	Ice cream	Roast beef	Roast beef

Table 12
Significant correlations between factor scores on 4 item by use
factors and frequency of use for 4 selected foods (adapted from
Schutz *et al.*, 1977)

	Pie	Roast beef	Hamburger	Candy bar
'Reward'	+	○	○	+
'High protein'	○	○	○	○
'Nutrition'	−	+	○	○
'Specialities'	○	−	−	−

From these studies the various hypotheses set forth earlier can now be addressed. Firstly, simple affect or preference is clearly not sufficient in explaining appropriateness for use; secondly, what is appropriate to consume, does vary widely depending on the nature and context of the consumption use situation; thirdly, by using a simple item by use appropriateness technique one can find the aggregate and individual cognitive structure for a class of items; fourthly, within a class of food items or uses consumers do have a simple cognitive structure relative to the total number of items or uses (the number of factors ranged from 3 to 7 and accounted for a high proportion of the variance); and finally, the cognitive structure of items from appropriateness data can predict product acceptance as represented by reported frequency of use.

The evidence to support these hypotheses does not mean that this is the only, nor necessarily the best, approach that can be used to measure cognitive structure, attributes, use intentions or appropriateness, but rather that this is one that has been demonstrated to have value in the understanding of food acceptance. An example of the use of the Kelly repertory grid approach to this general problem area can be seen in the research of Worsley (1980).

Although all the studies reported in this paper utilize food names, it would certainly be possible for individuals to make such judgements for any other type of food stimulus, including pure substances as well as the actual tasting of food items.

CONCLUSIONS

The concept of food acceptance is a complex one in which preference alone is only one factor in considering the actual acceptance of a food.

The various dimensions of external validity in the evaluation process should be carefully considered in the design and interpretation of research in this area. This is particularly important when information collected about foods is to be used in making decisions concerning actual food consumption situations. One productive way to obtain information concerning cognitive perceptions and food acceptance is to collect data on the appropriateness of a food or foods for a variety of uses, situations and attributes, from a representative group of the target population.

REFERENCES

Baird, P. R. & Schutz, H. G. (1976). The marketing concept applied to 'selling' good nutrition. *Journal of Nutrition Education,* **8**(1), 13–37.

Baird, P. C. & Schutz, H. G. (1980). Life style correlates of dietary and biochemical measures of nutrition. *Journal of the American Dietetic Association,* **76**, 228–35.

Bruhn, C. M. & Schutz, H. G. (1986). Consumer perceptions of dairy and related-use foods. *Food Technology,* **40**(1), 79–85.

Eindhoven, J. & Pilgrim, D. R. (1959). Measurement of preference for food combinations. *Food Technology,* **13**, 379–82.

Kamenetzky, J., Pilgrim, F. J. & Schutz, H. G. (1957). Relationship of consumption to preference under different field conditions. Quartermaster Food & Container Interim Report, December.

Krantzler, N. J., Muller, B. J., Schutz, H. G., Grivetti, L. E. & Meiselman, H. L. (1982). Validity of telephoned diet recalls and records for assessment of individual food intake. *American Journal of Clinical Nutrition,* **36**, 1234–42.

Lau, D., Hanada, L., Kaminskyj, O. & Krondl, M. (1979). Predicting food use by measuring attitudes and preference. *Food Product Development,* **13**, 66–72.

Martens, M., Schutz, H. G., Risvik, E. & Rodbotten, M. (1988). Consumer perceptions of nutritional value related to other quality attributes and to chemical components. In *Food Acceptance and Nutrition,* eds J. Solms, D. R. Booth, R. M. Pangborn & O. Raundhardt. Academic Press, London.

Olson, J. C. (1981). The importance of cognitive processes and existing knowledge structures for understanding food acceptance. In *Criteria of Food Acceptance,* eds J. Solms & R. C. Hall. Forster Verlag, Zurich, pp. 69–81.

Pilgrim, F. J. & Kamen, J. M. (1963). Predictors of human food consumption. *Science,* **139**, 501–2.

Resurreccion, A. V. A. (1986). Consumer use patterns for fresh and processed vegetable products. *Journal of Consumer Studies & Home Economics,* **10**, 317–32.

134 HOWARD G. SCHUTZ

Rucker, M. H. & Schutz, H. G. (1982). Development of consumer typologies from appropriateness ratings. *Proceedings of the Academy of Marketing Science*, **5**, 587.

Schutz, H. G. & Ortega, J. H. (1974). Consumer attitudes toward wine. *American Journal of Enology and Viticulture*, **25**, 33–8.

Schutz, H. G., Rucker, M. H. & Hunt, J. D. (1971). Hospital patients' and employees' reactions to food-use combinations. *Journal of the American Dietetic Association*, **60**, 207–12.

Schutz, H. G., Fridgen, J. D. & Damrell, J. D. (1975a). Consumer perceptions of rice and related products. *Journal of Food Science*, **40**, 277–81.

Schutz, H. G., Rucker, M. H. & Russell, G. F. (1975b). Food and food use classification systems. *Food Technology*, **29**, 50–64.

Schutz, H. G., Moore, S. M. & Rucker, M. H. (1977). Predicting food purchase and use by multivariate attitudinal analysis. *Food Technology*, **31**, 85–92.

Sidel, J. L., Stone, H., Wollsey, A. & Macredy, J. M. (1972). Correlation between hedonic ratings and consumption of beer. *Journal of Food Science*, **37**, 335.

Stefflre, V. (1971). Some eliciting and computational procedures for descriptive semantics. In *Explorations in Mathematical Anthropology*, eds P. Kay, P. Reich & M. McClaran. MIT Press, Cambridge, MA, pp. 211–48.

Worsley, A. (1980). Thought for food: investigations of cognitive aspects of food. *Ecology of Food and Nutrition*, **9**, 65–80.

Chapter 11

A Hedonic Price Index for Chocolate Chip Cookies

JILL R. JOHNSON and ZATA M. VICKERS

Department of Food Science and Nutrition, University of Minnesota, 1334 Eckles Avenue, St. Paul, MN 55108, USA

ABSTRACT

Five subjects, trained in descriptive analysis procedures, listed and quantified the attributes of 24 different chocolate chip cookies. Sixty-two attributes were identified; to have sufficient degrees of freedom for regression analysis, some of the attributes were eliminated by a selection process employing principal component analysis and Pearson correlations. The mean intensity scores for each of the selected attributes were regressed against the average prices of the cookies to determine which attributes had an effect on price. Many important attributes for chocolate chip cookies were lost during the variable selection procedure, and the regression models examined were not very satisfactory due to collinearity in the data set. This procedure may be useful for predicting price and determining the relative importance of attributes to consumers.

INTRODUCTION

A hedonic price index is a regression of the observed price of a product against its quality attributes. According to Lancaster's (1966) theory of consumer choice, people desire goods because of the functions these goods perform. Therefore, the basic underlying assumption of a hedonic price index is that goods are valued for their

135

characteristics which provide utility to a consumer, and the price of a product is a reflection of the amounts of each of the attributes the product contains (Eastwood, 1985).

Hedonic price functions have been developed for goods such as automobiles and homes (Griliches, 1968; Stinson, 1973). In a landmark study, Griliches (1968) developed a regression model to predict the price of a car based on its attributes and found that the price of a car could be predicted by its horsepower, weight, length, number of cylinders, etc. The beta coefficients corresponding to the attributes of the car could be used to determine the marginal valuation of the attributes. For example, a unit of increase in the horsepower of the car would increase the price of the car by the value of the beta coefficient for the car's horsepower.

Hedonic price functions have never been applied to food products and their sensory attributes. The purpose of this study was to see if the sensory attributes of chocolate chip cookies could be used to predict their price.

MATERIALS AND METHODS

Sample Selection
Twenty-four different brands of chocolate chip cookies were purchased from local supermarkets and bakeries. The brands were selected to include a wide range of prices, quality and sensory characteristics. Cookies were purchased the day before serving and stored at room temperature. Three stores were surveyed for chocolate chip cookie prices. If a cookie was available at more than one store the average price was used.

Subjects
Five students, two males and three females, ranging in age from 20 to 30 years, from the Department of Food Science and Nutrition at the University of Minnesota participated in the study. Selection was based on the subjects' willingness to participate and previous experience on taste panels. The subjects were paid for their participation.

Experimental Procedure
Six training sessions and nine tasting sessions were conducted as follows:

Training Session 1

A set of 4 different brands of cookies containing a wide range of characteristics was presented to the panel. From the set of cookies, the judges individually compiled a list of descriptors under the categories of appearance, aroma, flavour, and texture. The individual lists were combined to form a group list of descriptors. Through group discussion, the list of descriptors was edited for synonyms and the meanings of the descriptors were defined.

Training Session 2

The panellists individually scored the intensity of the attributes established in Session 1 for a sample chocolate chip cookie using a response form similar to Fig. 1. Panellists were allowed to write in attributes not previously identified. Large discrepancies between individual scores for an attribute were discussed to reach better agreement on the attribute's meaning. Modifications to the response form, including changes in some of the terms used for attributes, were suggested during the group discussion.

Training Session 3

This session was conducted as a practice taste test session in which the panellists evaluated different cookies using the response form, with modifications from Session 2 included.

Training Session 4

Panellists were given a list of the individual subjects' scores, group means and standard deviations associated with the group means for the attributes of the cookies evaluated in Session 3. Attributes whose ratings were highly variable were discussed to further clarify their meanings.

Training Session 5

This session was another practice taste test session conducted to further reduce some of the variability in ratings.

Training Session 6

The attributes with the highest variability in rating were identified to the panel and their meanings were further clarified through tasting and group discussion.

The remaining nine sessions were tasting sessions. Each panellist

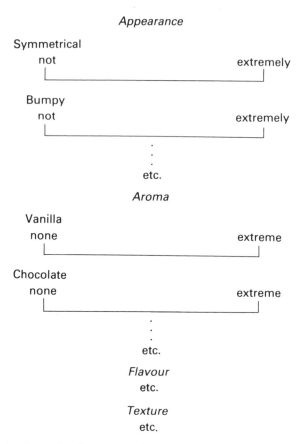

Figure 1. Example of response form used for descriptive analysis.

evaluated four brands of cookie per session. Twelve of the 24 brands of cookies were evaluated twice to determine the consistency of the judges' ratings.

Serving Procedure
Samples were served in random order on plastic plates labelled with three digit random numbers; each judge received the same four brands of cookies but in a different random order. Spring water (Glenwood) and spitcups were provided for rinsing between samples.

Data Analysis

Price was calculated per 100 grams of cookie. Scores for the attribute ratings were determined by measuring the distance in millimetres from the left end of the response scale. Mean attribute ratings were used for the remaining analyses.

Attribute Selection

The panel rated the 24 brands of cookies on 62 attributes. To have sufficient degrees of freedom for regression analysis, some of the attributes had to be eliminated.

During the first step of the elimination process, each category of attributes (appearance, aroma, flavour and texture) underwent principal component analysis (PCA) to identify attributes which were highly related to one of the principal components. The attribute loadings were examined to determine which attributes described the different dimensions (principal components) of the chocolate chip cookies. Attributes which loaded at 0·7 or greater with one principal component were selected. If an attribute loaded highly with a principal component and also loaded at 0·4 or greater with another factor, the attribute was not selected, since that attribute was not unique to one factor or dimension of chocolate chip cookies.

The next step was to examine the Pearson correlations of chosen attributes with high loadings on the same factor. If an attribute was highly correlated (0·7 or greater) with one or more of the other attributes within its factor, only one of the highly correlated attributes was chosen.

Regression Analysis

The 15 attributes remaining after the selection process are listed in Table 1. These attributes were used in regression analyses, using the program in SAS (1985) called Proc Rsquare. Proc Rsquare finds subsets of independent variables (attributes) that best predict a dependent variable (price), by linear regression based on R-Square. These models were searched to find an equation with a relatively high adjusted R-square, significant t-values for the beta coefficients and attributes reflecting the outstanding or important attributes of a chocolate chip cookie.

Table 1
Attributes remaining after variable selection procedure

Appearance	Aroma	Flavour	Texture
Symmetrical	Caramel	Chocolate	Cakey
Dense interior	Overall	Salty	Chewiness
Rounded top	Graham cracker	Baking soda	Sugary
Dark colour	White cake		
Number of visible chips			

RESULTS AND DISCUSSION

Almost 89% of the variability in price is explained by the attributes listed in the model equation (Fig. 2). Several other models were examined which were equally good.

Although the model equation in Fig. 2 has a relatively high R-square and all terms are significant, it does not include many of the attributes that are found in the higher priced chocolate chip cookies. For example, the hedonic price function lacked any attributes describing the texture of the cookies or the texture of the chocolate chips as well as important flavour attributes such as butter and caramel.

The models were not entirely satisfactory because many of the terms were eliminated during the attribute selection procedures, and other terms were eliminated by the regression analysis. The primary reason for most of the eliminations was that so many of the attributes were

$$PRICE = -0.451 + 0.006A - 0.006B + 0.006C$$
$$+ 0.009D + 0.013E - 0.016F + 0.007G$$

A = chocolate flavour
B = symmetrical shape
C = rounded top
D = graham cracker aroma
E = salty flavour
F = baking soda flavour
G = overall aroma

R-Square = 0.885   Adjusted R-Square = 0.835

Figure 2. Hedonic price index for chocolate chip cookies.

closely correlated to one another. This situation is referred to as collinearity (Weisberg, 1985). The collinearity in the data set was due to the design of the cookies in the marketplace. Bakeries which set out to make premium chocolate chip cookies produced cookies that were large with a homemade appearance, had butter, chocolate, and caramel flavours, with soft, non-waxy chocolate chips and a chewy texture. The grocery store brands lacked these characteristics.

Several things can be done to alleviate collinearity. Measurements can be taken in the areas lacking in the data set. For example, a cookie high in caramel flavour, but low in chocolate flavour could be developed and added to the data set. In this study, this approach was not possible since only cookies already existing in the marketplace, which had prices, were examined. A second option is to omit the variables which are related to another variable. This was the course of action taken in the data analysis. However, in omitting variables related to one another, characteristics important to chocolate chip cookies were lost, such as chewiness, caramel flavour, butter flavour and the texture of the chocolate chips.

Despite the collinearity in the data set, this procedure could have several applications. It is useful in predicting price; but only for those cookies having similar combinations of attributes to those products tested. The procedure itself, especially the variable selection process, helps to focus on the attributes important to the food product. The value of the beta coefficients in the model may theoretically be used to determine the relative value of a sensory attribute, but this application was not possible in this study due to the collinearity in the data set.

REFERENCES

Eastwood, D. B. (1985). *The Economics of Consumer Behavior.* Allyn and Bacon, Newton, Massachusetts.

Grilichos, Z. (1968). Hedonic price indexes for automobiles: an econometric analysis of quality change. In *Readings in Economics, Statistics and Econometrics,* ed. A. Zellner. Little, Brown & Co., Boston, pp. 103–30.

Lancaster, K. (1966). A new approach to consumer theory. *Journal of Political Economy,* **74,** 32–57.

SAS (1985). *SAS User's Guide: Statistics, Version 5 Edition.* SAS Institute, Inc., Cary, North Carolina.

Stinson, T. F. (1973). *The Demand for Education: an Hedonic Approach.* University of Minnesota.

Weisberg, S. (1985). *Applied Linear Regression.* John Wiley, New York.

Chapter 12

Too Many Cooks? Food Acceptability and Women's Work in the Informal Economy*

SALLE E. DARE

Science Policy Research Unit, University of Sussex, Falmer, Brighton, Sussex BN1 9RP, UK

ABSTRACT

Clearly women with families spend a large amount of time on food preparation. The foods they select to prepare are influenced by a range of factors including religious taboos, income, taste, habits and so forth. However, such is true for all people in their selection of food. An additional factor for women is the relationship between convenience food, and her domestic work in the informal economy. Convenience could thus be seen as a major determinant in food acceptability to women.

The background to this research project lies in the studies made of both domestic technology and the use of time through time budget analysis. The received wisdom among writers on domestic technology is that it has had little if any impact on the time spent on housework.

It is clear that convenience food represents an enormous technological contribution to domestic work, yet there have been few, if any, studies

---

* The term, 'informal economy' is problematic and the definition is the subject of much debate. Here it is used to mean that sector of the economy which is not subject to classical market forces and in this context reduces to unpaid domestic work.

carried out which are available in the public domain. Similarly the time budget research does not isolate food preparation and its associated technology, and thus we are unable to draw any conclusions about the way in which these particular food technologies impinge upon women's work. The research reported in this chapter was carried out in order to explore some of these issues and it is hoped that it will act as a pilot to a more extensive and detailed study.

INTRODUCTION

Food acceptability is determined by a variety of physiological, psychological, social and cultural factors, all of which interact so that ultimately the body is ensured an adequate supply of nutrients to maintain reasonable health. Yet food of course is much more than simply a fuel for the body. The very factors which shape taste also imbue food with social and cultural significance, from celebrating religious festivals to providing psychological comfort. For women in industrialised countries food has further significance: it is part of the daily work that they must perform in the informal economy to feed the family. (Of course not all women in Britain live in families but the vast majority, at some time in their lives, are part of a nuclear family taking on the role of wife and mother. Such women are the focus of the research described in this chapter.)

Women have always been responsible in varying degree for the provision of food. In early gatherer hunter societies, it is estimated that they supplied between 60% and 80% of the food, by gathering seeds, grasses, roots, nuts and trapping small animals. In the agricultural communities of pre-industrial Britain, women's contribution to food production was essential. In such subsistence economies, the production of food as an economic activity was inseparable from the processing of food and preparation of meals. Only with the Industrial Revolution did food production and processing become distinct from preparation. The mediating role of retailing marked the boundary between activity in the formal and informal economy. Agriculture and food processing took place in the formal economy and meal preparation became confined within the home, unpaid and hence invisible.

Women's domestic work was progressively eased throughout the nineteenth century as the utilities diffused, bringing piped water, mains sewerage and fuel supply to the home. In the twentieth century, innovations in domestic technology introduced refrigerators, washing machines and vacuum cleaners to the average home. In food preparation, developments were equally rapid. The food industry burgeoned in the nineteenth century supplying, through the new retailers, a wide variety of processed and convenience foods. No longer did women have to bake bread, salt their beans, make the jam. All were available in the shops along with ham, black pudding and bacon, none of which were processed in the urban home. The new techniques of canning, and later freezing were added to the traditional methods of preserving food by drying and pickling. Thus was the variety and quality of the diet improved. By the 1980s an unbelievably wide range of ready prepared meals and foods offer women an opportunity to minimise their time in the kitchen.

In addition then to the nature of the food itself, it is suggested that one dimension of the acceptability of food is the impact it has on women's work time and effort, both in preparing meals and clearing up afterwards. The discussion which follows examines this dimension in some depth, beginning with a brief overview of some findings from time budget research and examining food consumption patterns.

WOMEN'S WORK IN THE INFORMAL ECONOMY

In the early 1970s women's domestic work emerged as a subject for serious academic study. Until then such work had only been seen, if it had been visible at all, as an aspect of family life, conflated with notions of love and caring.

Feeding the family can be, of course, an expression of love and caring but it is also demanding work, involving time, effort and some (varying) level of skill. Meals and purchases have to be planned within the constraints of the family budget and taste, whilst keeping in mind the health and wellbeing of the household. The food must be bought, transported and stored; ingredients of meals must be assembled, prepared and cooked; the cooking and eating utensils must be cleared and if there are young children, mealtimes requiring supervision and feeding can become a time of stress.

Attempts have been made to understand how technology may have affected women's domestic work time, but the results are equivocal. Vanek (1974) concluded that there has been no decrease in work time for which various explanations have been advanced including:

• technology enables living standards to be raised so that modern foods allow much greater variety and choice for individuals rather than the 'pot au feu' of the peasant;
• the ideology of domesticity fostered by the domestic science movement imposes upon women the need to fill their time with domestic work.

Gershuny (1987) on the other hand maintains that there has been a decrease in women's domestic work time and the key explanatory variable is indeed domestic technology.

Food preparation is part of this domestic work but it differs significantly in the way it can be shifted out of the informal economy and back. Take-away meals, eating out, and school meals all remove food preparation from the informal sector to the formal economy. Effort and skill as well as time, can be partially transferred to the formal economy through the purchase of sundry processed foods, from frozen uncooked pies to ready chopped salads in the chill cabinet. Thus it can be appreciated how food acceptability in the informal economy is manifest.

Drawing on time budget surveys carried out over the last 25 years or so, it is possible to monitor changes in informal economic activity. Table 1 shows clearly how the time women spend in cooking and clearing up after meals has declined and how it varies with women's employment status. Unfortunately there is little comparative data on time spent by couples in cooking and washing up but the 1974/75 and the 1984 time budget surveys did examine couples. Table 2 shows

Table 1

Minutes per average day spent by women in the UK in cooking and cleaning up by women's employment status

Employment status	1961	1975	1981	1986[a]
Full time	56	56	35	56
Part time	138	114	92	69
Not employed	163	131	111	75

[a] Data from London Food Diaries. Source: Thomas & Zmroczek (1985).

Table 2
Minutes per average day spent in cooking and cleaning up by
men and women in couples by women's employment status

Employment status	1974/5		1986	
	Men	Women	Men	Women
Full time	14	77	21	56
Part time	11	112	7	69
Not employed	9	134	9	75

Source: as Table 1.

clearly the inequitable division of labour, and again how this varies by women's employment status, confirming the findings of Walker & Woods (1976), that women's employment status is a strong determining factor in the amount of time women spend on domestic work.

Women act as 'gate-keepers' of the larder, deciding what foods to buy and all family women are involved in food related activities. Thus foods which may reduce time and effort, either absolutely or by promoting a more equitable division of labour in the home, would be very acceptable. However, the acceptability of such foods is tempered by other considerations such as appropriateness of food. For example Charles & Kerr (1985) found that women will not serve convenience foods to their husbands. Herein lies a dilemma for women who rely on so-called convenience foods yet for whom these foods arouse feelings of guilt. The British Nutrition Foundation (1984) have shown that the foods which women can introduce into the family are limited by the tastes of the family, even when the women are primarily motivated by health considerations.

CONVENIENCE FOOD OR CONVENIENT MEAL

Convenience is a problematic concept. The common sense definition embodies assumptions which may not be valid. The UK National Food Survey (MAFF, 1960) began to enumerate convenience foods as a special category in 1960, and defines them as: 'Those processed foods for which a degree of culinary preparation has been carried to an advanced stage by the manufacturer and which may be used as labour saving alternatives to less highly processed products'. This definition introduces a further ambiguous term, 'labour saving' which takes no account of *when* the food is prepared, nor how much attention it requires during cooking, and of course how much clearing up is involved. Traub & Odland (1979) defined convenience food as foods which: 'require less preparation time or fewer preparation activities in the kitchen. Ease of storage, change in storage space requirements and ease of transporting the food from the market to the home because of lighter weight or reduced bulk are also convenience attributes'. Both these definitions ignore the cultural associations of food, so that bread and cheese are not considered convenience food although they are undoubtedly a convenient meal. It is not simply the processing level or production technology which must be considered but the nature of the product itself (Paulus, 1977).

Although there are difficulties in using the National Food Survey (NFS) definition of convenience foods, it is the best source of data in the UK on the national food consumption patterns. Combining the information from the NFS on convenience food consumption with time budget data, a clear picture emerges of the relationship between time spent in food preparation and consumption of convenience food. It would seem from Fig. 1 that convenience food has indeed had a profound impact on time spent in food preparation. Furthermore, it could be asserted that the received wisdom is correct; convenience

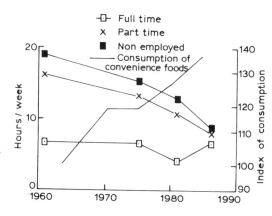

Figure 1. Time spent in food preparation and consumption of convenience food. (Source: MAFF, Thomas & Zmroczek, *London Survey*.)

food has been of most benefit to employed women, since the proportion of women in employment has risen over this period too.

Figure 1 shows that the relationship between the factors has changed over time. A more detailed exposition of the relationship at one point in time is now to be considered.

TIME, WORK AND FOOD ACCEPTABILITY

The discussion presented here is based on results from food diaries which were circulated to families in London. Families with school age children were selected because earlier research had shown that the presence of children within the family is a strong determinant of women's domestic work time (Walker & Woods, 1976).

The families were recruited through primary and secondary schools in what can be approximately called working and middle class areas of West London, hence the sample was in part self-selected. However, the diary method itself implies a certain degree of self-selection since there is a much greater commitment on the part of the respondents than in a more conventional questionnaire type of survey. Only couples were selected because one of the aims of the research was to examine the division of domestic labour in the home and to test the hypothesis of the symmetrical family. Eighty-seven diaries were distributed and 67 were returned, four of which were unusable. The respondents were asked to keep the diary for 3 days including 1 weekend day. The diaries were very complex and time consuming and it was believed that commitment to such detailed recording would not endure beyond 3 days.

The results below are based on the 63 diaries which covered 703 meals. The data were analysed using a specially written SPSSX program.

The mean time per meal, shown in Table 3, reveals quite starkly the unequal division of labour and the way convenience foods may play a role in reducing women's work time. Breakfasts and snacks are meals featuring a high proportion of convenience foods, where time is somewhat less unequally divided between family members, suggesting such meals are prepared by household members other than the woman. Yet other meals reveal the same high proportion of convenience foods used with a grossly unequal division of time. Indeed in preparing Sunday lunch women spend 14 times longer than men and

Table 3
Meal preparation time in minutes per meal for different household
members by meal

Meal	Woman (min)	Man (min)	Children (min)	Proportion of meals made with convenience foods (%)
All meals	19	3	2	n/a
Breakfast	12	4	3	97
Snack	5	2	3	97
Mid-day	16	3	1	74
Evening meal	35	3	2	87
Sunday mid-day	57	3	1	82
Sunday tea	19	2	1	90
Packed lunch	11	1	1	79

children combined. However what becomes apparent is that these meals are more complex, containing more separate ingredients, hence involving potentially more work. This work is reduced perhaps by the increased use of convenience food. What is not clear is whether there is a causal relationship. Does the relative ease of preparing meals with convenience food mean that women prepare more complex meals, confirming Szalai's hypothesis (1975) that living standards are being raised? Or do women turn to convenience food to lessen their burden when faced with having to meet the different expectations and tastes of the family, and perhaps the ritual of the Sunday Lunch? In either case it is obvious that convenience food makes a contribution to family wellbeing but in the former the woman does not derive direct benefit since she does not reduce her work time.

Women were involved in preparing about 80% of the families meals and of these meals about 63% take up to 30 min to prepare and cook, 13% between 30 min and 1 h and about 6% take more than 1 h to prepare and cook. As can be seen from Table 4, of those meals which take over 1 h to prepare 22% contain 7 or more items of convenience food and of those meals which take up to 30 min to prepare only 40% contain such a high proportion of convenience foods but about 60% contain up to 3 items of convenience food. Again there is an indication of the two separate processes at work: saving time and effort *and* raising standards.

Table 4
Women's preparation time by convenience food

Number of items convenience foods	Women's preparation and cooking time				
	None (% meals)	Up to 30 min (% meals)	30 min to 1 h (% meals)	Over 1 h (% meals)	Total Number
None	13	12	6	14	74
1–3	68	58	40	31	366
4–6	18	27	43	33	180
7 +	<1	4	11	22	33
	100 $N = 125$	100 $N = 410$	100 $N = 82$	100 $N = 36$	653

It has been suggested that convenience food is a significant benefit to women in employment yet from Table 5 it is clear that there is no difference in the use of convenience food by women's employment status. The partial explanation may lie in the fact that full time mothers cook more complex meals and hence may use more convenience food to raise or maintain a somewhat higher living standard, by providing a greater choice for the family at meal times. A further explanation might be that convenience foods are now so well integrated into the shopping patterns that they are not even conceived in time saving terms.

It must, however, be remembered that food is prepared and consumed in a social context and the family is the social and economic unit upon which the community is constructed. Food and meal times

Table 5
Proportion of meals (%) using convenience foods by mother's employment

No. convenience food items	Mother employed		Mother not employed
	Part time	Full time	
0	12	12	12
1–2	56	56	55
3–4	28	28	26
>5	4	4	7
	100	100	100

are an important means of establishing and reinforcing cultural and family norms. It has been suggested (Taylor Nelson, 1985) that there has been a general increase in snacking and a trend away from formal family meals. Within families this trend is not so marked. Seventy per cent of meals are eaten 'en famille' and only 13% are eaten separately while 14% of meals are those at which the children eat separately from the parents; a pattern slightly more marked in middle class homes. It was suspected that the pattern of eating might have shown some correlation with the type of food eaten but this in fact was not so. About 80% of snacks, which are predominantly convenience food, were eaten together as a family. If women are perceived as having greater commitment to the family unit, clearly this is not threatened by changes in food patterns.

It is evident from the few findings presented here that convenience foods are an immense asset to women who have the laborious duty of feeding the family. However, there is evidence of considerable ambivalence amongst women. Many women express concern over the nature of processed foods and particularly additives. In contrast to the findings of Charles & Kerr (1985) it was found that mid-day meals exhibited a lower consumption of convenience foods; the meal when the man of the house might be expected to be away from home. This might reflect the nature of the research instrument, in which a high proportion of week-end meals were recorded or a concern not to use processed food for young children.

A further dimension of food acceptability which has influence on low income families, is the cost of convenience foods. For women with low food budgets the cost of 'fresh' convenience foods, chilled salads and meats for example, are very high and this has implications for the diet and time use of poor families. The cheap convenience foods are those which attract the attention of the 'anti-additive' lobby (Millstone, 1986), who perceive additives as a way of disguising cheap ingredients.

There is clearly scope for more detailed investigation into women's response to foods which can profoundly affect their work time, and hence the characteristics of food of varying acceptability.

REFERENCES

British Nutrition Foundation (1984). *Eating in the Early 1980's*. British Nutrition Foundation, London.

Charles, N. & Kerr, M. (1985). *Attitudes Towards the Feeding and Nutrition of Young Children.* Health Education Council, London.

Gershuny, J. (1987). Paper presented to the British Sociological Association Conference in Leeds, April 1987 (available from the author, University of Bath).

MAFF (1960). *Domestic Food Consumption and Expenditure.* HMSO, London.

Millstone, E. (1986). *Food Additives.* Penguin, Middlesex.

Paulus, K. (1977). *How Ready are Ready to Serve Foods?* Karger, Basle.

Szalai, A. (1975). Women's time. *Futures,* **7** (5), 385–99.

Taylor Nelson (1985). *'Snacks' and Informal Eating.* Taylor Nelson Group, Epsom.

Thomas, G. & Zmroczek, C. (1985). Household technology: the "liberation" of women from the home? In *Family and Economy in Modern Society,* eds P. Close & R. Collins, Macmillan Press, London, pp. 101–29.

Traub, L. & Odland, D. (1979). *Convenience Foods and Home Prepared Foods: Comparative Costs, Yield and Quality.* USDA AER 429 August 1979, Washington.

Vanek, J. (1974). Time spent in housework. *Scientific American,* **231,** 116–20.

Walker, K. & Woods, M. (1976). *Time Use: A Measure of Household Production of Family Goods and Services.* Centre for the Family, American Home Economics Association.

Topic 4

Factors Influencing Food Choice— Consumer Related Factors

Chapter 13

Sweet and Bitter In the Mirror of Behaviour

JACOB E. STEINER

Department of Oral Biology, The Hebrew University, 'Hadassah'
Faculty of Dental Medicine, PO Box 1172, Jerusalem, 91-010 Israel

ABSTRACT

Sweet taste is preferred by many living organisms, while bitter is rejected. In animals, taste preference and hedonics can be tested by consumption, using a two-bottle design or by recording of physiological measures. In adult human subjects, cognitive testing can reflect on pleasure aspects of sensations. To indicate these in pre-verbal infants, in verbally disabled subjects as well as in animals, the elicitation of fixed, innate behaviour-features was found to be a valid and reliable method. Behaviours mirror taste hedonics with equal sensitivity to other methods. A major advantage of this testing method is that only minute amounts of stimulating substances are needed to trigger responses. Accomplished human and animal studies, using behavioural testing, are summarized. The further application of this method, in basic research, in applied studies as well as a clinical-diagnostic tool, is suggested.

INTRODUCTION

Sensory information, gathered and transduced by receptors, produces neural messages, which are transmitted to the brain. Central processing of this information may activate motor or secretory responses, as well as cognitive work-up and elicitation of *sensations,* or *feelings.* That domain, where feelings are aroused, is presumably the most 'private' amongst all territories of life. This *res privata* is only accessible to the sensing organism itself (Leibowitz, 1986).

The process of measuring is, from the view point of logic, that of direct comparison, therefore measurement can only be carried out in the public domain and never in the private domain. By direct measurement man is able to quantify distances, volumes or weights, expressing these in numeric terms. Sensations, feelings, likes or dislikes, in contrast, can never be subjected to direct and quantitative assessment, but indirect psychophysical estimation methods offer some semi-quantitative means of evaluation. Among all living creatures, man alone is capable of abstraction, and of putting his sensory experiences into words, or of using relative numerical scales of estimation. This human ability is restricted to fully conscious and co-operative subjects of verbal age. Furthermore, psychophysical testing is dependent on the knowledge of a common language, equally understood by tester and subject.

But there is also interest in exploring likes and dislikes in situations where no verbal communication exists, as in the pre-verbal infant, in patients with verbal disability or in animals. To mirror likes, dislikes and sensations in all these instances, means other than verbal are needed to penetrate the private domain.

Recording, and evaluation of stimulus-dependent events, may offer such an alternative approach. Among all event-related responses, the fixed, stereotyped, sensory-motor co-ordinations deserve special interest. These behaviours are in most cases innate, non-acquired (presumably inherited) and can be elicited in all members of a species, when stimuli are delivered under controlled conditions.

The fact that behavioural manifestations can truly mirror different emotions, was apparently recognized in ancient times. Motor events related to crying and laughing are, possibly, the most common examples. Moreover, behavioural manifestations were also used as research tools in ancient times. Gallenus, the famous, second century, Roman physician, investigated food preference in neonate animals, using the behavioural patterns of approach and rejection towards diverse food samples, which he presented in uniform dishes (Siegel, 1973). This behavioural experiment, of rather modern design, preceded the publication of the classic by C. Darwin (1872) by about 1700 years!

Sensations in general have a hedonic overtone, that is, they are pleasure-causing or displeasure inducing. Chemical sensations seem to have much greater hedonic impact than either vision or hearing (Pfaffman, 1960). Among gustatory qualities, those of 'sweet' and 'bitter' are not only polar and antithetic, but both have a very special, rather profound hedonic, motivational impact. This is reflected, among other things, by the fact, that in most languages 'sweet' has the connotation of 'good', 'likeable', 'pleasant' and 'desirable', while 'bitter' refers to 'bad', 'sad', 'unpleasant', 'aversive', 'painful', 'disgusting', etc. This remarkable metaphoric use of 'sweet' and 'bitter', is well known from numerous examples of the most ancient cultural documents (e.g. the Old Testament).

In animal experiments, differential consumption from simultaneously offered samples (two-bottle design), or the recording of stimulus-dependent changes in physiological parameters were also found as useful indicators of taste hedonics (e.g. Richter & Campbell, 1940; Carpenter, 1956; Ganchrow, 1977, 1979; Steiner & Reuveni, 1979).

Our attention was first called to behavioural reactions to sweet and bitter tastes when assessing gustatory function using a simple psychophysical method (Steiner et al., 1969). In these trials, the intra-oral presentation of even minute amounts of supra-threshold sweet and bitter solutions, was found to unlock fixed oral, peri-oral and facial motor behaviours. These reactions appeared involuntarily in all tested subjects, regardless of age, sex, ethnic, cultural or educational background, or state of health. The sweet- and bitter-induced reactions were found to be distinct, and different among themselves, as well as different from those induced by samples of water. The motion reactions appeared in response to minute amounts of stimulating solutions and always preceded verbal response. These taste-triggered oral and facial motion features have been named the gustofacial response (Steiner, 1973) and comprise the following features. (A) Water induced a fleeting swallow, not accompanied by any characteristic facial play. (B) Sweet samples induced a marked facial relaxation a quick licking movement in which the tip of the tongue is slid over the upper lip, accompanied by smacking and by retraction of the mouth corners to resemble a slight smile. Eyes were in most cases wide open. The overall facial expression was that of pleasure and satisfaction. (C) Bitter samples, in contrast, induced a sudden and tight closure of the eyes, depression of the mouth corners, followed by gaping and by an abrupt and sudden turn and elevation of the head. The overall facial expression was that of aversion or disgust.

It was assumed that these reactions are innate, fixed, reflectory responses. In subsequent studies, this neurobiological phenomenon was further explored and the results obtained are briefly summarized in the following paragraphs.

EXPERIMENTAL

Studies on Neonate Human Infants

(a) *Testing Normal Term-born Neonates*
The first question to be investigated was whether the gustofacial response is indeed innate (i.e. present at birth). In order to answer this, two groups of term-born, normal healthy infants were tested. In the first group 50 infants of 2–8 days of age and of both sexes were included. These infants displayed the differential orofacial behaviours to water, sweet and bitter samples, with most features similar to those of adults. It is noteworthy that neonatal responses were of shorter latency and of greater intensity than adults' responses. Since infants of several days of age might have gathered considerable gustatory experience, a second group of 100 normal term-born infants (50 of each sex), all of them of 4–12 h of age and prior to their first feeding (bottle or formula) were chosen. Here again, samples of distilled water containing 0·34 M sucrose (sweet) and 0·000 07 M quinine HCl (bitter) were presented, and the behavioural responses recorded. The analysis of the recordings revealed that the differential, taste-induced orofacial display is an innate ability of the nervous system. Some of these reactions are shown in Fig. 1.

(b) *Testing Neonates with Severe Developmental Malformations of the Brain*
Although intensive pre-natal care is known to reduce the incidence of birth of infants with severe brain-malformations, we have had the rather rare opportunity to test two infants with anencephaly and two others with hydroanencephaly during the course of the experiments. The malformed infants responded to gustatory stimulation exactly as normal infants did. Some examples of the gustofacial reflex in the malformed infants are also shown in Fig. 1. These observations (Steiner, 1973; 1979) firmly indicate that the gustofacial reflex is

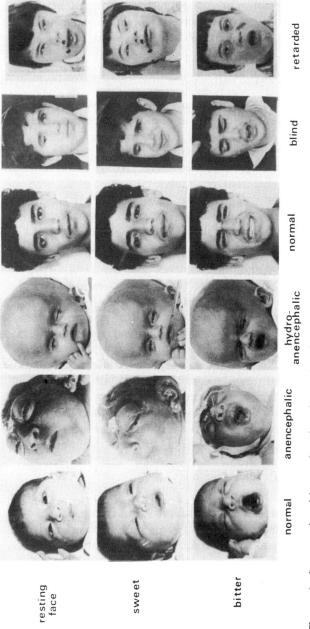

Figure 1. A synoptic tableau, showing the typical features of human gustofacial responses to sweet and to bitter in infants and in adolescents (photographs by J. E. Steiner).

primarily controlled at brainstem level, without mandatory involvement of higher brain structures; a finding confirmed later in animal
studies (Grill & Norgren, 1978a,b).

(c) *Testing Normal Adolescents and their Blind and Retarded*
Age-Mates
A group of healthy adolescents was tested (Steiner, 1979) in order to
assess whether the infantile appearance of the gustofacial response is
maintained up to adolescence. Furthermore, using these adolescents as
a control group, their congenitally blind and severely mentally
retarded (mean IQ score lower than 65) age-mates were also tested.
Results revealed that in adolescents the reflex, with its infantile
features, is also displayed. Testing the two other groups revealed that
the performance of reflectory display is independent of both visual
reinforcement and mental ability. Examples of the gustofacial display
in normal, blind and retarded adolescents are shown in Fig. 1.

Psychophysical Estimates and Behaviours Equally Indicate
Feelings
The assumption that behavioural displays reflect the hedonics of
sensations as reliably as psychometric estimates was studied by a
multidisciplinary approach. Cooperative adult volunteers were exposed to gustatory stimuli and psychometric and behavioural responses
were simultaneously recorded (Steiner *et al.*, 1982). This study
revealed a sizeable correlation between psychometric estimates and
behavioural manifestations. This indicates that the two methods are
equally sensitive in reflecting sensations. The same study showed that
even those subtle perceptual changes, which were induced by a natural
taste-modifying substance (miraculin), are reflected with equal sensitivity by both testing methods.

Is the Gustofacial Response Intensity Dependent?
A further experiment was designed to study whether frequency of
occurrence and intensity of the motion features which comprise the
gustofacial reaction, vary with stimulus intensity. This study by
Ganchrow and co-workers (1983) revealed that increasing concentrations of tastants, which presumably stimulate more peripheral receptors, induce a greater and more frequent activation of the motion
components. Some of the findings are illustrated in Fig. 2.

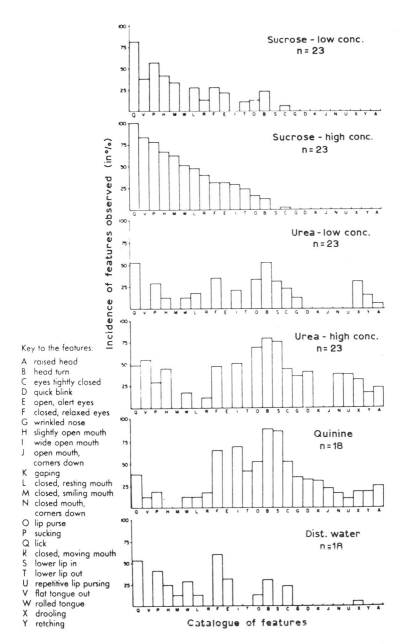

Key to the features:

A raised head
B head turn
C eyes tightly closed
D quick blink
E open, alert eyes
F closed, relaxed eyes
G wrinkled nose
H slightly open mouth
I wide open mouth
J open mouth,
  corners down
K gaping
L closed, resting mouth
M closed, smiling mouth
N closed mouth,
  corners down
O lip purse
P sucking
Q lick
R closed, moving mouth
S lower lip in
T lower lip out
U repetitive lip pursing
V flat tongue out
W rolled tongue
X drooling
Y retching

Figure 2. Distribution of percentages of the occurrence in each of the facial motion-features; with high (1·0 M) sucrose as reference (from: Ganchrow *et al.*, 1984).

163

The Gustofacial Reflex as a Clinical-diagnostic Tool

(1) Kalmus (1976) was the first to apply the gustofacial reflex as a diagnostic tool in testing neonates for PTC-tasting. He found that facial expressive features reliably differentiated between tasters and non-tasters of PTC in early infancy.

(2) Later, in our laboratory, patients affected with the hereditary condition of Usher's syndrome were tested for chemosensory functions using behavioural methods. The exclusive use of behavioural testing in these subjects is imperative, since the disease affects both vision and hearing. This study (Steiner & Abraham, 1978) was the first to demonstrate normal chemo-sensory functions in patients with Usher's syndrome.

(3) In another hereditary disease, Familial Dysauthonomia, disturbed tasting is, together with other signs, pathognomonic. The accurate diagnosis of disturbed tasting in neonatals who are suspected of having this hereditary disease is of great clinical importance. Here again non-cognitive testing is essential. In examining a group of adolescent patients, using the above mentioned multidisciplinary approach, we could demonstrate that cognitive estimates and behavioural testing, indicate the impaired taste functions with equal accuracy. Therefore behavioural testing can be used as a safe diagnostic tool in neonates suspected of having this hereditary disease (Steiner *et al.*, 1988).

The Gustofacial Response as a Research Tool

(a) *Human Studies*

(1) Classical conditioning in the perinatal human infant was investigated using intra-oral presentation of a sweet solution and the elicitation of the orofacial 'acceptance response' as an unconditioned stimulus (US) and unconditioned response (UR), respectively. A tactile cue was used as the conditioning stimulus (CS). The US and CS were initially presented together, with the aim of eliciting the 'acceptance response' by presenting the CS alone. This study, carried out by Blass and co-workers (1984) revealed that classical conditioning could easily be achieved in the perinatal (4–48 h old) human infant; a phenomenon hitherto inadequately demonstrated.

(2) College students, when stimulated with sapid samples, in the presence of fellow students, or when closely observed by the experimenter, were found to suppress the gustofacial reflex (Brightman

et al., 1975). This inhibition was most probably caused by social pressures. Therefore it was of interest to observe the gustofacial response in adult subjects of primitive cultures. By courtesy of Professor Irenaeus Eibl-Eibesfeldt and coworkers (of the Max-Planck Institute of Behavioural Physiology, Study-Group for Human Ethology; Seewiesen/W. Germany) some recorded sequences were recently made available to us, showing behavioural reactions of primitive Papua tribes to attractive and repulsive chemo-stimulation. Although these analyses are not yet complete the recordings convincingly indicate that adult members of these primitive tribes display both 'acceptance' and 'aversion' reactions in the most uninhibited manner. The intensity and latency of the responses was similar to those of neonates. Data from this study are not yet published.

(3) The gustofacial reflex of newborn human infants has also been used in applied studies. Investigation of the palatability of umami taste (that of nucleotides, amino acids and their salts) in the perinatal human infant revealed clear signs of 'like' and of 'acceptance' towards monosodium glutamate (MSG), a compound which typically causes the umami taste and is widely used as a seasoning and taste-enhancing food-condiment. The 'acceptance' response to MSG in perinatals suggests a special gustatory mechanism for umami taste (Steiner, 1987*a*). The palatability of non-caloric sweeteners to the neonate infant, is presently being investigated in our laboratory using behavioural testing.

(b) Animal Studies

The studies of Grill and Norgren (1978*a,b*) first indicated that taste-triggered behaviours occur as an across-species neurobiological phenomenon. Our studies have been aimed at comparison of the human gustofacial response and taste induced behaviours in different animal species. Though focusing mainly on mammals, some other vertebrates and also invertebrates were selected for testing. Findings are summarized in the following paragraphs:

(1) According to neonatal appearance and function, animals can be classified into 'precocious' and 'non-precocious' ('altricial') species. While the former have at birth (or at hatching), mature sensory and motor functions, the latter achieve maturity of these functions during postnatal development. Both rabbits and rats are good examples for the altricial type among mammals as they are born with incompletely

functioning vision and hearing. Elicitation of behavioural taste-reaction in pups of these species suggests fully functional perinatal gustatory ability, thus demonstrating, among other things, differences in embryonal development of the sensory systems (Ganchrow et al., 1979; 1984).

(2) Taste induced behaviours of non-human primates in general, and of apes in particular, were of special interest because of their phylogenical relation to man. The analysis of videotaped reactions in numerous primate species showed that the taste dependent behaviours are not only analogous, but almost identical to the human gustofacial reaction (Steiner & Glaser, 1984, 1985). Some selected frames from these studies are shown in Fig. 3 (B and C).

(3) A preliminary observation on the African Elephant living in captivity, revealed that this animal too, both in early infancy and in adulthood, also displays differential oral behaviours in response to sweet and bitter tastes. While samples of a 0·34 M sucrose solution induced licking and trunk-sucking, the bitter stimulation (0·0007 M quinine HCl) caused gaping, drooling and trunk-rubbing (Steiner & Glaser, 1987) (see Fig. 3(E)).

(4) Current studies on the domestic cat show that in this car-nivorous species also sweet and bitter tastes unlock differential oral and facial behaviours, analogous in their appearance and sequence to human orofacial reactions to the same stimuli (Steiner, 1987b) (see Fig. 3(D)).

(5) A further study showed that the domestic chicken also displays an array of differential oral (beak) movements and other behaviours, in response to intra-oral water, sweet and bitter stimuli, both in new hatchlings and in adults (Braun-Bartana et al., 1987).

(6) Among invertebrates, the feeding behaviour of the freshwater prawn (Macrobrachium rosenbergii) was extensively studied. By videotaping the ingestive process in this animal, the rejection display towards food samples, adulterated with a bitter substance was deter-mined and quantified (Steiner & Harpaz, 1987).

COMMENTS

All the findings strongly suggest that behaviour patterns truly mirror the sensations of sweet and bitter, both in man and animal. Beha-viours, triggered by sweet and bitter tastes are composed of strikingly

Figure 3. Characteristic responses to sweet and to bitter in: (A) the term-born normal human infant; (B) in a female Orang-utang infant; (C) in the adult chimpanzee; (D) in the domestic cat; (E) in an infant elephant of 4 weeks old. Attention is called to the similarity of the features in different species (photographs by J. E. Steiner).

analogous motion elements across many species and these occur in similar temporo-spatial organization. Furthermore, these reflectory reactions are innate, non-acquired and are closely related to ingestive behaviour. In general terms: sweet taste triggers a distinct set of motion sequences which promote, facilitate and enhance ingestion. By contrast, bitter taste triggers a different set of movements, which inhibit, interrupt or stop the ingestive process and aid the organism in eliminating the ill-tasting, probably dangerous substance from the oral and pharyngeal region. It should be mentioned that the bitter taste is also a potent sialogogue stimulus; copious salivation serves to dilute the bitter compounds and aids in removal from the mouth. All these biological phenomena emphasize that gustation should be considered as one of the main and the most efficient gate-keeper control mechanisms of ingestion. The findings on malformed infants and animals emphasize that the different qualities of sweet and bitter represent separate entities for the brainstem, where no cognitive recognition can be presumed (Faurion, 1987).

As to the fascinating, communicational aspect of taste triggered behaviours, it should be stressed that all the records on both human subjects and animals were evaluated only by untrained and completely naive reviewers in a double-blind manner. None of them have ever had any difficulty in 'reading' the behaviours correctly and interpreting them in terms of 'like' and 'dislike'. In many instances the inter-observer reliability was calculated and the correlation was found to be high $(0.65-0.85)$. Interestingly, 'dislike' reactions were recognized with even higher inter-observer correlation $(r = 0.86-1.0)$ indicating that communicational messages included in the taste-induced reactions represent a common signal-system, easily understood by everyone.

As to the role these signs might play in communication, one can speculate that the 'acceptance' display may alert other members of the species to the availability of nutrients while the 'rejection' display may warn of potentially harmful items. Furthermore, these signs might be of special value in interaction between generations (mother–offspring) especially in contexts of acquisition and reinforcement of food search and selection behaviours.

A simplified classification of stimulus-induced behaviours was suggested by Pfaffman and co-workers (1977) who suggested dividing them up into those of 'indifference' (O), 'acceptance' (+), 'rejection' (−). This concept is similar to that proposed by nineteenth century scientists (e.g., Jenning, 1906) who labelled the active migratory responses of single cell organisms towards chemical stimuli as 'positive and negative chemotaxis'. All such classifications imply a distinction-process made by the organism; a 'decision-making' (Adler & Tso, 1974). Indeed the decision to take a sweet compound and to leave a bitter one is of great biological, existential, survival value. Such 'decision-making' is, of course, non-cognitive, and should not be compared to learned, acquired distinctions between 'good' and 'bad' in the philosophical, ethical sense.

Decisions of existential, survival importance have to be taken at once, with the shortest possible delay, and involve mono- or olygosynaptic pathways. It is evident that the decision between 'take' of sweet and 'leave' of bitter is anchored in the brainstem, even in the nervous system of phylogenically advanced mammals. Additional neural control from higher brain structures may, of course, facilitate, suppress, and modulate such brainstem regulated decisions, making these reflectory, non-cognitive processes even accessible to volition.

Behaviours which mirror sweet and bitter are phenomena investigated by neurobiologists. Experts in food science, in nutrition or in clinical medicine may use these behaviours as research or diagnostic tools in applied studies. Advertisers can use the actual or posed behaviours, or their pictures, as non-verbal signs of communication, to draw attention to potentially attractive or harmful items, respectively.

REFERENCES

Adler, J. & Tso, W. (1974). 'Decision'-making in bacteria: Chemotaxis of *Escherichia coli* to conflicting stimuli. *Science*, **184**, 1292–94.
Blass, E. M., Ganchrow, J. R. & Steiner, J. E. (1984). Classical conditioning in newborn humans 2–48 hours of age. *Infant Behavior & Development*, **7**, 223–35.
Braun-Bartana, A., Ganchrow, J. R. & Steiner, J. E. (1987). Behavioral reactions to taste stimuli in hatchling chicks. In *Olfaction and Taste IX*, eds S. D. Roper & J. Atema, *J. Ann. N.Y. Acad Sci*, **510**, 196–8.
Brightman, V. J., Segal, A., Werther, P. & Steiner, J. E. (1975). Ethologic study of facial expressions in response to taste stimuli. *J. Dent. Res.*, **54**, special issue A, Abstr. No. L/564.
Carpenter, J. A. (1956). Species differences in taste preferences. *J. Comp. Physiol. Psychol.*, **49**, 139–44.
Darwin, C. (1872). *The Expression of the Emotions in Man and Animals.* Murray, London.
Faurion, A. (1987). Physiology of the sweet taste. In *Progress in Sensory Physiology, Vol. 8*, Springer, Berlin–Heidelberg, pp. 129–201.

Ganchrow, J. R. (1977). Consumatory responses to taste stimuli in the hedgehog *Erinaceus Europaeus*. *Physiol. Behav.*, **18**, 447–53.

Ganchrow, J. R. (1979). Taste preference in rabbits for acid, sucrose, saccharin and quinine. *Physiol. Behav.*, **22**, 457–60.

Ganchrow, J. R., Oppenheimer, M. & Steiner, J. E. (1979). Behavioral stimuli in newborn rabbit pups. *Chemical Senses & Flavour*, **4**, 49–61.

Ganchrow, J. R., Steiner, J. E. & Daher, M. (1983). Neonatal facial different qualities and intensities of gustatory stimuli. *Infant Behavior & Development*, **6**, 189–200.

Ganchrow, J. R., Steiner, J. E. & Canetto, S. (1984). Behavioral display to gustatory stimuli in newborn rat pups. *Develop. Psychobiol.* **19**, 163–74.

Grill, H. I. & Norgren, R. (1978*a*). The taste reactivity test. I. Mimetic responses to gustatory stimuli in neurologically normal rats. *Brain Res.*, **143**, 263–9.

Grill, H. I. & Norgren, R. (1978*b*). The taste reactivity test. II. Mimetic responses to gustatory stimuli in chronic thalamic and chronic decerbrate rats. *Brain Res.*, **143**, 281–97.

Jenning, H. S. (1906). Behavior of the lower organism. Republished in 1962: Indiana University Press, Bloomington.

Kalmus, H. (1976). PTC-testing of infants. *Ann. Human Genet.*, **40**, 139–40.

Leibowitz, Y. (1986). *Between Science and Philosophy* (in Hebrew). Academon Publisher, Jerusalem.

Pfaffman, C. (1960). The pleasure of sensation. *Psychol. Rev.*, **67**, 253–68.

Pfaffman, C., Norgren, R. & Grill, H. I. (1977). Sensory affect and motivation. *Ann. N.Y. Acad. Sci.*, **290**, 18–34.

Richter, C. P. & Campbell, K. H. (1940). Taste thresholds and taste preference of rats for five common sugars. *J. Nutrition*, **20**, 37–46.

Siegel, R. E. (1973). *Galen on Psychology, Psychopathology and Function and Diseases of the Nervous System*. Karger, Basel.

Steiner, J. E. (1973). The gustofacial response: observations on normal and anencephalic newborn infants. In *IV. Symposium on Oral Sensation and Perception*, ed. J. F. Bosma. US Dept. of HEW/NIH Bethesda/MD, pp. 254–78.

Steiner, J. E. (1979). Human facial expressions in response to taste and smell stimulation. In *Advances in Child Development, Vol. 13*, eds H. W. Reese & L. P. Lipsitt. Academic Press, New York, pp. 257–95.

Steiner, J. E. (1987*a*). What the neonate infant can tell us about umami. In *Umami: a Basic Taste*, eds Y. Kawamura & M. R. Kare. Marcel Dekker, New York, pp. 97–123.

Steiner, J. E. (1987*b*). Taste induced behavior displays in the domestic cat (unpublished).

Steiner, J. E. & Abraham, F. (1978). Gustatory and olfactory functions in patients affected by Usher's syndrome. *Chemical Senses & Flavour*, **3**, 93–8.

Steiner, J. E. & Glaser, D. (1984). Differential behavioral responses to taste stimuli in non-human primates. *J. Hum. Evol.*, **13**, 709–23.

Steiner, J. E. & Glaser, D. (1985). Orofacial motor behavior-patterns induced by gustatory stimuli in apes. *Chemical Senses*, **10**, 452 (Abstract No. 152 at AChemS-VII).

Steiner, J. E. & Glaser, D. (1987). Taste-induced behavior stereotypes in the African elephant (unpublished).
Steiner, J. E. & Harpaz, S. (1987). Behavior stereotypes of food acceptance and the rejection of a 'bitter' food in the freshwater prawn *Magrobrachium rosenbergii. Chemical Senses, 12,* 89–97.
Steiner, J. E. & Reuveni, J. (1979). Differential arousal response to gustatory stimuli in the awake rabbit. *Electroencephalogr. & Clin. Neurophysiol.,* **47,** 1–11.
Steiner, J. E., Rosenthal-Zifroni, A. & Edelstein, E. L. (1969). Taste perception in depressive illness. *Israel Ann. Psychiat. Rel. Discipl.,* **7,** 223–32.
Steiner, J. E., Reuveni, J. & Beja, Y. (1982). Simultaneous multidisciplinary measures of taste hedonics. In *Determination of Behaviour by Chemical Stimuli,* eds J. E. Steiner & J. R. Ganchrow. IRL-Press Ltd, London, pp. 149–16.
Steiner, J. E., Gadoth, N. & Abramowitz, D. (1988). A multidisciplinary approach to the taste dysfunctions, pathognomonic in familial dysauthonomia. *Isr. J. Med. Sci.* (submitted for publication).

Chapter 14

Explaining Individual Differences in Flavour Perception and Food Acceptance

DAVID A. STEVENS, DALE A. DOOLEY and JAMES D. LAIRD

Department of Psychology, Clark University, Worcester, Massachusetts 01610, USA

ABSTRACT

Attribution theories of personality, following William James and Carl Lange, argue that individuals determine their affective state by assessing cues. These cues come from the environment (situational cues) and from the person's behaviour (self-produced cues). Further, individuals differ in the relative extent to which they use one or the other of these two kinds of cues. Using this approach, Laird and associates have explained a variety of individual differences including those in the effectiveness of placebos, the role of facial expression in emotion, and extent to which people choose to suffer. We suggest differences in the use of cues will also explain individual differences in the perception of flavour, and in the acceptability of foods. Accordingly, we had subjects who differed in responsiveness to body cues, rate the flavour of soup samples which varied orthogonally in their salt concentration and the information given verbally about their flavour. Attribution theory applied to flavour perception would predict that those subjects most responsive to body cues would be more influenced by salt concentration whereas those least responsive to body cues would be more influenced by the verbal information.

Psychophysical studies and other evaluations of intensity and hedonic quality of taste, odour and flavour stimuli typically yield wide individual differences. These differences can be the source of several serious problems.

One problem is that when the sources of individual differences are not identified, the variation is included as error variance in statistical analyses of the data. The error estimate is then larger than if the variance were excluded, and Type II errors in interpretation will be made, i.e. no effects may be inferred when they exist, or effects are shown to be less vigorous than they are.

Another problem is that a failure to identify systematic individual variation results in generalizations from the data being made under the assumption that a simpler model accounts for the data than in fact is required. For example, a bi- or multi-modal population might be erroneously treated as unimodal. Measures of central tendency (for example, means and medians) would be incorrectly used to describe groups.

Simply using larger groups of subjects is not a solution if there are systematic individual differences. A larger number of subjects will indeed increase reliability, but not insure that the measures used are valid. For example, using a mean to represent a large bi-modal distribution will only give you a more reliable invalid measure than you would get from a smaller sample. The only solution is the identification of sources of individual variation and their control by an appropriate method.

A number of sources of individual variation have been identified. Pangborn (1981) listed subject variables that define genetic and biological differences, intellectual differences, semantic differences, and personality differences as known sources of individual differences. In the present chapter, we will argue from a self-perception theoretical position of personality, that stable individual differences in responses to taste, smell and flavour stimuli can be identified, and present evidence to support the argument.

Self-perception theory (Bem, 1967, 1972) asserts that we know our own feelings, moods, abilities, etc., by the same means that we know them in others; by inference from observed actions and their context. Furthermore, recent research indicates that individuals differ consistently in the types of information they use in making inferences about themselves. Two types of cues have been identified: (a) those that arise from the individual's actions and personal properties, including visceral responses, expressive behaviour, overt actions, and the consequences of those actions, and (b) those that come from the environment, and include normative expectations about what most people would feel in a particular situation. The former are called self-produced cues, and the latter, situational cues (Laird, 1984).

All persons seem to use situational cues, but there are reliable, stable differences among individuals in the extent they are affected by manipulations of self-produced cues. For example, when people are induced to perform the muscle movements associated with smiling and frowning, which produce self-produced cues, some subjects report strong emotional fluctuations corresponding to the manipulation of facial expression and some do not.

Self-produced cuers, those individuals who respond to self-produced cues in this facial expression manipulation situation, respond to self-produced cues in other situations as well. They change their impression of themselves as a result of changes in appearance (Kellerman & Laird, 1982), feel more romantic love after gazing into their partner's eyes (Kellerman *et al.*, 1985), and show reverse placebo effects—they feel *more* fear rather than less after taking placebos identified as relaxers, and *less* aroused rather than more after taking placebos identified as arousers (Duncan & Laird, 1980). Situational cuers (people who do not respond to facial manipulation) will accept more readily an experimenter's suggestion about what they should feel (Kellerman & Laird, 1982), and show the usual, positive placebo effects (Duncan & Laird, 1980).

This distinction between self-produced and situational cues is analogous to Schachter's distinction between internal and external cues. The latter are defined on the basis of location while the former are defined on the basis of whether the cues are something distinctive about the individual and his or her behaviour, or are normative expectations.

Taste, smell and flavour perception, and one's hedonic responses to those sensory experiences are the result of both self-produced and situational cues. Self-produced cues result in part from mouth and facial movements, salivation, swallowing, inhalation and other behaviours that accompany tasting and smelling. Situational cues are the normative expectancies produced by the situation, e.g. that roses have a floral odour and it is pleasant; that a syrup tastes sweet.

If there are these two kinds of cues used in evaluation of flavour, and if there are individual differences in the extent to which people use self-produced cues, it follows that manipulation of self-produced and situational cues will differentially affect evaluation of flavour by the different types of people. This was tested by a factorial experiment in which subjects identified as being more or less sensitive to bodily functions evaluated soup samples which orthogonally differed in the concentration of sodium chloride (a manipulation of a stimulus for the self-produced cues for flavour) and verbal information given about the flavour (a manipulation of situational cues).

Thirty-four men and 61 women voluntarily participated in the experiment. Their ages ranged from 17 to 43 years. They were paid for their services.

The flavour stimuli were samples of chicken soup having three levels of sodium concentration. They were made from a commercially available instant soup mix. The *low* sodium concentration, that of the soup mix as furnished, was 0·276% w/v. Reagent grade NaCl was added to the soups to produce sodium concentrations of 0·420% and 0·564% for the *medium* and *high* sodium samples. The 10 cl samples were served at 61°C in covered styrofoam cups.

Response sheets for the taste tests had seven line scales, each 15 cm long. On these scales the subjects indicated their ratings of the intensities of overall flavour, chicken flavour, saltiness, spiciness, oiliness, other flavours, and of hedonic quality. For all scales except hedonic quality, 'weak' was written on the left of the scale and 'strong' was written on the right. For hedonic quality, 'strongly dislike' and 'strongly like' were at the ends of the line. A subject made a mark on the line indicating their rating, and the score was the distance in centimetres from the left end of the line to that mark.

The subjects were given the Private Body Consciousness Scale (Miller *et al.*, 1981) to complete. This scale is composed of ratings of awareness of such events as heart beat, changes in body temperature and hunger contractions. The subjects were instructed on the rating of the soup samples on the seven scales, and then given the 9 samples to rate. Each of 3 samples of a given salt concentration was tasted under each of 3 information conditions: (a) told that the soup had 'flavour removed', (b) told that it had 'flavour added', and (c) told nothing about the level of flavouring. Greco-Latin squares were used to determine the sequences of the salt concentration × information combinations used.

The Private Body Consciousness test scores were rank ordered. Those subjects having the highest third of the scores were classified as

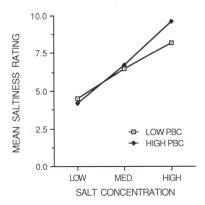

Figure 1. Ratings of saltiness as a function of salt content by subjects having high and low private body consciousness.

high body consciousness (high PBC) ($N = 32$) and those having the lowest third of the scores were classified low body consciousness (low PBC) ($N = 28$). Data from the remaining subjects were not used.

Analyses of variance showed that the level of subjects' private body consciousness was associated with differences in ratings of saltiness and of hedonic quality.

Subjects with high PBC rated the samples with the highest salt level as saltier and those with the lowest salt levels as less salty than did the subjects with low body consciousness. This interaction ($F_{2,116} = 3 \cdot 19$, $p < 0 \cdot 05$) between body consciousness and ratings of saltiness is shown in Fig. 1. The exponents of the psychophysical power functions describing the relation between salt concentration and perceived saltiness are $0 \cdot 846$ for the low body consciousness group and $1 \cdot 168$ for the high PBC group.

The interaction of level of body consciousness and salt concentration is consistent with predictions made from our extension of self-perception theory to sensory psychology. The subjects with high PBC, i.e. those who report paying the most attention to changes in bodily activities, were those who were the most sensitive to changes in the concentration of salt in the soup samples. The theory which influenced this work holds that people differ in the extent to which they used self-produced cues, not in the extent to which they use situational cues. There is evidence to support this notion. The situational cue manipulated in the present study was the verbal information given about the addition or removal of flavouring. If the groups differed in the extent to which they used these cues there would have been differences in the variance of the estimates within groups. This is because the verbal information was equally often consistent with the soup's ingredients (when the subjects were told flavour was added and reduced, and the salt concentrations were high and low, respectively) and inconsistent (when the subjects were told flavour had been added or reduced, and salt concentrations were low and high, respectively). A group responding more to the verbal information would be responding to both consistent and inconsistent cues, and thus would have higher variance within it than a group that was not responding to such information. The variance in estimates of saltiness made by the two groups did not differ (the ratio of mean group variances was 1·06:1). This suggests that the groups did not differ in the extent to which they used situational cues, but rather in the self-produced cues provided by the manipulation of salt concentration.

Level of body consciousness also affected our subjects' hedonic ratings of the soups. Analysis of variance indicated a significant three-way interaction between body consciousness, verbal information, and salt concentration ($F_{4,232} = 3 \cdot 030$, $p < 0 \cdot 025$), shown in Fig. 2. The low PBC group consistently liked samples identified as having

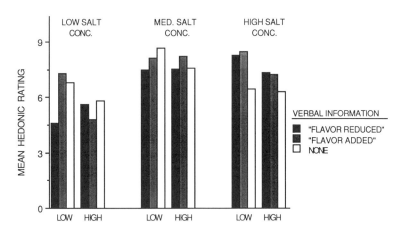

Figure 2. Hedonic ratings by subjects having high and low private body consciousness, as a function of salt concentration and verbal information.

flavour added more than it liked samples identified as having flavour reduced despite there having been no differences in ingredients. However, for the high PBC group, there was no consistent relationship between verbal information regarding flavour and hedonic ratings.

These results are based on comparisons of the effects of being told flavour was added or reduced, not on comparisons using the no-information condition. That condition was originally included as a control, but it seems likely that it is not an appropriate one. No information in a context where information is more often provided is not a neutral condition.

The results found with the low salt concentration samples are similar to those found in studies comparing responses by self-produced cuers and situational cuers to placebo treatments (Duncan & Laird, 1980; Brockner & Swap, 1983). The subjects characterized as not as likely to use self-produced cues showed the typical positive placebo effects, responding as suggested by the information accompanying the placebo, while those characterized as more likely to use self-produced cues showed reversed placebo effects. This is predicted by self-perception theory since self-produced cuers, but not situational cuers, are likely to note the lack of change in their body's state after having received the placebo. They conclude that their condition must be worse than previously thought since the placebo treatment did not produce the promised result. Our high PBC subjects also showed a reverse placebo effect; their relative hedonic judgements were in the opposite direction of that suggested by the verbal information. Presumably the subjects found the soup sample having less than the optimal level of flavour, heard it described as having flavour added, and concluded that a soup tasting like that after having flavour added cannot be a very good soup. They assigned it a low hedonic rating. However, the same soup described as having flavour reduced was given a higher hedonic rating. The subjects concluded that a soup having that much flavour left after flavour reduction must have redeeming qualities. This reverse placebo effect was not found at the higher concentrations, and this is consistent with placebo effects in general. As the sensory event being manipulated becomes stronger, placebos become less effective. Placebos are more likely to reduce a mild headache than the pain of a broken arm.

Most studies on individual differences in taste, smell and flavour have focused on individual differences in magnitude of sensory experience and the resulting hedonic response. The present study shows that in addition to these linear effects, there are individual differences responsible for complex interactions between those sensory variables and cognitive variables which produce hedonic responses.

ACKNOWLEDGEMENTS

This work was supported by a grant from Thomas J. Lipton, Inc. Charles Bresler participated in the early planning of the project. We are grateful to both.

REFERENCES

Bem, D. J. (1967). Self-perception: An alternative interpretation of cognitive dissonance phenomena. *Psychol. Rev., 74,* 183–200.

Bem, D. J. (1972). Self-perception theory. In *Advances in Experimental Social Psychology,* Vol. 6, ed. L. Berkowitz. Academic Press, New York, pp. 1–62.

Brockner, J. & Swap, W. C. (1983). Resolving the relationships between placebos, misattribution, and insomnia: An individual-differences perspective. *J. Pers. Soc. Psychol., 45,* 32–42.

Duncan, J. W. & Laird, J. D. (1980). Positive and reverse placebo effects as a function of differences in cues used in self-perception. *J. Pers. Soc. Psychol., 39,* 1024–36.

Kellerman, J. & Laird, J. D. (1982). The effect of appearance on self-perception. *J. Pers., 50,* 296–315.

Kellerman, J., Lewis, J. & Laird, J. D. (1985). Looking and loving: The effects of mutual gaze on feelings of romantic love. Unpublished MS.

Laird, J. D. (1984). The real role of facial response in the experience of emotion: A reply to Tourangeau and Ellsworth, and others. *J. Pers. Soc. Psychol., 47,* 909–17.

Miller, L. C., Murphy, R. & Buss, A. H. (1981). Consciousness of body: Private and public. *J. Pers. Soc. Psychol., 41,* 397–406.

Pangborn, R. (1981). Individuality in responses to sensory stimuli. In *Criteria of Food Acceptance: How Man Chooses what He Eats,* ed. J. Solms & R. L. Hall. Forster Verlag, Zurich, pp. 177–219.

Chapter 15

Psychological Determinants of Food Intake

NORBERT MAUS and VOLKER PUDEL

Department of Psychiatry, University of Göttingen, von-Siebold-
Str. 5, D-3400 Göttingen, FRG

ABSTRACT

Food intake in a newly born baby is almost exclusively controlled by physiological need. With increasing age, psychologically motivated needs become more important: within a few years they can in some cases even control the physiological need to a great extent (for example, anorexia nervosa). In short, physiological regulation of food intake gives way to external influences (externality hypothesis). Preferences for certain foods, culturally determined stereotype meals, educational strategies employing food as a means of reinforcement and information on nutrition, begin to compete with each other and must continually be countered with effective behaviour by children. Moreover, until puberty, children rarely have the comprehensive capability and cognitive structure to grasp rational decisions. Their consumption of sweets is a paradigmatic example for (spontaneous) childhood needs which continually come up against cognitive counter strategies. The 'psychology' of eating is, all too often, experienced as a conflict situation, in which they are unable to understand why the conflict has become relevant. Developmental psychology has not yet managed to propose methods of conveying information, necessary to make rational decisions and for training children how to cope with an over-abundance of food, which are best suited to the child's needs and their ability to comprehend.

A newborn baby is completely controlled by its physiological needs. Given an adequate supply of food, an infant is instinctively capable of controlling its selection of food and the intake of the necessary amounts according to its needs. Regulation occurs by way of inherent neurophysiological and biochemical mechanisms. This was demonstrated in a classical experiment by Davis, as early as 1928 (Davis, 1928).

However, a child's nutrition and its eating behaviour can sometimes become problematic, when emotional and situational (external) factors begin to exert an influence on the selection, supply and eating of food. Then, in addition to the *need for nourishment,* a secondary *need to eat* or, as in the case of anorexia nervosa, a strong need to refuse food, develops. These requirements, which are conditioned by taste stimulations, situational and emotional conditions, are primarily motivated by psychological variables and can thus, in the sense of a functional autonomy (Allport, 1960), sometimes cause intake which is in excess of the needs of the organism.

Bruch (1973) and Selvini (1967) have repeatedly pointed out the special roll of the mother–child interaction in the development of such nutritional requirements. Inadequately differentiated devotion reactions of the mother can contribute to a small child's inability to differentiate between hunger and other emotions. This leads to the general misinterpretation of all negative emotions as hunger. The effects of this over-protection have been widely discussed and their consequences for the development of stress conditioned eating, in the sense of oral compensation, are well known (Jung & Pudel, 1977). However, this should be qualified by pointing out that, at least when using representative survey procedures (Deutsche Gesellschaft fuer Ernaehrung, 1984), it has been impossible to correlate a specific educational style of mothers (e.g. employing food as a reward, forcing children to eat everything on their plates, etc.) to children with abnormal weights.

Nevertheless, with the exception of manifest eating disorders and their associated psychic syndromes, which are relatively rare in older children, the question of the importance of psychological factors in the nutrition of healthy children remains. A recent comparison of the nutritional and physiological parameters of German children has highlighted the need to consider ways of improving child nutrition. If the average consumption of energy-supplying foods in German elementary school children is compared with the recommendations of the

Table 1

Intake of energy-supplying nutrients by children between 7 and 9 years of age compared to the recommendations of the German Nutritional Society

	Nominal recommendations of the GNS, 1985		Actual consumption analysis (EB 1984)	
	% Nutritional energy	Weight (g)	% Nutritional energy	Weight (g)
Fats	35–40	78	38	87
Carbohydrates	50–55	240	49	245
Proteins	8–10	40	13	65
Calories	1 900		2 100	

German Nutritional Society (Deutsche Gesellschaft fuer Ernaehrung, 1985), there are relatively few deviations (Table 1). However, from a qualitative point of view, the intake of complex carbohydrates is too low, since at present 50% of all carbohydrates are eaten in the form of mono- and disaccharides. Although total energy intake appears to be excessive, this is open to question since, according to the most recent recommendations of the German Nutritional Society (Deutsche Gesellschaft fuer Ernaehrung, 1985), the desired energy input cannot be standardized, i.e. it depends on the development of the individual.

If the GNS's recommendations reflect children's actual nutritional requirements, it can then be concluded that need fulfilment is not guaranteed for all children and, in particular, that by choosing food with lower nutritional density, the theoretically optimal intake of essential nutrients may not be achieved.

These conclusions are complemented by a recent food consumption analysis. The basis of this study was a 3-day nutritional questionnaire that was filled out in a representative sample of 2900 German families. An excerpt of the data for 6–10-year-old children showed that they consumed sweet drinks more often than milk, that sweets more often enter their energy balance than potatoes or noodles and that, contrary to popular opinion, sausage ('wurst') and butter are the dominant spreads (Tables 2–4).

Table 2
Consumption frequency of milk and soft drinks by
elementary school children (proportion of children
who consumed a particular item during a three-day
period, expressed as %)

Food	Consumption (%)	Average intake/day (ml)
Milk	59	200
Cola/soft drinks	65	300

Table 3
Consumption frequency (see Table 2) of potatoes, noodles and
various sweets by elementary school children

Food	Consumption (%)	Average intake/day
Potatoes	68	1·2 pieces
Noodles	34	70 cm^3
Chocolate	49	1·6 pieces
Cookies	49	1·6 pieces
Sweets	46	1·9 pieces
Gummi bears	37	3·0 pieces
Chocolate bars	35	0·5 pieces

Table 4
Consumption frequency (see Table 2) of sausage ('Wurst'),
butter, honey and nougat cream by elementary school children

Food	Consumption (%)	Average intake/day
Sausage[a]	88	1·2 slices of bread
Butter[a]	75	1·9 slices of bread
Honey	29	0·7 teaspoons
Nougat cream	43	0·9 teaspoons

[a] Eaten on slices of bread.

The decisive questions are therefore: What factors influence the eating behaviour of children? What motivational structures determine their nutritional preferences which in turn influence consumption? According to the social learning theory (Bandura, 1973) it should, in principle be possible to explain the eating behaviour of children by studying the influence of their models; in this case their parents. This assumption is to some extent supported by a comparison of the nutritional composition of foods consumed by parents and their children. There are some broad similarities in the diets in that both are characterized as being 'too fat' and 'too sweet', but the specific nutriments which are preferred are frequently different for adults and children. In fact, a comparison of the preferred foods of mother and child showed that there is much better agreement on what is *not* eaten, rather than what is eaten. This can be clearly illustrated, for example, by preference for apples. If mothers like apples, and state that their children also like apples, the accuracy of the predicted consumption of apples by children is improved by 10%. If, on the other hand, mothers dislike apples, the accurate prediction of an aversion of their children to apples is improved by 60%. These distinctly closer parallels for non-consumption are valid for nearly all foods. The exception is, however, sweets: in this case a preference of the mother is more strongly correlated with a preference of her child (Deutsche Gesellschaft fuer Ernaehrung, 1984). Thus, social learning theory alone, is insufficient to understand the conditioning factors of the child's nutritional choice, even though the nutritional behaviour of the parents is not without influence.

A study of the literature dealing with the development of taste preferences, supplies few empirically consistent answers. According to Cowart's detailed survey (1981), it is at least possible to determine that newborn babies already possess highly differentiated sensitivity to extremely varied taste substances (Desor et al., 1975). Studies of taste preference, which primarily investigate the effect of different concentrations of sugar, allow the conclusion that newborn babies already possess a preference for sweet tastes which is independent of learning experience (Nisbett, 1970; Desor et al., 1975; Steiner, 1979). There is also a consensus of opinion that aversion is the general reaction to stimuli which cause bitterness (Cowart, 1981). It has however, also been determined that infants and children of elementary school age, initially have a positive reaction to 'salty' and 'bitter', which is attributable to conditioned learning (Cowart, 1981). In the

Table 5
Average energy intake of sweet and non-sweet food by
suckling babies from 8 to 111 days of age (after Ziegler,
1983)

Age of baby (days)	Sucrose ('sweet') energy intake (kcal/kg/d average)	Polycose ('bland') energy intake (kcal/kg/d average)
8–27	117	111
28–55	118	108
56–83	106	101
84–111	106	96

course of development, the acceptance of sugar also appears to be modified, in that the maximum preferred sugar concentration decreases (Grinker et al., 1976). As a general principle, boys seem to prefer higher sugar concentrations than girls (Greene et al., 1975). Ziegler (1983) reported on a cross-over study with 16 babies which, from the eighth to the one-hundred and eleventh day, were fed ad libitum with sucrose or non-sweet-tasting, polycose-containing, food. The results show (Table 5) that sugar preference leads to a significantly increased intake of food. In 2–6-year-old children, Filer (1978) found a significantly increased consumption of sweetened spaghetti. These studies prove that subjective preference can be considered as an important behaviourally affective motivation for actual food consumption.

There are indications in the literature, as in the study of Garb & Stunkard (1974), that the transition from late childhood to early adolescence should be considered as the decisive developmental phase in the differentiation of taste preferences. All people between the ages of 6 and 60, who were questioned, declared that their taste aversions developed between the ages of 6 and 12. According to a study by Greene et al. (1975) on 622 fraternal and identical twins, a hereditary component for the preference tendency to 'sweet' and/or 'salty' cannot be assumed.

In principle all of these preference studies suffer from a methodological problem in that they investigate the single taste dimensions of 'sweetness', 'sourness', 'saltiness' and 'bitterness', whereas the sensory qualities of food are multidimensional and result from interactions of various taste substances and their mediators (e.g. fats), as well as other sensory attributes such as texture, colour, smell, etc.

Although honey, nut nougat cream and jam all taste sweet, children's preferences for these sweet spreads are different (58% like to eat jam, 47% nougat cream and 43% honey). The importance of other primarily non-taste factors, such as consistency, bite, appearance and 'play value' of the food is illustrated by the high preference for rather bland tasting sphaghetti, which, with 70%, is only exceeded by roast chicken and chocolate (Deutsche Gesellschaft fuer Ernaehrung, 1984).

It appears as if, at least in the first 6 years of life, a child's nutritional choice is primarily distinguished by stereotypical, innate preference tendencies centred around the taste of sugar. However, mothers' continual attempts at corrective intervention in the spontaneous taste preferences of their children should not be overlooked, even though, as can be seen in the data analysis in the Nutritional Report of 1984, their strategies seem ineffective in the 'fight' against sugar preference. On the other hand, this should not be too surprising, since they have been offered, naturally from the manufacturers' side, pseudo-logical arguments for sweet foods, which are oriented toward their alleged health value. More than 50% of all German mothers stress the nutritional value of white chocolate because of its increased milk content, and just as many emphasize the value of 'sugar for the nerves'. Forty percent believe that nougat cream is nutritionally good for children. This leads to the situation that 15% of those children who do not prefer this nutriment receive it for breakfast (Deutsche Gesellschaft fuer Ernaehrung, 1984).

The development of children's taste preferences, which in the end play an important role in their choice of food, appears to become increasingly more amenable to change, with advancing age. Such changes are largely to be determined by intra-familial psychosocial processes, which once again are lastingly influenced by economic pressures and educational information as well as general cultural determinants.

Figure 1 serves to illustrate the developmental process. Nutritional intake, which was initially spontaneously regulated by innate mechanisms, becomes increasingly weaker from the first day of life onwards. This occurs because external conditions are superimposed on them and to some extent override them. These external influences on eating behaviour, whose increase in importance is inversely proportional to

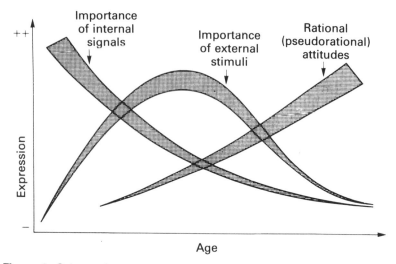

Figure 1. Schematic presentation of the reciprocal effect modification of internal signals, external stimuli and rational attitudes in the course of life.

that of innate control, modify children's eating behaviours. In spite of this preference for the sweet taste usually remains. Meyer & Pudel (1983) have reported that the influence of external factors may diminish in later adult life. It is conceivable that other cognitive factors could mediate between the two influences. As corrective measures for the controlled modification of children's eating behaviour, pedagógical concepts have been developed, which attempt to influence eating behaviour using a 'children's version of nutritional physiology' to convey the relevant facts (Gutezeit, 1985). Educational measures concerning caries and sugar consumption is a paradigmatic example of this, where it is hoped that by means of reports, contests, games and riddles (Bartsch, 1984) an appeal to the child's better judgement can be made to encourage rational behaviour.

From a child's point of view, however, it must appear, against the described background of preference development, 'unreasonable' to voluntarily give up sweets. Such an abstention would only seem judicious to the child, if the advantage won by abstaining could be anticipated. However, even this rationale is open to doubts. It is uncertain whether the child's cognitive structure and their intellectual capacity are sufficiently well developed by the tenth year of life, to even begin to understand such arguments. However, according to an

Table 6

Arrangement of foods according to their similarity, by elementary school children (method: cluster analysis). (Deutsche Gesellschaft fuer Ernaehrung, 1984). The groups are characterized as follows: Group 1: 'not very fattening', 'makes you very strong', 'healthy', 'unpopular'; Group 2: 'non-fattening', 'makes you very strong', 'very healthy', 'very popular'; Group 3: 'not too fattening', 'makes you strong', 'healthy', 'very popular'; Group 4: 'very fattening', 'doesn't make you strong', 'unhealthy', 'very popular'

Group 1	Group 2	Group 3	Group 4
Whole grain bread	Cocoa	Nut nougat cream	Pudding
Noodle soup	Whole milk	'Curry wurst'	Bonbons
Potatoes	Carrots	Fish sticks	Hamburger
Grey-bread	Peas	Chicken	Cola
Sausage ('Wurst')	Bananas	Spaghetti	Chocolate bar
Tomatoes	Eggs	Rolls	Jam
Cheese	Salad		Crackers
Pork chops	Oranges		Chocolate
	Pears		
	Apples		

investigation of 518 elementary school children (Deutsche Gesellschaft fuer Ernaehrung, 1984), children can consistently and accurately classify most foods using the criteria 'makes you fat', 'makes you strong' and 'is healthy'. Clearly, there are deep-rooted food stereotypes, with learned functional assignments (Table 6), which have been conditioned by information from parents and teachers.

In another explorative study with 89 children Seidenschwanz & Zeller (1983) came to the conclusion that these non-perceptible functional connections are not understood in their original sense. Especially since children have neither the necessary ability to make abstractions nor any real awareness of the long term effects of food on the metabolism. They therefore must develop their own images within their own way of thinking, in addition to the recitable stereotypes. To the child, the purpose of nutritional intake thus primarily comprises easily experienced functions, such as 'I eat so that I won't starve', or 'I eat so that I'll not be hungry'. It is already a paradoxical cognitive problem for 6–10-year-old children, on the one hand, to learn that 'everything that is eaten is later eliminated from the body', but on the other hand that 'food is stored in the body and one becomes overweight'. Without going into detail, it can be ascertained that concepts are necessary which orient themselves more closely to the child's intellectual capacity, in order to answer children's questions within their own conceptual framework. Models suitable for children which could better explain the preceptionally limited nutritional world, are lacking. A form of developmental psychology, similar to the state theory which Piaget presented for the interpretation of quantities, would surely be helpful for the development of the child's cognitive structure of nutrition.

In a comprehensive investigation of 451 children between 6 and 13 years of age, (Chome, 1984), the question was whether, and at what age, children are able to distinguish between the *energy content* and the *volume* of food, with respect to its satiation effect. The children were repeatedly given the task of collecting specific foods for a fantasy character. This creature ate a different type of food every day and it was important that it was always quickly satisfied. In this way it was possible to investigate the quantities of 'bratwurst' (fried sausage), chips, ice cream, rolls, chocolate bars and apples which, in the children's opinions, result in the same degree of satiation. In a second study the quantities of two different foods which would balance each other on a scale were estimated. The results were clear; at all age levels, the categorization according to satiation effect was similar to the classification according to weight and/or volume. Older children showed a slight tendency to take the energy content into considera-tion, although the correlations to volumes still clearly predominated. Hence, it can be inferred that, in their preceptionally limited world, children associate the term 'too much' almost exclusively with 'visible volume' or 'detectable weight' of food. It is thus not surprising that children claim that they do not eat many sweets, but that they eat a great deal of potatoes, even though their caloric intake of sweets is greater. Energy density is not directly comprehensible, hence it is not relevant to their actions. Indeed when it is important to motivate children with weight problems to eat 'less' or 'more', they consider this request only in terms of visible quantities.

The human organism was rarely confronted with an over-abundance of food during the course of evolution. In contrast to this, its adaptive mechanisms for coping with a lack of food were taxed and correspond-ingly developed. Nutrition regulated by primary need has been replaced by a secondarily motivated eating behaviour which, in children, is determined by preference for sweets. It is now a question

of utilizing their socially learned secondary needs in order to channel-
ize their food choice by setting trends and eating fads. That this can
occur with lasting effects, can be seen in the epedemic-like spread of
bulimia nervosa amongst young people, who abuse nutrition as a tool
to model their figures. In this case, a fad determines their eating
behaviour.

In an environment of an over-abundance of food, adults could
acquire the knowledge and motivation to nourish themselves properly,
but most do not bother! Children have neither adequate knowledge
nor the specific cognitive structures to do so. Hence, they do not
possess the necessary motivation to nourish themselves in an alternative manner which would still satisfy their preferences. As long as the
effectiveness of social learning is not used, it appears nearly arrogant
that adults preach concepts to their children which they consider
advantageous, but seldom practise themselves.

REFERENCES

Allport, G. W. (1960). The open system in personality theory. *J. Abnorm.
soc. Psychol.*, **6**(1), 301–10.

Bandura, A. (1973). *Social Learning Theory*. Prentice-Hall, Englewood Cliffs,
N.J.

Bartsch, N. (1984). Zucker—die suesse Verfuehrung. *Zahnaerztl. Mitteilg.*,
74, 1468–74.

Bruch, H. (1973). *Eating Disorders*. Basic Books, New York.

Chome, J. (1984). Entwicklung und Analyse kognitiver Denk- und Wahrneh-
mungsstrukturen von sechs-bis zehnjaehrigen Kindern bezueglich der
Ernaehrung. Research report on the ISFE, Goettingen.

Cowart, B. J. (1981). Development of taste perception in humans: sensitivity
and preference throughout the life span. *Psychol. Bull.*, **90**, 43–73.

Davis, C. M. (1928). Self selection of diet by newly weaned infants. *Am. J.
Dis. Child.*, **36**, 651–79.

Desor, J. A., Maller, O. & Andrews, K. (1975). Ingestive responses of human
newborns to salty, sour, and bitter stimuli. *J. Comp. Physiol. Psychol.*, **89**,
966–70.

Deutsche Gesellschaft fuer Ernaehrung. (1984). *Ernaehrungsbericht 1984*.
Heinrich, Frankfurt.

Deutsche Gesellschaft fuer Ernaehrung. (1985). *Empfehlungen fuer die
Naehrstoffzufuhr*. Umschau, Frankfurt.

Epstein, A. N. (1967). Oropharyngeal factors in feeding and drinking. In
Handbook of Physiology, Vol. 6, ed. C. F. Code. American Physiological
Society, Washington, D.C. pp. 197–218.

Filer, L. J. (1978). Studies of taste preference in infancy and childhood. *Pediatr. Basics*, **12**, 5–9.

Garb, J. L. & Stunkard, A. J. (1974). Taste aversions in man. *Am. J. Psychiat.*, **131**, 1204–7.

Greene, L. S., Dresor, J. A. & Maller, O. (1975). Heredity and experience: Their relative importance in the development of taste preference in man. *J. Comp. Physiol. Psychol.*, **89**, 279–84.

Grinker, J. A., Price, J. M. & Greenwood, M. R. C. (1976). Studies of taste in childhood. In *Hunger*, eds D. Novin, W. Wyrwicka & G. A. Bray. Raven Press, New York, pp. 441–457.

Gutezeit, G. (1985). Enaehrungsbezogene Kenntnisse, Einstellungen und Verhaltensweisen im Schulalter. *Sozialpaediatr. Prax. Klin.*, **7**, 301–9.

Jung, F. & Pudel, V. (1977). Zur Auswirkung von psychischer Aktivierung auf die Nahrungsaufnahme von Kindern. *Prax. Kinderpsychol. Kinderpsychiatr.*, **26**, 85–90.

Meyer, J. E., & Pudel, V. (1983). Das Ernaehrungsverhalten im Alter und seine Konsequenzen fuer die Ernaehrung. *Z. Gerontol.*, **16**, 241–7.

Nisbett, R. E. (1970). Weight, sex and the eating behaviour of human newborns. *J. Comp. Physiol. Psychol.*, **73**, 245–53.

Seidenschwanz, A. & Zeller, D. (1983). Wissen und Einstellung zu Thema Ernaehrung bie Kindern im Grundschulalter. Unpublished masters thesis, Goettingen.

Selvini, M. P. (1967). Die Bildung des Koerperbewusstseins—Die Ernaehrung des Kindes als Lernprozess. *Psychother. Psychsom.*, **15**, 293–312.

Steiner, J. E. (1979). Human facial expressions in response to taste and smell stimulation. *Adv. Child. Dev. Behav.*, **13**, 257–95.

Ziegler, E. E. (1983). *Nahrungs-(insbesondere-) Saccharose- aufnahme und Wachstum von Saeuglingen*. Nestle Wissenschaftlicher Dienst, Munich.

Chapter 16

Cuisines and Food Selection

CLAUDE FISCHLER

Chargé de Recherche au CNRS, CETSAP, 44, rue de la Tour, 75116 Paris, France

ABSTRACT

Social and cultural factors play an important part in the selection of foods by the omnivore Homo Sapiens. *The very definition of what is or is not food is subject to high intercultural variability (e.g. insects). Neither nutritional value nor sensory features of a potential food are reliable predictors for actual acceptance and consumption.*

Such cultural 'biases' in food selection are based on culture-specific, often implicit, classifications and rules of appropriateness, the nature and origins of which currently are an object of debate in the social sciences. Other biases, particularly class-specific differences in food consumption, have also been observed. Finally, a set of factors influencing food choice can be termed 'bio-social' for they either combine biological and social dimensions or their determinants cannot clearly be ascribed to one rather than the other. Such is the case of age and sex.

Why we eat what we eat is an apparently simple, if not simplistic, question. It usually elicits supposedly commonsensical answers such as the following:

—Because of the availability and cost. Indeed, if a given food were simply not available in the first place, or if its cost in terms of

193

money, time or energy were not affordable, one could think of few reasons why and how it could be consumed at all.

—Because we like the taste. Sensory quality is an obvious candidate when it comes to explaining why the foods are consumed. There is solid evidence, for instance, that preference or aversion for certain tastes (sweetness and bitterness for instance) have a strong innate biological basis across the human species.

—Because we have become accustomed to eating the food. Even in the absence of outstanding sensory quality, some foods are widely consumed and acquire prominence in our diet. A common, spontaneous explanation is that, in the words of Kurt Lewin (Lewin, 1943), 'people like what they eat rather than eat what they like', i.e. they acquire a preference for the foods they have had exposure to in their native environment and culture.

—Because it is 'good for us'—and our body knows it. According to this line of argument, which is in part substantiated by evidence, foods have post-ingestional effects which affect our likes and dislikes, hence in turn our patterns of consumption in the longer term.

Although each of the above statements can be supported at least in part by good arguments or even scientific evidence, they also take a lot for granted and raise serious questions. For instance, why do we like or dislike a taste in the first place? How do we (or our bodies) 'know' a given food is good for us? Some foods, though extremely hard to procure and outrageously expensive, are highly appreciated; in fact, their very rarity seems to make them attractive. Far from being naturally attractive to our palate, other foods (chili pepper for one) are actually painful and rejected by most naive subjects and young children; nevertheless, large human populations somehow come to crave them (Rozin & Schiller, 1980). How and why do we become 'accustomed' to eating foods we dislike in the first place?

It turns out that such simple answers to our initial simple question actually raise more issues than they solve. Phrasing an alternative question may help us put the issue into focus. The question is: Why *don't* we eat certain foods?

Table 1 provides a series of anecdotal examples of foods which are consumed by human groups in certain areas of the world, yet would never be thought of as food in other cultures. The mere definition of what is edible and what is not is subject to remarkable variability across cultures.

Table 1
Differential classifications of animal species (edible versus non-edible)

Species \ Location	Food	Non-food
Insects	Latin America, Asia, Africa, etc.	Western Europe, North America, etc.
Dog	Korea, China, Pacific Isles, etc.	Europe, North America, etc.
Horse	France, Belgium, etc.	Britain, North America, etc.
Rabbit	France, Italy, etc.	Britain, North America, etc.
Snail	France, Italy, etc.	Britain, North America, etc.
Frog	France, Asia, etc.	Europe, North America, etc.

How can we account for this variability? It seems difficult to assign a sensory basis, since across human cultures the same animal species are appreciated entirely differently. It seems equally difficult to explain rejections in toxicologic terms. After all, insects are good protein and they are widely consumed by vast numbers of humans in the world.

Another common answer to the question 'Why don't we eat certain foods that other cultures seem to relish?' could be phrased 'Because we don't have to'. Environmental pressure, such as shortage or famine, could lead us to overcome our reluctance and consume species we otherwise would not regard as edible (a potential problem here is that this explanation is based on the implicit assumption that the foods we consume on a regular basis are the better ones, as opposed to those eaten by remote, foreign cultures. Such hierarchy can be suspected to being based on cultural bias).

Differential ecological factors are an obvious candidate, and indeed much research indicates that they play an important role, which will be discussed further on in this chapter.

A distinctive feature of *Homo sapiens* is that he is a 'brainy' animal; he is endowed with a highly developed neo-cortex. The likelihood that cognitive factors play an important part in man's adaption to his environment, and in particular the selection of his food, is, to say the least, quite high. It seems that at least part of the answer to our question lies in the eater, not just the food, and in the eater's mind, not just his body. Indeed, there is evidence that humans select their food in accordance, for a good part, with food cultures, or cuisines.

The variability in human patterns of food selection is probably in part a reflection of the variability of cultural systems. In this respect, an analogy can be offered between language and cuisines: all humans speak, but they speak different languages; similarly, all humans eat, but they eat different cuisines.

THE NATURE OF CUISINES

Cuisine or cooking is usually defined as a set of ingredients and techniques used in collecting, preparing and consuming food. In this paper, however, cuisines are meant in a different, broader sense. In our definition, cuisines consist of mental representations and the practices associated with them, all shared by individuals in a culture or a group. Cuisines involve culture-specific taxonomies and complex sets of rules about how to collect, prepare, combine and consume foods. Cuisines are also associated with meanings. Meanings of food depend to a large extent on the way in which culinary rules are applied. As with language, again, grammatical errors can distort or even destroy meaning.

Culinary Taxonomies

That cuisines are based on taxonomies already became apparent as we discussed Table 1. A basic preliminary classification that every culture has to establish is which items in the environment are food and which are not. What the table shows is that cultures assign different species to the food and non-food categories.

Within the realm of what a culture accepts as food, another set of distinctions is drawn. One of these distinctions is the opposition between pure and impure. Tabooed items are usually categorized as food (if they were not, there would be little sense in tabooing them in the first place). Certain foods are tabooed only in certain circumstances, and/or for certain people.

Substances classified as edible are distributed across various categories, such as tastes (e.g. sweet versus savoury), shapes or textures, and miscellaneous culinary classes (pasta, a course in its own right in Italy, is somehow functionally part of the 'vegetable' category in

France, and in many cultures, chicken and poultry are a class of their own, not part of the meat category).

Dietary taxonomies are related to other taxonomies, such as those stemming from the local, traditional medical system. In many cultures, for instance, foods are categorized in terms of their medicinal properties and the effect they are supposed to have on the body and mind (e.g. 'hot' versus 'cold', 'dry' versus 'moist', yin versus yang).

Culinary Rules

In all cultures, complex rules govern food consumption and eating behaviour. The existence of strict culinary rules, mostly unconscious, can best be demonstrated *a contrario*, in circumstances when they are broken. A good anecdotal example is provided in a story recently published in the *International Herald Tribune* (Jaynes, 1988) about a Mexican-Scottish ethnic-culinary mish-mash in a Manhattan restaurant:

> The gentleman slowly began to take the measure of his surroundings. He was in a Mexican restaurant called Tortilla Flats. There was a man in a skirt deafening the dining area with the bagpipes as tradition dictates on *Bobby Burns' birthday piping in the haggis. They were celebrating the birthday of the national poet of Scotland. The appetizers, or *antojitos,* included haggis tamales. Haggis was also available as an entrée under the *platos grandes,* accompanied by* taddies and neeps. They were having a special on unblended, single-malt whiskies. A muddled look crossed his face. He got his hat and left.

> A little later there was an accident in the kitchen. 'So we dropped some pinto beans into the haggis' said the chef, Steve Smith. 'Plaid meets picante'.

Mr Smith, the chef, was apparently not as disturbed as the would-be patron. The explanation for that may be that, being a Texan, his internalization of the culinary cultures of either Scotland or Mexico was not quite as deep and thorough as that of a native of either country (whether the visitor himself was Scottish, Mexican or neither

---

* Possible examples of American–Scottish cultural 'mish-mash'? Scots normally refer to their National Bard as Robert, Robbie or Rabbie Burns—never as Bobby! Most Scots have a strong preference for *tatties* (potatoes) but *taddies* (tadpoles) do not, thankfully, feature in Scottish cuisine.

was left unspecified; in any case, the bi-ethnic syncretism did unsettle him).

The story went on to reveal how Mr Smith prepared haggis. Sheep or calf hearts and lungs being unavailable in New York, he 'settled for beef liver and kidneys'. For sheep stomach, he used 'vegetable parchment paper'. 'He boiled [the liver and kidneys] in milk, threw the milk away, added five pounds of chopped beef, steel-cut oats, onions and, against all rules, garlic. Mr Smith likes garlic.'

In this rather extreme case, a large number of rules and taxonomies in both Mexican and Scottish cuisines, some very obvious, others more subtle, clearly were disregarded, to say the least. A native of either culture would probably have found inappropriate a number of the features of the meals served at the Tortilla Flats. Culinary rules are, for a good part about contextural appropriateness: meals, dishes and foods are prepared, selected and served in accordance to context, intrinsic and extrinsic.

Intrinsically, sets of structural rules specify, among other things, the number and types (taxonomic classes) of foods served in the meal, as well as, of course, the ingredients in a dish. The Mexican–Scottish menu blatantly disregarded this. Haggis was indiscriminately proposed as an appetizer or an entrée. As to the garlic, its addition in the haggis probably sounds as disturbing to a native as, say, the substitution of Balinese gamelan for bagpipes (the actual taste, although probably beyond words, is relatively irrelevant; the concept is the problem).

Some of the common rules are about mutual exclusion of whole categories of foods. In classic French cuisine, for instance, sweet and salty are usually mutually exclusive, as are fish and meat in many catholic countries, or dairy and meat in the orthodox Jewish tradition.

Inversely, other rules are about mutual inclusion. In Chinese cuisines, for instance, a meal requires appropriate amounts of both *fan* (grain and other starch foods) and *ts'ai* (vegetable and meat dishes; Chang, 1977). Inclusion and exclusion are important in the understanding a given culture has of its overall food pattern. The difference between a snack and a meal in certain cultures, India for one, is a function of the presence or absence of certain elements, particularly a staple: 'unleavened bread and a raw onion is a meal, but a mixture of farina and vegetables is only a snack' (Katona-Apte, 1975).

Extrinsic appropriateness, on the other hand, involves a number of factors not directly related to food. For lack of space, they are not reviewed or discussed extensively in the context of this chapter.

Among others, they include time (time of day, day in week, season, etc.), location, occasion (social or other), and the people involved (age, sex, status, etc.) (see Douglas & Nicod, 1974; Douglas, 1979). A given food, for instance, may be appropriate for males, another for females (see for instance Dickens & Chappell, 1977). A type of dish may be fit for children more than old people or for festive rather than daily circumstances.

The requirements of appropriateness in cuisines are reminiscent of syntactic and grammatical constraints in language. In certain cultures, an inappropriately constructed eating pattern, or a meal such as the Mexican–Scottish aberration, could be qualified as absurd, nonsensical, meaningless, in much the same way that an incorrect linguistic utterance is received as a laughable distortion or an unintelligible jumble.

ORIGINS AND FUNCTIONS OF CUISINES: THEORIES AND HYPOTHESES

Culinary patterns (categories, rules, meanings) raise important and mysterious issues that have been hotly disputed in the social sciences for decades. Are culinary rules and norms, prescriptions and prohibitions, taboos in particular, essentially arbitrary, or do they stem from natural determinisms and serve material, identifiable functions? For a grossly oversimplified, impressionistic review of some of the views under discussion, I suggest a categorization based roughly on two types of approaches, which I shall try to illustrate with appropriate examples.

The Functionalist View

What I call the functionalist paradigm is that any given cultural trait can be shown to serve a specific function, and that function can be explained only by relating the trait to another, extra-cultural, order of determinism (biological, physical, economic, etc.). In other words, to explain culture, one must resort to natural explanations.

Functionalism Stricto Sensu

A typical example is the formerly popular hypothesis about the Jewish and Moslem taboo on pork. In the area of the world where the prohibition originated, it was commonly contended, undercooked pork was often a vector for trichinosis (but then why a taboo and not just a prescription to eat the meat only when well done?). Another, more recent example is provided by the British anthropologist Radcliffe-Brown who, discussing the issue of animal species with high symbolic value, proposed the hypothesis that it is essentially linked to the functional or anti-functional value of the animal in a local context. In other words, any animal important to a given human society, whether it is particularly useful or dangerous (functional or anti-functional), tends to acquire strong symbolic value, thus becoming an object of ritual attitudes (Radcliffe-Brown, 1952).

'Cultural Materialism'

A particular brand of functionalism calls itself 'cultural materialism'. To phrase its paradigm, one can resort to the work of its prominent advocate, American anthropologist Marvin Harris. The view he defends is that culinary rules (he actually refers to 'food preferences and avoidances') can always be explained by way of simple cost/benefit analysis. In this framework, 'Preferred foods (good to eat) are foods that have a more favourable balance of practical benefits over costs than foods that are avoided (bad to eat)' (Harris, 1985, p. 15). According to Harris, the origin of pork avoidance in the Middle East is the following: 'The pig had been domesticated for one purpose only, namely to supply meat. As ecological conditions became unfavorable for pig raising [due to ecological changes such as deforestation], there was no alternative function which could redeem its existence' (Harris, 1985, p. 76).

Structuralism

Structuralist views are in sharp contrast to those expressed above, which have been subjected to relentless attacks. The structuralist paradigm is best summarized in the words of Mary Douglas: 'Rules of edibility can only be understood structurally, not by following the cause-and-effect implications of particular rules. A structural interpretation traces how rules of conduct match together to constitute an intelligible pattern' (Douglas, 1979). Such a statement obviously is a direct refutation of the functionalist and cultural materialistic approaches. I would add that, whereas the functionalist view is that natural determinisms are needed to explain culture, structuralism believes culture can and must explain culture. Douglas's interpretation (let us note that the term is the one she uses herself) of the pork taboo is thus a purely cultural one: pork, she contends, fits nowhere in the taxonomies according to which ancient Hebrews divided the physical world. It is a taxonomic anomaly, an insult to order in the living world as it was construed in the thoughts of ancient Jews (Douglas, 1966).

The Problems with the Theories

Structuralist authors in the last 30 years have insisted that functionalism simply does not work. According to Lévi-Strauss (Lévi-Strauss, 1962), there is no clear correlation between practical and symbolic importance of animal species in specific cultures (Sperber, 1975). Harris' cost/benefit analysis, on the other hand, is probably not without its problems. One question it does not answer, for instance, is, if indeed pork avoidance made perfect cost/benefit sense in the Middle East, why did it have to take the particular form of a religious taboo instead of, for instance, a mere string of successful individual decisions by farmers? Also, the hypotheses of cultural materialism are almost as difficult to test as those from structuralism. When direct ecological determinisms do not seem to do the job, one can always resort to increasingly remote and indirect explanations—demographic or other. The main problem probably resides in the notion of optimal adaptation on which culture materialism is based. If it is suggested, *a priori*, that an apparently counter-productive culinary trait *must* have some form of hidden benefit, *must* in fact be a facet of optimal adaptation, it is probably always possible to suggest one, no matter how difficult it is to demonstrate. Finally, cultural materialism does not as yet deal at all with more complex and subtle aspects of culinary rules of appropriateness, of the kinds briefly discussed above, be they intrinsic or extrinsic.

The problems with structuralism are no less important. The first objection is that structural analysis is not really looking for deterministic 'explanations' for culinary traits. Rather, it is concerned with 'interpreting' or 'deciphering', meanings. But obviously, deciphering hidden meanings in the patterns says nothing about why and how they occurred in the first place (a criticism which Harris makes much of). The structuralists certainly would find this criticism unfair. 'A society's cookery', writes Lévi-Strauss, 'is a language into which it translates its structure, unless it reluctantly and no less unwittingly reveals there its contradictions' (Lévi-Strauss, 1968). If culinary patterns merely 'translate' the social structure, then the issue between materialism and structuralism really is which determinism is pre-eminent: ecological or social?

BEYOND THE ADAPTATION VERSUS ARBITRARINESS DEBATE

I would suggest that there might very well be some degree of arbitrariness in culinary traits, at least for those that bear no vital or critical relevance. It does not take a lot of heavy theorizing to come to the conclusion that a group with a totally counter-productive culinary pattern would not thrive, and would risk disappearing altogether. Biological evolution has been recently described by prominent authors in terms of 'tinkering' (Jacob, 1977). The notion of optimization, according to which every single trait in an organism tends to be the one optimally adapted to the particular environment in which the organism lives, does not figure among some of the more recent views on evolution (Gould & Eldredge, 1977; see also Sober, 1984). One author describes evolution by tinkering as 'Transient sub-optimal compromises, sometimes followed by long periods of relative stability which are, in turn, followed by rare sudden reorganizations' (Piattelli-Palmarini, 1987, p. 15). Of course cultural evolution, for its part, is a much more labile process than biological evolution and one could expect it to tend towards fine-tuned adjustments, at least for those traits that bear direct, critical relevance to the individual organisms or groups under consideration. But this very lability of culture might produce a vast array of traits that do not necessarily always have immediate critical bearing on biological or ecological balance and the way organisms adjust to it.

It is apparently a peculiarity of the human mind to lean towards the production of taxonomies, categories, norms and rules (Sperber, 1975). I do not know of any documented case of a culture without its set of categories and rules about food, without prescriptions on what to eat, not to eat and how. Small wonder it is hard to imagine culture without thought. The variability observed across the human species is in the nature and contents of the categories, not in the presence or absence of categorizing. Categorization is 'the main way that we make sense of experience' (Lakoff, 1987).

The point is that food selection seems to be a domain where this propensity to categorize and establish rules of behaviour based on the categories, (a) is exerted with particular prolixity, and (b) ties into affective, behavioural and even physiological manifestations in individuals: a mere culinary clash of rules can for instance result in aversion, disgust, even nausea and regurgitation (Rozin & Fallon, 1986; Fischler, 1988). To find out why this is the case, one must transcend the optimal-adaptation versus mere-arbitrariness debate. Because of limited space, I shall merely try to illustrate a possible *integrative* approach ('integrative' in the sense that it takes into account biological as well as social dimensions of the phenomena) to reach a better understanding of the nature and function of cuisines. To do this, I shall use Paul Rozin's analysis of omnivory and its paradoxical consequences (Rozin, 1976) and extend the conclusions to cuisines as a whole.

The Omnivore's Paradox

Figure 1 summarizes the implications of omnivory for the human eater. Omnivory means freedom of choice, but it also means a basic constraint, that of minimal variety in the diet, which is needed to provide all necessary nutrients. This latter consequence of the constraint of variety means the omnivore must be able to innovate and have ways of protecting himself against possibly toxic novel foods.

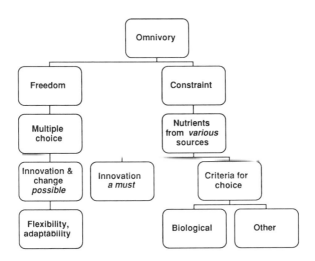

Figure 1. Implications of omnivory.

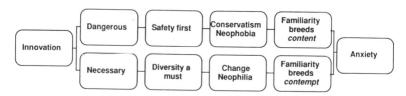

Figure 2. The omnivore's paradox.

From omnivory derives a paradoxical consequence. An omnivorous creature must be able to find new resources in case of necessity (neophilia) yet in order to protect itself against possible poisoning (neophobia) be extremely 'conservative' in its choices whenever possible. In Rozin's terms, familiarity breeds content *and* contempt. This dual, contradictory, constraint is represented on Fig. 2.

The omnivore's paradox lies in the tension, the oscillation, between the two poles of neophobia (prudence, fear of the unknown, resistance to change) and neophilia (the tendency to explore, the need for change, novelty, variety). Every omnivore, and man in particular, is subject to this double blind, which probably results in various forms of anxiety.

Cuisine as Resolution of the Paradox

Culinary patterns may be seen as helping resolve the paradox. Rozin & Rozin (1981) suggested that at the core of every cuisine are peculiar flavour combinations, or 'flavour principles', which function as ethnic markers, indicating familiarity. In fact, the whole of cuisine can be seen as serving this function. Through cooking, food acquires both familiarity and variety. A familiar, monotonous staple can be prepared in an almost infinite number of ways, while a novel food's potential menace can be 'tamed', as it were, by preparing it in familiar ways (Rozin, 1976; Fischler, 1981; Rozin & Rozin, 1981; Fischler, 1988).

SUMMARY AND CONCLUSION

This chapter has attempted to present, in an extremely compact and necessarily impressionistic form, a perspective on food acceptability and food selection as seen from the social sciences. After having shown that humans eat in accordance with cuisines, or culture-specific sets of categories, norms and rules, it has attempted to present the current debate in the social sciences about the origins, nature and function of rules of edibility. Beyond the functionalist view, which tends to see them as resulting from processes of adaptation, and the structuralist one, which insists on their internal coherence and arbitrariness, it is suggested that culinary patterns are a product of the human tendency to categorize and that a number of features that they include are sub-optimal, relieving or reducing the anxiety associated with the omnivore's paradox.

REFERENCES

Chang, K. C. (ed.). (1977). *Food in Chinese Culture.* Yale University Press, New Haven, Connecticut.

Dickens, J. & Chappell, B. (1977). Food for Freud? A study of the sexual polarisation of food and food products. *Journal of the Market Research Society,* **19**(2), 76–92.

Douglas, M. (1966). *Purity and Danger. An Analysis of Concepts of Pollution and Taboo.* Routledge and Keagan Paul, London.

Douglas, M. (1979). Les structures du culinaire. *Communications,* **31**, 145–70.

Douglas, M. & Nicod, M. (1974). Taking the biscuit: the structure of British meals. *New Society,* **30**, 744–7.

Fischler, C. (1981). Food preferences, nutritional wisdom, and sociocultural evolution. In *Food, Nutrition and Evolution,* ed. D. N. Walcher & N. Kretchmer. Masson International, New York, pp. 59–67.

Fischler, C. (1988). Food, self, and identity. *Social Science Information,* **27**(2), 275–92.

Gould, S. J. & Eldredge, N. (1977). Punctuated equilibria: the 'Tempo' and 'mode' of evolution reconsidered. *Paleobiology,* **3**(2), 115–51.

Harris, M. (1985). *Good to Eat. Riddles of Food and Culture.* Simon and Schuster, New York.

Jacob, F. (1977). Evolution and tinkering. *Science,* **196**, 1161–6.

Jaynes, G. (1988). With Haggis Tamales, a toast to Bobby Burns. *International Herald Tribune,* January 29, **32**, 635, 1.

Katona-Apte, J. (1975). Dietary aspects of acculturation: meals, feasts, and fasts in a minority community in South East Asia. In *Gastronomy. The Anthropology of Food and Food Habits,* ed. M. L. Arnott, Mouton, The Hague, pp. 315–26.

Lakoff, G. (1987). *Women, Fire, and Dangerous Things. What Categories Reveal about the Mind.* University of Chicago Press, Chicago

Lévi-Strauss, C. (1962). *Le Totémisme aujourd'hui.* PUF, Paris.

Lévi-Strauss, C. (1968). *Mythologiques 3. L'origine des manières de table.* Plon, Paris.

Lewin, K. (1943). Forces behind food habits and methods of change. *Bulletin of the National Research Council*, October, **108,** 35–65.

Piattelli-Palmarini, M. (1987). *Evolution, Selection and Cognition*: *from 'Learning' to Parameter-Fixation in Biology and in the Study of Mind.* Occasional Paper No. 35. MIT Center for Cognitive Science.

Radcliffe-Brown, A. R. (1952). *Structure and Function in Primitive Society.* The Free Press, Glencoe.

Rozin, P. (1976). The selection of foods by rats, humans, and other animals. In *Advances in the Study of Behaviour, Vol. 6,* eds J. S. Rosenblatt, R. A. Hinde, E. Shaw & C. Beer. Academic Press, New York, pp. 21–76.

Rozin, P. & Fallon, A. E. (1987). A perspective on disgust. *Psychol. Rev.,* **94,** 23–41.

Rozin, E. & Rozin, P. (1981). Culinary themes and variations. *Natural History,* **90**(2).

Rozin, P. & Schiller, D. (1980). The nature and acquisition of a preference for chili pepper by humans. *Motivation and Emotion,* **4**(1), 77–101.

Sober, E. (ed.) (1984). *Conceptual Issues in Evolutionary Biology.* Bradford Books/MIT Press, Cambridge, MA.

Sperber, D. (1975). Pourquoi les animaux parfaits, les hybrides et les monstres sont-ils bons à penser symboliquement? *L'Homme,* **XV**(2), 5–34.

Chapter 17

Salt and Sour Taste Intensity and Pleasantness Perception with Age

JAYA CHAUHAN* and ZENIA J. HAWRYSH

Department of Foods and Nutrition, University of Alberta, Edmonton, T6G 2M8 Canada

ABSTRACT

Salt and sour taste perception were investigated in 180 (randomly sampled, with additional volunteers) free-living, healthy, English-speaking Edmonton residents. Using magnitude estimation, subjects: 20–29, 70–79, and 80–99 years with 30 women and 30 men per group, assessed the perceived intensity and pleasantness of suprathreshold concentrations of (i) NaCl in solution and soup and (ii) citric acid (CA) in solution and in a drink. For each tastant, concentrations in the aqueous and food system were identical. All taste assessments were made in triplicate in separate sessions.

For both tastants in each system, psychophysical functions showed significant age effects. For NaCl and CA, respectively in solution and in the food system, compared to the young (Y), the very old (VO) gave lower intensity estimates (IE) for the weak tastant levels than the Y and old (O) adults. In contrast, the O gave lower IE for the high tastant levels than the Y and VO. For the lowest NaCl level in solution, the VO gave a significantly greater number of zero IE than the Y and O. There was a significant effect of sex on the IE, with the women giving higher IE than the men to the high tastant levels in both aqueous and food

* Present address: Department of Hotel Catering and Management, Oxford Polytechnic, Headington, Oxford, OX3 0BP, UK.

systems. The system also had a significant effect on the IE. Subjects gave lower IE to low tastant levels in solution than to comparable food systems, while at high concentrations, higher IE were given to solutions than the food systems. Thus, misleading conclusions regarding suprathreshold taste perception may be drawn if studies are confined solely to aqueous solutions.

Trend analyses of the pleasantness estimates (PE) indicated significant age group differences for both NaCl and CA. For solutions, the PE of the Y as a function of tastant concentration showed a clearly monotonic decreasing trend, whereas the PE of the older groups showed polytonic trends. The PE for the soup and drink, respectively of all age groups showed a major bitonic trend, but the breakpoints differed between groups. Further study of salt and sour taste intensity and pleasantness perception using a variety of food systems and much larger population samples than the present study is required to elucidate age-related changes in suprathreshold taste perception.

INTRODUCTION

The question of whether or not taste losses are a function of ageing is currently being explored. Taste defects have been reported to occur for both pure solutions and common foods. Early studies focusing on detection and recognition threshold determinations, using single-tastant aqueous solutions both support and contradict the theory that the sense of taste is adversely affected by ageing. Such data provide limited information on taste function as what is measured is only the lowest extreme of the perceptual range. Furthermore, the data cannot be extrapolated to complex interactive systems such as foods. Measures of suprathreshold taste perception provide a more comprehensive picture of taste function, but such reliable information is lacking. Common to many of the investigations of age effects on taste perception are the use of (a) small sample size of a wide age range, (b) no random population groups, (c) no young adults as controls, (d) inadequate psychophysical and stimuli presentation procedures and (e) no evaluation of food systems.

The present study focuses on salt and sour taste perception, using both aqueous and food systems and a large sample size of appropriate ages typical of the population. It is part of a study designed to examine interrelationships between taste perception and dietary intakes of nutrients in elderly versus young adults.

METHOD

Subjects

A total of 180 subjects, divided into three age groups, young (Y) 20–29 years, old (O) 70–79 years and very old (VO) 80–99 years, with 30 men and 30 women in each group, participated. Subjects, randomly sampled with additional volunteers, were all Edmonton residents, English-speaking, free-living, relatively healthy and ambulatory, with responsibility for their own provision of meals. All the young subjects came to the laboratory, while all the very old and some of the old were visited at home. All assessments were made in triplicate in separate sessions. Subject attributes such as education, food aversions and/or allergies, nasal abnormalities, dentures, smoking, alcohol use, prescription medication and salt use were obtained.

Taste Stimuli

These were six suprathreshold concentrations of (i) NaCl in solution and chicken soup base (0·02, 0·04, 0·08, 0·16, 0·32, 0·64 м) and (ii) citric acid (CA) in solution and apple drink (0·003, 0·006, 0·012, 0·018, 0·024, 0·036 м). Tastant concentrations in solution and the related food system were identical. The salt content of the soup base and the acid content of the drink were taken into account and appropriate amounts of tastant added to give the same stimuli concentrations as the aqueous solutions.

All samples were prepared in advance and stored at −15°C. These were brought to the appropriate temperature as required. For taste assessments, samples were dispensed as 10 ml samples in 30 ml disposable plastic medi-cups. Double-distilled deionised water for rinsing before and between samples was available in a 150 ml plastic tumbler which was refilled *ad lib* from glass storage bottles.

Poyohophyoiool Proooduroo

At the beginning of the first session, subjects were familiarised with magnitude estimation by means of a series of tasks in which line lengths and areas of shapes were estimated. Using the 'sip and spit' procedure and the fixed-modulus method of magnitude estimation (a reference sample, the middle range of concentration, being assigned a value of 10 and samples compared to this) subjects assessed the intensity and pleasantness of the taste stimuli. The reference sample was tasted at the start and again in the middle of the series, with a hidden reference being included in the series of samples. Before and between sampling each stimulus, each subject rinsed his/her mouth with deionised water. Male and female participants in each age group were treated as subgroups; half of the 30 subjects in each of the age groups began the first session by assessing the acid stimuli, while the other half began with the salt stimuli. Aqueous solutions were assessed first and a 10–15 min rest period preceded the tasting of the food stimuli. The aqueous solutions were assessed at room temperature, the soup at $50 \pm 5°C$ and the drink at $12 \pm 2°C$. Sample presentation was randomised both across subjects and across replicate sessions such that no extremes in stimuli concentrations were presented consecutively.

Data Analysis
Both parametric and nonparametric statistics were used. Subjects may not perceive magnitudes on a ratio scale and zero estimates skew the distributions making parametric statistics inappropriate for intensity and pleasantness data. For each tastant and each system (NaCl: solution/soup; CA: solution/drink) at each stimulus concentration, the taste assessments for intensity and pleasantness made in triplicate by each subject were averaged to give the mean individual response. The mean intensity estimates (IE) were not normalised as a reference was used and with large population samples, normalisation is not critical. Mean pleasantness estimates (PE) were normalised prior to analysis in order to discount any disparities in the use of numbers between subjects. The PE were normalized such that the sum of the PE for each subject equalled 100.

In the case of NaCl, the widespread use of zero estimates by the VO precluded the usual computation of geometric means (a better measure of central tendency than the arithmetic mean for magnitude estimation (Stevens, 1975)). For each NaCl concentration, the arithmetic mean of the IE for each system was computed across subjects and the mean fitted with a power function ($\log IE = a \log C + b$) according to Steven's Power Law (Stevens, 1957). For each age group the power functions, essentially linear plots of $\log IE$ against $\log C$ (C refers to the stimulus concentration), with the slopes as exponents, were examined.

Frequency of use of zero IE for the lowest NaCl concentration among age groups was compared two at a time using the Fisher Exact Probability test (Siegel, 1956).

Except for one VO subject's mean IE for the first ($0·003$ M) CA concentration in solution (which was treated as a missing observation), all subjects' mean IE were greater than zero. Therefore, for each system, each indvidual's mean IE were fitted with power functions. The effects of age and sex on individual slopes, intercepts and R^2 of the psychophysical functions were examined by a two-way analysis of variance (ANOVA).

The effects of sex and system on the IE for each of the tastants were examined using Mann–Whitney U-tests.

The normalised PE were analysed by nonparametric trend analysis, based on ranks and the utilisation of the sampling distribution of the statistic S as used in the definition of Kendall's coefficient of rank correlation tau (Ferguson, 1965). The trend analysis was restricted to age group mean PE as consideration of individuals would be unwieldy with a large population sample. Each age group's PE for each tastant and each system as a function of stimulus concentration could be objectively classified as monotonically increasing ($+$), monotonically decreasing ($-$), bitonic (one branch monotonically increasing and the other branch monotonically decreasing), tritonic (two branches increasing and one decreasing or vice versa), quadritonic (two branches increasing and two branches decreasing), etc.

RESULTS

The best-fitting regression lines for the intensity data were determined (using least squares) on the assumption that the data obey the power function ($\log \text{IE} = a \log C + b$). The slopes, a, i.e. exponents of the power functions, and intercepts, b, of these regression lines for each age group are given in Table 1. For both solutions and soup, age had a significant influence on group slopes and intercepts of the power functions. For both systems, the slopes and intercepts of the O subjects were significantly lower than those of the Y and the VO subjects, with the slopes and intercepts of the VO being even higher than those of the Y subjects. The R^2 values, a measure of the degree of agreement of the fitted regression model to the data, were similar for all age groups, except in one case. For NaCl in soup, the O group had a lower R^2 than the Y and VO. The VO gave a significantly (solutions: $p < 0.001$; soup: $p = 0.002$) greater number of zero estimates than the Y and O subjects.

Table 1
Mean slopes, intercepts and R^2 of the psychophysical power functions for NaCl intensity data

	NaCl solutions			NaCl soup		
	Young	Old	Very old	Young	Old	Very old
Slopes ($n = 60$)	0·63[b] (0·03)	0·45[c] (0·02)	0·75[a] (0·02)	0·47[b] (0·02)	0·36[c] (0·03)	0·66[a] (0·02)
Men ($n = 30$)	0·58 (0·04)	0·40 (0·03)	0·74 (0·03)	0·44 (0·02)	0·29 (0·04)	0·63 (0·03)
Women ($n = 30$)	0·68 (0·03)	0·50 (0·02)	0·76 (0·02)	0·51 (0·03)	0·42 (0·03)	0·68 (0·02)
Intercepts ($n = 60$)	1·75[b] (0·04)	1·57[c] (0·03)	1·82[a] (0·02)	1·58[b] (0·02)	1·46[c] (0·04)	1·77[a] (0·02)
Men ($n = 30$)	1·67 (0·04)	1·50 (0·03)	1·83 (0·03)	1·53 (0·02)	1·36 (0·04)	1·75 (0·03)
Women ($n = 30$)	1·82 (0·03)	1·64 (0·02)	1·82 (0·02)	1·63 (0·03)	1·55 (0·03)	1·78 (0·02)
R^2 ($n = 60$)	0·97 (0·06)	0·97 (0·05)	0·99 (0·03)	0·98 (0·04)	0·91 (0·06)	0·99 (0·03)
Men ($n = 30$)	0·98 (0·05)	0·98 (0·03)	0·99 (0·03)	0·99 (0·02)	0·94 (0·05)	0·99 (0·04)
Women ($n = 30$)	0·99 (0·04)	0·99 (0·02)	1·00 (0·02)	0·99 (0·04)	0·98 (0·04)	0·99 (0·03)

Mean (SEM).
Means in a row for slopes and intercepts, respectively not sharing a common superscript (a, b, c) are significantly different tested at $p < 0.05$ level using the Student–Newman–Keul test.

For the intensity data for CA, age by sex ANOVA on individual slopes, intercepts and R^2 of the psychophysical functions yielded significant age and sex effects (Table 2). For solutions, age ($F_{2,174} = 35.33$; $p < 0.001$) and sex effects ($F_{1,174} = 18.98$; $p < 0.001$) on the slopes were reflected in the steeper slopes of the Y and VO adults compared to the O adults, with the women having steeper slopes than the men. A similar pattern was also apparent for the intercepts (age: $F_{2,174} = 34.03$, $p < 0.001$; sex: $F_{1,174} = 21.36$, $p < 0.001$) and R^2 (age: $F_{2,174} = 9.46$, $p < 0.001$; sex: $F_{1,174} = 7.29$, $p = 0.008$). For CA in the drink, age had a significant effect on the slopes ($F_{2,174} = 40.18$; $p < 0.001$), intercepts ($F_{2,174} = 39.06$; $p < 0.001$) and R^2 ($F_{2,174} = 20.25$; $p < 0.001$). The Y and VO had significantly higher slopes, intercepts and R^2 than the O adults, with all three parameters even being significantly higher in the VO than the Y. Sex effects on the slopes ($F_{1,174} = 23.66$; $p < 0.001$), intercepts ($F_{1,174} = 233.39$; $p < 0.001$) and R^2 ($F_{1,174} = 3.87$; $p = 0.051$) for CA in drink were also significant, with all parameters examined being higher for the women than the men. For both systems, no age by sex interactions on the slopes, intercepts, or R^2 were observed.

For NaCl and CA, respectively in solution and in the food system, compared to the Y, the VO gave lower IE for the weak tastant levels than the Y and O adults. In contrast, the O gave lower IE for the high tastant levels than the Y and VO.

There was a significant effect of sex on the IE for both tastants in solution and the food system, with the women giving higher IE than the men to the high tastant levels.

System also had a significant effect on the IE (Table 3), with subjects giving lower IE to the weak tastant concentrations in solution than to comparable food systems. At high tastant levels higher IE were given to solutions than the food systems.

The trend analyses of the PE indicated significant age group differences for both tastants. For solutions, the PE of the Y as a function of tastant concentration showed a clearly monotonic decreasing trend whereas the PE of the older groups showed polytonic trends. The PE for soup and drink respectively showed a major bitonic trend for all age groups but the maximally rated; the breakpoint concentration varied slightly between groups. For the soup, all three age groups' breakpoint was around 0.008 M NaCl. For the CA, the breakpoint of the Y was higher (0.018 M) than the O (0.012–0.018 M) and the VO (0.012 M).

Table 2
Mean slopes, intercepts and R^2 of the psychophysical power functions for citric acid intensity data

	Citric acid solutions						Citric acid drink					
	Young		Old		Very old		Young		Old		Very old	
Slopes ($n = 60$)	0.71[a]	(0.04)	0.40[b]	(0.03)	0.69[a]	(0.03)	0.51[b]	(0.03)	0.26[c]	(0.02)	0.59[a]	(0.03)
Men ($n = 30$)	0.67	(0.05)	0.33	(0.03)	0.58	(0.03)	0.44	(0.05)	0.19	(0.02)	0.50	(0.03)
Women ($n = 30$)	0.75	(0.05)	0.47	(0.04)	0.80	(0.04)	0.58	(0.05)	0.32	(0.04)	0.69	(0.04)
Intercepts ($n = 60$)	2.44[a]	(0.07)	1.83[b]	(0.05)	2.39[a]	(0.05)	2.00[b]	(0.06)	1.52[c]	(0.05)	2.16[a]	(0.05)
Men ($n = 30$)	2.33	(0.10)	1.69	(0.06)	2.17	(0.06)	1.87	(0.09)	1.39	(0.05)	1.98	(0.06)
Women ($n = 30$)	2.54	(0.11)	1.97	(0.08)	2.62	(0.07)	2.14	(0.09)	1.65	(0.08)	2.34	(0.07)
R^2 ($n = 60$)	0.92[a]	(0.01)	0.86[b]	(0.01)	0.92[a]	(0.01)	0.84[b]	(0.02)	0.71[c]	(0.03)	0.92[a]	(0.01)
Men ($n = 30$)	0.90	(0.02)	0.84	(0.02)	0.90	(0.02)	0.81	(0.04)	0.67	(0.05)	0.91	(0.02)
Women ($n = 30$)	0.94	(0.00)	0.88	(0.01)	0.93	(0.01)	0.88	(0.03)	0.75	(0.03)	0.93	(0.01)

Mean (SEM).
Means in a row for slopes, intercepts and R^2, respectively not sharing a common superscript (a, b, c) are significantly different tested at $p < 0.05$ levels using the Student–Newman–Keul test.

Table 3
Comparison of intensity estimates for tastant in solution versus food system

	Young (n = 60)	Old (n = 60)	Very old (n = 60)
NaCl (M)			
0·02	$p < 0.001\ 0^{a,b}$	$p = 0.001\ 8$	$p = 0.000\ 9$
0·04	$p = 0.050\ 6$	$p = 0.526\ 6$	$p = 0.051\ 0$
0·08	$p = 0.000\ 8$	$p = 0.038\ 1$	$p = 0.205\ 1$
0·16	$p < 0.000\ 1$	$p = 0.104\ 6$	$p = 0.371\ 1$
0·32	$p = 0.002\ 4$	$p = 0.076\ 8$	$p = 0.502\ 4$
0·64	$p = 0.054\ 6$	$p = 0.190\ 2$	$p = 0.494\ 1$
CA (M)			
0·003	$p = 0.003\ 2$	$p = 0.047\ 6$	$p = 0.219\ 7$
0·006	$p = 0.137\ 3$	$p = 0.204\ 5$	$p = 0.286\ 1$
0·012	$p = 0.000\ 2$	$p = 0.000\ 9$	$p < 0.000\ 1$
0·018	$p < 0.000\ 1$	$p < 0.000\ 1$	$p = 0.000\ 1$
0·024	$p < 0.000\ 1$	$p = 0.000\ 1$	$p = 0.000\ 1$
0·036	$p = 0.000\ 4$	$p < 0.000\ 1$	$p = 0.000\ 3$

[a] Significance levels established by Mann–Whitney U-tests (one-tailed).
[b] $p > 0.05$ not significant.

DISCUSSION

For both systems at weak tastant concentrations, the Y and VO adults gave lower IE than the O adults; while at higher levels, the Y and VO gave higher IE than the O adults. The presence of a residual taste in the elderly (Bartoshuk et al., 1986), resulting in elderly subjects giving higher IE than the young subjects to weak tastant concentrations in solution, is supported by the results for the O, but not the VO, in the present study. The differential sensitivity between the O and VO for the low tastant concentrations cannot be readily explained. Perhaps the residual taste reaches a peak at a certain age and then progressively declines. If this were the case, then the IE of the VO at low tastant levels would have been lower than those of the O and possibly higher than those of the Y. However, deficits in perception of the low tastant levels in the VO could lead these subjects to assign lower IE than the Y and O.

All the subjects received similar rinsing instructions, but the likely variation between individuals in the rinsing procedure used is worth noting (O'Mahony & Wingate, 1974). The Y may rinse more efficiently than the O and VO subjects, so that adaptation in the elderly could render the low tastant concentrations less intense to them than to the Y. At high tastant levels adaptation effects would be minimal. Thus, at the low tastant levels, the low IE of the VO can be attributed to the loss of taste acuity and peaking of the residual taste and possibly poor rinsing. The O are suggested to be better at rinsing than the Y and VO; perhaps the O were conscientious in following the rinsing instructions. The effect of rinsing on taste intensity scaling merits further study.

For NaCl and CA in solution and food systems, the slopes and intercepts of the O were significantly lower than those of both the Y and VO. The low intercepts of the O are a result of their low IE at high suprathreshold tastant concentrations and as such do not reflect a constant percentage reduction in perceived saltiness/sourness at suprathreshold levels. This is in contrast to olfactory decline with age (Stevens & Cain, 1985).

Examination of the data suggested that the Y and VO adults in this study had similar taste functions. It should be noted that high IE cannot always be interpreted as high perceived intensity. The VO showed a taste deficit at lower tastant levels, which was more marked for NaCl, hence, the reference, given a value of 10, would be expected to taste weak to these particular subjects. The effect of this would be that, compared to the reference, high tastant concentrations would be given higher estimates than usual. Thus, high values given by the VO to the high tastant concentrations cannot be interpreted as an increased perceived intensity in the VO, but rather as indicative of a taste deficit of the low stimulus concentration.

For both tastants, there was a significant effect of sex, with the women giving higher IE than the men to the high tastant levels in both systems. Sex effects have also been demonstrated in smell identification tasks (Doty et al., 1984).

The use of food systems in studies examining age effects on taste perception is lacking. For perceived intensity, compared to the same concentrations in solution, low tastant levels in the related food system were assigned higher estimates, while high tastant levels in the food system were assigned lower estimates. Perhaps, familiarity with low tastant levels in the food system as opposed to water, resulted in the assignment of appropriate IE to the foods but not the solutions. The effect of high tastant levels in solution may be greater than in food, so that subjects were not conservative in giving large numbers to the solutions. Thus, misleading conclusions regarding taste perception are likely to be drawn if studies are confined solely to aqueous solutions.

The Y adults' PE showed a clearly monotonic decreasing trend for NaCl/CA in solution, whereas the older subjects' PE showed polytonic trends. The functions at low tastant levels in solution suggest that the older subjects perceived something different to the Y subjects, and in comparison to the Y, they considered it more pleasant. For the food systems, age effects on PE were not as marked as for the solutions. The maximally rated levels of NaCl in soup was similar for all groups, but for CA in the drink, the breakpoint concentration was lower in the VO than the Y and O.

In conclusion, for both NaCl and CA, the O adults showed deficits in taste perception at high tastant levels, while the VO showed decreased perception at low tastant levels. Compared to the men, the higher IE of the women at high tastant levels in both systems suggest that with age, taste function in women may diminish less than in men. The elderly subjects in this study were all free-living and healthy, with the over 80 years group representing the survivors and taste function may well remain intact in this group. Further study of the influence of dietary intakes and subject attributes on taste perception is required.

ACKNOWLEDGEMENT

Supported by Alberta Heritage Foundation for Medical Research.

REFERENCES

Bartoshuk, T. M., Rifkin, B., Marks, L. E. & Baro, P. (1986). Taste and aging. *J. Gerontol*, **41**, 51–7.

Doty, R. L., Shaman, P. & Dann, M. (1984). Development of the University of Pennsylvania smell identification test: A standardized microencapsulated test of olfactory function. *Physiol. Behav.*, **32**, 489–502.

Ferguson, G. A. (1965). *Nonparametric Trend Analysis*. McGill University Press, Montreal.

O'Mahony, M. & Wingate, P. (1974). The effect of interstimulus procedures on salt taste intensity functions. *Perception and Psychophysics*, **16**, 494–502.

Siegel, S. (1956). *Nonparametric Statistics for the Behavioral Sciences.* McGraw-Hill, New York.

Stevens, S. S. (1957). On the psychophysical law. *Psychol. Rev.,* **64,** 153–81.

Stevens, S. S. (1975). *Psychophysics: Introduction to its Perceptual, Neural and Social Prospects.* John Wiley, New York.

Stevens, J. C. & Cain, W. S. (1985). Age-related deficiency in the perceived strength of six odorants. *Chem. Senses,* **10,** 517–29.

Chapter 18

Behavioural Variables Influencing the Consumption of Fish and Fish Products

DAVID W. MARSHALL

Department of Agricultural & Food Marketing, University of Newcastle upon Tyne, Newcastle upon Tyne NE1 7RU, UK

ABSTRACT

This chapter is based on a substantial piece of qualitative research carried out at the end of 1986, as part of an ongoing 3-year investigation into behavioural variables influencing the consumption of fish and fish products. It serves to illustrate that food choice is under a wide range of influences which extend beyond purely sensory considerations, and is related to age, lifestyle characteristics and time availability.

Food habits are acquired over a long period of time and experience serves to condition consumer responsiveness to new foods, and their place in the meal system. The chapter considers the place of fish in the meal structure and the way in which the meal occasion influences food choice, and determines the appropriateness of particular types of product.

The role of different products is evaluated, and the relationship between the fresh and manufactured products examined.

INTRODUCTION

Consumption of fish in the UK has been on the decline since shortly after the War, and despite a slight recovery in recent years, our consumption of fish and fish products remains consistently low. We eat a mere 5·6 kg per capita and spend around 4% of our food income on fish and fish products, well behind many of our European neighbours, such as Spain, with consumption around 23·3 kg per capita. The difficulty with marketing the fish that we land in the UK seems to arise both from a consumer resistance to fish in general, and a preference for a narrow range of demersal species.

Today, with the emphasis increasingly on health and diet, fish appears to be in a potentially strong position. Nutritionists stress its healthy qualities and role in reducing risk of cardiovascular disease. Despite these benefits, consumption remains low. Perhaps current research has failed to understand fully the dimensions involved in consumption, and approached the problem from the wrong perspective. We need to identify new products, and to specify key product features, in order to formulate a marketing plan for British-caught fish. To do so will require us to concentrate on more than 'objective' measurements of sensory evaluation. Some attention needs to be directed towards the implications of actual usage and an understanding of how fish fits into food habits.

CURRENT RESEARCH

Current research practice tends to focus on 'objective', tangible and measurable product attributes, but in doing so fails to address wider social and cultural influences. When food is bought, prepared and served, other things are going on apart from satisfying hunger. Foods do not exist in isolation as single products, which is often how current sensory research treats them; they must fit into a meal system which has evolved over generations. Mary Douglas (1979) draws our attention to the fact that food, like all goods and commodities, serves as a social marker reinforcing social order.

Food has social uses in ritual, custom and everyday habit, often with divergent usage in different cultural settings, and widely different significance for the people who use them—for example, the significance of pork to the Jewish religion, or meat to a vegetarian. To understand fully the role of a foodstuff such as fish in the eating habits of specific groups, requires an examination of how it is actually *used* and *regarded* and the way in which it *fits* into all aspects of food habits. It is not enough to assume that attitudes to fish are based on simple calculation of its relative cost, nutritional value, taste or appeal in terms of other characteristics. This is not to deny their importance, but rather to insist that the use of food, and its meaning as part of a food system, can *only* be understood by considering it in the context of the system as a whole. We need to consider which foods are used, how, when and why, which combinations are acceptable, and what influential factors are changing food habits.

The preoccupation with quantification and 'objective' measurement of attributes via the questionnaire method, fails to allow investigative manoeuvrability. It is too rigid an approach and inappropriate at a stage in the research when the method needs to determine exactly what we need to be investigating, rather than what we think we should be investigating. The very design accentuates the idea of objectivity and reduction of the problem to a series of independent identifiable areas, when it is more relevant to determine what is and is not acceptable to consumers, and their general expectations of food. A White Fish Authority (WFA) study (1975) attempted to measure consumer attitudes by examining reasons for serving or not serving fish, followed by a series of attitudinal statements. The reasons offered related to the product characteristics, price considerations and family approval. The main appeal of fish was in its high nutritional value, and perceived ease of preparation; but each statement is examined in isolation and this method prevents an exploration of meanings attached to terms like 'nourishing', 'tasty', and 'freshness'. Until we examine the range of influences on these food purchase decisions, their relative importance and the meanings attached to particular food beliefs, we cannot start the quantification stage. Both qualitative and quantitative approaches serve useful purposes, and should complement rather than compete with one another. Thus, the qualitative work discussed in this chapter aims to examine how fish is regarded in the meal system.

NEED TO EXAMINE FOOD HABITS

This problem of researching the behavioural variables and their contribution to the understanding and specification of product features, related to the usage context, necessitated an approach which was open and allowed some scope to probe areas of interest. The utilisation of focus groups, and incorporation of projective or enabling techniques, seemed most appropriate. (Their use in market research was popularised in the 1950s by psychologists, such as Dichter, and suffered with the growing demands for increased quantification during the 1970s. However, the growth in qualitative research over the last 8 years or so has seen an increased confidence in the qualitative approach and a realisation of the benefits of complementary qualitative and quantitative research designs.) The group discussions encourage rapport between the respondents, and are as non-directive as possible, with the discussion leader operating as a 'moderator' to ensure particular topics are covered, rather than as a formal interviewer. Ten groups were run throughout the UK, selected on a specific quota control. Each group discussion was recorded and later transcribed for analysis.

FISH IN THE MEAL SYSTEM

Any food taking involves a series of stages (Table 1), which range from acquisition through to disposal. Each stage in this process is conditioned by our expectation of what is appropriate for the type of food occasion involved. Our thesis is that fish embodies a number of negative features which extend through all stages.

Acquisition. Due to a decline in the number of fishmongers, and limited availability of fresh fish, the decision to use fish will, for the majority of UK consumers, involve extra time investment and effort, plus extensive search. In choosing fish, additional knowledge is required to determine which species to choose, and its form, according to the meal occasion. Many respondents displayed a limited knowledge of how to evaluate the freshness of fish, although the older respondents were more familiar with fish in this form. The presence of a whole fish in its raw natural state is alien to many consumers, and in some cases evokes disgust, accentuated by a negative reaction to the smell of the product on display. For those who do purchase fresh fish, it poses a problem because it is thought difficult to store and keep, and the product must be used immediately and this makes it less convenient than other foods.

Preparation. Cleaning and gutting a whole fish was out of the question for many respondents, especially the young. This was as much a function of unfamiliarity and lack of the relevant skills as

Table 1
Fish in the food system

Stages in the food system	Negative features of wet fish
Acquisition	Limited availability
	Display of whole fish
	Smell
	Freshness evaluation
	Limited species knowledge
	Poor keeping qualities
↓	
Preparation	Large time, skill investment
	Aversion towards gutting
	Smell
	Dislike handling raw product
↓	
Cooking	Smell
	Limited knowledge on cooking time
	Restricted range of cooking method
	Product breaking up
↓	
Consumption	Delicate, fiddly to eat
	Inherent product problems (bones, etc.)
	Perceived insubstantiality
	Not suitable for young children (bones)
	White = too bland
	Dark = too strong
	Limited combinations, meal variation
↓	
Disposal	Unusable leftovers
	Smell
	Confined to one meal occasion

disgust at the thought of handling the innards of fish. Disgusting objects are usually of animal origin, and Angyal (1941) notes (see also Levi-Strauss (1984), Douglas (1966) and Elias (1983)) that removal of the animalness in preparation reduces the disgust. Hence the removal of the eyes and head diffuse this association. The respondents did not like to handle a wet, cold, slimy fish, and smell was again cited as a negative product feature. Fish is thought by many to require more skills in terms of preparation than most other foods.

Cooking. Smell in cooking again presented a problem, and the lack of knowledge of cooking methods and times was apparent in all but the most regular fish users. The most commonly cited cooking method was frying, but this was thought unhealthy and somewhat damaging to the image of fish as a healthy food. It is perceived as a delicate food, liable to breaking up on cooking. We formed the opinion that standard cooking methods and times in the UK are relatively simple, and based on a central element of red meat whose characteristics and features are different to fish. The limited use of fish is reflected in the lack of common beliefs relating to fish preparation and the perceived need to carefully monitor cooking (when is it 'done'?). Fish is generally thought less versatile or resilient in cooking than meat, and meat is believed tolerant of a range of cooking times.

Consumption. Fish is perceived as delicate and fiddly to eat; a 'feminine food' lacking substantiality. Part of this difficulty in eating ties in with the need for confidence over the safety of foods and a heightened awareness of the presence of bones in fish. Even frozen products, although regarded as safer, are believed to be not entirely free of bones. This concern is even greater where children are involved. The rules of 'appropriate' eating are relaxed to allow them to consume 'safer' products like fish fingers and fish cakes.

We believe that taste, flavour, appearance and the combinations in which food is served all interrelate in consumer perceptions. The appearance of white fish is associated with a bland flavour; dark fish is seen as 'too strong', but more substantial. The level of etiquette required at different types of meals reflects the appropriateness of different fish products. The frozen fish fillet is consistent, but appears rather uniform and boring, unsuited to more special or formal occasions. The importance of retaining this identifiable fish shape is reflected in the problems of serving fish which breaks up due to textural qualities. The demands for a 'flaky' white fish seems to conflict with the textural requirements for cooking and serving where appearance is important.

Disposal. Unlike red meat and chicken, fish does not offer very much in terms of usable leftovers. It is confined to one meal, and requires more careful evaluation of exact quantities required at the acquisition state. The disposal of bones, skin, head and leftovers creates a problem in terms of smell, which is seen to be strong and lingering.

FOOD VARIETY AND COMBINATIONS

The food system is relatively simple and repetitive as noted. For Mary Douglas (1984), complexity within the system is not necessarily related to the range of items used, or the use of more unusual foods, but rather to the sequencing and ordering of these foods within the meal pattern. We believe that fish usage will be directly related to the degree of complexity in the UK meal system. Establishing meal patterns convincingly could only be accomplished by quantification which is currently being carried out in the form of a food diary study. However, the qualitative work illustrates the limited role of fish in the system and the need for variety.

Fish was thought only to go with a limited range of vegetables; chips, peas and one or two others, unlike meat or chicken which offered a wider range of combinations, and hence the opportunity for variety within the meal. Fish provided variety in the meal pattern, but was considered a complementary meal to be used with much less frequency. Variety is not only the spice of life, it is an essential part of our meal system. Rozin (1976) has shown the need for variety to induce consumption in animal diets, and Fischler (1980) echoes this idea that 'familiarity may breed contempt'. Variety is viewed as a necessary condition in order to demonstrate what could be termed cultural competence; lack of variety implies a lack of culinary skill, limited repertoire of recipes and meal ideas, inefficient use of resources and purely utilitarian treatment of foods. Fish in the UK meal system represents a problem because it is thought to offer little scope for meal variation. Meal formats and menu negotiation start from the expectation of what food on a particular occasion should be like, and this is expressed in various social cues.

SOCIAL CUES AND FOOD OCCASIONS

A variety of social cues signify the appropriateness of particular meal formats and structures. The main cues relate to:

1. time of day;
2. presence of other guests, family members;
3. time availability.

Time of day. The main meal has come to be located, for the majority of people, in the early part of the evening (Palmer, 1984). Primary meals are closely related to the work patterns, and tend to be standardised, more ritualised, and involve more household members. It is this meal which embodies the most formal structure, and it is supported by a series of secondary or light meals at other times. These secondary meals are less structured, but still contain the basic elements of the standard meal format. Secondary meals are much more individualistic, and less predictable in terms of the varieties of foods used, participants, frequency and duration. Although fish may feature in a main meal, only certain types are conventionally used. Fish cannot just be substituted for meat—and the meals where it is used are seen as having a distinctive character. The use of fish in the main meal is likely to indicate a 'special' event, with the emphasis on entertainment and use of the fresh product. While the frozen product may take the central role, it is unlikely to be used in the main meal for more important occasions in the presence of guests or non-family members.

The use of particular types of fish, such as frozen or convenience products, altered the state of this meal to that of a secondary food event. Fish was not thought suitable for 'hot-pot' type meals, since it broke up in cooking, and did not 'produce' gravy. Fish was associated with sauces, meat with gravy; as a result, the latter was appropriate for one-pot meals.

Presence of guests. This introduces a level of extraneous social control, heightening the importance of providing the correct foods, in the correct order at the right place and time. The appearance of food on the plate also takes on a greater significance. Fish is thought risky as a meal for guests, since it is believed to be disliked more often than most of the standard meat meal centres. Fish presents a problem here in two areas. First, only fresh fish is thought appropriate, but this involves greater risk due to the problems at all stages from acquisition through to disposal.

Second, inherent product characteristics in fish, such as bones, skin, eyes, head, tail, etc., are not readily acceptable to many consumers. This may relate to the idea of disgust expressed earlier. It appears also that the manner of consumption requires particular kinds of 'social graces' and may present problems for some eaters in actually handling the food, particularly children.

Time availability. The increase in working women in Britain has seen a decreasing willingness to spend time in the kitchen, and shopping, and a search for foods which are convenient to buy, store, prepare, present and consume, as well as simply easy to cook. Whilst fish is considered quick and convenient in terms of cooking time, it is perceived as inconvenient in terms of adaptability. Particular products such as fish cakes and fish fingers were thought to be convenient, but not appropriate adult foods, or main meal centres, because of low status associations, and identification as children's food. They were not thought a 'serious' food.

SUBSTANTIALITY AND THE ROLE OF MEAT

Despite the higher incidence of snacking and lighter meals, one main meal a day is still an essential part of our meal system. Given its physiological, psychological, social and cultural importance, the main meal must be substantial.

But substantiality involves much more than quantity. The foods themselves must be 'filling', with the right colours, chewy texture, or mouthfeel. This has underlying associations with masculinity (a 'man's' meal). Femininity in food suggests lightness, a lack of seriousness, temporary replenishment and relation to secondary meals. Fish is not regarded as a substantial food. White for most respondents signified lightness in texture, blandness in flavour, and a boring appearance. Fish lacked the 'meatiness' of red meat, and even chicken; its bland flavour required the accompaniment of sauces. The ideal texture for fish was perceived to be flaky; it 'melted in your mouth', and required minimal chewing. But the demand for substantiality requires a chewy texture, something to 'get your teeth into'. The presence of bones in fresh fish demands a degree of caution and delicacy when eating, necessitating smaller mouthfuls and stripping the flesh from the bones. The use of fish was perceived as beneficial for the invalid or the sick where strong flavours were not desired and digestion was easy. But such associations do little for its general appeal.

FRESHNESS AND SAFETY

Here we have come up against the paradox in the fish story. We demand substantiality in our foods, but the symbolism associated with freshness, which we also demand in fish, evokes an image of insubstantiality. Fish represents, for many people, an unknown entity. They are very different from the other sorts of animals we eat, and require special methods of preparation, cooking and serving. In this respect, they do not readily fit into our meal system with relatively restricted methods of cooking, combination and eating. This creates a degree of uncertainty in their usage, especially with younger housewives. We demand an element of safety in the decision to utilise any unfamiliar food. With fish, safety is translated into a heightened awareness of freshness. This repeatedly emerged in groups as a restrictive factor. Fresh fish has clear, bright eyes, shiny skin, and smells of the sea. These evaluations were used by the older consumers with more confidence.

Most fish were purchased and consumed on the same day, certainly no longer than 24 h elapsed between purchase and consumption. It was considered unsafe to reheat fish, which lost any recognisable shape second time round. Safety concerns were also expressed about bones, based either on direct or second-hand experience, particularly with children, where fish fingers offered a safe alternative.

PRODUCT APPROPRIATENESS

The appropriateness of different types of fish product for different meals seemed more relevant than any difference between species. Table 2 illustrates the positive and negative associations of the different types of products. By relating these to the type of meal and the social cues, it is possible to establish the appropriateness of different types of fish product.

Table 2
Positive and negative features of fish and products

	Fresh fish	Frozen fish	Prepared fish	Canned fish
Positive features	Healthy Light Quick to prepare A change Nutritious Non-fattening No waste Variety of species	Convenient to Acquire Store Prepare Easy to eat Informal Good value Nutritious No waste Consistent	Convenient to Prepare Store Tasty High status Good quality Exciting/novel No waste Well packaged 'Safe' Attractive	Convenient to Prepare Store Tasty Easy to eat No waste Consistent Good for Sandwiches Salads
Negative features	See Table 1	Poor taste/bland Less nutritious Not adult Not main meal Quality uncertain Frying—unhealthy Additives Not versatile Limited combinations Boring	Expensive Insubstantial Unfamiliarity Requires additional ingredients Small portions	Limited usage Old fashioned Unfamiliar Oily/dark fish

NEW POSSIBILITIES

Historically, the formal meal pattern in the UK has been dominated by meat, with fish characteristically in the hor'-d'oeuvre or starter course, seldom promoted to centre-stage (Beeton, 1864). Given the restricted appropriateness of fish products to the main meal format, light meals and snacks offer a more promising area for new product development. Fish is well regarded in these meals where substantiality is not so crucial, and an element of lightness is required. It is suitable for salad meals, snacks—witness the success of surimi (crabsticks). Dark fish and tuna are associated with sandwiches. It is readily acceptable to many as a starter or less serious meal, as one infrequent user stated, 'suitable for women because they do not like to eat so much'.

If freshness can be associated with chilled foods, then this may be a way forward for fresh fish; freshness can then be evaluated by the more adventurous young consumer using sell-by dates. It does seem that a niche exists for a new fish product which embodies meaty qualities and suggests an element of substantiality; a necessary condition for admission to the main meal format. Specific fish products, like tuna steaks, possess these qualities, and may offer new potential; that remains to be seen. Any new product needs to be presented in a form which offers good combination possibilities, and ease of cooking, but without appearing processed.

The shopping regimes of the younger housewife and her requirements for added convenience offer greater potential for new product development at this end of the market.

CONCLUSION

Fish exists in a hierarchy of foods, relevant to our meal system. It is regarded in its fresh form as a suitable substitute for meat in the main meal. However, meat is central to this meal system, and it determines our expectations of serious foods. In comparison, fish scores poorly in terms of substantiality, and the symbolic meaning of those signifiers associated with substantiality conflict with those for freshness. Fish gains to some extent in its perception as a healthy food. Its limited appeal is also a function of the restricted forms of fish usage in meal patterns, confined mainly to the 'platter' type meal. Given the need for variety in the diet, this further hinders its more widespread appeal. The meal format demands a 'proper meal' each day, in theory, though it is unlikely this is adhered to in practice, and fish is not really perceived as being 'proper'—certainly in the presence of a male head of household. We regard fish as second best. Appeals to the rationale of health and nutrition fail to take into account the other demands of a food system, and we as individuals neglect an abundant food source which is there for the taking.

REFERENCES

Angyal, A. (1941). Disgust and related aversions. *Abnormal. So. Psychol.*, **36**, 393–412.

Beeton, M. I. (1864). *Household Management*.

Douglas, M. (1966). *Purity and Danger: An Analysis of Concepts of Pollution and Taboo*. Routledge and Keagan Paul, London.

Douglas, M. (Ed.) (1984). *Food in the Social Order: Studies of Food and Festivities in Three American Communities*. Russel Sage Foundation, New York.

Douglas, M. & Isherwood, B. (1979). *The World of Goods*. Allen Lane, London.

Elias, N. (1983). *The Civilising Process (Vol. 2): Vol. 1 The History of Manners*. Basil Blackwell, Oxford.

Fischler, C. (1980). *Food Habits, Social Change and the Nature/Culture Dilemma*, Fifth International Congress of the International Organisation for the Study of Human Development, Campione, Italy.

Levi-Strauss, C. (1984). *Le cru et le cuir*, translated 1970. Jonathan Cape, London.

Palmer, A. (1984). *Moveable Feasts: Changes in English Eating Habits*. Oxford University Press, Oxford.

Rozin, P. (1976). The selection of food by rats, human and other animals. In *Advances in the Study of Behaviour, Vol. 6*, eds J. S. Rossenbalt *et al.* Academic Press, London/New York.

White Fish Authority (1975). Attitudes to Fish, Frequency of Serving Fish and Other Foods, Fisheries Economic Research Unit mimeographed papers.

Chapter 19

Hunger and the Satiety Cascade—Their Importance for Food Acceptance in the Late 20th Century

JOHN E. BLUNDELL, ANDREW J. HILL and PETER J. ROGERS

Biopsychology Group, Department of Psychology, University of Leeds, Leeds, LS2 9JT, UK

ABSTRACT

The ways in which foods may increase willingness to eat or satisfy our desire for further food is an issue of great theoretical and practical significance. Products whose palatability has been raised in order to promote consumption may have the potential for causing overnutrition. In addition new types of foods and additives are constantly being added to the food supply although little is known about their effects on appetite. Consequently there is a considerable need to provide information about the appetite enhancing and satiating capacity of food items. First, knowledge of how the composition of food alters energy intake and food selection throws light upon the mechanisms of appetite control. Food itself can be used as an experimental tool to investigate the mode of operation of appetite mechanism. Second, this knowledge can be employed to develop a coherent strategy of nutritional intake for everyday use in the home, at work and in the clinic. Knowledge about the effect on appetite control exerted by particular components of food can help industry to provide appropriate foods for specific requirements and can allow the consumer to rationally select a suitable diet. Despite the importance of these issues only a little is known about the satiating properties of foods in general and only a few studies have examined the effects of individual food components. Various research strategies and experimental designs are available for investigating these matters. The management of hunger via the processes of satiation and satiety is important for maintaining good nutrition and may therefore be of considerable significance for food acceptance.

'It could be of great value to have tables showing the energy-satiety ratio of all the common foods to indicate their potential for causing over nutrition'

K. W. Heaton (1981), p. 288

SATIATING POWER OF FOODS—PRACTICAL SIGNIFICANCE

The ways in which foods may increase the willingness to eat or satisfy our desire for further foods is an issue of great theoretical importance and of considerable practical significance in these last decades of the the 20th century. Products whose palatability has been raised in order to promote consumption may have the potential for causing over- nutrition. In addition new types of foods and additives are constantly being added to the food supply although often little is known about their effects on appetite. Consequently there is a considerable need to provide information about the appetite enhancing and satiating capacity of food items. First, knowledge of how the composition of food alters energy intake and food selection throws light upon the mechanisms of appetite control. Food itself can be used as an experimental tool to investigate the mode of operation of appetite mechanisms. Second, this knowledge can be used to develop a coherent strategy of nutritional intake for everyday use in the home, at work and in the clinic. Knowledge about the effects on appetite control exerted by particular components of food can help industry to provide appropriate foods for specific requirements and can allow the consumer to rationally select a suitable diet. Despite the importance of these issues, only a little is known about the satiating properties (or appetite enhancing capacity) of foods in general and only a few studies have examined the effects of individual food components. However, various research strategies and experimental designs are available for investigating these matters.

Uncoupling Sensory and Nutritional Characteristics

Why have the above issues become particularly important in the last quarter of the 20th century? There are two prominent reasons. First, advances in food technology have made it possible to develop and produce foods with precisely defined sensory characteristics. These characteristics are designed to make foods particularly attractive for the consumer (the eater and the purchaser). At the same time it is clear that the sensory characteristics of foods can be manipulated quite independently of the nutrient or calorific content of food. This disengagement (or uncoupling) of the sensory and nutritional components of food is likely to have effects upon the control of appetite and the pattern of ingestion.

Second, in well developed economic cultures such as North America and Europe the last 10 years has seen increased attention directed to the problem of obesity and the effects of excess weight on health. This concern has been reflected in the extent to which the media has promoted the doctrine of slimness—particularly amongst women. In turn these circumstances have provided the conditions for an epidemic of eating disorders ranging from mild but uncontrolled dieting to the disabling disorder of bulimia nervosa (e.g. Stunkard & Stellar, 1984). A sizeable proportion of the population is therefore greatly concerned with body shape and weight and is actively attempting to undereat. This type of behaviour and the associated eating patterns, brings to importance the way in which foods satisfy hunger and provide for bodily requirements.

Taken together these two factors—the increased sophistication of strategies in food product development and the prevalence of dietary concern in the consumer market—suggest that mechanisms of appetite control are being subjected to considerable pressures. These pressures may be quite dissimilar to those biosocial problems which directed the functional properties of appetite mechanisms during the course of evolution. Consequently, this is a particularly appropriate time to investigate the roles of hunger and satiety in the overall expression of appetite and the control of eating.

Some Simple Practical Issues

One major objective in nutrition research is to examine ways in which properties of foods influence their long term pattern of consumption and therefore affect the nutritional status of individuals. This enterprise is vital since it is possible that strongly held positive beliefs about a food, economic factors or very attractive taste qualities, may stimulate and maintain consumption but, if the commodity is not nutritionally appropriate, then long term effects may not be beneficial. It is clear that a complex interacting system of variables modulates long term patterns of intake. Within this system distal and proximal variables can be distinguished. Distal variables are made up of those enduring habits, attitudes and opinions about the value and suitability of foods. The proximal variables are those in which certain major dimensions of food such as perceived palatability, total caloric value, amount of fibre and the proportions of macronutrients, may exert a potent action on ingestion. These proximal effects also include those cognitions induced by the sight or thought of food. These effects are therefore concerned with the way in which the properties of foods influence the short term processes controlling the pattern of consumption. The issue involves the way in which particular qualities of foods alter feelings of hunger and fullness, control how much of a food will be consumed and modulates preferences for certain classes of foods— either similar to or different from those being consumed. Do these matters influence food acceptance? They appear to be important since it has been argued that three quarters of the variation in intake is predictable from knowledge of food preference, the subjective satiety or 'fillingness' of food, and the amount of two major nutrients, fat and protein, the food contains (Pilgrim & Kamen, 1963).

In simple terms the aim of investigating the proximal actions of foods is to disclose how the attributes of foods influence the motivation to eat in the short term. If eating a particular food produces a powerful feeling of fullness, will this affect the acceptability of the product? If a particular food augments hunger but eating the food leaves the consumer feeling empty, will this affect acceptability? If a food immediately changes an individual's preference for that or other foods, how will this influence acceptance? It is assumed that the action of foods upon the feelings of hunger, fullness and preferences for taste will have some bearing on overall acceptability and upon long term profiles of consumption. It is widely accepted that the sensory evaluation of foods is important in predicting acceptability; how important is the evaluation of appetite modulating effects?

HUNGER, APPETITE, SATIATION AND SATIETY

The terms hunger, appetite, satiation and satiety are widely used in both the scientific literature and in non-technical discourse to refer to states and processes which control and guide food consumption. For a full discussion of these issues see Blundell (1979) and Blundell & Burley (1987). It is useful to clarify the use of these terms. Satiation and satiety can be functionally distinguished. Satiation can be regarded as the process which brings a period of eating to a close whereas satiety is the state of inhibition over further eating once a period of eating has ended. Satiety therefore has a precise technical definition. Although there are many vicarious reasons why eating could be halted, satiety refers only to the inhibition of eating as a result of prior food ingestion. The terms satiation and satiety, as distinguished above, appear to be identical to the notions of 'intra-meal satiety' and 'inter-meal satiety' defined by Van Itallie & Vanderweele (1981). In research on animals the operation of these two processes can be distinguished by effects upon meal size (satiation) and inter-meal interval (satiety). This distinction can also be used in the description of human eating patterns, if the experimental designs permit the disclosure of these effects (see Hill & Blundell, 1986a).

The logical status of the term hunger often causes confusion since it is widely used in more than one sense. Hunger is clearly a word which implies a drive or motivational impetus to eat. On the one hand, hunger is a motivational construct with the logical status of a mediating concept or intervening variable (McQuorquodale & Meehl, 1948; Royce, 1963). That is the term refers to an explanatory principle which itself cannot be directly measured but which is inferred from other observable and measurable events. For example hunger can be operationally defined as the number of hours since a person or animal was last fed. The number of hours without food therefore quantifies the intensity of the (hunger) drive without reference to any further mental or physiological phenomena. On the other hand, hunger may be used to refer to certain conscious sensations or feelings linked to a desire to obtain and eat food. This is the sense in which the layman recognises the notion of hunger and reflects the way in which the term is used in day to day discourse. The term is given understanding through a social consensus; that is, use of the term is generally understood as implying a willingness or desire to eat. It is this articulated hunger which researchers attempt to capture by means of rating scales and other devices.

Hunger the motivational construct and hunger the perceived desire to eat can both be seen to be biologically functional. Hunger is a force which impels organisms to seek food to satisfy nutritional requirements. Consciously perceived hunger is one aspect of this and partly exists as detectable physical sensations provoked by physiological events. This may occur in animals but there is no way of revealing this so objective measures of hunger drive are employed (e.g. measuring the amount of effort expended to obtain food). With humans we can ask directly about hunger feelings.

Hunger and Satiety—a Clarification

In much of the literature on the control of eating and body weight regulation, hunger and satiety are used as if they were polar opposites. For example the question has been posed as to whether obese people eat because of excessive hunger or defective satiety (e.g. Blundell, 1977 for discussion). This implies that the reason must be one or the other. However, when hunger is used as a motivational construct it can be seen that hunger and satiety really refer to the same process; hunger is the force impelling eating (arising from lack of food) and satiety is the resistance to eating (arising from having eaten). The strength of hunger and satiety are therefore reciprocally related.

However, in considering hunger the conscious sensation or articulated desire to eat, it is clear that the perception of this feeling can be assessed before eating, during eating or after eating. Therefore the intensity of perceived hunger can reflect the tendency to start eating (hunger construct) the willingness to stop eating (satiation) and the maintenance of inhibition over further eating (satiety). The measured sensation of hunger therefore becomes one index of the strength of satiety. If hunger sensations are weak or low then satiety will be maintained; the restoration of perceived hunger represents the dissipation or weakening of satiety. This conceptualisation reflects the different status of these two terms; hunger a conscious sensation and satiety a state or process. Measuring the hunger feeling can therefore be used to evaluate the development of satiation and the durability of satiety. But of course this assessment will be most powerful when combined with the actual measurement of food consumed.

The Satiety Cascade

Eating food has the capacity to take away hunger and, after satiation has occurred, further eating is inhibited for a period. What mechanisms are responsible for these processes? It is likely that the mechanisms involved in terminating eating and in maintaining inhibition range from those which occur when food is initially sensed, to the effects of metabolites following digestion and absorption. By definition, satiety

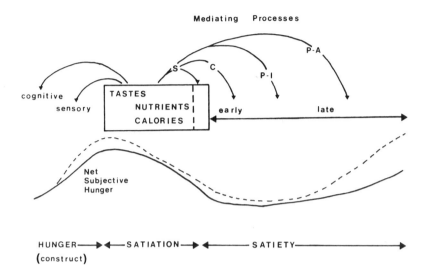

Figure 1. Illustration of the major components of the satiety cascade. S, sensory; C, cognitive; P-I, post-ingestive; P-A, post-absorptive; and postulated changes in motivation (perceived hunger) accompanying the ingestion of a meal. The diagram also shows the anticipatory effects of food consumption.

is not an instantaneous event but occurs over a considerable time period; it is therefore useful to distinguish different phases of satiety which can be associated with different mechanisms. This concept is illustrated in Fig. 1. Four mediating processes are identified: sensory, cognitive, post-ingestive and post-absorptive. These maintain inhibition over eating (and hunger) during the early and late phases of satiety. Sensory effects are generated through the smell, taste, temperature and texture of food and it is likely that these factors help to bring eating to a halt and inhibit eating (of foods with similar sensory characteristics) in the short term. Such a mechanism is embodied in the idea of sensory-specific satiety first disclosed by Le Magnen (1960). Cognitive effects represent the beliefs held about the properties of foods and their presumed effect upon the eater and, under certain experimental conditions, they have been demonstrated to operate (e.g. Wooley, 1972). The category identified here as post-ingestive processes includes a number of possible actions including gastric distension and rate of gastric emptying, the release of hormones such as cholecystokinin from the duodenum, and the stimulation of physico-chemically specific receptors along the gastro-intestinal tract (see Mei, 1985). The post-absorptive phase of satiety includes those mechanisms arising from the action of metabolites after absorption across the intestine and into the blood system. This category embraces the actions of chemicals such as glucose and the amino acids which may act directly upon the brain after crossing the blood–brain barrier or which may influence the brain indirectly via neural inputs following stimulation of peripheral chemo-receptors.

The approximate anticipated moment of action of these mediating processes is shown in Fig. 1 but of course the mechanisms will overlap and their effects will be integrated to produce a conjoint effect. It should also be kept in mind that the psychobiological system for appetite control has the capacity to learn. That is, to form associations between the sensory and post-absorptive characteristics of foods (e.g. Booth, 1977; Le Magnen, 1985). Therefore the sensory aspects of a food may come to predict the absorptive consequences thereby allowing the sensory-mediating processes to exert an augmented effect. (This effect will of course be weakened or distorted when there is uncoupling of the sensory characteristics and nutritional properties of foods.) All of these factors add to the importance of measuring the strength of satiety at various times after the end of ingestion, in order to throw light upon the effect of individual mediating processes. Good experimental designs will be required to analyse the operations of the satiety cascade. However, it is clear that the effects of foods upon the satiety cascade have important consequences for appetite control and for the subjective feelings associated with eating. It is therefore likely that the expression of the satiety cascade will have implications for food acceptability.

Role of Hunger in Food Consumption

It is clear that food itself is a potent and natural anorectic substance; eating food takes away our hunger and being deprived of food generally leads to a build up of hunger (although there are one or two special circumstances where this does not occur). The processes responsible for the inhibition of hunger are shown in Fig. 1. Since the intensity of hunger feelings is one major component of satiety, hunger is influenced by the processes identified. However, a dilemma arises when foods are produced to deal with a popular demand for low calorie items in support of an obsession with dieting and slimming. It can be seen from Fig. 1 that reducing the amount (or nature) of food eaten will weaken those processes (post-ingestive and post-absorptive) which maintain a low level of hunger and postpone further eating. Changing food composition will alter the capacity of food to influence the satiety cascade. It is well known that casual or planned dieting leads to chronic low levels of hunger and acute intense hunger episodes. This illustrates well the biological function of the hunger sensation which is to motivate eating. Hunger reminds us that the body requires food. The importance of this is reflected in the nature of hunger; it is a nagging, irritating feeling whose presence constantly serves to stimulate thoughts of food and eating. These attributes of hunger are one reason why casual dieting almost always ends in failure. It appears to be very difficult to cope with unregulated hunger. It also draws attention to the fact that reducing the calorie content of foods in order to reduce overall energy intake will probably only be effective as a weight controlling strategy if the individual has some capacity for the management of hunger.

Facilitatory and Inhibitory Effects of Foods

The satiety cascade in Fig. 1 illustrates those processes which mediate the inhibitory effects of food upon further consumption. This diagram also shows that some attributes of food act pro-actively. These responses are called cephalic phase reflexes and they involve the mouth, stomach, duodenum and lower intestine together with related endocrine glands. In man the sight and smell of food are sufficiently potent to trigger cephalic phase insulin responses (Sjostrom *et al.*, 1980; Simon *et al.*, 1986), and the response in obese subjects is four times that in lean people. The taste of saccharin can provoke a cephalic phase insulin response in rats (Berthould *et al.*, 1981) and in man (Halter *et al.*, 1975). The stimulus-induced cephalic phase responses are accompanied by an augmentation of the desire to eat. Consequently one action of salient sensory components of food is to provoke physiological responses which anticipate ingestion and which may facilitate appetite. Therefore in assessing the overall effect of individual foods on appetite control it is necessary to take into account both facilitative and inhibitory actions. Moreover, it is worth noting that this dual action of food may have important implications when a potent sensory dimension—for example, sweetness—is combined with a weak (low energy) inhibitory component (e.g., Blundell & Hill, 1986).

EVALUATING THE SATIATING CAPACITY OF FOOD

The ability to assess the satiating effectiveness of foods depends upon having valid monitoring procedures and appropriate experimental designs. It will also be useful to monitor the motivation to eat along with actual caloric intake, the distribution of eating episodes and the selection of particular nutrients. In addition since the overall satiating capacity of food will depend upon facilitatory and inhibitory effects it will be helpful to measure the various parameters before, during and after eating. The temporal profiles of motivation (e.g. hunger) and behaviour (e.g. eating) should provide the most complete description of satiation and satiety.

Recently, a model system has been developed to monitor the profile of changes which take place over time and which are associated with the consumption of a meal (Hill & Blundell, 1986a; Blundell & Hill, 1987c). These assessments include visual analogue rating scales, food preference checklists and forced-choice preference tests, checklists of bodily sensations, ratings of hedonic responses and food intake diaries (see Blundell *et al.* 1988). These procedures constitute a relevant battery extracted from a much broader range of dietary and nutritional assessment devices (see Blundell, 1987; Blundell & Hill, 1988). This procedure for the analysis of motivational variables accompanying eating provides a profile of characteristics illustrated in Fig. 2. The profile disclosed by the model system provides a baseline for evaluating the consequences of various types of experimental manipulations of eating. Agents believed to intensify satiation should clearly influence the constellation of changes associated with the end of a meal. Changing the properties of particular foods would be expected to produce shifts in the profile of variables and to change immediate or later intake.

Some Effects of the Components of Food

Four properties of food which are of considerable significance are the level of palatability, the energy value (calories), the proportions of the macronutrients protein, carbohydrate and fat and the quantity of indigestible material present. In order to describe the consequences of manipulating any one of these features it is of course necessary to hold the others constant. For example, if palatability is experimentally manipulated then total calories and the proportion of macronutrients should be held at constant values. When working with real foods this

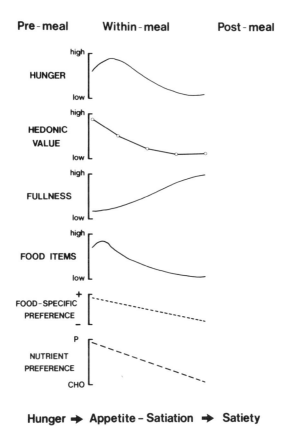

Pre-meal   Within-meal   Post-meal

Hunger → Appetite – Satiation → Satiety

Figure 2. Diagram illustrating how monitored motivational variables may be tracked during the course of a meal. These temporal profiles provide a baseline for assessing the effects of nutritional manipulations. Effects on satiety can be evaluated by continuing the monitoring during the post-prandial period. P: protein, CHO: carbohydrate.

methodological requirement can present the experimenter with some difficult nutritional problems. Investigations which have experimentally manipulated these features have disclosed interesting consequences. For example raising the palatability of food augments the perceived hunger sensations (Hill *et al.* 1984). Moreover, palatability affects the recovery from satiation. Increasing the protein content of a meal (whilst maintaining the level of palatability and value of calories) increases feelings of fullness at the end of a meal and maintains the intensity of these sensations (Hill & Blundell, 1986*b*; Blundell & Hill,

1987*a*). This finding confirms the widely held belief that protein has greater satiating power than the equivalent caloric value of carbohydrate. Food preferences are also adjusted along with the general satiating or de-satiating effects of these manipulations.

Of course, not all nutritional manipulations can be expected to produce effects instantly or within the space of a meal. Different types of experimental design are required in order to demonstrate the power of pre- or post-absorptive effects of food. One procedure has been termed the pre-loading strategy (Kissileff, 1984) which can take the form of a measured nutritional manipulation or a precisely controlled meal (Blundell *et al.*, 1987). Motivational changes can be tracked during the preload or meal and the consequences followed in subsequent test meals (Kissileff *et al.*, 1984) or by means of diary records of eating patterns and meal profiles. These designs incorporate the necessity of validating the changes in ratings and checklist response by measuring actual intake of energy and the selection of particular nutrients. For example, if the total number of calories consumed at a meal is experimentally manipulated whilst the appearance and palatability of the food remains unchanged then the cognitive effects on motivational parameters may prevent any instantaneous change in these variables. However, an effect should become apparent as the post-absorptive effects of the food take effect. This is exactly what was demonstrated when subjects ate calorically different meals similar in other respects. After 3 h the consequences of eating the low calorie meals were reflected in higher levels of hunger sensations (Hill *et al.*, 1987*a*). Energy intake was also greater once subjects resumed eating.

Further studies have indicated that the amount of fibre in a meal can cause certain adjustments in motivational parameters and food consumption (Burley *et al.*, 1987) and it appears that fibre may exert effects on both satiation or satiety depending upon the experimental manipulation employed (Blundell & Burley, 1987). In the case of fibre much depends upon the timing and mode of delivery of the product. Fibre administered as a preload may exert different effects compared with fibre delivered as part of a meal. The same food may also exert differing effects depending on its physical (liquid or solid) form (Kissileff, 1985).

Implications of Dietary Action on Satiating Efficiency

The studies outlined above have indicated that some major dimensions of foods clearly influence subjectively perceived sensations as reflected in analogue ratings or checklist scores. What is the relevance of these findings? It is clear that the nature of the transcription process between a subjective experience and making a response on an experimental device is not known. The quantification involved can be regarded only as an ordinal scale (although for statistical purposes interval measurement is assumed). Consequently the numerical data should not be used to infer the absolute intensity of a subjectively perceived sensation. The status of the ratings and other forms of quantification is given credibility by their correlation with actual behaviour. For visual analogue ratings of the type described above correlations with the amount of food consumed vary between 0·7 and 0·9 (Hill et al., 1987a; Hill, 1987). Moreover the tracking of sensations across meals and over various periods of time accords well with actual eating behaviour. It is the temporal profiles of rated sensations which add a further meaningful dimension to the use of these procedures. Tracking the course of satiation and the recovery from satiety increases the sensitivity of these devices to detect the effects of particular experimental manipulations. It is also clear that satiating capacity is reflected in actual food consumption as well as in motivational dispositions.

It is important that assessment of satiating efficiency begins before eating is initiated, continues through consumption and is maintained through the post-ingestive phase. Analysing satiation and satiety entails knowing what changes are occurring both *during* eating and when no eating is taking place. Depending upon the particular circumstances, a major action may be upon meal size—altering the point of meal termination (De Castro & Kreitzman, 1985) or upon the interval between meals (Kissileff et al., 1984).

The capacity of a food to limit intake of the product itself and to inhibit further consumption of other foods has both social and economic importance. In certain cases it may be necessary or desirable to keep satiating power low in order to ensure a high consumption. In other instances a food may be attractive because it possesses high satiating power. There is widespread agreement that the combination and proportions of macronutrients in a food have an important influence on the satiating effect of a product. As noted above the amount of protein appears to be particularly effective and this has been demonstrated with real foods (e.g. Blundell & Hill, 1987a) and with composite formulas (Booth et al., 1970).

The question of satiating capacity is particularly relevant to the development of low-calorie products which have a ready market in a culture obsessed with dieting. It is known that calories from any source constitute a major source of satiating capacity. The question therefore arises whether the reduction in the caloric content of low-calorie products will automatically lower the satiating effect of the food and leave a residue of hunger following consumption. Alternatively, the lower caloric content could lead to the more rapid rehabilitation of hunger over time. Naturally, the interaction between the cognitively and physiologically-induced effects of the food will be important in determining which, if either, of these above effects actually take place. However, it is worth considering whether it is possible to design low-calorie foods which produce immediate feelings of satisfaction (and satiation) and which, in addition, prevent compensatory consumption in the intermediate or long-term. The theoretical issue pertaining to the capacity of the biological system to monitor calories and to adjust intake so as to maintain a constant input has received considerable experimental attention. Much depends upon the methodology and design of the investigation. However, when real food products have been used evidence indicates at least a partial compensation for the calories omitted from the low-calorie product (Hill et al., 1987a; Porikos et al., 1982). In the case of low calorie intense sweeteners it has been shown in one experimental model that non-caloric solutions, in contrast to solutions of glucose or sucrose, reduced the perceived pleasantness of sweet fluids but did not suppress hunger or augment fullness (Blundell & Hill, 1987b). Indeed in certain cases there appeared to be a facilitation of some measures of appetitive motivation.

Sensory Evaluation and Appetite Evaluation

The sensory evaluation of foods is an obligatory step in the development of a product from the food technology laboratory to the market place. Should the evaluation of appetite have equal importance? Some findings noted above indicate that various characteristics of food such as palatability, caloric content, actual and inferred, proportions of macronutrients, physical form and fibre content exert effects on measures of motivation and the degree of satiation. Differences between foods in satiating capacity means differing effects upon the control and expression of appetite. Since food products may vary markedly in salient characteristics, it is not easy to predict in advance the response to any particular product. Each food probably needs to be investigated separately and with differing experimental designs in order to distinguish between effects on satiation and satiety, and to detect the relative strengths of facilitatory and inhibitory actions. The tools currently available, combined with a rigorous experimental methodology and meaningful research designs, can provide some useful information about the short-term effects of foods. In turn these close range effects may have some bearing on long-term patterns of acceptability and consumption. It should of course be kept in mind that the effects of a food on the short-term control of eating may alter with repeated exposure as cognitions and physiological responses to the product may change.

It is highly likely that the demonstrated effects of food will vary between different groups of individuals whose psychological state and physiological processes may be different. For example there is evidence that lean and obese subjects show different responses to administered nutrients such as glucose (Hill *et al.*, 1987*b*). The obese display no negative gustative alliesthesia but show a very sensitive response on rated motivational parameters. Another group likely to respond idiosyncratically are dieters. Because of the constant or periodic voluntary inhibition of eating, dieters (restrained eaters) experience both acute and chronic hunger. Consequently, the system may well be primed and particularly sensitive to the facilitatory characteristics of food. Restrained and non-restrained subjects behave differently under a variety of experimental circumstances (Polivy & Herman, 1985). In more extreme cases of disordered eating—as in anorexia nervosa or bulimia—the prandial profiles of feelings of hunger and fullness are completely disrupted (Owen *et al.*, 1985). Accordingly, the facilitatory or satiating capacity of foods may be different in individuals exercising self-imposed food restriction. Considering the number of people who fall into this category the consequences for acceptability seem worth investigating. In the present cultural milieu focused upon dieting and weight regulation it is certain that the acceptability of a product can be raised by its *believed* helpfulness in controlling eating and body weight. To what extent would the acceptability of a product be influenced by its *measured* or *perceived* effect upon hunger and appetite control?

REFERENCES

Berthould, H. R., Bereinter, D. A., Trimble, E. R., Siegel, E. G. & Jeanrenaud, B. (1981). Cephalic phase, reflex insulin secretion. *Diabetologia*, **20**, 393–401.

Blundell, J. E. (1977). Hunger and satiety in the control of food intake: implications for the treatment of obesity. *Clin. Deitolog.*, **23**, 257–72.

Blundell, J. E. (1979). Hunger, appetite and satiety—psychological constructs in search of identities. In *Nutrition and Lifestyles*, ed. M. Turner. Applied Science Publishers, London, pp. 21–42.

Blundell, J. E. (1987). Research methodologies for the study of human feeding behaviour. In *Medicaments et Comportements Alimentaires*, eds P. Meyer, F. Chaouloff, J-C. Gilbert & Y. Rolland. Masson, Paris, pp. 147–64.

Blundell, J. E. & Burley, V. J. (1987). Satiation, satiety and the action of fibre on food intake. *Int. J. Obesity*, **11**, Suppl. 1, 9–25.

Blundell, J. E. & Hill, A. J. (1986). Paradoxical effects of an intense sweetener (aspartame) on appetite. *Lancet*, **i**, 1092–3.

Blundell, J. E. & Hill, A. J. (1987*a*). Influence of tryptophan on appetite and food selection in man. In *Amino Acids in Health & Disease: New Perspectives*, ed. S. Kaufman. Alan Liss & Co., New York, pp. 403–19.

Blundell, J. E. & Hill, A. J. (1987*b*). Artificial sweeteners and the control of appetite: implications for the eating disorders. In *The Future of Predictive Safety Evaluation*, eds A. Worden, D. Parke & J. Marks. MTP Press, Lancaster, pp. 263–82.

Blundell, J. E. & Hill, A. J. (1987*c*). Serotonergic modulation of the pattern of eating and the profile of hunger-satiety in humans. *Int. J. Obesity*, **11**, Suppl. 3, 141–53.

Blundell, J. E. & Hill, A. J. (1988). Descriptive and operational study of eating in man. In *Modern Concepts of the Eating Disorders: Research, Diagnosis, Treatment*, eds B. J. Blinder, B. F. Chaitin & R. Goldstein. PMA Press, New York, pp. 65–86.

Blundell, J. E., Rogers, P. J. & Hill, A. J. (1987). Evaluating the satiating power of foods: implications for acceptance and consumption. In *Food Acceptance and Nutrition*, eds J. Solms, D. A. Booth, R. M. Pangborn & O. Raunhardt. Academic Press, London, pp. 205–19.

Booth, D. A. (1977). Satiety and appetite are conditioned reactions. *Psychosom. Med.*, **39**, 76–81.

Booth, D. A., Chase, A. & Campbell, A. T. (1970). Relative effectiveness of protein in the late stages of appetite suppression in man. *Physiol. Behav.*, **5**, 1299–302.

Burley, V. J., Leeds, A. R. & Blundell, J. E. (1987). The effect of high and low fibre breakfasts on hunger, satiety, and food intake in a subsequent meal. *Int. J. Obesity*, **11**, Suppl. 1, 87–93.

De Castro, J. M. & Kreitzman, S. M. (1985). A microregulatory analysis of spontaneous human feeding patterns. *Physiol. Behav.*, **35**, 329–35.

Halter, J., Kulkosky, P., Woods, S., Makous, W., Chen, M. & Porte, D. (1975). Afferent receptors, taste perception and pancreatic endocrine function in man. *Diabetes*, **24**, 414.

Heaton, K. W. (1981). Dietary fibre and energy intake. In *Regulators of Intestinal Absorption in Obesity, Diabetes and Nutrition*, eds P. Berchtold, A. Cairella, A. Jacobelli & V. Silano. Societa Editrice Universo, Roma, pp. 283–94.

Hill, A. J. (1987). Investigation of some short-term influences on hunger, satiety and food consumption in man. Ph.D. thesis, University of Leeds.

Hill, A. J. & Blundell, J. E. (1986a). Model system for investigating the actions of anorectic drugs: effect of d-fenfluramine on food intake nutrient selection, food preferences, meal patterns, hunger and satiety in healthy human subjects. *Advances in the Biosciences*, Pergamon Press, Oxford, pp. 377–89.

Hill, A. J. & Blundell, J. E. (1986b). Macro-nutrients and satiety: the effects of a high protein or a high carbohydrate meal on subjective motivation to eat and food preferences. *Nutrit. Behav.*, **3**, 133–44.

Hill, A. J., Magson, L. D. & Blundell, J. E. (1984). Hunger and palatability: tracking ratings of subjective experience before, during and after the consumption of preferred and less preferred food, *Appetite*, **5**, 361–71.

Hill, A. J., Leathwood, P. J. & Blundell, J. E. (1987a). Some evidence for short term caloric compensation in normal weight human subjects: the effects of high and low energy meals on hunger, food preference and food intake. *Human Nutrit.: Appl. Nutrit.*, **41A**, 244–57.

Hill, A. J., Wales, J. K. & Blundell, J. E. (1987b). Do 5-HT drugs reduce food intake through taste hedonics or hunger? Studies in lean and obese humans. *Inter. J. Obesity*, **11**, 308A.

Kissileff, H. R. (1984). Satiating efficiency and a strategy for conducting food loading experiments. *Neurosci. Behav. Rev.*, **8**, 129–35.

Kissileff, H. R. (1985). Effects of physical state (liquid-solid) of foods on food intake: procedural and substantive contributions. *Am. J. Clin. Nutrit.*, **42**, 956–65.

Kissileff, H. R., Gruss, L. P., Thornton, J. & Jordan, H. A. (1984). The satiating efficiency of foods. *Physiol. Behav.*, **32**, 319–32.

Le Magnen, J. (1960). Effets d'une pluralite de stimuli alimentaires sur le determinisme quantitif de l'ingestion chez le rat blanc. *Arch. Sci. Physiol.*, **14**, 411–19.

Le Magnen, J. (1985). *Hunger*, Cambridge University Press, Cambridge.

McQuorquodale, K. & Meehl, P. E. (1948). On the distinction between hypothetical constructs and intervening variables. *Psychol. Rev.*, **55**, 95–109.

Mei, N. (1985). Intestinal chemosensitivity. *Physiol. Rev.*, **65**, 211–37.

Owen, W. P., Halmi, K. A., Gibbs, J. & Smith, C. P. (1985). Satiety responses in eating disorders. *J. Psychiat. Res.*, **19**, 279–84.

Pilgrim, F. J. & Kamon, J. M. (1963) Predictors of human food consumption. *Science*, **139**, 501–2.

Polivy, J. & Herman, C. P. (1985). Dieting and bingeing: a causal analysis. *Am. Psychol.*, **40**, 193–201.

Porikos, K. P., Hesser, M. F. & Van Itallie, T. B. (1982). Caloric regulation in normal-weight men maintained on a palatable diet of conventional foods. *Physiol. Behav.*, **29**, 293–300.

Royce, J. R. (1963). Factors as theoretical constructs. *Am. Psychol.*, **18**, 522–8.

Simon, C., Schlienger, J. L., Sapin, R. & Imler, M. (1986). Cephalic phase insulin secretion in relation to food presentation in normal and overweight subjects. *Physiol. Behav.,* **36,** 465–9.

Sjostrom, L., Garellick, G., Krotkiewski, M. & Luyckx, A. (1980). Peripheral insulin in response to the sight and smell of food. *Metabolism,* **29,** 901–9.

Stunkard, A. J. & Stellar, E. (1984). *Eating and its Disorders.* Raven Press, New York, p. 280.

Van Itallie, T. B. & Vanderweele, D. A. (1981). The phenomenon of satiety. In *Recent Advances in Obesity Research III,* eds P. Bjorntorp, M. Cairella & A. N. Howard. Libby, London, pp. 278–89.

Wooley, S. C. (1972). Physiologic versus cognitive factors in short term food regulation in the obese and non-obese. *Psychosom. Med.,* **34,** 62–8.

Topic 5

Investigations of Consumer Attitudes and Behavioural Intentions

Chapter 20

Consumer Attitudes and Food Acceptance

RICHARD SHEPHERD

AFRC, Institute of Food Research, Norwich Laboratory, Colney Lane, Norwich NR4 7UA, UK

ABSTRACT

The concepts of attitudes and beliefs have been used to try to understand many forms of behaviour but often a poor relationship has been found between assessed attitudes and a behaviour of interest. The use of attitudes and beliefs in the area of food acceptance will be reviewed. In order to arrive at a clearer picture of the role played by attitudes and beliefs, it is necessary to investigate the relationship within a clear conceptual framework. The attitudes model of Fishbein and Ajzen ((1975) Belief, Attitude, Intention and Behaviour: An Introduction to Theory and Research, *Addison-Wesley, Reading, Mass.) will be described and its usefulness in the food area will be discussed. This model is useful for integrating diverse influences on food choice. Hence beliefs about the sensory attributes of foods, the perceived nutritional benefits and functional and price factors can all be investigated and the relative importance of these factors determined. Likewise perceived social pressure to eat particular sorts of foods can also be investigated. Examples of applications in predicting the use of table salt, the consumption of high fat foods and low fat milk will be described.*

INTRODUCTION

Food choice is a complex phenomenon influenced by many different factors. It has been suggested that attitudes and beliefs may prove

253

useful concepts in trying to integrate these different factors (Shepherd, 1988).

The chemical and physical properties of foods are perceived as sensory attributes; these will influence food selection but operate only through the person's preference for (or attitude towards) that sensory attribute in the particular food. Hence two people may perceive samples as equally high in saltiness intensity, but one person may like this level of saltiness whereas the other may not. It is only by understanding the preferences (or attitudes) of the individuals that the role of sensory factors in food choice may be understood. Other factors such as price and nutritional benefits will likewise operate through the person's beliefs and affects.

Many of the inconsistencies in the literature on attitudes and beliefs stem from the lack of clear and adequate definitions. Allport (1935) defined an attitude as 'a mental and neural state of readiness to respond, organized through experience exerting a directive and/or dynamic influence on behavior'. Krech and Crutchfield (1948) and other workers have conceptualised attitudes as having three components: (a) cognitive, i.e. information or beliefs about the object; (b) affective, i.e. feelings of like or dislike towards the object; (c) conative, i.e. the tendency to behave in a certain way towards the object. The affective component is often seen as being the central component of attitude; beliefs may be thought of in this framework as being the cognitive component. It is important to distinguish between the cognitive and affective components.

ATTITUDES AND FOOD CHOICE

The role of attitudes in food choice has been reviewed by Foley *et al.* (1979) and Khan (1981). The findings have generally not been clear. There are two main approaches to investigating attitudes in this area. The first involves investigating preferences for the food or for specific sensory attributes of the food (Piggott, 1979; Randall & Sanjur, 1981), and has included much work on the food preferences of American soldiers (e.g., Meiselman, 1984). In these studies there is evidence for liking predicting consumption of foods. However, when the preferences for particular attributes are investigated these do not relate so closely to consumption; for example, salt intake is related to preferences for saltiness in foods only to a limited extent (Shepherd *et al.*,

1984; Shepherd and Farleigh, 1986b), with some studies showing no relationship (e.g. Pangborn & Pecore, 1982; Mattes et al., 1983). Likewise with sweetness preference and sugar consumption the relationships are not so clear (Pangborn & Giovanni, 1984; Mattes, 1985).

There are other attitudes and beliefs concerning food consumption, such as beliefs about the nutritional benefits or harm which might result from such consumption. In the nutritional literature there have been many attempts to investigate the relationships between nutritional knowledge, attitudes and behaviour. Whilst it might be supposed that there will be a causal relationship between these variables the results are far from clear.

In those cases where a significant relationship between knowledge and attitudes has been found (Eppright et al., 1970; Schwartz, 1975; Sims, 1976; Grotkowski & Sims, 1978; Werblow et al., 1978; Foley et al., 1983; Perron and Endres, 1985), the attitudes have either been general attitudes towards nutrition (e.g. nutrition is important) or have apparently contained cognitive belief items, which would tend to lead to a greater similarity between the knowledge and attitude items. Again when the behaviour of interest is specified in the form of a score for 'nutritional practices' there tends to be a relationship between attitudes and behaviour (Jalso et al., 1965; Schwartz, 1975; Carruth et al., 1977; Foley et al., 1983; Douglas and Douglas, 1984). However, assessing behaviour in terms of consumption of specific foods or nutrient intakes, Grotkowski & Sims (1978) and Eppright et al. (1970) found only a small number of statistically significant relationships, and Perron and Endres (1985) and Werblow et al. (1978) found no relationships. Looking at the relationship between knowledge and behaviour shows an association when the behaviour is a general practice score (Carruth et al., 1977; Foley et al., 1983; Allen & Ries, 1985), but when the consumption of specific foods or nutrients is investigated there are again no relationships (Grotkowski & Sims, 1978; Perron & Endres, 1985), or relationships for only a small number of nutrients (Eppright et al., 1970).

It would thus appear that nutritional knowledge may be related to attitudes and to behaviour, but only when the behaviour is one of general dietary practices. This relationship breaks down when the consumption of specific foods is assessed. It is difficult from these studies to determine how nutritional beliefs might be related to attitudes or to behaviour because of the lack of a clear conceptual framework within which to study such relationships, and the confusion over the use of terms in the literature.

In the following section the attitudes model proposed by Fishbein & Ajzen (1975) will be described. This offers a framework for assessing attitudes, beliefs and values, and can be used to investigate the relative importance of different types of beliefs, including sensory and nutritional, in determining behaviour.

THE FISHBEIN AND AJZEN ATTITUDE MODEL

Fishbein & Ajzen (1975; Ajzen & Fishbein, 1980) presented a model of beliefs, affect and behavioural intention. They argued that beliefs and affect should not be assessed as directed towards an object but should be assessed as directed towards a behaviour. The components of the Fishbein and Ajzen model are shown schematically in Fig. 1, and will be explained in more detail below.

With rational behaviour, the best predictor of a person's behaviour is assumed to be his or her conscious decision to perform that behaviour, i.e. behavioural intention. Since the model is related to rational behaviour it has been called the theory of reasoned action; it may be less applicable in circumstances where the behaviour is less under the conscious control of the individual. In general there will be choices open to the individual, e.g. choosing to buy one food rather

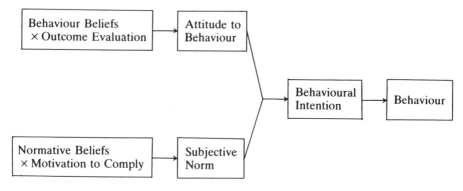

Figure 1. Schematic representation of the components of the Fishbein and Ajzen attitudes model.

than another, and at the very least this might be a decision to perform the behaviour against the decision to do nothing. The behavioural intention is predicted by two components, the person's attitude towards the behaviour (A_{act}) and the subjective norm (SN). The attitude to the behaviour is an evaluation of whether it is seen as good or bad, harmful or beneficial, etc. The subjective norm is the perceived social pressure (from important other people) to perform the behaviour. The attitude to the behaviour and the subjective norm predict behavioural intention (I) according to the equation:

$$I = w_1 \times A_{act} + w_2 \times SN$$

The relative weightings (w_1 and w_2) for the components can be derived from a multiple regression of the standardised scores (z-scores) for the two components against behavioural intention. These weightings give an indication of the relative importance of the two components in predicting behavioural intention.

The attitude to the behaviour is predicted by beliefs about the expected outcome of the behaviour (behaviour beliefs). For any individual there will be a set of salient beliefs (b_i); these can be elicited during short interviews, before the questionnaire is designed, with a small group of people similar to those to be tested in the main study. The beliefs will not be the same for everyone, but the most frequently expressed beliefs can be used in order to derive a standard list for a questionnaire. In addition to the beliefs about the outcome of the behaviour, the individual's evaluation of the expected outcome (e_1) will be important. Thus, if an individual says that eating chocolate bars will make him fat, but is not at all concerned about getting fat, then this belief would be unlikely to exert much influence on his behaviour. An overall belief-value measure is derived from the sum of each belief score multiplied by the evaluation of the outcome. This relationship is expressed as:

$$A_{act} = \sum b_i \times e_i$$

Because of the use of this type of function in the model, it is called an expectancy-value model, making use not only of beliefs about the expected outcome but also the value attached by the individual to such an outcome.

The subjective norm is predicted in a similar way from a set of normative beliefs (NB_j) about whether the individual thinks specific other people (e.g. spouse, doctor) or groups of people (e.g. government, medical profession) would prefer him or her to perform the behaviour, hence breaking down the subjective norm component so that the role played by specific others can be investigated. As with the behaviour beliefs, the normative beliefs are also modified, in this case by how much the individual wants to comply with the wishes of these other people (i.e. the motivation to comply Mc_j). Again there will be a set of salient beliefs for each individual and the most frequent salient beliefs can be formed into a general set to be included in a standard questionnaire. The normative beliefs are multiplied by the motivation to comply and summed in order to predict the subjective norm:

$$SN = \sum NB_j \times Mc_j$$

This approach has been used widely in social psychology (e.g. Ajzen & Fishbein, 1980) and has recently been applied in the food choice area.

EXAMPLES OF USE IN FOOD RESEARCH

The Fishbein and Ajzen attitude model has been used in several studies of food selection. It has shown good prediction of behavioural intention from the attitude and subjective norm components. The attitude to behaviour component has generally been found to have greater predictive power than the subjective norm. Where belief items have been assessed, these have shown good prediction of the appropriate attitude and subjective norm components. Where actual behaviour has also been measured, behavioural intention has proved a good predictor of this.

Bonfield (1974) showed relatively good prediction of the choice of soft drinks from belief items. Axelson *et al.* (1983) investigated eating in fast-food restaurants and found the subjective norm component did not significantly predict behavioural intention, but this was well predicted by the attitude component. The summed belief-evaluation score predicted the attitude component. A factor analysis of the belief items showed two factors, which the authors described as organoleptic-nutritious and economic. There were some beliefs such as having limited selection, involving no cooking and the location of the restaurant, which did not load heavily on either factor.

Tuorila-Ollikainen *et al.* (1986) studied choice of low-salt bread, calculating the regression of the belief items directly against behavioural intention. The belief-value items were more closely related to behavioural intention than were the normative beliefs.

Tuorila (1987) investigated consumption of milks varying in fat content. The beliefs included sensory, nutritional, suitability and price items. Except for price these were reasonably related to the attitude score. Likewise the beliefs were most positive for the type of milk generally consumed, indicating the role played by these beliefs in determining behaviour. None of the evaluations differed for different milk users. The normative beliefs for family members most closely related to the subjective norm score and to the type of milk consumed.

Feldman & Mayhew (1984) used a model derived from that of Fishbein and Ajzen, but incorporating aspects of the Health Beliefs Model and Triandis' model. This adaption showed good prediction of self-reported meat and sodium consumption. Lewis & Booth (1985) likewise incorporated elements of the Fishbein and Ajzen model with aspects of the Health Beliefs Model to study dieting and weight loss. Schifter & Ajzen (1985) have used the theory of planned behaviour (an extension of the original Fishbein and Ajzen model) also to study weight loss.

Shepherd & Stockley (1985) reported a study on the consumption of foods contributing highly to fat intake in the average UK diet. Attitude was the better predictor of behaviour, with weights of $w_1 = 0.46$ and $w_2 = 0.15$ from the multiple regression and a multiple correlation of $R = 0.59$. The measure of frequency of consumption was also reasonably predictive of measured intake of fat as a percentage of energy over a 7-day period in a separate group of 30 subjects ($r = 0.58$). These findings were replicated by Shepherd and Stockley (1987), who found a score for nutritional knowledge was not related to either the attitude or behaviour scores.

Table Salt Use

Shepherd & Farleigh (1986*a*) investigated attitudes towards adding table salt to foods in a group of 81 subjects, and in a separate study (Shepherd & Farleigh, 1986*b*) 36 further subjects completed the same questionnaire. The data from all 117 subjects were analysed together.

Initially belief items were generated from short interviews. The belief items were that adding table salt to food (a) makes it taste better, (b) increases the risk of ill health, (c) replaces lost body salt,

(d) increases the risk of high blood pressure, (e) improves the food (other than taste). The responses were on seven-category scales labelled disagree and agree at the extremes. There were five corresponding items on each of these outcomes with seven-category scales labelled good and bad at the extremes.

Five normative belief items were chosen from the same interviews, on (a) members of the family (other than parents), (b) doctors, (c) food manufacturers, (d) parents, (e) nutritionists and dietitians. There were five corresponding items on motivation to comply. The questionnaire also included three attitude questions on whether adding table salt to food was good/bad, unpleasant/pleasant and harmful/beneficial, and a subjective norm item on whether most people who are important to the individual think he or she should add table salt to food. There was one question on how frequently the individual added table salt to food, which served as a measure of behavioural intention.

All of the responses were on seven-category scales and were scored from -3 to $+3$, except for the motivation to comply items which were scored from 0 to 6, since it has been suggested that responses on this scale tend to be unipolar rather than bipolar (Ajzen & Fishbein, 1980).

There was generally good prediction of table salt use from the components of the model. There was a multiple correlation of $R = 0.73$ for attitude and subject norm against behaviour, with the weighting for attitude being greater ($w_1 = 0.63$, $w_2 = 0.19$). The sum of the behaviour belief-evaluation scores correlated well with the overall attitude ($r = 0.59$), as did the normative component with subject norm ($r = 0.60$). In the 36 subjects where actual behaviour was measured over 7 days, this was well predicted by the behavioural intention score ($r = 0.64$).

Low-fat Milk Use

In the model proposed by Fishbein & Ajzen (1975), the beliefs are seen as being unitary; that is if a person holds some positive beliefs then the other beliefs should also be positive. This can be tested using statistics such as Cronbach's alpha coefficient (McKennell, 1970). This will be true for some behaviours but it might not be true in the case of choice of foods. For example, it is possible that a person might believe both that a food is very tasty and enjoyable but that it is also bad for health. Thus it might be predicted that there will be different belief structures related to different aspects of consumption of the food.

In order to test this assertion a questionnaire on consumption of low-fat milk was designed, based upon that by Tuorila (1987). One hundred and three subjects completed the questionnaire. The questionnaire included questions on the frequency of consumption of skimmed milk, semi-skimmed milk and whole-fat (silver top) milk; these consisted of seven categories labelled from '1 (or less) pints per week' to '7 (or more) pints per week'. There were three corresponding questions on behavioural intention to purchase each type of milk when next shopping for milk. There were four questions on attitude of whether buying low-fat milk was bad/good, unpleasant/pleasant, harmful/beneficial and undesirable/desirable.

There were no questions on the subjective norm or normative beliefs but instead the questionnaire concentrated on behaviour beliefs. Thirteen belief items were included which could be broken down into four groups of sensory attributes, nutritional, functional properties and price/value (see Table 1). The responses were on seven-category scales labelled 'strongly disagree' and 'strongly agree' at the extremes. There were thirteen corresponding outcome evaluation questions with responses on seven-category scales labelled 'bad' and 'good' at the extremes. All responses were scored from -3 to $+3$ (Ajzen & Fishbein, 1980), and were converted so that a positive score corresponded to a positive feeling towards consuming low-fat milk.

Scores were calculated for the relative intention towards low-fat milks by summing the scores for skimmed and semi-skimmed milks and subtracting the score for whole-fat milk. This was done for the intention scores and for frequency of behaviour. The belief-evaluation scores were summed for all thirteen beliefs and the correlation between this sum and the attitude score was found to be $r = 0.80$. In turn the attitude score was related to the score for behavioural intention ($r = 0.70$) and this was related to the behaviour score ($r = 0.68$).

In order to test how well the belief items did fall into the supposed separate groups, a principal components analysis (with varimax rotation) was calculated on the belief-evaluation scores. The solution involving two components was the most interpretable. These components accounted for 52% of the variance and the loadings on the components are shown in Table 1. The scores did not fall into four separate groups but rather the nutritional items formed a separate component, the sensory and functional items tended to relate on the first component but the price items were not so clear. Even in the

Table 1

Component loadings for the belief-evaluation scores from the principal components analysis of responses on the low-fat milk questionnaire ($n = 103$). All responses were scored to have a high score for a positive belief-evaluation

	Component	
Item	1	2
Sensory		
Tastes nice	0·70	0·40
Tastes watery	0·67	0·18
Can have off flavours	0·49	0·11
Leaves a greasy taste in the mouth	0·55	0·00
Nutritional		
Healthy	0·21	0·84
Fattening	0·12	0·77
Reduces my fat consumption	0·06	0·75
Functional		
Suitable for drinking by itself	0·63	0·35
Suitable for cooking	0·62	0·10
Suitable for tea or coffee	0·73	0·23
Price		
Expensive	0·04	0·21
Stays fresh for a long time	0·21	−0·06
Good value for money	0·52	0·28

three component solution where the items on 'stays fresh' and 'good value for money' loaded on the third component, the item on being expensive was not related to any of the components. This probably reflects the lack of a price differential for milks of different fat content.

The relative degree of prediction by these components was tested by calculating a multiple regression of the component scores against attitude. The multiple correlation was $R = 0.84$, with simple correlations and weightings for the two components shown in Table 2; it can be seen that the second component (relating to nutritional beliefs) was more closely related to the attitude. A separate multiple regression was calculated on the sums of the belief-evaluations split into the four original groups. These are also shown in Table 2. It can be seen that

Table 2
Correlations and multiple regression weights from regressions against attitude to behaviour of (1) scores on the first two components from the PCA on belief-evaluation items, (2) sums of belief-value scores on sensory, nutritional, functional and price aspects ($n = 103$). All correlations are significant at $p < 0.001$.

	Simple correlation	Weighting in multiple regression
Regression 1		
Component 1	0·73	0·18
Component 2	0·83	0·69
Regression 2		
Sensory	0·61	0·19
Nutritional	0·73	0·52
Functional	0·63	0·25
Price	0·40	0·13

the nutritional beliefs are most closely related to the attitude, followed by the functional and sensory attributes. There is a great deal of collinearity in these measures and the multiple correlation was $R = 0·84$.

These analyses show that the beliefs are not unitary but tend to differentiate between nutritional and other beliefs and that the nutritional beliefs tend to be more important in determining attitude towards the choice of low-fat milks. This is in contrast to other behaviours investigated (e.g. Shepherd & Farleigh, 1986*a*) and probably means that people who choose low-fat milks do so for health reasons rather than because of the sensory attributes. The relative importance of such factors will vary between foods.

CONCLUSIONS

The literature on attitudes, beliefs and food choice is confused. Part of the reason for this is that many of the studies lack a clear conceptual framework within which to study these relationships. One such attitudes model has been described here and has proved successful in a number of applications in the food area. In general the person's own attitude outweighs perceived social pressure. It would appear that the belief-values held by the individual are probably not unitary in the area of food choice and that people may hold beliefs which are inconsistent. Further exploration of this belief-value structure should reveal how important different types of beliefs (e.g. sensory and nutritional) are in determining food choice in particular contexts.

REFERENCES

Ajzen, I. & Fishbein, M. (1980). *Understanding Attitudes and Predicting Social Behavior*. Prentice-Hall, Englewood Cliffs, N.J.

Allen, C. D. & Ries, C. P. (1985). Smoking, alcohol, and dietary practices during pregnancy: Comparison before and after prenatal education. *J. Am. Dietet. Assoc.*, **85**, 605–6.

Allport, G. W. (1935). Attitudes. In *A Handbook of Social Psychology*, ed. C. Murchison. Clark University Press. Worcester, Mass, pp. 789–844.

Axelson, M. L., Brinberg, D. & Durand, J. H. (1983). Eating at a fast-food restaurant—A social-psychological analysis. *J. Nutr. Educ.*, **15**, 94–8.

Bonfield, E. H. (1974). Attitude, social influence, personal norms, and intention interactions as related to brand purchase behavior. *J. Marketing Res.*, **11**, 379–89.

Carruth, B. R., Mangel, M. & Anderson, H. L. (1977). Assessing change-proneness and nutrition-related behaviors. *J. Am. Dietet. Assoc.*, **70**, 47–53.

Douglas, P. D. & Douglas, J. G. (1984). Nutrition knowledge and food practices of high school athletes. *J. Am. Dietet. Assoc.*, **84**, 1198–202.

Eppright, E. S., Fox, H. M., Fryer, B. A., Lamkin, G. H. & Vivian, V. M. (1970). The North Central Regional study of diets of pre-school children. 2. Nutrition knowledge and attitudes of mothers. *J. Home Econ.*, **62**, 327–32.

Feldman, R. H. L. & Mayhew, P. C. (1984). Predicting nutrition behavior: The utilization of a social psychological model of health behavior. *Basic Appl. Soc. Psychol.*, **5**, 183–95.

Fishbein, M. & Ajzen, I. (1975). *Belief, Attitude, Intention and Behavior: An Introduction to Theory and Research*. Addison-Wesley, Reading, Mass.

Foley, C., Hertzler, A. A. & Anderson, H. L. (1979). Attitudes and food habits—a review. *J. Am. Dietet. Assoc.*, **75**, 13–18.

Foley, C. S., Vaden, A. G., Newell, G. K. & Dayton, A. D. (1983). Establishing the need for nutrition education: III. Elementary students' nutrition knowledge, attitudes, and practices. *J. Am. Dietet. Assoc.*, **83**, 564–8.

Grotkowski, M. L. & Sims, L. S. (1978). Nutritional knowledge, attitudes, and dietary practices in the elderly. *J. Am. Dietet. Assoc.*, **72**, 499–506.

Jalso, S. B., Burns, M. M. & Rivers, J. M. (1965). Nutritional beliefs and practices. *J. Am. Dietet. Assoc.*, **47**, 263–8.

Khan, M. A. (1981). Evaluation of food selection patterns and preferences. *CRC Critical Rev. Food Sci. Nutr.*, **15**, 129–53.

Krech, D. & Crutchfield, R. S. (1948). *Theory and Problems in Social Psychology*. McGraw-Hill, New York.

Lewis, V. J. & Booth, D. A. (1985). Causal influences within an individual's dieting thoughts, feelings and behaviour. In *Measurement and Determinants of Food Habits and Food Preferences*, eds J. M. Diehl & C. Leitzmann. EURO-NUT Report Number 7, Wageningen, The Netherlands, pp. 187–208.

Mattes, R. D. (1985). Gustation as a determinant of ingestion: Methodological issues. *Am. J. Clin. Nutr.*, **41**, 672–83.

Mattes, R. D., Kumanyika, S. K. & Halpern, B. P. (1983). Salt taste responsiveness and preference among normotensive, prehypertensive and hypertensive adults. *Chem. Senses*, **8**, 27–40.

McKennell, A. C. (1970). Attitude measurement: Use of coefficient alpha with cluster or factor analysis. *Sociology*, **4**, 227–45.

Meiselman, H. L. (1984). Consumer studies of food habits. In *Sensory Analysis of Foods*, ed. J. R. Piggott. Elsevier Applied Science, London, pp. 243–303.

Pangborn, R. M. & Giovanni, M. E. (1984). Dietary intake of sweet foods and of dairy fats and resultant gustatory responses to sugar in lemonade and to fat in milk. *Appetite*, **5**, 317–27.

Pangborn, R. M. & Pecore, S. D. (1982). Taste perception of sodium chloride in relation to dietary intake of salt. *Am. J. Clin. Nutr.*, **35**, 510–20.

Perron, M. & Endres, J. (1985). Knowledge, attitudes, and dietary practices of female athletes. *J. Am. Dietet. Assoc.*, **85**, 573–6.

Piggott, J. R. (1979). Food preferences of some United Kingdom residents. *J. Hum. Nutr.*, **33**, 197–205.

Randall, E. & Sanjur, D. (1981). Food preferences—Their conceptualization and relationship to consumption. *Ecol. Food Nutr.*, **11**, 151–61.

Schifter, D. E. & Ajzen, I. (1985). Intention, perceived control, and weight loss: An application of the theory of planned behavior. *J. Pers. Soc. Psychol.*, **49**, 843–51.

Schwartz, N. E. (1975). Nutritional knowledge, attitudes, and practices of high school graduates. *J. Am. Dietet. Assoc.*, **66**, 28–31.

Shepherd, R. (1988). The effects of nutritional beliefs and values on food acceptance. In *Food Acceptance and Nutrition*, eds J. Solms, D. A. Booth, R. M. Pangborn & O. Raunhardt. Academic Press, London, pp. 387–402.

Shepherd, R. & Farleigh, C. A. (1986a) Attitudes and personality related to salt intake. *Appetite*, **7**, 343–54.

Shepherd, R. & Farleigh, C. A. (1986b). Preferences, attitudes and personality as determinants of salt intake. *Hum. Nutr: Appl. Nutr.*, **40A**, 195–208.

Shepherd, R. & Stockley, L. (1985). Fat consumption and attitudes towards food with a high fat content. *Hum. Nutr: Appl. Nutr.*, **39A**, 431–42.

Shepherd, R. & Stockley, L. (1987). Nutrition knowledge, attitudes, and fat consumption. *J. Am. Dietet. Assoc.*, **87**, 615–19.

Shepherd, R., Farleigh, C. A. & Land, D. G. (1984). The relationship between salt intake and preferences for different salt levels in soup. *Appetite*, **5**, 281–90.

Sims, L. S. (1976). Demographic and attitudinal correlates of nutrition knowledge. *J. Nutr. Educ.*, **8**, 122–5.

Tuorila, H. (1987). Selection of milks with varying fat contents and related overall liking, attitudes, norms and intentions. *Appetite*, **8**, 1–14.

Tuorila-Ollikainen, H., Lahteenmaki, L. & Salovaara, H. (1986). Attitudes, norms, intentions and hedonic responses in the selection of low salt bread in a longitudinal choice experiment. *Appetite*, **7**, 127–39.

Werblow, J. A., Fox, H. M. & Henneman, A. (1978). Nutritional knowledge, attitudes, and food patterns of women athletes. *J. Am. Dietet. Assoc.*, **73**, 242–5.

Chapter 21

Behavioural Models in the Prediction of Consumption of Selected Sweet, Salty and Fatty Foods

HELY TUORILA* and ROSE MARIE PANGBORN

Department of Food Science and Technology, University of California, Davis, CA 95616, USA

ABSTRACT

Fishbein and Triandis' models of intention, and the Triandis model of behaviour and nutritional locus of control, were applied in a study on determinants of the consumption of milk, cheese, ice cream, chocolate, and regular and diet sodas amongst 100 females. Both the Fishbein and Triandis models gave good predictions, with multiple correlations varying from 0·45 to 0·90. The magnitude of the multiple correlation varied with product rather than model, and was highest for diet sodas and lowest for ice cream. Externality, as estimated on the locus of control scale, was a poor predictor of consumption behaviour for milk, cheese and regular sodas. The concepts applied, and the general usefulness of the models, are discussed

INTRODUCTION

In the present state of abundance of the western food supply, marketers, who are concerned with increasing sales, and public health

* Present address: Department of Food Chemistry and Technology, University of Helsinki, SF-00710, Helsinki, Finland.

agencies, who are aware of the contribution of diet to health, are interested in factors underlying and influencing human food selection. When studying these relationships, behavioural research information should be utilized, since food selection and consumption are a natural and integrated part of human behaviour.

The data discussed in this chapter were collected in order to explore and compare three social psychological approaches for food selection research: the Fishbein model of reasoned action (Ajzen & Fishbein, 1980), the Triandis models (Triandis, 1977, 1980) and the locus of control (Rotter, 1966). Various commonly used and nutritionally relevant sweet, salty and fatty foods (milk, cheese, ice cream, chocolate, regular and diet sodas) were studied.

THE APPROACHES USED

The Fishbein Model
In its shortest form, the Fishbein model of reasoned action (Ajzen & Fishbein, 1980) states that behavioural intention (I) is determined by a person's attitude (A_{act}) towards the behaviour and by his/her subjective norm (SN), i.e. by perceived social pressure, according to the equation:

$$I = w_1 \times A_{act} + w_2 \times SN \qquad w_1, w_2 = \text{relative weights, obtained by regression analysis}$$

According to Ajzen & Fishbein, when measuring behavioural intention, we obtain information also on actual behaviour (B), since intention is the best single predictor of behaviour.

The Fishbein model has been widely applied in research in social psychology (Fishbein & Ajzen, 1975) and marketing research (Ryan & Bonfield, 1975). Recently, it also has been applied in several food and nutrition related research studies, with reasonably good results (Axelson *et al.*, 1983; Shepherd & Stockley, 1985; Shepherd & Farleigh, 1986; Tuorila-Ollikainen *et al.*, 1986; Matheny *et al.*, 1987; Tuorila, 1987).

The Triandis Model
Triandis (1977, 1980) developed two equations for the description of the determinants of human behaviour. The first equation states that behavioural intention (I) is determined by affect associated with the

behaviour (A), by perceived consequences of the behaviour (C) and by social factors (S), which Triandis (1980) defines as an individual's conceptions of appropriate, desirable and morally correct behaviours:

$$I = w_3 A + w_4 C + w_5 S \qquad w_3, w_4, w_5 = \text{relative weights}$$

According to the second equation, the probability of an act (B) depends on the strength of the habit emitting the behaviour (H), intention (I) to emit the behaviour, and on facilitating conditions (Fc) which regulate the impact of H and I, by making them either easier or more difficult:

$$B = w_6 \, \text{Fc} \, H + w_7 \, \text{Fc} \, I \qquad w_6, w_7 = \text{relative weights}$$

According to Triandis, when a particular act is new for an individual, intention is relatively the most important factor in predicting behaviour. As the behaviour occurs more and more frequently, it tends to become more and more controlled by habit. He also points out the methodological limitation of the use of regression coefficients as indicators of relative weights, since inter-correlations which naturally occur between independent variables, can often lead to unreliable or biased regression coefficients.

Triandis (1980) cites numerous studies which support these equations. However, we located no published reports using the Triandis' equations in the food and nutrition area. The most closely related study is a comparison of the Fishbein and the Triandis models by Brinberg & Durand (1983) who studied intention and behaviour to eat in fast-food restaurants. Visits to these restaurants could be better predicted by a combination of habit and intention alone, rather than by the original equation which includes the facilitating factors ($R = 0\cdot41$, $R = 0\cdot28$, respectively).

Locus of Control

The locus of control theory (Rotter, 1966) deals with a human tendency to perceive one's own behaviour as being controlled by oneself (internally) or by others (externally). The external control can be exerted by 'powerful others' or by 'chance'. The theory has received much attention by those interested in health-related behaviour because of its potential to increase understanding of people's dispositions to their own health care (Wallston & Wallston, 1978). Scales specifically designed to measure the nutritional locus of control have been developed by Eden et al. (1984), and by Drewnowski (personal communication); the latter for the measurement of locus of control of obese patients, in particular. Pangborn (1987) and co-workers have used the nutritional locus of control scale in several food and nutrition related studies. The results indicate correlations between the locus of control and some intake and preference measures for sweet and salty tastes as well as shifts in the locus of control during a weight reduction diet.

METHOD

The subjects ($N = 100$) were young females who were mainly students at the University of California, Davis. These are described in detail elsewhere (Tuorila & Pangborn, 1988). They completed a question-naire in which various aspects of their consumption practices of the foods under study were queried. The parts of the questionnaire which were designed to test the two models, were constructed following, as closely as possible, the guidelines provided by Ajzen & Fishbein (1980) and Triandis (1977, 1980). Table 1 gives examples of items used to operationalize the components of the models.

There were several departures from the operational definitions suggested by the authors of the models: (1) Degree of liking was used as the operational definition of attitude in the Fishbein model, since previous research (Tuorila, 1987) had shown high correlations between this and the other evaluative scales, such as good-bad or pleasant-unpleasant, suggested by Ajzen & Fishbein (1980). (2) In the present experimental design, it was not possible to measure actual behaviour, as required by Trandis' second equation. Therefore, this variable was constructed as a mean of frequency of consumption, and consumption compared to others, which were highly correlated (range of $r = 0.58$–0.87). Frequency of consumption, in its various modifications, is a commonly utilized technique for the measurement of dietary intakes (Mullen *et al.*, 1984). (3) Frequency of consumption was not con-sidered to be an appropriate measure of habit for reasons which are discussed later. Besides, in this experimental design frequency of consumption was used for the estimation of the dependent variable.

For the measurement of nutrition locus of control, a shortened version of Drewnowski's scale was applied. Items specifically related to overweight were omitted, since these were not directly relevant for the present population, and only externality ('powerful others' and

Table 1
Items used in the study, with an example for ice cream

Component	Operationalization
Attitude/ affect	Rate your degree of liking of ice cream. Base your rating on the types, flavours or brands you use most frequently. Dislike extremely 1 2 3 4 5 6 7 Like extremely
Subjective norm	Most people who are important to me think that I should eat ice cream. Strongly disagree 1 2 3 4 5 6 7 Strongly agree
Consequences	Rate ice cream according to how good or bad it is for you. Extremely bad 1 2 3 4 5 6 7 Extremely good
Social norm	According to nutritionists, I should eat ice cream. Strongly disagree 1 2 3 4 5 6 7 Strongly agree
Facilitating conditions	Rate the ease or difficulty in obtaining ice cream when you feel like eating it. Extremely difficult 1 2 3 4 5 6 7 Extremely easy
Habit	I eat ice cream out of habit. Not at all 1 2 3 4 5 6 7 Very much so
Intention	I intend to have ice cream whenever I get the next opportunity, either as part of a meal or as a snack. Extremely unlikely 1 2 3 4 5 6 7 Extremely likely
Frequency of consumption (subscale of B)	How often do you eat ice cream? (Never or almost never = 1, 1–2 times a month = 2, Once a week = 3, 2–3 times a week = 4, At least once a day = 5)
Consumption compared to others (subscale of B)	Estimate your consumption of ice cream when compared to the consumption of other people of your age. (Very low = 1, Low = 2, The same = 3, High = 4, Very high = 5)
Nutritional locus of control	My family's food choices often determine what I eat. Strongly disagree 1 2 3 4 5 6 7 Strongly agree
Nutritional locus of control	My choice of foods is greatly influenced by unpredictable circumstances. Strongly disagree 1 2 3 4 5 6 7 Strongly agree

'chance') was measured. This resulted in eight items, two examples of which are given in Table 1.

Data analysis showed significant correlations between items related to powerful others and chance, and these items did not load on separate factors in factor analysis. Therefore, a scale of externality, based on all eight items, was constructed, resulting in a Cronbach's $\alpha = 0.72$.

RESULTS

Mean values obtained for each of the components of the models are presented in Table 2. The affect/attitude ratings (A) were highest for cheese, ice cream and chocolate, and lowest for sodas, with milk being intermediate. Milk and cheese were considered good for you (C) and as being approved by 'most important people' (SN) and by nutritionists (S), whereas the remaining items were, on average, 'bad for you' and disapproved of by 'important others' and nutritionists. Intention to consume (I) was highest for milk and cheese and lowest for regular sodas. Product-to-product variation of mean ratings of habit (H) and facilitating factors (Fc) was relatively small. Cheese was consumed most frequently, sodas least frequently (B). Of the six foods, cheese was the only one with reported average consumption higher than 'people of my age' (B).

The multiple correlations obtained for the Fishbein and Triandis equations ranged from 0.45 to 0.90 (Table 3). The prediction was highest for diet sodas and lowest for ice cream. Both models of intention (I) showed approximately equal predictive power.

Affect, or attitude (A), was the predominant predictor in the intention models. However, the subjective norm (SN) of the Fishbein model was also a significant predictor in four cases (ice cream, chocolate and sodas). Perceived consequences (C) of the Triandis model was likewise, a significant predictor in four cases (milk, ice cream, chocolate and regular sodas). Social norm (S) was the weakest predictor, being significant only in one case (diet sodas).

Triandis' model of behaviour (B) gave better prediction without the 'facilitating factors' (Fc) than in its original form. Intention (I) was more important than habit (H) in these models, with the exception of sodas, for which habit was equally or more important.

The correlations between consumption variables (I, B) and externality, were significant in only five out of twelve cases, which is in line

Table 2

Mean responses to components of Fishbein and Triandis' models. For scales, see Table 1

Product	Attitude/ affect (A)	Subjective norm (SN)	Consequences (C)	Social norm (S)	Facilitation (Fc)	Habit (H)	Intention (I)	Behaviour (B) Frequency	Behaviour (B) Compared to others
Milk	4·8	5·2	6·1	6·4	6·0	4·0	4·7	2·8	2·8
Cheese	5·8	4·6	5·4	4·8	5·5	3·5	4·9	4·2	3·3
Ice cream	5·7	3·7	3·4	3·4	4·7	3·4	3·1	3·1	2·5
Chocolate	5·7	2·9	2·7	2·0	4·8	3·4	3·0	3·2	2·7
Regular sodas	3·1	2·8	2·0	2·1	5·1	2·4	2·2	2·4	1·5
Diet sodas	3·6	3·3	2·3	2·6	5·3	3·1	3·1	2·5	2·2

Table 3

Standardized regression coefficients and multiple correlations (R) for the Fishbein and Triandis' models, and correlations between consumption behaviour (I, B) and external locus of control

Food equation	Attitude/ affect (A)	Subjective norm (SN)	Conse- quences (C)	Social norm (S)	Habit (FcH/H)	Intention (FcI/I)	R/r
Milk							
$I = A + SN$	0·62[c]	0·09					0·65[c]
$I = A + C + S$	0·62[c]		0·18[a]	0·00			0·67[c]
$B = FcH + Fcl$					0·19[a]	0·63[c]	0·75[c]
$B = H + I$					0·22[b]	0·69[c]	0·82[c]
$I \times$ External							0·15
$B \times$ External							0·24[b]
Cheese							
$I = A + SN$	0·64[c]	0·06					0·65[c]
$I = A + C + S$	0·65[c]		0·09	0·15			0·68[c]
$B = FcH + Fcl$					0·07	0·70[c]	0·75[c]
$B = H + I$					0·11	0·75[c]	0·80[c]
$I \times$ External							−0·23[b]
$B \times$ External							−0·28[b]
Ice cream							
$I = A + SN$	0·33[c]	0·26[b]					0·45[c]
$I = A + C + S$	0·30[b]		0·26[a]	0·05			0·47[c]
$B = FcH + FCl$					0·14	0·43[c]	0·53[c]
$B = H + I$					0·23[a]	0·47[c]	0·63[c]
$I \times$ External							0·16
$B \times$ External							0·07
Chocolate							
$I = A + SN$	0·37[c]	0·35[c]					0·54[c]
$I = A + C + S$	0·39[c]		0·36[c]	−0·12			0·53[c]
$B = FcH + Fcl$					0·20[a]	0·51[c]	0·66[c]
$B = H + I$					0·28[c]	0·57[b]	0·74[c]
$I \times$ External							0·04
$B \times$ External							−0·04
Regular sodas							
$I = A + SN$	0·63[c]	0·17[a]					0·67[c]
$I = A + C + S$	0·55[c]		0·20[a]	0·13			0·70[c]
$B = FcH + FCl$					0·49[c]	0·38[c]	0·82[c]
$B = H + I$					0·57[c]	0·40[c]	0·90[c]
$I \times$ External							0·25
$B \times$ External							0·23

Table 3   (continued)

Food equation	Attitude/ affect (A)	Subjective norm (SN)	Conse- quences (C)	Social norm (S)	Habit (FcH/H)	Intention (FcI/I)	R/r
Diet sodas							
I = A + SN	0·75^c	0·19^b					0·84^c
I = A + C + S	0·84^c		−0·03	0·13^a			0·83^c
B = FcH + FcI					0·43^c	0·50^c	0·88^c
B = H + I					0·43^c	0·53^c	0·90^c
I × External							0·14
B × External							0·12

^{a} Significant at $p > 0.05$.
^{b} Significant at $p > 0.01$.
^{c} Significant at $p > 0.001$.

with the low predictive value of subjective norm (SN) and social factors (S) of the Fishbein and Triandis equations. In the case of milk and regular sodas, the consumption or intention to consume increased with externality, whereas for cheese, the consumption and externality were inversely related.

DISCUSSION

Method
Although the potential biases in verbal reports are well recognized (Nisbett & Wilson, 1977), asking questions is still a useful method, provided that the limitations are acknowledged (Ericsson & Simon, 1980). However, richer and more truthful or valid information on food selection would result from a combination of data from various sources, e.g. surveys, observations of behaviour, qualitative interviews and sensory tests with specific products. It is likely that with a one-level measurement, such as the present one, the measures tend to converge and results appear more consistent than the connections between measured variables really are.

Models
In a study by Shepherd & Stockley (1985), the amount of milk consumed and frequency of consuming cheese were predicted by the

Fishbein model with multiple correlations of 0·49 and 0·45, respectively. The subjective norm was significant only for the prediction of milk consumption. Another study on different types of milk yielded multiple correlations varying from 0·43 to 0·60. Subjective norm was significant only for the consumption of regular fat milk (Tuorila, 1987). The multiple correlations obtained in this study, using the Fishbein model, are comparatively high ($R = 0·65$ for both milk and cheese). The relative importance of the components corresponds well with all earlier food-related results obtained using this model, showing the importance of attitude and the minor role of norm. There is no immediate explanation for the fact that prediction varies according to the product, being high for sodas and lower, particularly for ice cream. Possibly, the predictability of the consumption of regular and diet sodas was based on established practices to favour either one or another, which may polarize any evaluations or ratings related to them.

A few studies have compared the Fishbein and Triandis models. Brinberg & Durand (1983) found that the Fishbein model (as a matter of fact the attitude component of it) was superior to the Triandis model of behaviour for the prediction of visits to fast-food restaurants. Moreover, they reported an improved prediction by the Triandis model when the facilitating conditions were excluded from the equation; a finding also obtained in this study.

The predictions obtained by both models of intention generally correspond to results obtained in a study on church attendance which compared the Fishbein and Triandis models of intention (Brinberg, 1979). However, in this study, the Triandis model yielded slightly better predictions. Interestingly, both social factors and perceived consequences were important predictors, indicating the variability of factors which control divergent human activities.

Of the approaches used, the Triandis models seem to be most relevant for food selection research for two reasons. The model of intention includes parts which people customarily use as reasonings for their food selection (liking, good for you; Tuorila & Pangborn, 1988). Also, Triandis takes habits into consideration, defining them as situation-behaviour sequences that are or have become automatic, so that they occur without self-instruction. Habit is probably very important in the case of activities such as eating which is repeated several times every day. If habits were not developed for such behaviours, considerable mental resource would be tied up in making detailed decisions on non-productive issues. Thus, habit can be viewed as a way of rationalizing and simplifying everyday life. But what is habit? Triandis' objective was to develop a theoretical framework which 'includes variables that are general and abstract enough to be relevant to any investigation, in any culture' (1980, p. 198). He is less concerned about measurement techniques. His suggestions for the operational definition of habit (frequency of occurrence of behaviour, subjects' judgements of the likelihood that behaviour will take place in different situations, or frequency of behaviour in the past) does not cover his conceptual definition, or, at least, covers only a small portion of it. Wittenbraker et al. (1983), when studying attitudes to seat belts, criticized the operational definition and ended up by asking their subjects to rate frequency of wearing seat belt 'by force of habit'. A somewhat similar approach was used in this study when subjects were asked to state the degree of habit involved in their consumption. Our modification does not adequately correspond to the conceptual definition either, although it was considered sufficient for exploratory purposes. Also, it is possible that, by adopting a slightly different definition, the influence of habit has changed in the prediction models.

The characteristics of habit, as described by food habit researchers, shows its many dimensions. When outlining food habit research, Grivetti & Pangborn (1973) described seven major approaches, which dealt with many possible relationships between people, communities and food. In nutrition education, food habits are defined as 'the kinds of food eaten, when and how much; considered in terms of what people eat on a fairly consistent basis' (Anon., 1980). Perhaps the concept of habit is so complex and fluctuating that its adequate operational definition becomes an obstacle for the utilization of the Triandis model.

Application of Models

Although liking was found to be the predominant, and social factors only a minor predictor in established consumption situations, it is not justified to conclude that social factors can be excluded from an analysis of food-related problems. For instance, if the models were applied in the measurement of psychological processes during a dietary change, it is possible that social forces rather than liking would control intakes. Liking, as a concept, can be viewed as a general disposition which is formed and modified through internalization (Rozin, 1982).

The internalization can take place under different pressures, for instance in mere exposure or social reinforcement.

Finally, in food and nutrition research, our ultimate task is not to prove that we can produce multiple correlations as high as the original authors of models. Rather, we should use these models, and explore which of them is most helpful in increasing our understanding of food selection processes. Thus, models which were developed in another research area have provided the opportunity to approach our research problems from a different angle, thus enriching the analysis.

REFERENCES

Ajzen, I. & Fishbein, M. (1980). *Understanding Attitudes and Predicting Social Behavior*. Prentice-Hall, New Jersey.

Anon. (1980). Eating patterns. In *Directions for Nutrition Education Research—the Penn State Conferences,* eds L. S. Sims & L. Light. College of Human Development and United States Department of Agriculture, Pennsylvania, pp. 27–38.

Axelson, M. L., Brinberg, D. & Durand, J. H. (1983). Eating at a fast-food restaurant—a social-psychological analysis. *J. Nutr. Educ., 15*, 94–98.

Brinberg, D. (1979). An examination of the determinants of intention and behavior: a comparison of two models. *J. Appl. Social Psychol., 9*, 560–75.

Brinberg, D. & Durand, J. (1983). Eating at fast-food restaurants: an analysis using two behavioral intention models. *J. Appl. Social Psychol., 13*, 459–72.

Eden, I., Kamath, S. K., Kohrs, M. B. & Olson, R. E. (1984). Perceived control of nutrition behavior: a study of the locus of control theory among healthy subjects. *J. Am. Dietet. Assoc., 84*, 1334–9.

Ericsson, K. A. & Simon, H. A. (1980). Verbal reports as data. *Psychol. Rev., 87*, 215–51.

Fishbein, M. & Ajzen, I. (1975). *Belief, Attitude, Intention and Behavior: an Introduction to Theory and Research.* Addison-Wesley, Reading, MA.

Grivetti, L. E. & Pangborn, R. M. (1973). Food habit research: a review of approaches and methods. *J. Nutr. Educ., 5*, 204–7.

Matheny, R. J., Picciano, M. F. & Birch, L. (1987). Attitudinal and social influences on infant-feeding preference. *J. Nutr. Educ., 19*, 21–31.

Mullen, B. J., Krantzler, N. J., Grivetti, L. E., Schutz, H. G. & Meiselman, H. L. (1984). Validity of a food frequency questionnaire for the determination of individual food intake. *Am. J. Clin. Nutr., 39*, 136–43.

Nisbett, R. E. & Wilson, T. D. (1977). Telling more than we can know: verbal reports on mental processes. *Psychol. Rev., 84*, 231–59.

Pangborn, R. M. (1987). Relationship of personal traits and attitudes to acceptance of food attributes. In *Food Acceptance and Nutrition.* eds J. Solms, D. A. Booth, R. M. Pangborn & O. Raunhardt. Academic Press, London, pp. 353–70.

Pilgrim, F. J. & Kamen, J. M. (1963). Predictors of human food consumption. *Science,* **139,** 501–2.

Rotter, J. B. (1966). Generalized expectancies for internal versus external control of reinforcement. *Psychol. Monogr.,* **80** (whole No. 609).

Rozin, P. (1982). Human food selection: the interaction of biology, culture and individual experience. In *The Psychobiology of Human Food Selection,* ed. L. M. Barker. Ellis Horwood, Chichester, pp. 225–54.

Ryan, M. J. & ·Bonfield, E. H. (1975). The Fishbein extended model and consumer behavior. *J. Consumer Res.,* **2,** 118–36.

Shepherd, R. & Farleigh, C. A. (1986). Attitudes and personality related to salt intake. *Appetite,* **7,** 343–54.

Shepherd, R. & Stockley, L. (1985). Fat consumption and attitudes towards foor with a high fat content. *Human Nutr. Appl. Nutr.,* **39A,** 431–42.

Triandis, H. (1977). *Interpersonal Behavior.* Brooks/Cole, Monterey.

Triandis, H. (1980). Values, attitudes, and interpersonal behavior. In *Nebraska Symposium on Motivation,* eds H. E. Howe & M. M. Page. University of Nebraska Press, Lincoln/London, pp. 195–259.

Tuorila, H. (1987). Selection of milks with varying fat contents and related overall liking, attitudes, norms and intentions. *Appetite,* **8,** 1–14.

Tuorila, H. & Pangborn, R. M. (1988). Prediction of consumption behavior of selected fat-containing foods. *Appetite* (in press).

Tuorila-Ollikainen, H., Lähteenmäki, L. & Salovaara, H. (1986). Attitudes, norms, intentions and hedonic responses in the selection of low salt bread in a longitudinal choice experiment. *Appetite,* **7,** 127–39.

Wallston, B. S. & Wallston, K. A. (1978). Locus of control and health: a review of the literature. *Health Educ. Monogr.,* **6,** 107–17.

Wittenbraker, J., Gibbs, B. L. & Kahle, L. R. (1983). Seat belt attitudes, habits, and behaviors: an adaptive amendment to the Fishbein model. *J. Appl. Social Psychol.,* **13,** 406–21.

Topic 6

Food Acceptability and Quality
as a Basis for Marketing

Chapter 22

Using Sensory Resources to Identify Successful Products

HERBERT STONE

Tragon Corporation, 365 Convention Way, Redwood City, CA 94063, USA

ABSTRACT

Determining that a product will be successful in the marketplace is a difficult and costly process. Competition and the complexities of the marketplace dictate that use is made of available resources and particularly those that can provide an early indication of a product's potential. Sensory evaluation and the acceptance model represent resources that are under-utilized and often misused in an attempt to be successful. Sensory information can be obtained quickly and at minimal cost compared to other product information sources.

This presentation focuses on how sensory evaluation should be used to be more effective in the introduction of successful products. The unique features of the sensory model, and in particular the acceptance model, will be described, including respondents, test designs and questionnaires, and the analyses of responses. This will be contrasted with the marketing research model. Various examples of tests will be presented and discussed.

INTRODUCTION

Today's competitive marketplace dictates that a comprehensive approach is used to develop quality products that are well liked and satisfy specific consumer needs. A comprehensive approach to product development should be both global in the technology that is used and in the sources of information that are developed. At the same time, it must be very specific in the nature of that information, particularly as it relates to the individual for whom the product is intended. A comprehensive approach to product development must make use of technology to yield a product that has unique sensory characteristics. This reduces product vulnerability in the marketplace and forces competition to invest more capital in their marketing effort. Much has been written in the technical, marketing and advertising literature about techniques for the development of products (for an extensive list of this literature, see Meyer, 1984). In recent years attention has been given to the use of statistical models to delineate consumer behaviour with regard to products, identifying optimal products, and so forth. It is clear that there are no single or easy options for developing successful products; however, there are possibilities for reducing risk and, at the least, minimizing failure because of product deficiencies. It is also clear that there is only limited appreciation for the different information sources and how they can be used to facilitate the product development process. This situation leads most observers to conclude that developing successful products is a high risk venture or alternatively, the testing process is a risk that must be taken. This risk is not resolved by technology alone nor is it solved by the marketplace alone. Each year hundreds of products are introduced (usually preceded by thousands of individual projects) and at least 90% quickly disappear not to be seen again for at least another few years.

The reasons for continued development and introduction of new products are numerous, including the business need for growth and profits, the impact of new technology, and the consumer's willingness to try new and innovative products that offer an alternative to what they now purchase. For some companies the risk of new product failure is thought to be minimized by extensive testing with consumers such that the testing develops a life of its own, continuing for many months and in some instances, several years. With so much information, significant effects are easily obtained and often for variables unrelated to that specific test objective. This is particularly true of tests with large numbers of respondents or when results from tests done many months apart are combined. After all, tests are fielded in numerous locations and the potential for conflicting information is high. Perhaps even more critical is the product which may be difficult to prepare consistently while development is in progress. Product is never the same from one test to another. This leads to relatively high scores in one test and much lower scores on another test, causing uneasiness among project management. In many instances this can be traced to product differences about which management is unaware. Unfortunately, this leads to even more testing in an effort to reassure management, but merely adds more confusion because the product formulation issue is not resolved. Alternatively, products can be introduced with no testing and the cost savings that are realized are used to introduce the next new product with the expectation that (sooner or later) one of the products will be successful. While this approach might have considerable initial appeal, it too has not proven to be very successful and in the long term is more costly because of the expense of manufacturing and distributing product to the marketplace with no indication of its potential. As might be expected, most companies fit within these extremes and are always considering alternatives that will increase the likelihood for product success.

This discussion focuses on selected aspects of the evaluation of products with particular emphasis on the use of sensory evaluation as a timely and cost effective resource for assessing products.

THE CONSUMER TEST

Measuring consumer responses to products is considered as a critical part of the development effort and major emphasis is given to this activity. Regardless of the amount of testing, there are several particularly important issues that are often overlooked in the rush to obtain a response from the consumer. The first is to know what kind of information (and type of test) is needed; the second is the ability to fully understand the relative strength of a test and of the result; and the third is to be able to juxtapose all the results to reach actionable recommendations. All these issues are operating within an environment in which objectives and target population often are changed or, in the case of the target population, is not well defined. In addition, given the inclination to ask everything of a respondent, questions are included in a test that are not fully understood, often to the detriment of both the development effort and the evaluation process.

There are numerous examples of consumer test practices that can lead to conflicting information and it is worthwhile to describe a few of them (see also Stone & Sidel, 1981). The first is to field a study in multiple cities, obtaining responses from about 20 consumers in each location. Results are pooled and a generalized conclusion is reached without any determination that the pooling is justified. Without considering the nature of the test, it is obvious that this is as much a test of differences in fielding practices as it is a test of products within and across test locations. Cell sizes in each location are generally so small that any skewed response patterns would not be recognized. The popularity of this approach derives from the generalized finding and the knowledge that the test will be fielded in all locations within the same time, thus enabling a deadline to be met. It takes considerably less time to recruit 20 than it does 150 or more people at a single location. This is probably the least important basis for selecting a test protocol.

A second, equally suspect procedure is use of the consumer to provide detailed information about a product's sensory attributes as a basis for reformulation, improvement, and so forth. This is probably the single most difficult of problems to contend with and reflects confusion as to what the consumer is capable of communicating versus the consumer's ability to complete a scorecard. It also represents a lack of familiarity with sensory evaluation procedures, and the mistaken belief that responses obtained from consumers are equated with validity, or alternatively, validity is a function of the number of consumers who participate in a test.

That an individual is capable of responding to questions asked by an interviewer or of completing a scorecard on their own regardless of its length should come as no surprise to anyone who has fielded a consumer test. After all, the consumer is compensated to complete this task. Completion of a scorecard is not, by itself, evidence that the task was understood. If it requires as many as 10–12 h to screen and train an individual to function reliably as a subject in a descriptive test (only about 50% of those who volunteer pass screening), how is it possible that an inexperienced and untrained consumer can operate with the same degree of precision and reliability within the space of 30 or 40 min? The example shown in Table 1, albeit an abbreviated one, is very typical of the differences between the naive consumer and the trained subject in their use of words to communicate perceptions about a product, let alone understand the meaning of those words. Besides the greater detail provided by the trained panel in describing the sensations, word meaning is clarified and differences between products are more easily obtained. These are important issues; they

Table 1
Examples of product attribute descriptions developed by
consumers and trained subjects for a beer/beverage[a]

Consumer	Trained subject
Filling	Fruity-similar to banana
Thick	Reference
Consistent	Sour (acid)-similar to citrus
Lot of alcohol	(not spoiled or decomposed)
Rich	Yeast-like sourdough bread
Refreshing	Aroma
Clean	Papery-stale, old beer,
	reminded of paper or
	cardboard
	Gummy-sensation of coating tongue,
	somewhat like cooking oil

[a] See text for explanation of the listing of words.

directly impact on the validity of the final result. It also is pertinent to note that the consumer tends to provide conceptual rather than perceptual terms when asked to describe a product. The ability to separate conceptual and perceptual comes with training and practice and evidence in the form of responses obtained in a controlled test situation. Some investigators have proposed that this time and training and the inherent weakness in consumer sensitivity and reliability can be overcome either through use of increased numbers of respondents or through use of various inferential statistical techniques. While there are data reduction techniques and multivariate models to identify product characteristics important to preference, the assumption that statistical methods can be used to substitute for recognition of specific characteristics, without regard for individual differences in sensitivity and reliability is, at best, questionable.

Consumer testing is an essential element in the overall decision-making process with regard to the likelihood for product success. While it is relatively easy to identify and criticize the weaknesses of the consumer and particularly the consumer testing process, sensory methods are not without their own weaknesses. Consider those listed for the three categories of sensory methods, as shown in Table 2. The limitations of each are a reflection of the type of information required and the specific type of subject skills that are required. The consumer

Table 2
Limitations of sensory test methods

Discrimination
  Result limited to whether difference is perceived
  Requires qualified subjects
  Judgement criterion (or criteria) unknown
  Methodology can be product specific
Descriptive
  Provides no measure of preference
  Requires qualified and specially trained subjects
  Requires several sessions to obtain reliable results
  Sensitivity may exceed the technology
  Provides no measure of the importance of each attribute
Affective
  Passive response
  Limited number of subjects
  Results can be extrapolated but not generalized

may not have the level of skill for the specialized sensory task; however, the consumer can provide information not obtainable in an unbiased form from the trained subject; for example, preference, purchase intent, and so forth. All participants are important and have something to contribute; it is the responsibility of the test specialist (sensory or market research) to be sure that the test is planned to address the specific problem and that the responses are not misunderstood or misused. This is true whether one is working with consumers or trained subjects; however, the action that is taken will not necessarily be the same. Consider the example shown in Table 3 which contains summaries from three tests. The first is typical of a consumer test, in which a series of attributes (as many as ten or more) are listed along with three- or five-point just-about-right scales (one per attribute). The proportion of responses is listed, providing obvious direction for product change. There are recommended statistical procedures for the analysis of just-about-right responses; however, for this discussion the most commonly used procedure, comparison of percentages, is used (see Stone & Sidel, 1985). For most food products, a 70% proportion in the just-about-right category constitutes evidence that the particular attribute does not need changing, and conversely, lower percentages constitute a basis for product change. The second set of values are the mean preference scores (using the

Table 3
Consumer and trained panel responses to a specific product attribute and preference[a]

	Product	
	A	B
Consumer descriptive, $N = 100$		
Not enough vanilla	34[b]	33
Just about right	57	50
Too much vanilla	9	17
Consumer preference, $N = 100$		
9-point hedonic scale	7·0[c]	6·5
Trained panel, $N = 12$		
Vanilla flavour	28·3[d]	35·6
Flavour intensity (0–60 intensity scale)	31·6	39·5

[a] Results excerpted from a study of frozen dairy dessert item.
[b] Entries are percentages.
[c] Mean scores based on 9-point hedonic scale with 9-like extremely and 1-dislike extremely.
[d] Mean scores based on 60-pt scale with 0-no detection and 60-maximum, obtained from 12 subjects and 4 replicates per subject.

9-point hedonic scale) from these same consumers, and the third are mean intensity scores for two of the attributes from a QDA test (Stone & Sidel, 1985). Considering only the just-about-right results, the recommendation would be for an increase in vanilla flavour with the expectation that preference also will be increased. Inasmuch as Product A was preferred (i.e. it was scored significantly higher than B) it would be reasonable to focus development attention on this product. However, the trained panel results do not support this decision, as Product A had significantly lower scores for vanilla flavour and flavour intensity and any formulation change leading to an increase in the intensities would likely result in reduced preference (A, 28·3 and 31·6 versus B, 35·6 and 39·5, and the preferences were 7·0 and 6·5, respectively). Taken together, these results raise several issues: one is the assumption that the just-about-right scale provides more than what is 'about-right'; another is the assumption that specific product changes can be directed from this type of response. This is not to suggest that results from the just-about-right scale are invalid or any less useful than the intensity results from the trained panel (a second and equally important question). Both are providing different kinds of information and both should be used for different purposes. The just-about-right scale is a dichotomous, discrete type of scale with three categories, two of which provide direction and the third is the neutral or just-about-right category. The use of this scale is an adaption from its use in surveys of social attitudes and opinions. While it has been adapted to provide direction for product change as in the case of the aforementioned example, the results can be deceiving. As Payne (1951) noted, . . . 'it makes the replies seem definite when they may not be; it forces their answers to conform to the questioner's preconceived notion of the issue'. Consider the vanilla, for which 34% of the respondents indicated it was too strong. The questions confronting the experimenter are: (1) are the 34% stating that the flavour is too strong, or that the quality of the flavour is not correct; (2) will a change in vanilla intensity satisfy most of the 34% but dissatisfy an equal proportion of the 54% who thought vanilla was about right; (3) do the respondents know what is meant by vanilla flavour? What may appear obvious to the product specialists may not be clear to the respondent who has had no prior training or specialized knowledge about the product and its ingredients. Much of the difficulty associated with the product development process can be directly traced to either improper use of resources or an inability to understand the limitations of one's resources.

This brief assessment of the product evaluation process serves as a basis for discussing how sensory resources can impact favourably on the product development process. The next section focuses on the use of sensory resources as an integral part of this process. It also includes a brief description of specific methods but with emphasis on their applications.

DEVELOPING SENSORY RESOURCES

For sensory evaluation to contribute in a meaningful way, it must have the resources and a management commitment that is clear and unambiguous. Sensory evaluation is a relatively new function and most companies do not have a clear understanding of its purpose nor is there a full appreciation for its importance in the overall decision-making process. Sensory information is unique and cost effective and is not easily obtained by other means. Because it is unique there is always interest in control of this information; hence the emphasis on having independent sensory resources.

Developing sensory resources derives from a well organized, management-approved plan, knowledgeable sensory staff, qualified subjects, methods, facilities and support services. For the purposes of this discussion, professional staff, facilities and support services are assumed to be in place and fully operational. The importance of having an organized and fully integrated sensory resource that is supported by management cannot be emphasized enough. Too often sensory resources are based on nothing more than a single test method in the mistaken belief that problems are solved by methods alone. Such resources never contribute in a meaningful way nor do they survive for very long. For a more comprehensive discussion on all the organizational issues involved in developing and operating sensory resources, the reader is referred to Stone & Sidel (1985) and Sidel & Stone (1986). As shown in Table 4, there are three basic types of methods used in product development. The latter two are relied on almost exclusively because the type of information provided is more helpful.

In addition to methods, qualified subjects are a necessary part of the evaluation process. Just as there are different kinds of test methods, there also are different kinds of subjects, all of whom have varying levels of skill. Inasmuch as sensory tests use limited numbers of subjects (20 or fewer for analytical and not more than 50 for affective tests), it is extremely important that those selected for a test are qualified (empirically) for the product and the method. Table 5 lists

Table 4
The three types of sensory test methods

Discrimination	Are product differences perceived at the appropriate level of significance?
Descriptive	What are the perceived sensory characteristics and their relative intensities?
Affective	How well is the product liked?

Note: There is no universal test method.

Table 5
Characteristics of subjects

• There is no universal or all-purpose subject
• All individuals have varying levels of sensory skill
• Sensory skills require practice to develop
• Sensory skills may be product specific
• The skill of an individual must be monitored on a regular basis

key factors to consider when developing subject resources. For example, about 30% of those individuals who express an interest in sensory testing will fail to meet minimum discrimination test qualifying criteria (specific product discrimination ability). A further 20% will fail to meet descriptive qualifying criteria. For affective testing the failure percentage is smaller, reflecting the less stringent nature of the task. It is clear that selecting the appropriate subjects for a test is difficult and time-consuming and individuals exhibit considerable variation in terms of sensitivity, reliability and rate of learning a sensory task. Failure to appreciate the consequence of including unqualified subjects will increase the risk of reaching incorrect product decisions.

SENSORY APPLICATIONS

As already noted, developing products is difficult and time-consuming. In many instances the objective is not well-defined or it changes as a result of new information (or new project management) in the course of the development effort. Sensory resources are particularly helpful because they provide information quickly and in a quantitative context.

Descriptive

The descriptive test enables a product benchmark to be obtained from a product concept or from the more traditional product itself. Such a benchmark is helpful when comparing prototypes and other early versions of a product, as well as for comparison when the concept or the project focus changes. Since the descriptive method provides quantitative results within 2 or 3 days or less, it provides project managers with rapid decision-making. Once a project shifts from the concept stage to actual product formulation using commercially available ingredients, the descriptive model is used to determine how current formulations differ from a target, and the effects of ingredient amounts and types on finished product quality. The descriptive model helps focus the development effort particularly when linked with preference results. Product formulation efforts can easily yield more products than can be tested in a reasonable time period and an independent assessment is useful to determine if the effort is justified. Because the descriptive model is a multiproduct resource, there are considerable efficiencies to be realized throughout the development process.

The descriptive information has other applications, including input to quality control and to marketing research. For the former, the results help establish the sensory effect of a specific ingredient while for the latter, it identifies which attributes are likely to be detected by the consumer. Equally important is the permanent sensory record of a product which can now be used to address questions such as: has product changed since last tested or what are the effects of a series of cost reductions on specific product attributes.

Acceptance

Use of the sensory acceptance model also contributes in a timely and cost effective manner. It provides an early measure of preference, the effect of ingredients and process variables on preference and determines whether external testing is warranted. Testing requires no more than 2 or 3 h and results are obtainable shortly thereafter. The sensory affective model is particularly useful because it can be used with limited numbers (about 40 to 50) of qualified employees or local residents, multiple products can be evaluated, and the results used as a basis for action relative to larger scale testing. For sensory evaluation the 9-point hedonic scale is the method of choice based on research, an extensive data base, and its validity in product decision-making (Peryam & Pilgrim, 1957; Moskowitz & Sidel, 1971) As shown in Table 6, results can be presented in different ways to better understand which product is the most likely candidate for further development. It is clear from the analysis that the means for the products were not different; however, the response patterns by serving order suggest that Products B and C exhibited an advantage. Of the two, Product C experienced the least amount of change (0.3 scale points versus 0.8 for B) as a function of serving order. The ranks and average magnitudes of difference confirmed the rejection of A but the differences between

Table 6
Results derived from use of the 9-point hedonic
scale[a]

	Serving order			
Product	1	2	3	Total
A	6·8	6·3	6·4	6·5 ⎤ [b]
B	7·3	6·7	6·5	6·8 ⎥
C	7·0	6·7	6·7	6·8 ⎦
Total N = 48	7·0	6·6	6·5	

Scores converted to ranks and magnitudes of
difference

A:B	2:12 (2 ties)	1·02:1·97
A:C	3:12 (1)	1·13:2·02
B:C	5:8 (3)	1·43:1·50

[a] Also available: frequency distribution, magnitude of differences and their frequencies. See text for more information about the entries.
[b] Means within bracket are not significantly different.

B and C were too small to identify a clear, winning candidate. If only one product were selected then it would be C. Such a detailed examination of results is essential if the development specialist is to have meaningful direction from sensory evaluation. This is part of the overall scheme of minimizing risk and enhancing the likelihood for success in any larger scale testing.

This discussion has focused on selected applications for specific sensory methods. However, there is considerably more involved in use of sensory resources in the product development process. For example, the acceptance model emphasizes a response obtained from limited product exposure by the respondent but does not address the longer term issue of product preference as a function of extended use. This latter issue can best be addressed through a home-use test, keeping in mind that the home-use test should be considered only after one is satisfied that the product meets testing criteria and does not have any obvious sensory deficiencies. A product not well liked in a sensory acceptance test will not improve with continued usage as occurs in the home-use test. Also, the home-use test can be done on a limited scale through sensory evaluation or on a larger scale through marketing research. The decision is usually a function of time, cost and the credibility of each group.

Optimization

In addition to assessing product acceptance as a function of consumption over time and other specific product-related issues, sensory resources also can be used on a broader basis. The most useful of these is in sensory optimization, i.e. developing models that identify specific sensory attributes that are most important to product preference (Schutz, 1983; Sidel & Stone, 1983). Developing optimal products derives from the concept that some sensory attributes will have a greater effect on preference than others and by identifying those attributes, development efforts are better focused and the likelihood for success is significantly improved. Optimization programmes rely on multivariate design techniques and the use of physical and sensory analyses of products in combination with consumer preference measures to provide a sufficiently broad data base for model development. With today's computer sophistication and ease of access to data processing, the development of models is not an impediment for sensory evaluation. While optimization methods and the resultant models are a useful resource in developing products, they are not the end to the process. The model provides directions that must be translated into product change and then tested in the marketplace. Almost any data file, regardless of its quality, will yield a model with all the outward measures of significance; however, its true value is measured in the marketplace.

EPILOGUE

For sensory evaluation, involvement in the product development process is an opportunity to contribute in a meaningful way, to demonstrate responsiveness and cost effectiveness. Beginning with the concept and carrying through to identifying the important and unique product attributes, sensory resources should be an integral part of the development effort, particularly in providing quantitative direction to that effort. To operate effectively, however, sensory evaluation must have the necessary resources, a management commitment to support the effort, and the knowledge to know when to apply these resources to best advantage. While there has been limited success to date, it is clear that its uses in the future will increase.

REFERENCES

Meyer, R. S. (1984). Eleven stages of successful new product development. *Food Technol.*, **38**(7), 71–8, 98.

Moskowitz, H. R. & Sidel, J. L. (1971). Magnitude and hedonic scales of food acceptability. *J. Food Sci.*, **36**, 677–80.

Payne, S. L. (1951). *The Art of Asking Questions.* Princeton University Press, Princeton.

Peryam, D. R. & Pilgrim, F. J. (1957). Hedonic scale method of measuring food preferences. *Food Technol.*, **11**(9), 9–14.

Schutz, H. G. (1983). Multiple regression approach to optimization. *Food Technol.*, **37**(9), 46–8, 62.

Sidel, J. L. & Stone, H. (1983). An introduction to optimization research. *Food Technol.*, **37**(9), 36–8.

Sidel, J. L. & Stone, H. (1986). Using panel results for management decisions. *Proc. 39th Ann. Recip. Meat Conference, J. Amer. Meat Sci. Assoc.* Vol. 39, pp. 97–100.

Stone, H. & Sidel, J. L. (1981). Theoretical and practical aspects of consumer testing. In *Quality of Poultry Meat,* eds R. W. A. W. Mulder, C. W. Scheele & C. H. Veekamp. Spelderholt Inst. for Poultry Res., Beekbergen, Netherlands, pp. 231–9.

Stone, H. & Sidel, J. L. (1985). *Sensory Evaluation Practices.* Academic Press, Orlando.

Chapter 23

Procedures and Problems in Optimizing Sensory and Attitudinal Characteristics in Foods and Beverages

ANTHONY A. WILLIAMS

Sensory Research Laboratories Ltd, 4 High Street, Nailsea, Bristol, BS19 1BW, UK

ABSTRACT

To optimize sensory and attitudinal characteristics in foods and beverages, the food acceptance scientist should have information on a product's acceptability, its sensory and attitudinal characteristics, the influence, on the latter, of production and environmental factors together with chemical and physical data on the product itself. Regression modelling of the acceptance information on raw sensory or analytical data, or in the multivariate case, principal axes following some form of rationalization, provides a means of identifying important attributes and characterizing ideal products. When only a few variables are under consideration simplex optimization approaches can also be used to provide similar information with minimum sample assessment hence shortening the time consuming data acquisition stage. This chapter reviews, with examples, the various approaches currently being used for product optimization, highlighting some of the problems.

INTRODUCTION

With the increasing affluence of the western world, consumers are becoming more discriminating in respect to what they eat and drink.

Food and beverage manufacturers, if they are to survive, must therefore be aware of the factors which customers perceive in their products and the importance they are attaching to them when selecting and purchasing foods for consumption. Without such information it is impossible to have meaningful quality control or for product formulation, packaging, advertising or promotion to be properly optimized and targeted. A knowledge of the characteristics which consumers are looking for in a particular product range, also considerably helps in defining research objectives and new product development.

The acceptance of a product is the consequence of its interaction with the person consuming it. This in turn may be viewed as depending on two factors:

(i) How the product is perceived by the consumer.
(ii) The consumer's hedonic response to the characteristics he or she perceives in the product.

How a product is perceived depends on its chemical and physical properties together with the sensitivity, awareness, needs and attitudes of the person consuming it (Williams, 1983, 1985, 1986). Those aspects of acceptance to which the product makes a major contribution include the sensory characteristics, together with less obvious factors such as nutritional value, inherent safety, versatility and convenience in use, shelf-life and price. Factors which are more consumer dependent (i.e. extrinsic to the food) include appetite, nutritional needs, expectations, cultural and ethnic backgrounds, desire to experience new foods, social pressures and the desire to project a certain personal image.

The former of these factors can obviously be influenced by raw material and production variables and to some extent are directly under the control of the food and beverage technologist. The more extrinsic factors too can also be manipulated, although in less obvious ways by such factors as education, advertising, packaging and promotion as well as the environment and context in which the product is consumed.

The aim of the present chapter is to examine a number of the procedures currently available for bridging the gap between this perceived or 'objective' information and hedonic information, hence determining what aspects of a product are significant to consumers when they select products and how such characteristics may subsequently be optimized by manipulating production, product benefit and promotional factors.

GENERAL CONSIDERATIONS IN RELATING PRODUCT PERCEPTION AND HEDONIC INFORMATION

Determining How the Consumer Perceives a Product

Before any attempt can be made to determine which attributes of a product are significant to the consumers, it is first necessary to provide a meaningful description of its sensory, imagery or analytical characteristics and how it relates in respect to these, to other similar samples. Such information then needs to be coupled with some form of hedonic evaluation indicating the relative acceptance of these products.

On the sensory side, several approaches are available for providing a picture of a product and how one product relates to another:

1. Conventional profiling.
2. Free choice profiling.
3. Similarity/dissimilarity scaling.

Profiling approaches, whether free choice or conventional, enable the food acceptance scientist to provide a reasonably accurate description of how a product is perceived. By subjecting the results of such investigations to multivariate statistical examinations such as principal component or generalized Procrustes analysis (GPA), it is possible to determine how one sample relates to another in a perceptual sense. With profile data, the application of GPA also enables groups of people who perceive these inter-relationships in a similar way, to be isolated, independent of the terminology and the scales used for deriving them.

An example taken from the free choice profiling of the appearance of ports (Williams & Langron, 1984) demonstrates how assessors can vary in their perception of a product. Examination of the scatter of the individual sample positions around the consensus following GPA (Fig. 1) provides a measure of the degree of agreement between assessors; those who are grouped together perceiving the ports in a similar way. In this instance the assessors at the top of the diagram are experts involved in the day to day production of ports in Portugal, whereas those in the lower half are UK based personnel, with varying experience in port evaluation. In making their evaluations the experts are obviously taking into account aspects of the ports which the UK assessors do not consider important. From the point of view of product acceptance, if groups of assessors perceive products in different ways, there is a strong possibility that they will be weighting characteristics

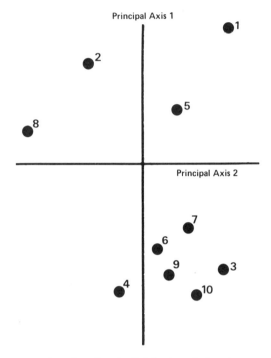

Figure 1. Assessor plot showing individual variation in the perception of
the appearance of ports.

differently when it comes to evaluating the acceptance of the product
as a whole.

Unlike conventional profiling, free choice profiling does not require
the derivation of a formal list of defined descriptive terms. As a
consequence, descriptive information and perceptual maps can be
obtained directly from consumer panels without the need for excessive
formal training. Apart from being easy to generate, such results also
have the advantage that they relate more directly to, and hence
provide a more realistic explanation of, consumer generated hedonic
information, than those derived from more conventional trained
profile panels.

Hedonic Information
To find out the importance of perceived characteristics to acceptance,
profile type information must be related to some form of consumption

or hedonic data providing a measure of the relative acceptance of a set of products. This is normally obtained either directly from the consumer, or from experts (deemed by their experience to reflect consumer opinion) by simple ranking or scaling approaches. Such information may be of a general nature or a measure of the acceptance of a product for a particular function, for eating or drinking in a particular environment, or at a particular meal or on a particular occasion, depending on exactly what one is trying to evaluate.

Just as people may perceive products differently in an 'objective' sense, they may also attach different weights to these characteristics when arriving at a decision regarding their acceptability and hence provide different ratings or rankings on the acceptability of a range of products. As well as isolating groups of assessors who perceive products in different ways one also needs to be able to explore this variation and isolate groups of people who rate samples in the same way. Only when one has homogeneous populations in this sense can meaningful causes of food acceptance be discovered and as a consequence, the properties of optimal products predicted.

When attempting to relate hedonic and perceived or 'objective' data it is also important to realize that factors, both sensory and imagery, interact and don't have the same importance over the whole hedonic range, that a given level of acceptance can be achieved in more than one way and finally, as far as the manufacturer is concerned, that people's tolerance to changes in characteristics and composition are equally as important as people's ideal or optimal values.

Once meaningful relationships have been derived between hedonic and perceived information, comparison of important characteristics with variations produced by production, labelling, advertising and educational factors, enables one to determine how important these latter factors are to the acceptance of the product.

METHODS FOR RELATING HEDONIC TO PERCEPTUAL AND COMPOSITIONAL INFORMATION

Fitting Hedonic Data to the Perceptual Space

Regression of acceptance information against the 'objective' data is one approach which enables the food acceptance scientist to find out the significance of attributes and compositional variables. This may be

Table 1
Regression models used in product optimization

Linear model	$y = a + \sum\limits_{i} n_i x_i$
Circular model	$y = a + \sum\limits_{i} n_i x_i + k \sum\limits_{i} x_i^2$
Elliptical model	$y = a + \sum\limits_{i} n_i x_i + \sum\limits_{i} k_i^2 x_i$
Rotated elliptical model	$y = a + \sum\limits_{i} n_i x_i + \sum\limits_{i} k_i x_i^2$
	$+ \sum\limits_{j} l_i x_i x_j$

carried out against the raw data (analytical or sensory), or against principal axes following some form of multivariate examination.

Models may be linear, or involve squared or interactive terms (Table 1), the latter enabling surfaces to be constructed and if appropriate, maxima and minima values isolated (Schiffman *et al.*, 1981).

A typical example of the type of results obtained, is shown in Fig. 2, in which wines of different ages were examined both 'objectively' and hedonically. In this case (linear model) the arrows represent directions of preference for individual consumers.

In another example, a set of beverages were profiled and the information related to consumer data. In this case the population broke down into a number of groups within which individual assessors produced similar hedonic response patterns. With one group, elliptical and surface response models provided the best solution (Fig. 3). To provide a more visual interpretation of such data and a clearer indication of peoples' tolerances to alterations in various attributes as one moves from the ideal, response surfaces may be fitted to the data (Fig. 4).

As already stated, when producing such relationships it is important to handle individual data or at least groups of respondents who react hedonically to the products in the same way. When handling individual data (Fig. 5), ideally results will cluster and groups of respondents can be identified who like the same thing. Taking the mean response of

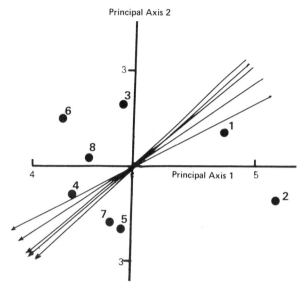

Figure 2. Example of product optimization: linear model. Numbered points represent wines and vectors (arrows) represent directions of preference for individual consumers.

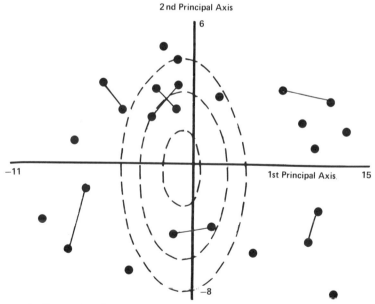

Figure 3. Example of product optimization: elliptical model. The centre of the ellipse represents the ideal point (position of real or hypothetical product of optimum preference) for a particular group of consumers.

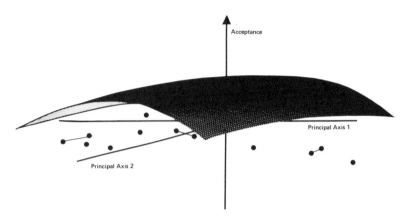

Figure 4. Example of product optimization: elliptical model response surface.

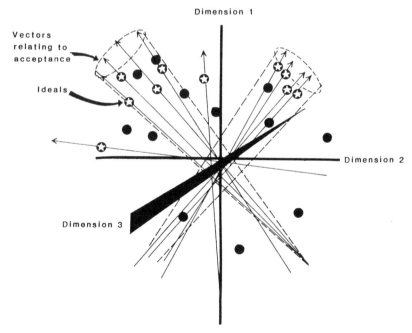

Figure 5. Clustering of individual ideals and dimensions relating to acceptability. Centre vector (next to Dimension 1 axis) represents the hypothetical 'average' consumer.

respondents as a whole or who conform to some predefined demographic criteria, as is often done, may well provide misleading information, predicting an acceptable product which satisfies no one (see centre vector in Fig. 5).

Exploring a Preference Space

An alternative procedure which may be used to investigate hedonic information is to produce a sample space based on the acceptance information alone (Coxon, 1981). In such cases the axes become subject preferences and the position of the samples in the space, the relative acceptance of the products for the panel as a whole. The application of PCA type analysis enables this space to be referred to principal axes and the information to be reduced to a meaningful number of dimensions. Projecting the original assessor ratings onto such a map also enables vectors to be placed in it, which reflect the direction of acceptance for each individual assessor (Fig. 6). Again

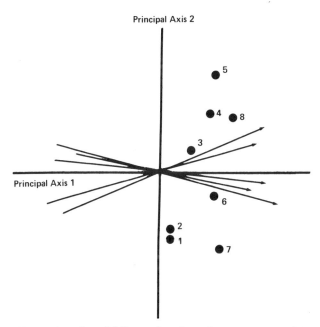

Figure 6. Example of multidimensional preference map of flavour acceptance. Vectors (arrows) represent directions of preference for individual consumers.

vectors (arrows) may be clustered and groups of people who respond in the same way to the products identified.

Reasons for preference however, must be obtained by regressing axis scores against sensory or imagery information, either in its raw form or following rationalization by other multivariate analyses. In such procedures models involving quadratic as well as linear terms should always be investigated to avoid misinterpretation of data and significant characteristics being overlooked due to the fact that their optima lie within the product range.

Alternatively pairwise or generalized Procrustes analysis may be used to match the acceptance and 'objective' spaces and hence provide an interpretation of the dimensions of the preference map.

A problem with all preference models of the type described, as with any regression approach, is that results are sample dependent and as a consequence, in certain circumstances can lead to misleading conclusions being drawn. In the example given above (Fig. 2), there was a clear indication that the most preferred wines were those which had undergone the most ageing. On the basis of the data this implied that assessors liked those wines both low in astringency and bitterness and low in fruitiness. In the sample set presented however, fresh fruity aromas were highly correlated with astringency and bitterness. Discussions with the assessors who provided the hedonic information indicated that fruitiness, as well as the lack of astringency and bitterness, were desirable characteristics of a good wine. Providing profiles of imaginary ideal products supplies useful additional information over simple hedonic ratings on existing products and helps to overcome such problems.

Examination of data by surface response modelling provides information on both an individual's ideal and his or her rate of change of acceptance with change in important attributes. Difficulties are however experienced when trying to pool such data in order to provide a meaningful picture for a population as a whole. Summation of ideal points, either as obtained by regression modelling or ideal profiles, and applying fresh surface response models provides an answer but information on the true rate of change of acceptance with changes in attribute level for individuals is lost.

Simple Approaches when Only a Few Variables are Being Investigated

All preference mapping approaches as described above are exploratory in nature and require a relatively large number of samples, covering as many possible variable combinations as are practical, to be examined, if useful information is to be obtained. In certain circumstances when the food acceptance scientist is aware of the important variables or when he or she has limited variables under his or her control, reduced models using only a limited sample matrix may be used and linear or surface response models derived based on the raw data. Where the number of variables to be investigated is limited, simplex optimization approaches utilizing the processing power of the modern computerized sensory laboratory also provide a rapid means of producing information on ideal products (Williams & Brain, 1986).

In the simplex approach a matrix of samples covering 1, 2 or 3 variables is normally made available to the assessor. He or she is presented with one of the samples chosen at random from the matrix, this being scored arbitrarily on an hedonic scale. A second sample, providing a contrast with the first, is then presented to the assessor who is asked to score its acceptance relative to the first, using a ratio scaling approach. A third sample is then presented, chosen in the same fashion as the second and the exercise repeated. In a two or three variable system, simplex optimization algorithms can then be used to predict the next most appropriate set of variables to be presented to the assessor in order to move closer to his or her ideal product. Once this sample has been assessed the computer again uses the information from the last three samples to again predict the next best sample to present and so on until the assessors ideal composition has been reached. In a matrix of some 60–70 sample variations, this normally takes 7–8 assessments.

The simplex method (Deming, 1983) on which this approach relies, provides a means of moving through a matrix according to a set of defined rules. The simplex itself is a simple geometric figure, the number of dimensions of which are one more than the number of variables one is investigating. In the example given in Fig. 7 this is a triangle constructed by the first three observations. Using this information the algorithm constructs a new simplex by projecting the least liked sample through the line joining the most liked pair of samples. In this example, the first samples (ABC) were scored as indicated. 'A' being the lowest score is projected to construct a second triangle on the opposite side of 'B' 'C' creating a new simplex 'B' 'C' 'D'. On assessment we find 'D' has a similar value as 'C' and we form a third simplex by reflecting 'B' through the line 'D''C'. The exercise is repeated until the optimum is reached. Simplex rules provide contingencies for cases when a new simplex wishes to move back on to the

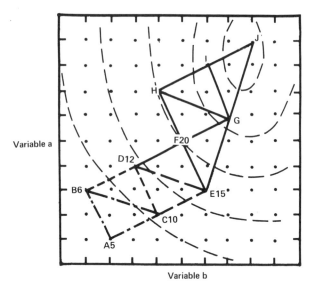

Figure 7. Construction and movement of simplex through a sample matrix.

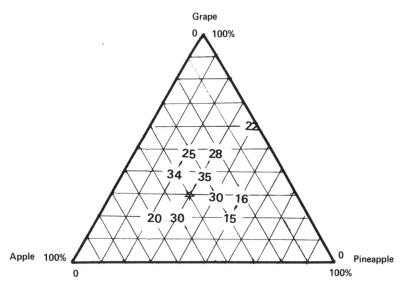

Figure 8. Typical response for an individual during the simplex optimization of a fruit juice blend (pineapple, grape and apple). Star represents optimal preference.

old one, when the projected new sample falls outside the matrix, for weighting projections to improve efficiency and for differentiating between local and global optima.

This approach has already been successfully used for the optimization of sugar and acid in a lime juice (Williams & Brain 1986) and for optimizing a blend of three fruit juices; pineapple, grape and apple (Williams & Brain, unpublished data). The results for one assessor in the case of the fruit juice example showing that assessor's optimum blend are given in Fig. 8.

Surface response models can of course be applied to these data but the requirements for good surface response modelling completely conflict with the concepts of simplex optimization in which the minimum number of samples is presented. Interpretation and presentation of pooled data also has problems similar to those associated with the modelling of preference spaces.

REFERENCES

Coxon, A. P. M. (1981). The MDS(X) series of multidimensional scaling programmes. Report No. 51. Inter University/Research Council's Series. University of Edinburgh, Programme Unit Library.

Deming, S. M. (1983). Experimental design: response surfaces. In *Chemometrics, Mathematics and Statistics in Chemistry*, ed. B. R. Kowalski. D. Reidel Publishing Company, Dordrecht/Boston/Lancaster, pp. 251–66.

Schiffman, S. S., Reynolds, M. L. & Young, F. W. (1981). *Introduction to Multidimensional Scaling. Theory, Method and Application*. Academic Press, New York/London.

Williams, A. A. (1983). Defining sensory quality in foods and beverages. *Chemy Ind.*, 740–5.

Williams, A. A. (1985). The use of perceptual space approaches for determining the influence of extrinsic and intrinsic factors in food choice. In *Consumer Behaviour Research and Marketing of Agricultural Products*, ed. J. E. R. Frijters. National Council for Agricultural Research, The Hague, Netherlands, pp. 29–38.

Williams, A. A. (1986). Some new ideas for measuring customer attitudes to wines. In 10*th Wine Subject Day, Quality Assurance in the Wine Industry*. AFRC Institute of Food Research, Reading Laboratory, pp. 85–91.

Williams, A. A. & Brain, P. (1986). The scope of the microcomputer in sensory analysis. *Chemy Ind.*, 118–22.

Williams, A. A. & Langron, S. P. (1984). The use of free choice profiling for the examination of commercial ports. *J. Sci. Food Agric.*, **35**, 528–69.

Chapter 24

Sensory Segmentation and the Simultaneous Optimization of Products and Concepts for Development and Marketing of New Foods

HOWARD R. MOSKOWITZ

Moskowitz/Jacobs Inc., Valhalla, New York 10595, USA

ABSTRACT

Traditionally, product developers have used an inefficient back and forth development and testing method to create new products. After lengthy development the consumer researcher may test the product to determine whether it fits a specific concept. Then, the product and concept may undergo further refinement to insure that they fit together, and that they appeal to a large or a targeted population. This chapter presents a rapid, alternative approach to accomplish the same objectives, as well as to highlight key characteristics of the product, the concept, and the consumer population. It combines experimental design of both products and concepts, multiple product and concept evaluation by a small group of consumers, early in the development cycle, and in-depth analysis and modelling of the data. The approach uncovers new segments of consumers, who differ in the sensory profiles that maximize consumer acceptance. The approach generates optimal products and concepts within constraints, such as cost, desired sensory profile limits, or multiple objectives (e.g. satisfying two segments simultaneously). The approach provides both technical knowledge

311

about the product, and a proactive development system for these products.

INTRODUCTION

During the past decade, beginning in the middle 1970s, sensory analysis began to grow dramatically in scope and impact. We can trace this growth to foundations laid down by researchers in a variety of fields, such as food science, experimental psychology (especially psychophysics), statistics and quality control. Along with this growth has come the beginnings of a scientific maturity. Sensory analysts no longer simply describe the 'perceptual attributes' of a product. In their expanded role in science and technology, sensory analysts also play a key role in the design and development of products.

This chapter focuses on new approaches in sensory analysis, including the discovery of underlying 'taste preference segments' in the population, and the design of 'optimal' products and advertising concepts for the total population and for these revealed segments. Readers familiar with the literature of statistical 'experimental design' will find this an expanded application of the techniques known collectively as 'response surface analysis' (Box *et al.*, 1978).

EXPLICATING THE APPROACHES USING A
CASE HISTORY

In order to clarify the approaches, this chapter uses the case history method, which presents a specific 'real-world' problem, and the methods used to solve the problem. The case history concerns the manufacturer of a chocolate bar, who faces an increasingly competitive market. In order to enter this market with a new product, the manufacturer recognized that he had to offer a product which demonstrated clear superiority to competition, or at least identify a segment of the population (of sufficient size), who would prefer to purchase this new product more than they would purchase competition. The manufacturer also had to develop a 'positioning concept' or statement about the product which would strongly appeal to the target population.

One might approach the problem in a simplistic fashion, without looking for 'structure', or models. The test requires evaluation of one's prototypes (versus competition) on a head to head basis, or the evaluation of an array of products by consumers along a series of attributes. Analytically, one then processes the data by several different methods to discover which attributes 'drive acceptance' (as measured by overall liking). This information helps the product developer 'understand' the key dimensions of a product, in terms of those correlated with liking, but does not tell the developer what to do, physically, in order to develop a product possessing a specific sensory profile or generating a high level of acceptance.

An alternative approach develops systematically varied products, according to an experimental design, and tests these among consumers. Furthermore, the researcher can vary statements about the candy product (e.g. names, taste messages, health benefits, price, etc.) and test systematically varied 'concept positionings'.

Stimulus Design—Prototypes and Concepts

Table 1 shows the design for 3 variables, systematically varied according to a Box–Behnken design. The design calls for 15 prototypes products, with each physical variable present at either high, medium or low levels. The experimental design creates an efficient set

Table 1
Example of experimental design for three physical variables

Prototype	Sweetener	Colour	Texturizing agent
101	High	High	High
102	High	High	Low
103	High	Low	High
104	High	Low	Low
105	Low	High	High
106	Low	High	Low
107	Low	Low	High
108	Low	Low	Low
109	High	Medium	Medium
110	Low	Medium	Medium
111	Medium	High	Medium
112	Medium	Low	Medium
113	Medium	Medium	High
114	Medium	Medium	Low
115	Medium	Medium	Medium

Table 2
Considerations for developing test concepts from elements

(1) Select as many elements as possible for inclusion in the test
(2) Categorize the elements into discrete categories (e.g. names)
(3) Count up the number of elements across all categories, and multiply by 2 (or more). The product equals the total number of concepts one must develop
(4) This study generated 25 elements, requiring a minimum of 25×2 or 50 concepts
(5) Decide how many times each element in each category will appear among the total number of concepts. For instance, with 4 names, each one would appear equally often, or 12–13 times (randomly allocated to the 50 concepts)
(6) If one desires to measure the absolute contribution of each element, add an additional element into each category, called the 'null element'. The 'null element' represents a space-holder. For 4 names, one has 4 elements and a fifth (the null element). The five elements each appear 50/5 10 times (randomly across the 50 concepts)
(7) Create the concepts in a randomized fashion, so that each element appears approximately equally often as every other element in its category. However, the allocation of the elements to the concept should follow a randomization scheme, so that the correlation between elements from different categories approaches 0

of products, which substitute for many hundreds of samples that one would otherwise have to produce. In this study, each of 80 panellists evaluated a randomized 10 of the 15 prototypes (all in a randomized order).

Table 2 shows the design considerations for the concept positionings. In contrast to the actual formulations (whose variables lay along a continuum), the concept elements behave as discrete wholes. One has a variety of different names, taste messages, etc., to combine into an efficient set of test concepts. Statistical design issues involve the number of combinations, with the recognition that the elements must appear independently of each other in the test concepts, so that the researcher can estimate their partwise or marginal contributions to consumer reactions.

Questionnaire Design
The questionnaire for the products probes a variety of attributes, including sensory (nonevaluative judgements, viz. 'amount of'), liking

(overall acceptance, acceptance of specific sensory attributes, such as appearance), and cognitive attributes (which focus on more complex dimensions, such as 'quality', 'nutritious', etc.). Panellists use a fixed, 0–100 scale (although any scale with sufficient discriminating power would suffice). The scale has anchors at both ends reducing ambiguity. Consumers rate purchase intent (which often differs from overall liking) using a different scale, viz. the conventional five point verbal scale, ranging from 'definitely would buy', down to 'definitely would not buy'. This limited category scale yields a different type of data. The 0–100 point scale provides average ratings of each product on each attribute. The five point purchase intent scale allows an estimate of the percentage of consumers positively disposed to each product (as gauged by the percentage of the consumer population, who rated each prototype as 4 or 5 on the purchase intent scale).

Test Implementation

Conventional consumer research involving 'taste tests' or concept evaluation, require short exposure times to the product or concept. Panellists test a limited number of samples in a brief session (often no more than 30 min, total). For developmental projects, which involve dozens of products or concepts, short test sessions prove unproductive. Instead, the sessions described in this chapter last 4 h, during which time the panellists evaluate many products and concepts, on the different scales. Rather than recruiting panellists from a mall to participate for a short test, a local interviewing service recruits the panellists by telephone, screens them to insure proper qualifications (viz. eats chocolate, positive to a basic description of the product), and invites the panellists to participate for the 4-h session. Panellists receive payment for their participation, and work in noninteracting groups of 20–30 individuals. (Although the sessions run with large groups, each panellist works at his/her own preferred pace.) Attending interviewers monitor the panellist's progress, check the incoming data, and give the panellist the appropriate products, or concepts, according to a randomized order. The sessions follow a choreographed sequence of activities, designed to acquire the data under careful, continual control by the supervising research 'monitor' (usually a paid interviewer, hired by the research company). Ongoing 'checking' of ratings by an attending interviewer (who does not know the 'correct answer') keeps the panellists actively involved in the evaluations, even over an extended period. Paying the panellists for their participation insures cooperation, and forces the panellists to set aside time to participate in the study, without other distractions (which often plague the shorter, 'mall-intercept' tests).

RESULTS

Basic Data and Validity Check

The basic product evaluation data consist of a product × attribute matrix, comprising the average rating of each product on every attribute, by those panellists who tried the product. For purchase intent, on the 1–5 scale, the entry for each product consists of the proportion of panellists who, having tried the product, scored the product as either 4 or 5 (probably or definitely would buy). In marketing research parlance, these two rating points constitute the 'top two box purchase intent', and constitute the conventional measure of 'interest in the product'. Ratings for the concepts also generate a rectangular matrix of concept by attribute.

Often, researchers in sensory analysis and marketing question the

Table 3
Validating the product attribute ratings

A. Order effects: F ratios from two way analysis of variance

Attribute	Product	Position	Interaction
Liking	8·26	0·58	0·91
Sweetness	19·33	0·39	0·42
(df)	14	10	140
residual = 635, total = 799			

B. Correlation of sensory attributes and formula ingredients

	Sweetener	Colouring	Texturizer
Darkness	0·12	0·80	0·52
Flavour strength	0·74	0·27	−0·09
Sweetness	0·77	0·23	0·15
Hardness	0·47	0·07	0·83

reliability and validity of such extended test sessions, averring that an untrained panellist cannot evaluate all these products in a limited time span, without losing sensitivity and rating the products in an increasingly random fashion. To answer these criticisms requires evidence from the data itself. Table 3 shows two analyses. The first assesses the effect of product versus position, by a two way analysis of variance. If the position effect achieves significance, then a critic could argue that the data exhibit substantial bias due to order. Two way analyses of variance show little or no position effect, however, as assessed by the F ratio. Position (order) effects occur, if at all, in the first position.

A second method to demonstrate the validity of the data correlates the sensory attribute ratings with the formula variables. Since the experimental design presents the ingredients in an uncorrelated fashion, the linear correlation of sensory attribute ratings with ingredients should lie closer to 1·00 (or −1·00) than to 0. Table 3 also shows these correlations for the chocolate data, and demonstrates that the panellists perceived differences among the products, because their sensory attribute ratings 'tracked' the physical formulations.

SEGMENTING CONSUMERS ON THE BASIS OF THEIR LIKING PATTERNS

Traditional psychophysics deals principally with measures of central tendency (mean or median rating). Some researchers recognize the pervasiveness of individual differences in liking (Pangborn, 1970). Consumer research, focusing on segments in the consumer population who show different preference patterns, cannot afford to ignore these individual differences which generate variability in liking. Consumer researchers divide the population by various breaks, including demographics (e.g. age, sex, market), usage pattern (what product(s) the panellist uses most often, etc.) or attitudes (answers to questionnaires probing general attitudes or attitudes toward the specific product category). Sometimes these segments display different patterns of liking ratings to an array of products. Typically they do not show large differences from subgroup to subgroup across the array of products, even though these groups differ dramatically, based upon the pattern of answers to the attitude questionnaire. Furthermore, dividing people into subgroups using attitudinal measures only, does not yield further insight into why people differ in what they like.

Table 4
Algorithm for segmenting consumers on the basis of the relation
between sensory attributes and liking (sensory segmentation)

(1) Assume that the panel has rated *S* stimuli on *P* sensory attributes.
Furthermore, the same panel (or even another panel) has rated each
of the stimuli on overall liking
(2) Compute the mean attribute rating for each stimulus on each sensory
attribute
(3) For a given attribute, and for a given panellist who rated some or all
of the stimuli on liking, create a table. The first column of this table
contains the mean rating of each stimulus on one particular sensory
attribute. (The mean sensory rating comes from the entire panel, or
may even come from ratings assigned by an expert panel, who
evaluated the same stimuli, and scored it on their particular scale.)
The second column of this table contains the liking rating, assigned
by the panellist to the products that each panellist evaluated. (The
panellist need not evaluate all of the stimuli in the set)
(4) Relate liking (*L*), rated by panellist, to the sensory intensity (rating) of
the particular attribute, using a quadratic equation:

$$\text{Liking} = A + B(\text{sensory rating}) + C(\text{sensory rating})^2$$

(5) Find the sensory rating, for the panellist, at which that panellist's
equation for liking reaches its maximum. Save this *optimal sensory
level*. Make sure that the range of sensory ratings matches the range
obtained in the actual study (viz. if the sensory ratings lie between 30
and 70 for darkness, then look for that sensory level of darkness,
between 30 and 70, at which the panellist's rating reaches its
maximum)
(6) Each panellist generates a profile of optimal sensory levels, one per
sensory attribute
(7) Factor analyse the optimal levels, to remove redundancy
(8) Cluster panellists on the reduced factor scores
(9) The outcome consists of a set of clusters, with panellists in the same
cluster showing similar profiles of optimal sensory levels (at which
liking reaches its peak, versus the sensory attributes, holding all
other attributes constant)

One alternative way consists of segmenting the population by the
pattern of liking ratings, described in Table 4 (Moskowitz *et al.*, 1985).
This method clusters consumers together based upon similar profiles
relating overall liking to sensory characteristics. The segmentation
differs from traditional methods because it uses reactions to an array
of perceptually different stimuli, and divides consumers into homogeneous groups, based upon how their sensory impressions covary
with rated 'liking'.

Figure 1 shows schematic curves. Figure 1(a) shows the data from a typical 'full panel'. Segmenting the population may reveal the existence of two or more segments, each of which generates its own unique pattern relating liking to sensory characteristics. Figure 1(b) compares two curves, one per segment, that might emerge from such a segmentation. Note the difference in the pattern relating sensory attribute level to overall liking.

The segmentation revealed two distinct segments, which one could label 'high sweet seekers' (68%) and 'dark, texture seekers' (32%). Consumers may or may not know to which category they belong, but the pattern of liking as shown in Table 5 clearly reveals two distinct groups. Furthermore, sensory segmentation generates larger differences in the liking rating (from segment to segment) than do other methods which divide the population. Table 5 shows the differences in liking ratings for several products, first for the sensory segments, and second for the same panel divided by what product they use most. As a check on the validity of the segmentation, one can perform a two way analysis of variance, with Factor 1 comprising products, and Factor 2 comprising subgroups. One can then compare different methods for dividing the population, in terms of the F ratio. Typically (albeit not always), the F ratio for Factor 2 corresponding to 'sensory segments' exceeds the F ratio for Factor 2 defined by other means (e.g. product used most often).

DEVELOPING PRODUCT MODELS FOR FORMULATIONS VERSUS RATINGS

The next step in analysis consists of developing product models, or equations, relating the consumer ratings (as well as objective measures, such as cost of goods or product stability) to the ingredients. For model systems the relation often describes an inverted U curve (Moskowitz, 1982). Generalizing this principle to products with 3 components (varying independently) generates the following equation:

$$\text{Rating} = A + B(X) + C(X^2) + D(Y) + E(Y^2) + F(Z) \\ + G(Z^2) + H(XY) + I(XZ) + J(YZ)$$

The equation states that the rating describes a surface, defined by linear, square and cross terms. Generally, only pair-wise interactions (e.g. XY) enter into the equation for parsimony. Otherwise, with

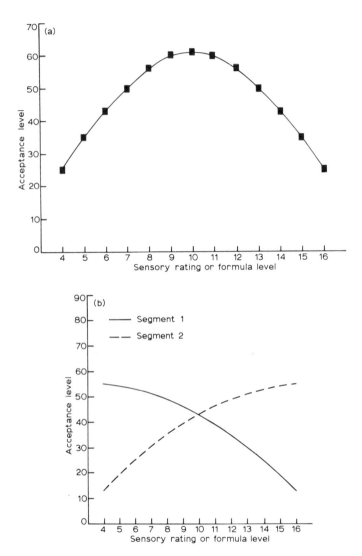

Figure 1. (a) Schematic curve relating overall liking (dependent variable) versus the sensory attribute or formula level (independent variable). The data come from the entire panel. The curve represents fitted data, with all points brought to the curve. In actuality, the points will scatter around the best fitting curve. (b) Example of a pair of curves, similar in nature to Fig. 1(a), with the difference that the curves come from the same set of independent variables, but fitted to ratings from two different segments.

Table 5
Comparison of liking ratings for selected products by subgroups

Prod.	Total panel	Sensory segment		Product used		Gender	
		Sweet(1)	Texture(2)	A	B	Male	Female
101	60	66	54	58	62	63	55
105	51	44	60	48	54	52	47
109	61	66	53	64	58	63	56
115	58	63	55	57	59	53	61

several different formula variables, one could generate equations having many additional terms, with these terms adding neither predictability in a statistical sense, nor meaning in a mechanistic sense. One can use the quadratic function to summarize the relation between ratings of a sensory attribute and physical formula variables, even though the quadratic terms may not reach significance (because we expect little in the way of an optimal level of a sensory attribute lying in the mid-range of the formula variables) (Box *et al.*, 1978).

The product model or set of equations allows one to estimate the likely rating of a product for given formula levels. Furthermore, the equation enables the investigator to uncover that combination of formula variables within the range tested which generates the highest level of liking, as well as to estimate the highest level of liking achieved. Finally, the equation allows the investigator to set constraints, such as cost of goods, or sensory attribute levels, and then uncover that combination of formula variables maximizing liking, while satisfying the imposed constraints. Thus, the product model replaces many intermediate, potentially disjointed tests. It becomes a proactive device, permitting the developer to assess many alternatives, based upon the results of one larger scale developmental study.

Optimizing Products

Table 6 shows the optimization results, using the product models. The product developer can use the models and specify various goals. Optimizing then proceeds, using the equation for the appropriate dependent variable. One can also specify constraints, either in terms of upper and lower levels of the three independent variables, or in terms of levels of dependent variables. When specifying dependent

Table 6
Optimization runs

	Total panel only	Seg 1 light sweet	Seg 2 dark texture	Total cost <140	Total cost <130	Total segs like > 60
Formula X 10						
Sweetener	47	68	38	43	39	53
Colour	42	39	52	48	44	45
Texturizer	39	32	47	32	31	42
Objective						
Cost	153	186	147	140	130	169
R&D/Stability	40	52	38	35	21	54
Liking						
Total	66	60	56	63	61	60
Segment 1	75	78	44	67	65	60
Segment 2	57	42	68	59	57	60
Sensory						
Darkness	58	52	68	56	54	55
Sweetness	62	72	54	60	57	66
Chocolate	60	70	58	58	56	66
Hardness	47	42	59	47	46	45

variables as 'constraints', the product developer provides an upper and a lower limit for each dependent variable to act as a constraint. The optimization procedure searches the allowable range of independent variables, while maintaining the constrained dependent variables within the limits specified.

In contrast to conventional back-and-forth research, which generates costly and inefficient time delays between development, test and feedback, the product modelling approach advocated here provides the developer with a set of products to develop, and specific predictions in terms of sensory characteristics, acceptance, etc. Furthermore, the approach quickly indicates whether the desired constraints on the optimal solution prevent a viable product from emerging. From time to time, developers work on products having so many properties and constrained so tightly that the product really cannot exist within the range of ingredients tested, or the constraints imposed.

Developing and Optimizing Concept Models

Although marketers and product developers recognize the need for a product to 'taste good' or otherwise please the senses, they realize that a product will not meet with success unless one can successfully entice the consumer to purchase the product, try it, and then return to buy and consume. One could 'sample' the product, placing it in many homes, hoping that this placement will generate sufficient interest to yield repeat purchase.

An alternative, and very common method, advertises the product, and provides the consumer with sufficient enticement to purchase the product, often by offering a coupon or a product at reduced cost. The concept evaluation and optimization approach in this research develops a combination of messages (e.g. name, taste, heritage, price) which consumers find acceptable. Such advertising messages motivate consumers to buy the product.

In this study, consumers rated a set of 50 concepts. Each consumer rated a randomized subset (32) of the test concepts. Each test concept comprised combinations of different elements, or messages.

Analytically, the design of the concepts (viz. randomized combinations of elements) enables one to determine which specific elements in the concepts generate consumer purchase intent, or communication of taste, health, or other benefits. First, the investigator knows what elements appear in each concept. Second, the database shows the proportion of consumers who, having read a concept, rate it 4 or 5 on the purchase intent scale (corresponding to probably or definitely would buy, respectively). Additionally, the databases show the mean rating for each concept on the other scales (e.g. uniqueness, communication of good taste, etc.).

It is possible to relate the presence/absence of the concept elements to consumer acceptance. One first codes each concept according to the presence (code '1') or absence (code '0') of each concept element (Moskowitz & Rabino, 1983). By 'dummy variable' regression analysis, one solves for the coefficients in the equation. The coefficient of each independent variable (viz. each concept element) shows the marginal, or partwise contribution of that element to purchase intent, or to any other dependent variable in the regression analysis.

Table 7 presents the coefficients for the additive model first for the total panel, and then for the two segments. The numbers for purchase intent show the marginal percentage of consumers in the panel who would rate a concept as a 4 or a 5, if the concept contained the element. Sometimes a coefficient has a negative value, implying that using the element in the concept actually decreases purchase intent. The additive constant serves as an adjustment factor, and shows the 'intercept' or the expected score of the concept without any elements. Furthermore, Table 7 shows the contributions of each element to the score of a concept on the other attributes, scaled with the 0–100 scale. We interpret the coefficient as the marginal additional rating scale points that a concept would obtain with the specific element present in the concept.

The sensory preference segments differ in their reactivities to the concepts. In this study (as in others) the sensory segmentation generates groupings of consumers who differ both in what they like sensorially, and what they want to hear about a product, both intellectually or emotionally.

The table of coefficients for the 'additive model' (Table 7) provides direction to generate a concept which yields consumer acceptance. The winning concept should (but need not) have one element from each category. Furthermore, the winning concept should incorporate only those elements having high coefficients. If a category of elements exhibits only low coefficients for the elements, then this means that the elements in that category do not add appreciably to purchase intent. One need not include them in the final concept.

AN OVERVIEW

This chapter presents an alternative approach to product development. The approach integrates sensory analysis in two ways. First, the sensory analyst designs the test for evaluation, using the panellist to provide a relatively large amount of information, in an extended test session. Second, the statistical design of the study allows the sensory analyst to play a dynamic role in guiding reformulation. Whereas traditionally sensory analysis has taken a passive role, acting primarily as the evaluator of the product, this approach allows the sensory analyst a far more active role. By incorporating concept evaluation and optimization into the experiment, the sensory analyst adds substantial value to the research. Since concepts 'promise' certain sensory characteristics, the sensory analyst can now direct the product

Table 7

Coefficients of additive model showing partwise contributions of elements to ratings

	Buy tot panel	Buy seg1 sweet	Buy seg2 crunch	Total like taste	Total value money
Additive constant	43	39	42	51	36
Name					
Choco-Crunch	4	2	9	2	0
Sweet-n-Crunchy	3	6	0	4	1
Crunch Delight	4	3	6	3	0
Chocolate Delight	3	3	4	3	1
Flavour/texture					
Rich, chocolaty taste	3	3	2	7	0
Chocolate, crunchy, rich taste	5	4	8	8	1
Delicious chocolate flavour	3	2	5	2	2
Sweet, rich, and a great texture	4	9	2	3	0
Support					
Milk chocolate, and pure nuts for a crunchy texture	15	13	21	8	2
100% real chocolate, and pure crushed nuts	10	2	14	9	3
Real chocolate, rich sweetener, and a crunchy texture	10	14	7	4	2
Milk chocolate, smooth texture	9	5	8	5	1
100% real chocolate, and a smooth texture	2	3	2	2	0
Real chocolate, rich sweetener and smooth texture	8	12	6	4	2
Sweet chocolate, and a crunchy texture	7	9	5	2	1
Sweet chocolate and a smooth texture	8	12	7	3	1
Bittersweet chocolate, and a crunchy texture	6	4	14	9	2
Bittersweet chocolate and a smooth texture	8	2	10	6	0
Usage occasions					
Great as a snack	7	7	5	3	2
Buy them when you want to treat yourself	11	14	10	9	4
Good after meal, as a dessert	3	3	4	3	1
Price					
Costs only $1.29 per package	11	9	13	0	18
Costs only $1·59 per package	8	7	8	1	13
Costs only $1·89 per package	3	4	3	1	3
Costs only $2·19 per package	−3	−2	−4	−1	−9

model and product optimization method to generate a highly acceptable product which also delivers the requisite sensory characteristics. The sensory analyst can also modify the optimal concept, so that it only promises what the actual product can really deliver.

REFERENCES

Box, G. E. P., Hunter, J. & Hunter, S. (1978). *Statistics for Experimenters.* John Wiley, New York.
Moskowitz, H. R. (1982). Sensory intensity vs hedonic functions: Classical psychophysical approaches. *Journal of Food Quality, 5,* 109–38.
Moskowitz, H. R. & Rabino, S. (1983). The trading of purchase interest for concept believability. *International Journal of Advertising, 2,* 265–74.
Moskowitz, H. R., Jacobs, B. E. & Lazar, N. (1985). Product response segmentation and the analysis of individual differences in liking. *Journal of Food Quality, 8,* 169–81.
Pangborn, R. M. (1970). Individual variations in affective responses to taste stimuli. *Psychonomic Science, 21,* 125–8.

Topic 7

Techniques for Measuring and Modelling Acceptability

Chapter 25

Objective Factors in the Appeal of a Brand During Use by the Individual Customer

DAVID A. BOOTH and ALAN J. BLAIR

Food Response Research, Department of Psychology, University of Birmingham, PO Box 363, Birmingham B15 2TT, UK

ABSTRACT

The success of a brand of food ultimately depends on what is actually going on in the mind of each purchaser and eater. The Appetite Triangle is a model for measuring discrete linear causes of an individual's acceptance behaviour in familiar food-choice situations. Naturalistic tests, run according to this model, estimate the objective multifactor response function for each person. The individuals' probabilities of choosing any variant can then simply be summed across a representative panel, to generate operational specifications for competitive formulations and presentations of the brand.

The principles of this psychologically scientific approach to brand optimization are illustrated here by applying it to one customer's choices among variants of a coffee drink.

CAUSAL MECHANISMS IN FOOD APPEAL

Acceptance is an Individual's Decision

The actual causal processes operating in the food market go on in the mind of each customer faced with a choice among brands. Scientific guidance to brand development therefore requires estimates of the

329

real-life purchasing or eating responses by the individuals in a representative panel to variations in formulation and marketing mix.

Even the best of the established methods of brand optimization fly in the face of these facts. This may be a major reason for the continued high rates of new product failure.

Verbal scores of conscious sensations or affect are treated as though they measured the strengths of influences on acceptability. Yet, at best only a part of the control of behaviour comes to consciousness (Ericcson & Simon, 1980). Also, raters vary indeterminately in their uses of words and numbers, as well as in their analytical awareness (Lundgren, et al., 1986).

Consensus approaches to hedonic ascriptive spaces, response surfaces and ideal-point modelling are likely to mislead. For the habitual mental processes of acceptance do not have qualitatively the same structure in all or most consumers. These approaches can provide only a bogus 'individualization'—namely, the positions of assessors within the alleged segment-consensus space. Descriptive factor analysis (Williams & Arnold, 1985) and the more causally oriented partial least squares approach (Martens & Martens, 1987) can provide individuals' response patterns. Even so, currently these approaches still aggregate by seeking to force a statistical consensus onto the individual data. What is needed, rather, is a sum of the predicted effects in the market of the operation of whatever mechanisms happen to be important within each individual.

In addition, all these research data are distorted by test conditions which happen to be convenient to the investigator. Many tests fail to simulate common usage situations adequately. None of the standard techniques unbiasedly samples the range of the particular preferences of each panellist (Conner et al., 1987). These inaccuracies, plus the grouping of the data, create nonlinearities, susceptible to only polynomial regression analyses (Moskowitz, 1983). These cannot establish principled and generalizable conclusions about a range of competing brands.

Therefore, the research base for successful food marketing would be much strengthened by a method for measuring the effects on an individual in a common purchase or use situation of relevant variations in operationally definable factors, either inherent in the product or presented with it during marketing. The test procedure must also preserve any linearities in this behavioural causation. The resulting definiteness of interpretation and quantitative precision would be unparalleled. With luck, sound conclusions would often be manageably simple too.

Just such a methodology can be built from a measurement model for naturalistic linear causal analysis. In the food-use context in which it was first developed, the model has been called the Appetite (or Acceptance) Triangle.

Theory and Method of Causal Measurement

Booth *et al.* (1983) described a linear causal theory of discrete determinants of the acceptability of a food to an individual consumer. They also specified an experimental design to protect the assessor's performance from systematic and random errors that conventional sensory tests and market research interviews are liable to introduce. These errors were well-known in academic psychophysics and psychometrics (Poulton, 1979). Booth *et al.* (1983) showed that data collected and analysed according to this model did indeed usually produce rather precise linear relationships. Hence, a rich database can be obtained from testing only a modest number of samples by each consumer (Conner *et al.*, 1986).

Booth *et al.* (1983) used graphic scoring of assessor-tuned selections of bread or soup salt levels for the position of their saltiness between maximum appeal and unacceptably high or low sensory magnitudes. They found that these scores were, as theoretically expected, linear against equally discriminable levels of salt. The linearity of such bias-minimized intensity ratings relative to ideal against an objective factor's discriminability, has since been abundantly confirmed in our own (Booth *et al.*, 1986; Booth *et al.*, 1987*a*; Conner *et al.*, 1986, 1987; Marie, 1987; Conner *et al.*, 1988*a,c*) and colleagues' (Shepherd *et al.*, 1984; Griffiths *et al.*, 1985) tests of one or more sensory factors in ordinary foods with untrained assessors (Conner *et al.*, 1988*b*).

This measurement model is not limited to factors inherent in foods or drinks, however. The influence of any observable factor can be estimated by identifying a linear function of its levels onto the acceptability of the product to the individual tested. This applies both to the socio-economic context of purchase or ingestion (e.g. price, labelled level of a constituent, breakfast-time, etc.) and to the assessor's nutritional physiology (e.g. stomach fill, glucose absorption rate or protein need) as much as to sensory factors (Booth, 1985, 1987*a,b*; Booth *et al.*, 1986). That is, the model is applicable to consumer tests of the influences of sensory, image, price and usage factors, and their interactions, on brand choice. The method delivers measures of the strength of a causal factor in objective units (i.e. the individual's ideal points, rejection points and tolerance sensitivities: Booth, 1987b; Booth et al., 1986, 1987a; Conner et al., 1988a,c). From these personal motivational parameters can be estimated the relative acceptability to the individual in the tested situation of different particular mixes of factor levels.

The grouping of the data does not then need any statistical calculations. The estimates of relative acceptabilities of different mixtures of factor levels to each individual are merely summed across a representative panel of users or purchasers. If the major influences on purchases of a range of competing brands have been tested, the relative popularities of the available brands and of any new variant of interest can be predicted.

The question of validity then arises. However, the requirements for naturalistic testing, operationalized objectivity for image factors as well as sensory factors, personally suited ranges of test brands, and quantitative analysis of real behavioural causation (i.e. at the individual level), all confer an internal face-validity beyond that aspired to by any established method. Furthermore, the quality of such data exceeds descriptor spaces or response surface methodology, for the aggregate is a cumulation of individuals' choice tendencies, not an average of raw verbalizations. Yet preference estimates are not limited to the brands or formulations actually tested; popularity among the panel can be interpolated to any level of a tested factor.

To Illustrate: a Drinker of Vended Coffee

Since the aggregation of individualized causal analyses is merely a matter of simple addition, the approach can be fully explained using data from only one person.

We use the example of consuming a machine-vended coffee drink because, unlike many groceries, the differences between the situations of purchase and of use are minimal. Foods and beverages are repeatedly purchased goods that everybody has to use for herself or himself. The view of the individual user on the performance of a food product during its consumption is therefore sure to dominate the brand's longer-term competitiveness. Nevertheless, use tests of packaged goods must be supplemented by introductory and post-use tests simulating common in-store presentations.

Variants of a cup of instant hot coffee as vended are also easily formulated during individual testing. We chose a purchaser of sweet, white coffee during breaks from work. This provided three potentially influential constituents. Also, some of the image factors in sugar and creamer are health-related. This connected to other aspects of our research programme.

OBJECTIVE ANALYSIS OF ACCEPTANCE DETERMINANTS

First, we give an example of causal analysis without profiling data. Our illustrative assessor's first two sessions in fact included descriptive scoring but initially we ignore these data and treat the tests as though they had been purely objective, i.e. assessing the effects of the three solids in the coffee on only observable choices among the white and black and the sweet and unsweetened coffees from the vending machine. Thus, we are now considering only the choice scores she gave for each of 12 variants which had been formulated to minimize distortions and noise in scaling.

Uncharacterized Acceptability Differences
The Appetite Triangle model relies on the existence of a personal norm for the test situation. This norm is the most strongly motivating configuration which the test situation recalls for the assessor of causal-factor levels in the food item and in the context of its use. If use of the food is sufficiently familiar, this ideal point can serve as a personal internal standard for comparisons which is as sensitively discriminable from a test sample-situation as is an external physical standard (McBride & Booth, 1986), even when a novel combination of familiar attributes is involved (Marie, 1987).

Performance in this decision task can be objectively measured as the sensitivity of the choice behaviour to differences between levels of an influence on acceptability (Booth et al. 1986; Booth, 1987b; Conner et al., 1988a,c). The model is that equal differences in causal-factor levels in units of 'just tolerable difference' generate equal reductions in acceptability below and above the ideal point. That is, the ideal-relative behaviour is linear (Booth et al., 1983) and the Appetite Triangle is isosceles. Properly tested choices lie on a determinate inverted V, not on a quantitatively atheoretical inverted U-function which can only be represented by a polynomial specific to the data set (e.g. Frijters & Rasmussen-Conrad, 1982; Moskowitz, 1983).

Identification of Discrete Causal Factors

The simplest theory we could test is that each constituent independently influences choice. For tastants such as sugar and caffeine in pure solution (Schutz & Pilgrim, 1957), equal ratios of concentrations are equally discriminable and logarithm of concentration has been found to be linear against unbiased ratings for these and several other sorts of constituents in real foods and drinks (Booth *et al.*, 1983; Conner *et al.*, 1986, 1988*a,c*; Marie, 1987). So the 'straight-through' (Booth, 1979), three-constituent theory can be tested by partial regression of the log-concentration difference of each variant from its ideal point onto the choice score for that coffee variant.

(The ideal point for each factor can be estimated by optimizing it for minimum residual partial variance, perhaps starting with the drink variant that was given the highest choice score. In fact, as we shall see, this assessor had also provided ideal-relative ratings of 'sweetness', 'milkiness', and 'strength' for these coffees. So, purely as a matter of convenience for this presentation, these descriptive ideal points were used.)

The three-constituent theory of coffee appeal is therefore tested by a simple multiple regression when bias-minimization has yielded linear performance. Whitener levels were triangularly predictive of overall acceptability in these first two sessions (Table 1, column 1). In addition, sugar accounted for about 30% of the variance and coffee solids for about 10%.

Furthermore, this non-interactive theory accounted for virtually all of the variance in choice scores. Interactive effects of constituents

Table 1

Control of an individual's choice by three constituents acting independently

Constituent	Partial reg'n coeff.	TDR	Accept/reject points (g/200 ml)			
			Ideal	Deficit	Excess	(Vended)
Coffee	36	1·47	1·2	0·03	40	(0·5)
Whitener	77[a]	0·33	2·7	0·25	27	(1·6)
Sugar	56	0·47	4·1	1·3	12	(4·5)

TDR = Tolerance discrimination ratio (the Weber ratio of the choice scores' sensitivity to the constituent).
[a] $p < 0.01$ for entry into multiple regression; other entries forced.

cannot therefore be demonstrated using these data. They might, however, be refutable. To test this, various hypothetical sensory integrations were tested, i.e. whitener minus coffee (colour), whitener plus coffee (strength), and/or sugar minus coffee (net sweetness). A potential caloric percept (sugar plus whitener) was also tested. In the event, no better than 10% of the variance in choice was predicted by any hierarchical regression, even when collinearity was not avoided.

Causal Parameter Values

Each partial regression provides an estimate of a determinate linear equation for that hypothetical causal relationship. The intercepts of this line give an ideal point and deficit and excess rejection points for each constituent for this assessor under these test conditions (Table 1, right-hand columns). These results indicate that she may like coffee stronger and milkier than vended, but not sweeter.

The slope of the regression together with its residual variance provides an estimate of the sensitivity of choice responses to differences in level of that causal factor (Booth, 1987b; Conner et al., 1988a,c): we apply the discrimination ratio named after Weber to the tolerance judgement—hence 'TDR' (Table 1). On this thoroughly objective measure of personal motivation, differences in coffee level were not nearly as important to this assessor as differences in whitener or sugar levels.

Causal Integration into Choice

These discrete influences combine in some fashion to cause choice. In group data, simple algebraic rules have been shown to characterize such integration of information (Anderson, 1982). These include averaging, addition and multiplication of orthogonal inputs.

With choice expressed as a frequency score (always to never), one obvious possibility to test is that choice is a joint probability, i.e. the overall response is predicted by the crossproduct of the three partial probabilities for each combination of factor levels. The choice scores calculated on this decision model correlated ($r = 0.70$, $p < 0.01$) with the observed scores, both when zero probability of choice was taken to be at the rejection points (rejection intolerance) and when zero choice was taken to be at one TDR on either side of the ideal point (threshold intolerance).

Averaging these three 'probabilities of choice' also gave a correlation of 0.7 for threshold intolerances. Using rejection-point intolerances, however, the correlation of the averaging rule with

Table 2
Percentage probabilities of an individual's choice of drinks containing coffee solids at vended level, estimated by an averaging model with zero tolerance at one TDR from ideal

Whitener concentration (g/200 ml)	Sugar concentration (g/200 ml)				
	0	2·8	3·4	4·0	4·5
3·6	0	1	16	31	27
2·7	0	34	50	65	60
2·0	0	1	18	31	27
1·6	0[a]	0	0	12	8[a]
0	0[a]	0	0	0	0

[a] The concentrations currently vended in plain black and white coffee and sweet white coffee.

observed scores was 0·79 ($p < 0·01$). Thus, unless a still more realistically performing decision model can be found (e.g. Euclidean or city-block metrics), and shown to be robust in replication, this assessor may be taken to be averaging in this test situation.

On this basis, we can estimate what her choice score would be for any formulation of the three constituents in this test situation. That gives us a continuous choice-response surface for any pair of the three constituents.

This assessor's averaging-modelled response to various levels of sugar and whitener, with coffee solids at the vended level, is illustrated in Table 2 for TDRs and in Table 3 for rejection points. The TDR intolerances give a sharper peak, because for both constituents the TDR is considerably smaller than the ratio of ideal point to rejection point (Table 1). Nevertheless, as we have seen above, this may be a slightly worse model of what the assessor was doing.

Aggregation without Consensus
This choice-score based response surface predicts the probability of this customer accepting any combination of levels of the measured factors in the familiar market situation simulated by the test conditions. Predictions of the market response to any set of combinations in the tested context can therefore be calculated simply by adding up these individual response surfaces across a representative panel of assessors.

Table 3

Percentage probabilities of an individual's choice of drinks containing coffee solids at vended level, estimated by an averaging model with zero tolerance at rejection points

Whitener concentration (g/200 ml)	Sugar concentration (g/200 ml)				
	0	2·8	3·4	4·0	4·5
3·6	30	61	70	77	77
2·7	31	62	72	79	78
2·0	22	52	62	69	69
1·6	16[a]	47	57	64	63[a]
0	0[a]	25	35	42	42

[a] Concentrations vended in the machine used by this consumer.

Unlike the consensus-forcing approaches, the aggregate from individual causal analyses omits no interindividual variance and so yields unrivalled precision. The aggregate is also transparent to any psychographic segmentation method and immediately yields quantitative objective guidance, i.e. operationalized positioning strategies.

DESCRIPTIVE EXPLORATION OF INFLUENCES ON ACCEPTANCE

Uncharacterized preference analysis was not the first use of the Appetite Triangle, however. The personally ideal configuration in a familiar use situation is a very efficient and informative basis for qualitative research that can at the same time yield truly quantitative descriptive analysis.

Qualitative/Ethnographic Assessment

Detailed, open-ended discussion of a single brand or concept can be structured relative to ideal. This will elicit the customer's own descriptions of salient merits and defects. Such qualitative data elicited from the consumers separately are unlikely to miss any idea that a member of a discussion group would come up with. The group process is likely to bury crucial individual differences in the content of awareness.

The individualized procedure also provides the qualitative report with quantitative breakdowns of common elements and idiosyncratic variations in integrated personal viewpoints. The frequencies of deficiencies or excesses of customer-named attributes can be added up and cross-tabulated across a modest-sized representative sample of individual records, without the distortions of group interaction or preformulated questions.

Psychological Quantification of Ethnography

Furthermore, genuine quantification of the strengths of individual opinions can be built into the ideal-relative attribute elicitation procedure, using just a concept or only one or two physical samples. The key procedure is to use only two category points to anchor the scores of an attribute (Booth et al., 1987a, 1988). The assessor can, for example, state in her own words what level of an attribute she would always choose, other things being satisfactory, and what levels she would reject. Only a pair of such descriptions at a time should be presented to score a sample.

Our illustrative assessor (and other users) evaluated the concept of a drink of coffee from the machine, before testing any actual drinks. She expressed her attitudes to drinking machine coffee in the terms 'sweet', 'milky', 'strong', 'dark', 'hot', 'fattening' and 'bad for health'. Other assessors in this study have evinced images such as 'refreshing', 'satisfying', 'stimulating' and 'bad for teeth', as well as coming up with some other apparently sensory terms.

There is no evidence that such one-word or phrase descriptions of aspects of the situation which are perceived as relevant to choice differ in substance from reasons for doing such an action which are expressed in whole sentences. Overtly affective reactions to a situation need be no different either. Thus, the cognitive models built on ideal-relative descriptors are rivals to conventional attitude models, whether topic-specific (Huba et al., 1981; Lewis & Booth, 1986) or initially constructed according to a formal scheme (Becker, 1977; Fishbein & Ajzen, 1975).

Descriptive Model within a Test of Sensory Factors in Choice

The assessor followed the choice score for each coffee sample (Table 1) with a personally scaled ideal-relative magnitude on each of her verbally elicited descriptors. The descriptive scores, choice scores and

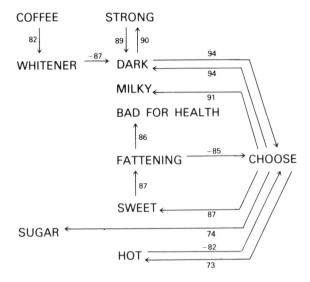

Figure 1. Linear relationships of ascribed magnitudes to and from constituent levels and choice scores for 12 samples by an individual assessor. Only and all the coefficients (%) of partials entering multiple regressions at $p < 0.01$ are given. Partial regressions from choice scores are unfolded.

levels of constituents were all analysed for linear relationships indicative of potentially causal connections. Each variable was regressed onto every other, partialling out the remaining variables. The resulting statistically significant partials are given in Fig. 1.

A fault in experimental design was exposed by a correlation between coffee and whitener levels. Such collinearity renders the data of Tables 1–3 and Fig. 1 less reliable as diagnostics of causal connections. This weakness was avoided in subsequent sessions by ensuring that the bias-minimization included combinations of high and low levels of factors as well as jointly high or jointly low levels.

The conventional assumption that certain descriptors are objectively 'sensory' is not necessarily sound. The only case of a relationship between levels of a constituent and magnitudes of an apparently sensory descriptor was a regression between 'dark' and whitener levels (Fig. 1), and this was paradoxically from a response variable to a controlled variable. Verbal reference to an entity does not guarantee real description of it: what a rating measures can be established only by causal (psychophysical) experiment (Booth, 1987a).

By the same criterion, choice scores were better sensory assessments of sugar levels than 'sweet' ratings (Fig. 1). A causal influence from sugar to choice could be responsible for the regression of choice onto sugar level: accidents of the small amount of data may throw up only the 'paradoxical' partial. Alternatively, the generally higher prevalence of significant regressions from choice than to choice (Fig. 1) may be the result of rating choice before descriptors. Even so, the effect is not likely to be peculiar to such a test procedure. There is reason to suspect that analytical thinking generally comes after an overall 'straight-through' reaction (Booth, 1979, 1987b; Booth et al., 1987a). The analysis often could be more a rationale for the degree of acceptance already expressed than a valid description of its actual causation or a neutral mapping of sensations.

Descriptive analysis, even when properly quantified, is therefore purely exploratory. Introspection may not reveal the effective mental processes. Any objective research into the determinants of acceptability must move from naive treatments of raw ratings to causal analysis of the relationships between controlled or measured variations in potential influences and the individual's responses.

We illustrate this strategy by an experiment in the next three sessions for this assessor which tested an hypothesis inspired by the descriptive data from the first two sessions (Fig. 1). There was some redundancy between 'fattening' and 'bad for health' (as also between 'dark' and 'strong'; not unexpectedly for coffee). The single direction of regression, from 'fattening' to 'bad for health', is consistent with weight concern being primary. We noted, furthermore, that 'fattening' was predicted by 'sweet' and that both these ratings were connected to the choice scores. This gave grounds for wondering whether a fattening health image of the drink could influence acceptance, with this assessor's concern being salient for sugar rather than for whitener (which also contains energy). The hypothesis was, therefore, that perceived caloric content of the coffee sweetener would substantially influence preference.

The analytical model also indicated that serving temperature might be worth examining (Fig. 1). The assessor was observed to sip a new sample immediately it was presented, at vended temperature. Thus, she might prefer it vended still hotter. This mechanism we have not examined here.

ASSESSMENT OF AN IMAGE FACTOR WITH THE SENSORY FACTORS

We therefore replaced sugar in nearly half the drinks by a low-calorie sweetener, and labelled each drink accordingly on a card presented with the cup of coffee. Each type of sweetener was tested with bias-minimizing selections of levels of sweetener, whitener and coffee solids, scoring choice first for each variant and then the assessor's own descriptors relative to ideal.

Descriptive Analysis
The causal structure inferred from multiple regressions involving descriptive responses is summarized in Fig. 2. Correlations between factor levels had been successfully avoided. A colour term was again controlled by a constituent, although this time it was coffee solids levels reducing 'milky' intensities. This time, in addition, sweetener level strongly influenced 'sweet' magnitude score.

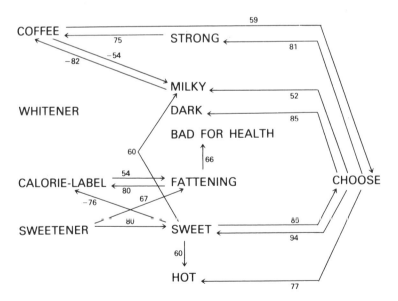

Figure 2. Significant ($p < 0.01$) linear relationships (with % partials) of ascribed magnitudes to and from constituent levels and choice scores for an individual tested on 26 variants of a coffee drink.

The assessor attributed some of her choice scoring to the temperature of the coffee (Fig. 2). The sweetener-driven sweetness rating was much more strongly related to choice, nevertheless, as might be expected now that sweetener had been given high verbal salience. Also, coffee levels influenced choice scores. The assessor seemed to be expressing her awareness of this in the terms 'strong', 'milky' and 'dark', although they did not relate significantly to each other as they had in the first two sessions (Fig. 1).

The hypothesis that sugar had a fattening image was strongly supported (Fig. 2): both sweetener level and caloric label influenced the 'fattening' score, and there was some sign of inverse attribution from 'sweetness' to labelled calories. A rational estimate of a drink's fattening potential should indeed combine information on levels of sweetener and of caloric labelling. There was evidence of such integration. 'Fattening' correlated more highly with cross-products of label with sweetener (0·73) or with 'sweet' (0·62) than with any of the controlled factors by itself. However, the crossproducts did not significantly multiple-regress onto 'fattening'.

Objective Measurement of Influences on Appeal

Objective analysis of these data is feasible by ignoring the descriptive data. The objective measurement may be distorted, though, by the effects on choice of the descriptive scoring of previous coffee samples. With this reservation, Table 4 presents causal strengths (partials) and parameters (TDRs and intercepts) for the four controlled inputs acting independently. Considerable variance in choice remains unaccounted

Table 4

Effects of three constituents and of sugar/low-calorie labelling, acting independently on the choice scores for 26 variants of coffee, by a drinker of sweet, white coffee

| Constituent | Partial reg'n coeff. | TDR | Accept/reject points (g/200 ml) | | | |
			Ideal	Deficit	Excess	(Vended)
Coffee	51[a]	0·60	1·25	0·13	12	(0·5)
Whitener	3	>k	5·3	0·02	1·3k	(1·6)
Sweetener	35	0·61	4·2	1·9	9	(4·5)
Labels	8	>k	400	<1/k	>k	—

TDR = Tolerance discrimination ratio (choice difference threshold).
[a] $p < 0.05$ for entry into multiple regression; other entries forced.

for. Therefore, likely interactions mediating the effects of these factors on choice should be tested, such as multiplication of label and sweetener level or differences in coffee and whitener levels.

There was no evidence that this form of caloric labelling, acting by itself, affected the appeal of these coffee drinks to this assessor (Table 4). That is, the response surface from this orthogonal model would be flat in the labels dimension. Nevertheless, this analysis indicates that it could be a serious error to conclude that such labelling has no impact on purchases by customers like her. Choices might be sensitive to a combination of sweetener and label levels. In addition, caloric labelling of the sweetener could be increasing the salience of the sweetener and its fattening potential, as the descriptive results suggest, and thereby altering the assessor's attitudes to the different aspects of coffee: she still likes her coffee almost as sweet as vended, even if with sugar (compare sweetener ideal points in Tables 1 and 4), but in this new context may be more disposed to focus on the coffee's good hot and strong taste!

Different causal structures could be identified in different customers, with or without the help of descriptive analysis. Hence, different combinations of formulation and image could be positioned for distinct preferences or uses.

CONCLUSIONS

Operational Guidance to Brand Design

The principles of experimental design and data analysis provided by the Appetite Triangle are the basis for a research system which is capable of identifying and measuring influences on the competitiveness of a brand. The output is as objective about image factors as sensory factors. Thus, the interpretation of research results is fully operational for both product development and marketing, expressed in terms which are meaningful both within the company and in advertising.

Construction of a scientific theory often much reduces the previous mathematical and statistical problems. Serious application of the Appetite Triangle system would remove the need to rely on large databases and complex statistical software. Yet it faces us with the intellectual challenge of becoming fully scientific about food acceptability. The comforts of simplistic interpretation of expert number-crunching are gone. The new method demands the technical inventiveness and behavioural insight to design naturalistic tests that

344DAVID A. BOOTH AND ALAN J. BLAIR

increase our understanding of the important factors in what individuals actually do with food and drink.

Implications for Customer Health Behaviour

The precision of psychological measurement made possible by design and analysis according to the Appetite Triangle also opens up opportunities for fundamental advances in behavioural nutrition. Recent applications of this approach have demonstrated, for example:

—the reality of the individual characteristic of a 'sweet tooth' but its dependence on snackfood consumption habits (Booth, 1987c,d; Conner & Booth, 1988; Conner et al., 1988c);
—the irrelevance of the congenital sweet-acceptance reflex to likings for sweetness in foods (Booth et al., 1987a);
—dependencies of food-specific cravings and satisfactions on learning bodily cues to need for or repletion of a specific nutrient (Booth, 1985; Baker et al., 1987);
—relationships of likings for food salt to blood pressure (Booth et al., 1987b) and food butterfat and total fat intakes to overweight and the dieting syndrome (Lewis & Booth, 1986; Booth, 1987d; Blair, Lewis & Booth, unpublished).

REFERENCES

Anderson, N. H. (1982). *Methods of Information Integration Theory.* Academic Press, New York.
Baker, B. J., Booth, D. A., Duggan, J. P. & Gibson, E. L. (1987). Protein appetite demonstrated: learned specificity of protein-cue preference to protein need in adult rats. *Nutr. Res., 7,* 481–7.
Becker, H. (1977). Health Belief Model and predictions of dietary compliance: a field experiment. *J. Health Soc. Behav., 18,* 348–66.
Booth, D. A. (1979). Preference as a motive. In *Preference Behaviour and Chemoreception,* ed. J. Kroeze. IRL Press, London, pp. 317–34.
Booth, D. A. (1985). Food-conditioned eating preferences and aversions with interoceptive elements: learned appetites and satieties. *Ann. N.Y. Acad. Sci., 443,* 22–37.
Booth, D. A. (1987a). Cognitive experimental psychology of appetite. In *Eating Habits,* eds R. A. Boakes, M. J. Burton & D. A. Popplewell. John Wiley, Chichester, pp. 175–209.
Booth, D. A. (1987b). Individualised objective measurement of sensory and image factors in product acceptance. *Chem. Ind. (Lond.),* 441–6.

Booth, D. A. (1987c). Evaluation of the usefulness of low-calorie sweeteners in weight control. In *Developments in Sweeteners—3*, ed. T. H. Grenby. Elsevier Applied Science, London.

Booth, D. A. (1987d). Relationships of diet to health: the behavioral research gaps. In *Healthy Eating—a Scientific Perspective*, ed. C. A. Manley, Allured, Wheaton, IL.

Booth, D. A., Thompson, A. L. & Shahedian, B. (1983). A robust, brief measure of an individual's most preferred level of salt in an ordinary foodstuff. *Appetite*, **4**, 301–12.

Booth, D. A., Conner, M. T., Marie, S., Griffiths, R. P., Haddon, A. V. & Land, D. G. (1986). Objective tests of preference amongst foods and drinks. In *Measurement and Determinants of Food Habits and Food Preferences*, eds J. M. Diehl & C. Leitzmann. University Department of Human Nutrition, Wageningen, pp. 87–108.

Booth, D. A., Conner, M. T. & Marie, S. (1987a). Sweetness and food selection: measurement of sweeteners' effects on acceptance. In *Sweetness*, ed. J. Dobbing. Springer-Verlag, London, pp. 143–60.

Booth, D. A., Thompson, A. L., Shepherd, R., Land, D. G. & Griffiths, R. P. (1987b). Salt intake and blood pressure: the triangular hypothesis. *Med. Hypoth.*, **24**, 325–8.

Booth, D. A., Eastman, C. & Blair, A. J. (1988). Quick measurement of psychological states and changes in the individual's own terms. Submitted.

Conner, M. T. & Booth, D. A. (1988). Preferred sweetness of a lime drink and preference for sweet over non-sweet foods, related to sex and reported age and body-weight. *Appetite*, **10**, 25–35.

Conner, M. T., Land, D. G. & Booth, D. A. (1986). Very rapid, precise measurement of effects of constituent variation on product acceptability. *Lebensm.-Wiss.-Technol.*, **19**, 486–90.

Conner, M. T., Land, D. G. & Booth, D. A. (1987). Effect of stimulus range on judgments of sweetness intensity in a lime drink. *Br. J. Psychol.*, **78**, 357–64.

Conner, M. T., Booth, D. A., Clifton, V. J. & Griffiths, R. P. (1988a). Individualized optimization of the salt content of white bread for acceptability. *J. Food Sci.*, **53**, 549–54.

Conner, M. T., Booth, D. A., Clifton, V. J. & Griffiths, R. P. (1988b). Do comparisons of a food characteristic with ideal necessarily involve learning? *Br. J. Psychol.*, **79**, 121–8.

Conner, M. T., Haddon, A. V., Pickering, E. S. & Booth, D. A. (1988c). The sweet tooth demonstrated: individual differences in preference for both sweet foods and foods highly sweetened. *J. Appl. Psychol.*, **73**, 275–80.

Ericcson, K. A. & Simon, H. A. (1980). Verbal reports as data. *Psychol. Rev.*, **87**, 215–51.

Fishbein, M. & Ajzen, I. (1975). *Belief, Attitude, Intention and Behavior*. Addison-Wesley, Reading, MA.

Frijters, J. E. R. & Rasmussen-Conrad, E. L. (1982). Sensory discrimination, intensity perception and affective judgement of sucrose-sweetness in the overweight. *J. Gen. Psychol.*, **107**, 233–48.

Griffiths, R. P., Clifton, V. J. & Booth, D. A. (1985). Measurement of an

346 DAVID A. BOOTH AND ALAN J. BLAIR

individual's optimally preferred level of a food flavour. In *Progress in Flavour Research 1984*, ed. J. Adda. Elsevier, Amsterdam, pp. 81–90.

Huba, G. J., Wingard, J. A. & Bentler, P. M. (1981). Comparison of two latent variable causal models for adolescent drug use. *J. Pers. Soc. Psychol.*, **40**, 180–93.

Lewis, V. J. & Booth, D. A. (1986). Causal influences within an individual's dieting thoughts, feelings and behaviour. In *Measurement and Determinants of Food Habits and Food Preferences*, eds J. M. Diehl & C. Leitzmann. Department of Human Nutrition, Wageningen, pp. 187–208.

Lundgren, B., Pangborn, R. M., Daget, N., Yoshida, M., Laing, D., McBride, R. L., Griffiths, N. M., Hyvonen, L., Sauvageot, F., Paulus, K. & Barylko-Pikielna, N. (1986). An interlaboratory study of firmness, aroma and taste of pectin gels. *Lebensm.-Wissensch.-Technol.*, **19**, 66–76.

Marie, S. (1987). Ph.D. thesis, University of Birmingham.

Martens, M. & Martens, H. (1987). Partial least squares regression. In *Statistical Procedures in Food Research*, ed. J. R. Piggott. Elsevier Applied Science, London, pp. 293–359.

McBride, R. L. & Booth, D. A. (1986). Using classical psychophysics to determine ideal flavour intensity. *J. Food Technol.*, **21**, 775–80.

Moskowitz, H. R. (1983). *Product Testing and Sensory Evaluation of Foods*. Food & Nutrition Press, Westport, CT.

Poulton, E. C. (1979). Models for biases in judging sensory magnitude. *Psychol. Bull.*, **86**, 777–803.

Schutz, H. G. & Pilgrim, F. J. (1957). Differential sensitivity in gustation. *J. Exp. Psychol.*, **54**, 41–8.

Shepherd, R., Farleigh, C. & Land, D. G. (1984). The relationship between salt intake and preference for different salt levels in soup. *Appetite*, **5**, 281–90.

Williams, A. A. & Arnold, G. M. (1985). A comparison of the aromas of six coffees characterised by conventional profiling, free-choice profiling and similarity scaling methods. *J. Sci. Food Agric.*, **36**, 204–14.

Chapter 26

An Investigation of the Factors Influencing Consumer Acceptance of Chocolate Confectionery Using the Repertory Grid Method

JEAN A. MCEWAN* and DAVID M. H. THOMSON

Department of Food Science and Technology, University of Reading, Whiteknights, P.O. Box 226, Reading RG6 2AP, UK

ABSTRACT

Conventional market research techniques, applied to the study of confectionery, suggest that people have difficulty in articulating the factors which influence their decision to buy and consume these products. As acceptability is greatly influenced by the way in which a consumer perceives a product, it is essential to be able to elicit and quantify such perceptual attributes for any particular product type. Previous experimentation has suggested that an application of the repertory grid method may offer a possible solution.

As part of a much larger study on chocolate confectionery, 26 housewives from High Wycombe volunteered to participate in this study. Photographs of 31 chocolate confectionery products were presented to each subject in a series of 15 triads. Subjects were asked to

* Present address: Department of Quality, Campden Food and Drink RA, Chipping Campden, Gloucestershire GL55 6LD, UK.

describe similarities and differences between products within a triad, as required by this application of the repertory grid method. They provided a name for each of their own constructs, corresponding definitions and verbal anchors to label the extremities of 100 mm visual analogue scales. Subjects then rated their own constructs for each of the 31 products.

Generalized Procrustes analysis, on the resultant data, revealed a consensus perceptual configuration. Interpretation of the four-dimensional space was made, both visually and using the vector loadings obtained from the analysis. Results suggest that the first principal component represented an 'easy to divide' and 'good for sharing' dimension, the second principal component represented a textural dimension from 'light and airy' to 'solid', the third was a 'biscuit-like' dimension, while the fourth distinguished between products according to 'milkyness'.

For 22 of the subjects, acceptability (consumption) and preference data were obtained for the 31 products. PREFMAP (preference mapping) suggested that none of the four perceptual dimensions were directly related to acceptability. The preference data fitted the space well, suggesting several directions of preference.

INTRODUCTION

From a marketing angle, a critical starting point in the investigation of food acceptability is the determination of those attitudinal/perceptual factors affecting consumer choice. Although there may be a number of general factors which influence consumers' perception of food (McEwan, 1986; Thomson & McEwan, 1986), it is necessary to determine unique lists of perceptual factors, tailored to suit each type of food.

Approaches involving pre-structured questionnaires or free elicitation procedures are often used by market researchers (Oppenheim, 1966; Moser & Kalton, 1971). In the former approach, limited response options may shield important information. In the case of free elicitation, some consumers find it difficult to describe the attributes of products when considered in isolation, and sometimes any information that is elicited, is of no practical importance. This is particularly true of chocolate confectionery, where people often have difficulty in articulating the factors which influence their decision to buy and consume these products (Todd, 1986).

Previous experimentation (Thomson & McEwan, 1988), using meat products, has indicated that an application of the repertory grid method may be useful in the study of chocolate confectionery. The repertory grid method was developed by Kelly (1955), and recently applied in consumer research by Olson (1981) to investigate nutritional aspects of food. As originally implemented (Kelly, 1955), the repertory grid method was used to investigate 'personal constructs' with the aim of determining how individuals perceived the world in which they lived. Such perceptions may either be at a general level, or with respect to particular objects (e.g. church and religion). The principle of this method is the elicitation of so-called 'constructs', which are usually defined as '. . . the way in which two things are alike and in the same way different from a third . . . ' (Kelly, 1955; Oppenheim, 1966). Elicitation of such constructs allows the experimenter to form a picture illustrating relationships between the constructs (perceptual attributes) which influence an individual's overall perception of a particular type of object.

This chapter reports an investigation using an application of the repertory grid method (Thomson & McEwan, 1988) to elicit and evaluate consumer perceptions of chocolate confectionery. In previous studies (Olson, 1981), information extracted from elicitation procedures was typically presented in the form of Knowledge Structure diagrams. While these show the inter-relationships between the various constructs, it has several drawbacks in the study of food acceptability. Firstly, there is no indication of the relative importance of each construct in relation to the food product under investigation. Secondly, on the basis of the information elicited, it is not possible to provide a visual map illustrating the relationships between products, with respect to the constructs. Finally, it would be useful to quantitatively relate consumption and preference data to the main perceptual attributes, for particular product types.

The constructs elicited using the repertory grid method are similar in concept to the attributes obtained in free-choice profiling (Williams & Langron, 1984). Therefore, by producing bi-polar scales for each of the constructs, generalized Procrustes analysis (Gower, 1975) can be used as a statistical tool to provide a perceptual map of the products. This technique also evaluates the relative importance of each construct, for each individual subject.

MATERIALS AND METHODS

Subjects

Twenty-six housewives (subjects) from High Wycombe volunteered to participate in the repertory grid experiment.

Products

Thirty-one products (Table 1) were selected in consultation with Cadbury Schweppes plc, to cover 5 categories of chocolate confectionery. These were Milk Moulded Blocks, Plain Blocks, Countline Chocolate Biscuits, Milk Moulded Recipe Blocks and Countline/Filled Blocks. The number of products in each category was determined according to sales figures for 1983 and 1984 (courtesy of Cadbury Schweppes).

Separate photographs of the 31 products were taken, each displaying the product with and without its wrapper. Care was taken to ensure that each product was as near as possible to its actual life size.

Table 1
Thirty-one chocolate confectionery products

Milk moulded blocks	Milk moulded recipe blocks
1 Aero	13 Fruit and nut
2 Cadbury's Dairy Milk	14 Toblerone
3 Galaxy	15 Whole Nut
4 Nestle	16 Yorkie Raisin and Biscuit
5 St Michael Milk	17 Yorkie Roast Almond
6 Yorkie	
	Countline/filled blocks
Plain blocks	18 Aero Chunky
7 Bournville Dark	19 Boost
8 Terry's Plain	20 Bounty (milk)
	21 Caramel
Countline chocolate biscuits	22 Crunchie
9 Drifter	23 Double Decker
10 Kit Kat	24 Flake
11 Twix	25 Lion Bar
12 Waifer	26 Mars Bar
	27 Marathon
	28 Picnic
	29 Topic
	30 Fry's Turkish Delight
	31 Wispa

The Repertory Grid Method

The 31 (n) products were arranged into a series of 15 triads ($(n-1)/2$). The first triad comprised 3 products chosen at random from the 'pool' of n. The second triad contained one product from the first and another two, chosen at random from those ($n - 3 = 28$) remaining in the 'pool'. The product common to the first two triads was discarded, and one of the remaining two chosen at random and carried forward to the third triad. This procedure was continued until all triads were complete. Four selections of 15 triads were made to overcome possible order effects.

Subjects were presented with the first triad and asked to say in what ways any two of the products (a and b) were similar to each other, and in the same way different from the third (c). The interviewer recorded their responses (constructs) as they were elicited. When no new constructs were forthcoming the other two combinations (a and c versus b; b and c versus a) were presented. This procedure was repeated for the remaining 14 triads. In another interview, subjects provided anchors representing the two extremities of each of their own constructs on a 100 mm bi-polar visual analogue scale. These rating scales, unique to each subject, were then used to quantify the perceptual characteristics of the 31 confectionery products.

As part of the interview procedure, detailed definitions for each construct were obtained from the subject who described them. This information was used in the development of a construct classification scheme (McEwan & Thomson, 1988), designed to aid interpretation of the statistical analysis.

Interviews

Interviews were conducted in the subject's home by the same experienced interviewer. Two interviews, each lasting approximately 45 min, were conducted to elicit the constructs. A further interview of 1 h was needed to define the constructs and provide anchors for each bi-polar scale.

Diary Study and Preference Measurement

As part of the confectionery project, a diary study spanning a 22 week period was conducted. Subjects were asked to list the name and size of every confectionery product they consumed, except non-chocolate biscuits, chewing and bubble gum. From this, unit consumption per 10 week period was calculated for the 31 products (Table 1), for 22 of the

26 subjects. Also, as part of the confectionery project, preference ratings on a 100 mm visual analogue scale were obtained for the 31 products.

Data Treatment

Using a newly developed data reduction procedure (Krzanowski, 1987) each subject's data matrix (N products by V constructs) was reduced to comprise only 15 and then 10 constructs, respectively (where appropriate). For subjects with less than the required number of constructs, dummy (zero) constructs were added to the data matrix.

Generalized Procrustes analysis was performed on the full and reduced data sets. Consensus perceptual spaces for the 31 products were then obtained for each. Further generalized Procrustes analysis on the 3 sets of consensus scores, determined if data reduction influenced the resultant perceptual space. From this analysis, a decision was made as to which of the 3 data sets should be used for interpretation.

For the chosen data, vector loadings were examined for each subject to determine the important constructs on the first 4 principal components. Interpretation was aided by the construct classification scheme and a table showing the number of times each construct class occurred, for the first 4 principal components. Significant construct classes were determined using the binomial statistic (Danzart, 1986), with $n = 26$ (number of subjects) and $p = 1/c$ (where c is the number of construct classes).

Principal coordinate analysis (Chatfield & Collins, 1980) on the distances between each assessor's perceptual space was used to identify any possible sub-groups or outliers in the population (Arnold & Williams, 1986).

Preference mapping (Schiffman et al., 1981; Davies & Coxon, 1983) was performed to determine if any of the perceptual dimensions, from the generalized Procrustes analysis, were related to acceptability and/or preference.

RESULTS

Between 8 and 31 constructs were elicited across the group of subjects.

A consensus perceptual space was obtained using generalized Procrustes analysis for each of the three data sets (31, 15 and 10

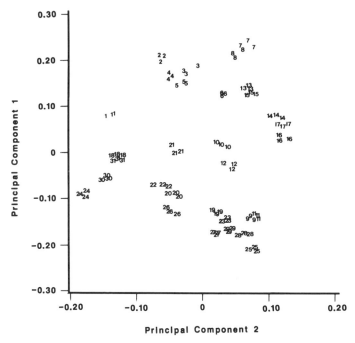

Figure 1. Geometrical similarity between the 3 perceptual spaces derived from data sets with 31, 15 and 10 constructs. (Numbers 1–31 represent the products.)

constructs, respectively). The two-dimensional similarity between these three spaces, as derived using generalized Procrustes analysis, is shown in Fig. 1. In all cases, the three numbers for each product are tightly clustered, indicating that no significant change in the product configurations has occurred because of data reduction. Figures 2 and 3 show the consensus spaces for Principal Components 1 and 2 and for Principal Components 3 and 4, respectively, for the smaller (10 constructs/subject) data set. The first 4 principal components explained 43·1%, 16·3%, 9·5% and 9·2% of the total variation in the data, respectively.

An abbreviated construct classification scheme (Table 2), comprising only terms which have vector loadings (10 constructs data set) of greater than 0·4 or less than −0·4 was used to aid interpretation. (The full classification scheme comprising 37 classes ($c = 37$) can be found in McEwan, 1988; McEwan & Thomson, 1988). Table 3 shows the

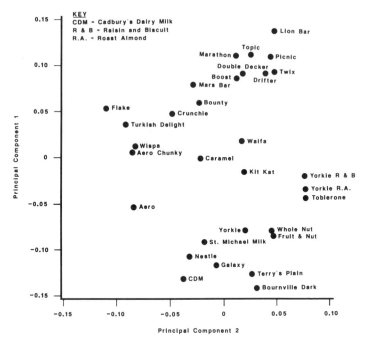

Figure 2. Consensus perceptual space for Principal Components 1 and 2, using 10 constructs.

number of occurrences of each construct class, on the first 4 principal components.

The subject plot, obtained by principal coordinate analysis, is shown in Fig. 4.

Preference mapping, using the acceptability data, indicated that none of the 4 models (3 ideal point models and 1 vector model), fitted the four-dimensional perceptual space. In the case of the preference data, all 4 models fitted the perceptual space. The latter model (Phase IV—vector model) fitted best of all, with a root mean square value of 0·61. Figure 5 shows the two-dimensional preference space for the vector model.

DISCUSSION

Subjects found the format of the repertory grid method helped them elicit perceptual attributes.

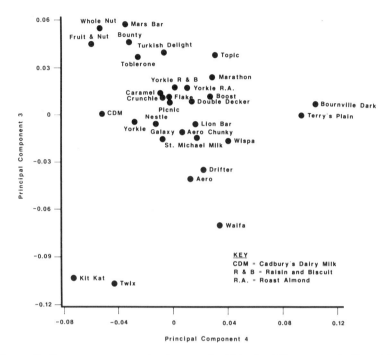

Figure 3. Consensus perceptual space for Principal Components 3 and 4, using 10 constructs.

Whilst data analysis could have been performed using the complete data set (31 constructs), the results would have been difficult to interpret, due to the large number of constructs; 31 constructs × 26 subjects. For this reason it is advantageous to reduce the number of constructs used in the analysis, while still retaining the original structure of the data. The technique proposed by Krzanowski (1987) gives better recovery of structure than previous methods (Jolliffe, 1973). In this experiment, minimal loss of structure occurred on reduction from 31 to 10 variables (Fig. 1).

The results shown in Table 3 indicate that the first principal component (Fig. 2) was dominated by 'sections' and 'good for sharing'. This is perhaps not surprising, as these two characteristics are probably the main distinguishing features between the moulded blocks, and most countline/filled blocks. The textural attributes 'light/airy' and 'soft/hard' were most important in Principal Component 2 (Fig. 2), with 'smoothness', 'biscuit-like' and 'percentage

Table 2
Abbreviated construct classification scheme

Class number	Construct class
1	Attractive wrapper
2	Informative label
3	Colour of chocolate
4	Visual texture
8	Milky chocolate
12	Smoothness
13	Light/airy
17	Texture: soft/hard
18	Crunchy
22	Biscuit-like
25	Sections
27	Good for sharing
29	Treat/special occasion
30	Adult/child product
34	Percentage chocolate
36	Good for packed lunch/snack

Table 3
Number of occurrences of each construct class for the first 4 principal components

Class	Principal component			
	PC1	PC2	PC3	PC4
1	1	3^a	5^c	6^c
2	2	2	3^a	0
3	0	0	1	3^a
4	4^b	3^a	3^a	1
8	1	0	0	7^c
12	0	4^b	0	0
13	0	5^c	0	2
17	3^a	5^c	2	0
18	1	1	3^a	1
22	2	4^b	7^c	0
25	15^c	4^b	4^b	3^a
27	8^c	3^a	3^a	2
29	1	0	2	5^c
30	2	2	3^a	2
34	3^a	4^b	0	1
36	3^a	2	5^c	1

$^a p < 0.05$; $^b p < 0.01$; $^c p < 0.001$.

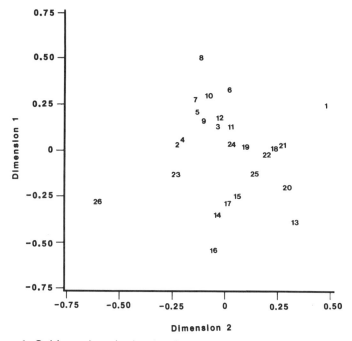

Figure 4. Subject plot obtained using principal coordinate analysis on the 10 construct data set.

chocolate' only slightly less important. 'Biscuit-like' was the main attribute in Principal Component 3 (Fig. 3), along with 'attractive wrapper' and 'good for packed lunch/snack'; 'sections' was only slightly less. Principal Component 4 (Fig. 3) comprised 'attractive wrapper', 'milky chocolate' and 'treat/special occasion'.

These results indicate that each principal component comprises a number of perceptual attributes. This is primarily due to individual differences in their perceptual interpretation of the 31 products, and the relative importance which they attach to their perceptual attributes. The subject plot (Fig. 4) indicates that Subjects 1 and 26, for example, are outliers, and thus may have behaved differently from the rest, though at present there is no indication as to why this might be.

It was not possible to relate acceptability to the 4 perceptual dimensions using PREFMAP. It may not always be the case that attributes used to discriminate samples in a complex multivariate space relate to consumption, or indeed preference. However, for preference,

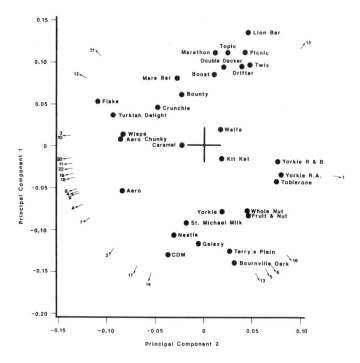

Figure 5. Two-dimensional preference mapping using the vector model.

in this case, the vector model and ideal point models fitted the space, for many of the subjects. As most subjects fitted the vector model, and since examination of the F-values and R-squared values (Schiffman *et al.*, 1981) indicated that no improvement in fit occurred on moving from Phase IV to III, the vector model was chosen for further consideration.

Figure 5 shows that there are several directions of preference. (Subjects 1, 3, 6, 7, 14 and 20 did not fit the vector model.) Most subjects have preference vectors running in the negative directions of Principal Components 1 and 2. This suggests that some subjects have a preference for products perceived as being 'sectioned' and 'good for sharing', while others prefer products which are 'light/airy' and 'soft/hard' (Table 3). The main cluster, on Principal Component 2, includes four subjects (3, 7, 14 and 20) who did not fit the model. It may be that while these subjects are inconsistent in their preference judgements, they like products with the same attributes as others in the group. Another explanation is that the perceptual space does not contain their preference dimensions, and that they have been positioned by chance. Subject 15 seems to have a preference direction which is unique to her, in this space (positive direction on Principal Components 1 and 2), suggesting a preference for the hard countline and filled products. While some general comments about this PREFMAP space have been made, it is important to look at the individual differences which are evident. Examination of the third and fourth principal components would also provide additional information about individual preferences (McEwan & Thomson, 1988).

One important aspect of acceptability on which the repertory grid method does not directly focus is the sensory characteristics of the product (Amerine et al., 1965). These are important influential factors for preference and acceptability (Williams, 1985). However, Principal Components 2 and 4 comprise, in part, textural and taste attributes, respectively. This suggests that these are the main sensory attributes discriminating between samples, though sensory profiling would yield a more in-depth analysis of these.

It is interesting, that despite the common assumption that acceptance and preference are highly correlated (Cardello & Maller, 1982), only preference is related to the perceptual dimensions of Figs. 2 and 3. In fact, only 3 out of the 22 subjects' acceptability and preference data were correlated. In this study it appears that those perceptual attributes which discriminate between samples, are those influencing consumer preference of the confectionery products. Thus, it is reasoned that the gap between preference and acceptability must be bridged by considering non-discriminatory factors such as 'cost', 'value for money' and 'fattening'. For example, some people may like chocolate confectionery, but seldom consume it since they perceive it as being too expensive for the pleasure it gives (McEwan, 1988).

When interpreting these results, it should be remembered that the population investigated was a group of housewives. So, it may be that the emphasis of preference for light/airy products, for example, is a feminine preference characteristic. This sample of 26 consumers is small in comparison with those used in the more traditional market research methods. However, in a previous study on meat products (Thomson & McEwan, 1988) similar perceptual spaces and conclusions were obtained using 2 different groups of 16 and 30 subjects.

CONCLUSIONS

The repertory grid method has proved a useful and valuable tool for eliciting perceptual information on chocolate confectionery products. Using generalized Procrustes analysis, the data yielded a four-dimensional perceptual space which could be interpreted using a construct classification scheme. The results provided a useful indication to the main perceptual differences between the 31 products investigated.

Preference mapping allowed consumer preference to be related to the perceptual space, identifying several directions of preference.

Future research in chocolate confectionery should be aimed at bridging the gap between preference and acceptability, by considering non-discriminatory perceptual attributes such as cost.

ACKNOWLEDGEMENTS

The authors are grateful to the Agricultural and Food Research Council UK and Cadbury Schweppes plc for financial support.

REFERENCES

Amerine, M. A., Pangborn, R. M. & Roessler, E. B. (1965). *Principles of Sensory Evaluation of Food.* Academic Press, New York.

Arnold, G. M. & Williams, A. A. (1986). The use of generalized Procrustes techniques in sensory analysis. In *Statistical Procedures in Food Research,* ed. J. R. Piggott. Elsevier Applied Science, London, pp. 233–53.

Cardello, A. V. & Maller, O. (1982). Relationships between food preferences and food acceptance ratings. *J. Food Sci.,* **47,** 1553–7, 1561.

Chatfield, C. & Collins, A. J. (1980). *Introduction to Multivariate Analysis.* Chapman and Hall, London.

Danzart, M. (1986). Univariate procedures. In *Statistical Procedures in Food Research,* ed. J. R. Piggott. Elsevier Applied Science, London, pp. 19–59.

Davies, P. M. & Coxon, A. P. M. (1983). *MDS(X) User Manual: the MDS(X) Series of Multidimensional Scaling Programs.* University of Edinburgh, Edinburgh.

Gower, J. C. (1975). Generalized Procrustes analysis. *Psychometrika,* **40**(1), 33–51.

Jolliffe, I. T. (1973). Discarding variables in a principal component analysis, II: real data. *Appl. Statist.,* **22,** 21–31.

Kelly, G. A. (1955). *The Psychology of Personal Constructs: a Theory of Personality.* Norton, New York.

Krzanowski, W. J. (1987). Selection of variables to preserve multivariate data structure, using principal components. *Appl. Statist.,* **36,** 22–33.

McEwan, J. A. (1986). Investigation of hedonic scaling techniques. *J. Sci. Food Agric.,* **37,** 1053–4.

McEwan, J. A. (1988) Methodology and new applications in food acceptance research. Ph.D. thesis, University of Reading, UK.

McEwan, J. A. & Thomson, D. M. H. (1988). The repertory grid method and preference mapping in market research: A case study on chocolate confectionery. *Food Quality and Preference,* (submitted).

Moser, C. A. & Kalton, G. (1971). *Survey Methods in Social Investigation.* Gower, Aldershot.

Olson, J. C. (1981). The importance of cognitive processes and existing knowledge structures for understanding food acceptance. In *Criteria of Food Acceptance,* eds J. Solms & R. L. Hall. Forster-Verlag, Zurich, pp. 69–81.

Oppenheim, A. N. (1966). *Questionnaire Design and Attitude Measurement.* Gower, Aldershot.

Schiffman, S. S., Reynolds, M. L. & Young, F. W. (1981). *Introduction to Multidimensional Scaling.* Academic Press, New York.

Thomson, D. M. H. & McEwan, J. A. (1986). Predictive modelling and evaluation of food acceptability. In *Consumer Behavior Research and Marketing of Agricultural Products,* ed. J. E. R. Frijters. National Council for Agricultural Research, The Hague, pp. 63–82.

Thomson, D. M. H. & McEwan, J. A. (1988). An application of the repertory grid method to investigate consumer perceptions of foods. *Appetite,* **10,** 181–93.

Todd, L. (1986). Personal communication. Market Research, Cadbury Schweppes, plc.

Williams, A. A. (1985). Recent developments in sensory analysis. *Food,* **7**(6), 28–31, 59.

Williams, A. A. & Langron, S. P. (1984). The use of free-choice profiling for the evaluation of commercial ports. *J. Sci. Food Agric.,* **35,** 558–68.

Chapter 27

Free-choice Profiling in Cognitive Food Acceptance Research

JAN-BENEDICT E. M. STEENKAMP and
HANS C. M. VAN TRIJP

*Department of Marketing and Marketing Research, Wageningen
Agricultural University, Hollandseweg 1, 6706 KN Wageningen,
The Netherlands*

ABSTRACT

*One of the key determinants of food acceptability is the way products
are perceived by the consumers. If a food product is perceived
favourably, its likelihood of acceptance increases. On the other hand,
less favourably perceived food products are less acceptable to
consumers.*

*Perceptual mapping techniques have been used extensively in market-
ing and sensory research to obtain an insight into consumers'
perceptions of food products. The strengths and weaknesses of the
major perceptual mapping techniques, factor analysis and multidimensional scaling, will be described briefly.*

*The limitations of these traditional approaches to the construction of
perceptual maps can be overcome by allowing the subjects to describe
and evaluate the products explicitly in their own terminology. An
efficient integrated procedure for constructing common perceptual maps
on the basis of completely individualised sets of data is presented. In
this procedure, generalised Procrustes analysis is integrated with a
technique called 'natural grouping'.*

*The integrated procedure will be described and illustrated empirically
by an application to consumer perceptions of meat cuts.*

INTRODUCTION

One of the key determinants of food acceptability is the way products are perceived by the consumers (e.g. Olson, 1981; Thomson & McEwan, 1986). If a food product is perceived favourably (e.g. tastes good, is nutritious, not fattening, etc.), its likelihood of acceptance increases. On the other hand, less favourably perceived food products are less acceptable to consumers. Perceptual mapping techniques have been used extensively in marketing and sensory research to obtain an insight into consumers' perceptions of food products. The aim of a perceptual mapping study is to obtain an insight into the basic cognitive dimensions consumers use to distinguish between the 'products' in the category under investigation, and the relative positions of the products with respect to these dimensions (Hauser & Koppelman, 1979). The major perceptual mapping techniques are factor analysis and multidimensional scaling, each with their own merits and short-comings. For both methods the strengths and weaknesses will be described briefly.

Factor analysis usually requires a two-stage data collection procedure. First, a pilot study is conducted to identify the attributes on which consumers base their perceptions. In the second stage, subjects rate each product on each attribute. The resulting aggregate data matrix serves as input to factor analysis. The perceptions of the products are represented by factor scores which are based on the attribute ratings. The dimensions are interpreted by examining the correlations between attribute ratings and the newly constructed dimensions. A major advantage of factor analysis is that the dimensions are usually readily interpretable in terms of the original attributes. Further, it can also be used if the number of products is small. Major disadvantages are: (1) it is a rather expensive method since qualitative research is usually required to generate the relevant attributes; (2) the attributes must be specified *a priori*; (3) all subjects evaluate the same set of attributes. Thus, the factor analysis approach to perceptual mapping implicitly assumes that all attributes used in the study are relevant to all subjects. However, an individual subject's set of relevant attributes may not be identical to the set of attributes presented (e.g. Williams & Langron, 1984; Böcker & Schweikl, 1986; Boivin, 1986). Some of the attributes presented may not be relevant to the subject whereas he or she can base his or her perceptions on attributes which are not included in the set of attributes presented.

Besides, subjects may attach different meanings to the same attribute and/or describe the same product aspect by different words (e.g. Williams & Arnold, 1985).

A second approach to perceptual mapping involves *multidimensional scaling*. In multidimensional scaling (Schiffman *et al.*, 1981) judgements are made with respect to the actual products rather than to specific attribute scales. The subject is asked to judge the perceived similarity or dissimilarity between (all) possible pairs of products. A perceptual configuration is constructed on the basis of the (dis)similarity judgements. A vast array of computer algorithms is available for this purpose. Similarly a perceptual configuration can be found from preference judgement of products. The most important advantages of multidimensional scaling are: (1) the subject is allowed to use his or her own attributes to discriminate between the products; (2) the data can be obtained in a single session. Multidimensional scaling also suffers from a number of limitations. The most important limitations are: (1) the judgement task becomes very time consuming and expensive if the number of products exceeds, say, 10; (2) the dimensions of the perceptual map are often very difficult to interpret without external information; (3) the number of products should be at least 7 or 8.

The reader is referred to Hauser and Koppelman (1979) and Shocker & Srinivasan (1979) for a more detailed discussion on the relative advantages and disadvantages of the major perceptual mapping techniques.

The limitations of the traditional approaches to the construction of perceptual maps can be overcome by allowing the subject to describe and evaluate the products explicitly in his or her own terminology. This approach, usually called free-choice profiling, has successfully been applied to sensory analysis (e.g. Williams & Langron, 1984; Williams & Arnold, 1985) The employment of free-choice profiling in the area of consumer research seems both straightforward and attractive as it is in line with the trend towards individualised data collection. Given the considerable costs of data collection in consumer research, a less time consuming approach than the one usually applied in sensory studies is required. Such an approach is presented in this chapter. We describe an efficient integrated free-choice profiling procedure for constructing common perceptual maps on the basis of completely individualised cognitive data. The procedure is illustrated empirically by an application to consumer perceptions of meat cuts.

A NEW PROCEDURE FOR CONSTRUCTING PERCEPTUAL SPACES

Data Collection

The data collection part of the procedure consists of 2 phases. In the first phase, attributes are generated by a technique called 'natural grouping'. In the second phase, each subject rates all products on all of his or her own attributes. Below, we shall describe each phase of the proposed procedure in more detail.

The subject is presented with a number of products. Verbal or pictorial description or actual products can be used. He or she is asked to split the set into 2 groups according to their perceived similarity, so that products which appear to the subject to be similar are placed in the same group. The subject is asked to verbalise the aspect or aspects on which the 2 groups differ. Further, he or she is asked to indicate the pole of the aspect that describes each group best (e.g. the aspect is type of meat and the poles are beef for group 1 and pork for group 2). Experience with natural grouping revealed that prompting for attribute levels is frequently not necessary as subjects show a natural tendency to describe groups with poles of attributes. The attribute(s) and poles are written down by the interviewer. The procedure is repeated for each of the 2 groups separately and continued until the subject indicates that no further partitions are possible because the products in a group are similar to him. Subsequently, each product is rated on each attribute; a five-point semantic differential scale is used. The pairs of adjectives are the poles of the attributes used by the subject.

Data Analysis

With the data collection procedure described above, a completely individualised perceptual configuration is obtained for each subject. Each product has a unique position in this configuration. The position of a product is given by the ratings of the product on the attributes. However, when the number of subjects is large, completely individualised perceptual representations make analysis and understanding of the results cumbersome and managerially less useful. It is preferable to search for communalities in the individual perceptions while retaining individual differences. Generalised Procrustes analysis (Gower, 1975; Ten Berge, 1977) is particularly suited for this purpose as it calculates a centroid or 'group' perceptual space, while allowing for individual variation. This procedure is an extension of simple

Procrustes analysis in which only two configurations are matched (Hurley & Cattell, 1962).

Generalised Procrustes analysis starts with a set of individual matrices X_i $(i = 1, \ldots, p)$. X_i is of the order $n \times m_i$ where n indicates the number of products and m_i is the number of attributes used by subject i. Thus, an element of X_i, x_{ijk} denotes subject i's rating of product j $(j = 1, \ldots, n)$ on attribute k $(k = 1, \ldots, m_i)$. It is assumed that the meaningful information of X_i is contained in the relative distances among the n products (cf. Lingoes & Borg, 1978; Coxon, 1982). The centroid configuration Y of the order $n \times m$ $(m = \max_i(m_i))$ is derived from the X_i's. Zero-element columns are appended to each X_i that initially has fewer than m columns. Y is computed as the average of all X_i's after they have been fitted optimally to each other under the admissible transformations (i.e. transformations that leave the relative distances between the products unchanged). The optimisation criterion is to minimise the residual sum of squares between Y and the X_i's. The individual configurations are brought into maximum correspondence to one another by translation, rotation/reflection and central dilation. Each X_i is centred at the origin to neutralise effects due to different subjects scoring at different levels of the scale. Rotation/reflection is applied to account for the effect that subjects use different words or combinations of words to describe the same stimulus. Differences in the range of scores used by different subjects are adjusted for by central dilation. Thus, the transformations used in generalised Procrustes analysis do not affect the relative distances among the products.

The overall communality in individual perceptions can be assessed by the average percentage of variance in the individual configurations that can be explained by the centroid configuration. The residual sum of squares can be partitioned both for products and for subjects (Gower, 1975). Product residuals are derived from the sum of squared distances (over all subjects) from the centroid position to individual subject's final position for each stimulus. Similarly, subject residuals are derived from the sum of squared distances (over all products) for each subject. A smaller residual sum of squares for any product indicates greater agreement among subjects with respect to the relative perceptual position of that stimulus. The residual sum of squares per subject provides information on the communality between the individual configuration and Y. Thus, subjects whose perceptions are poorly explained by Y can be identified.

For ease of interpretation, the centroid configuration may be referred to new orthogonal dimensions, accounting successively for decreasing amounts of variation in the data (Gower, 1975; Williams & Langron, 1984). These new uncorrelated dimensions may be interpreted in terms of each subject's original attributes by calculating the correlations of the original attributes with the new dimensions.

The New Procedure as an Alternative to the Traditional Approaches

The major features of the new procedure introduced above will be summarised briefly. First, this procedure starts with a set of completely individualised perceptual spaces, that is, each individual's configuration is built on individually generated attributes and therefore is meaningful to that person. While searching for communalities among individuals, this individual information is maximally taken into account both for construction and for interpretation of the centroid configuration. Second, the respondent's task is placed within the context of the total set of products under study. When generating attributes, the subject can derive information from all stimuli simultaneously. Third, the procedure takes into account differences in perceptual acumen among subjects. Subjects that do not perceive many differences between products, are not forced to perform a time consuming task as they score only those attributes on which differences are perceived. On the other hand, maximum information is obtained from subjects that show more involvement in the product being investigated. Thus the proposed procedure is a very efficient one. Fourth, the procedure allows for the identification of respondents whose perceptions are poorly explained by the common space. Factor analysis does not provide this possibility, as individual perceptions are not strictly kept separate from the group space.

In comparison to factor analysis the new procedure (1) does not require a pilot study for attribute generation, saving time and costs, (2) subjects use only attributes that are relevant to them, (3) differences in perceptual acumen are taken into account and (4) individual differences are retained and each individual's fit to the common space can be evaluated. As compared to multidimensional scaling, (1) the data collection task is less time consuming, (2) the perceptual dimensions are more readily interpretable, as they can be related directly to the original attributes used by each subject and (3) the data collection task remains manageable for the subject when the number of stimuli is large.

A potential weakness of the proposed procedure is its basic assumption that consumers are capable of verbalising differences between products. To date, experience has not given any indication that this problem is a serious one, but more research is needed before this can be concluded with confidence.

APPLICATION

Data Collection

Subjects and Materials
Sixty-four female purchasers of meat were interviewed at two different facilities of a market research agency. None of them had prior experience with the task involved, and no training was conducted. All subjects were interviewed individually by an experienced interviewer of the market research agency. Subjects were provided with colour photographs of 15 different meat cuts. The photographs were made by a professional photographer who had prior experience with the photography of meat cuts. Table 1 provides a list of the 15 meat cuts used.

Procedure
Data collection consisted of two phases: natural grouping and rating of the products on attributes. Both phases are described in more detail below.

For each subject the fifteen colour photographs of the different meat cuts were spread out on a table in random positioning in such a way that the subject could view all photographs at one time. All photographs were provided with the name of the meat cut depicted. As described above, subjects were asked to divide the photographs into two homogeneous groups (not necessarily of equal size) and were asked to verbalise both the criterion used for the partition made and the poles best describing the 2 groups formed. Subjects continued doing so until no further partitions were possible, as she perceived the products in the group as being similar. In practice, subjects varied in the number of attributes mentioned; it ranged from 2 to 9, with an average of 5.

For each partition made, newly generated attributes and the poles associated with the groups were written down by the interviewer.

After completion of the natural grouping task, each subject rated all 15 meat cuts on all the attributes generated. Thus a completely individualised m-dimensional configuration was obtained for each subject, whereby m (i.e. the number of attributes used by a particular subject) may vary amongst subjects. Subjects were allowed to work at their own pace. On average, the data collection procedure (comprising both natural grouping and rating) took about 20 min to complete.

Results

Data were analysed using generalised Procrustes analysis. The computer program used was kindly provided to us by the Institute of Food Research, Bristol, UK and is a slightly modified version of the Rothamsted Experimental Station version.

As the maximum number of attributes used by any of the subjects was nine, a nine-dimensional centroid configuration was obtained in the first instance. The nine-dimensional centroid configuration accounted for 63·1% of the total amount of variation in the data. This implies that 63·1% of the variance in all individual configurations can be explained by the centroid configuration. The residual sum of squares was partitioned for both products and subjects. Product residuals for the 15 meat cuts used are shown in Table 1.

Examination of the product residuals in Table 1 reveals that subjects show most agreement with respect to their perceptions of beef meat cuts such as blade steak, fore rib steak, roast beef and brisket beef

Table 1

Residual sum of squares in the centroid configuration for the fifteen meat cuts used in this study

Meat cut	Residual SS	Meat cut	Residual SS
Sirloin steak	1·548	Pork rib chop	1·597
Brisket beef steak	1·372	Pork sausages	1·750
Fore rib steak	1·271	Pork belly steak	1·681
Pork shoulder chop	1·607	Blade steak	1·202
Minced beef	1·825	Pork fillet	1·842
Minced meat (pork with beef)	1·492	Rolled pork	1·729
Hamburger	1·735	Roast beef	1·365
Pork steak	1·584		

steak, while they show a relatively strong heterogeneity with respect to their perception of minced beef and pork fillet.

Information on how well each subject's perceptual space is represented by the perceptual positions of the meat cuts in the centroid configuration can be obtained from the subject residuals. Most subjects appear to perceive the meat cuts rather similarly, although they described them using different words. However, a number of subjects had relatively large residual sum of squares. For 14 subjects the residual sum of squares was more than one standard deviation larger than the mean residual sum of squares (5 subjects even had a residual sum of squares that was more than two standard deviations larger). These subjects might attach differential weighting to the attributes or have a different point of perspective (see also the Discussion section of this chapter). This might be an indication that not all 64 subjects form a homogeneous group with respect to their perception of meat cuts.

The nine-dimensional centroid configuration was subjected to principal components analysis (PCA). The first 3 principal components accounted for 92·6% of the variation in the centroid configuration. The fourth principal component accounted only for 4·9% of the variance. When relating the three-dimensional PCA solution to the individual data, it accounts for 58·4% of the variance. A plot of the centroid configuration after PCA is given in Fig. 1.

The interpretation of this orthogonalised centroid configuration is based on the correlation coefficients obtained by correlating the scores on the principal components with each individual's original attribute scores. Thus, the centroid is interpreted on the basis of each individual's own vocabulary. Table 2 gives the most frequently used attributes for each principal component. Most frequently used was defined as: correlating higher than 0·70 for at least 5 subjects. Scale poles were reversed, where necessary, so that the poles first mentioned correlate positively with the principal component in question.

Table 2 reveals that the interpretation of the centroid configuration is straightforward. The first principal component refers to the type of meat, beef being considered leaner, of better quality and more expensive than pork. Other verbalisations used to describe this dimension were colour (red versus not red), tenderness and appreciation of taste. The second dimension refers to the perceived quality of the different meat cuts. Good quality is obviously associated with leanness, pure meat, good taste and being more expensive. The third

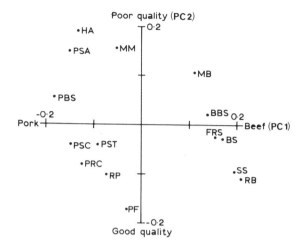

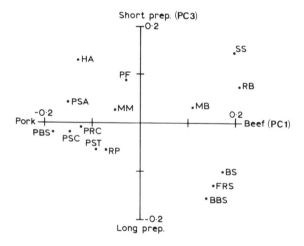

SS	Sirloin Steak	MM	Minced Meat	PBS	Pork Belly Steak
BBS	Brisket Beef Steak	HA	Hamburger	BS	Blade Steak
FRS	Fore Rib Steak	PS	Pork Steak	PF	Pork Fillet
PSC	Pork Shoulder Chop	PRC	Pork Rib Chop	RP	Rolled Pork
MB	Minced Beef	PSA	Pork Sausage	RB	Roast Beef

Figure 1. Centroid configuration after principal component analysis. (PC1, PC2, PC3: Principal Components 1, 2 and 3, respectively.)

Table 2
Interpretation of the centroid configuration in terms of subjects' original
descriptions (number of times correlations > 0·70 were obtained)

Principal Component 1		Principal Component 2		Principal Component 3
Beef vs pork	(46)	Fat vs lean	(23)	Long time of preparation
Lean vs fat	(23)	Minced vs pure	(15)	vs short time of
Expensive vs cheap	(8)	Poor quality vs good quality	(13)	preparation (48)
Good quality vs poor quality	(7)	Poor taste vs good taste	(11)	
		Cheap vs expensive	(11)	
		Rarely used vs often used	(6)	
		Common vs exclusive	(5)	
		Tough vs tender	(5)	

dimension is exclusively described by duration of preparation of the
meat.

DISCUSSION

The integrated procedure presented in this study appears to be both a
reliable and easy to handle method for the construction of a common
perceptual space, while retaining individual differences. Reliability is
apparent from the consistency of the results obtained in this study with
other studies concentrating on consumer behaviour with respect to
meat (Steenkamp & van Trijp, 1986). Further, reliability was assessed
by comparing the results of generalised Procrustes analysis to those
obtainable from INDSCAL. Euclidean distances between the products
were computed for each subject separately and analysed via
INDSCAL. The C-match index of fit (Cliff, 1966) between
INDSCAL's three-dimensional group space and generalised Procrustes
analysis' centroid space was 0·966. This indicates high agreement
between the two solutions. Moreover, INDSCAL's subject space
revealed a relatively homogeneous group of subjects.

In the integrated procedure presented in this study, natural grouping
was used for the generation of individually relevant attributes. As
such, this method is comparable to other methods for eliciting
attributes, Kelly's Repertory Grid method (Kelly, 1955) being the best
known among these. When compared to Kelly's Repertory Grid, the
natural grouping procedure has the advantage that it is less time
consuming and that partitions are being made within the context of the

total group of products under study. In Kelly's Repertory Grid judgements are made within the context of only 3 products (though in varying combinations), which may lead to attributes which are not that relevant within a larger context. Further, within the natural grouping task, subjects who do not perceive much difference between products, are not forced to perform a long-winded (and therefore boring) task, as they only score those attributes on which they perceive differences amongst the products. Subjects that show more involvement with the product under study will differentiate among the products in more detail and as such, a multi-layer organisation of the relevant attributes is obtained. For these the maximum amount of information is obtained, without the respondent getting bored.

It remains in question, whether natural grouping can be applied to small numbers of products. It is possible that Kelly's Repertory Grid would be preferable under these circumstances.

Natural grouping is fast and easy to understand but also rather rigid. Once products are placed into different groups, they cannot be placed into the same group with respect to other attributes. Clearly, the first partition especially, exerts a considerable influence on the outcome of the process. Possible modifications may render the natural grouping procedure more flexible.

Generalised Procrustes analysis is a versatile approach, of which in this study only the basic approach is used. Not all of the subjects are equally well represented by the centroid configuration, obtained on the basis of admissible transformations. The reasons for this can be investigated within the generalised Procrustes framework by extending the basic model to inadmissible transformations of the data. It can be investigated whether individuals attach greater salience to certain (fixed) aspects of the difference between products than to others (differential dimensional weighting) or whether individuals have idio-syncratic frames of reference (i.e. use different spatial directions as a result of using different attributes). Further, it can be investigated whether individuals have different points of perspective. Based on these additional individual parameters, subjects could be partitioned into relatively homogeneous subgroups, if necessary. However, other research has shown that the admissible transformations generally account for the largest share of the total variance explained in the individual data (Borg, 1977; Coxon, 1982).

Future research could apply the proposed data collection and analysis procedure to other products in order to investigate its possibilities and limitations. In this study the products were, for most subjects, perceptually very different. It would be worthwhile to examine whether subjects are able to verbalise their attributes and whether the centroid configuration is stable, when the products are perceptually closer to each other.

In summary, the results appear encouraging. It was possible to construct a readily interpretable common perceptual map on the basis of each subject's own vocabulary. The methods used in this study, to obtain an individualised perceptual product map, deserve further investigation.

REFERENCES

Böcker, F. & Schweikl, H. (1986). Better preference prediction with individualized sets of relevant attributes. *Proceedings of the 15th Annual Conference of the European Marketing Academy*, pp. 525–40. Helsinki.

Boivin, Y. (1986). A free response approach to the measurement of brand perceptions. *International Journal of Research in Marketing*, **3**, 11–17.

Borg, I. (1977). Geometric representation of individual differences. In *Geometric Representation of Relational Data*, ed. J. C. Lingoes. Mathesis Press, Ann Arbor, pp. 609–55.

Cliff, N. (1966). Orthogonal rotation to congruence. *Psychometrika*, **1**, 33–42.

Coxon, A. P. M. (1982). *The Users Guide to Multidimensional Scaling*. Heinemann Educational Books Ltd, London.

Gower, J. C. (1975). Generalized Procrustes analysis. *Psychometrika*, **1**, 33–51.

Hauser, J. R. & Koppelman, F. S. (1979). Alternative perceptual mapping techniques: Relative accuracy and usefulness. *Journal of Marketing Research*, **16**, 495–506.

Hurley, J. L. & Cattell, R. B. (1962). The Procrustes program: producing direct rotation to test a hypothesized factor structure. *Behavioral Science*, **7**, 258–62.

Kelly, G. A. (1955). *The Psychology of Personal Constructs*. Norton, New York.

Lingoes, J. C. & Borg, I. (1978). A direct approach to individual differences scaling using increasingly complex transformations. *Psychometrika*, **43**, 491–519.

Olson, J. C. (1981). The importance of cognitive processes and existing knowledge structures for understanding food acceptance. In *Criteria of Food Acceptance*, eds J. Solms & R. L. Hall. Forster, Zurich, pp. 69–81.

Schiffman, S. S., Reynolds, M. L. & Young, F. W (1981). *Introduction to Multidimensional Scaling*. Academic Press, New York.

Shocker, A. D. & Srinivasan, V. (1979). Multiattribute approaches to concept evaluation and generation: A critical review. *Journal of Marketing Research*, **16**, 159–80.

Steenkamp, J-B. E. M. & Van Trijp, H. C. M. (1986). *Consumer Evaluation of the Sensory Quality of Meat.* P. V. V., Rijswijk (in Dutch).

Ten Berge, J. M. F. (1977). Orthogonal Procrustes rotation for two or more matrices. *Psychometrika*, **42**, 267–76.

Thomson, D. M. H. & McEwan, J. A. (1986). Predictive modelling and evaluation of food acceptability. In *Consumer Behavior Research and Marketing of Agricultural Products.* ed. J. E. R. Frijters. NRLO, The Hague, pp. 63–82.

Williams, A. A. & Arnold, G. M. (1985). A comparison of the aromas of six coffees characterised by conventional profiling, free-choice profiling and similarity scaling methods. *Journal of the Science of Food and Agriculture,* **36**, 204–14.

Williams, A. A. & Langron, S. P. (1984). The use of free-choice profiling for the evaluation of commercial ports. *Journal of the Science of Food and Agriculture,* **35**, 558–68.

Chapter 28

Practical Application of Preference Mapping

GEOFFREY R. NUTE, HALLIDAY J. H. MACFIE

Agricultural and Food Research Council, Institute of Food Research, Bristol Laboratory, Langford, Bristol BS18 7DY, UK

and

KEITH GREENHOFF

Mobile Sensory Testing Services, 54–62 Station Road East, Oxted, Surrey RH8 0PG, UK

ABSTRACT

Preference mapping was used to study natural segmentation of a consumer population in terms of their sensory evaluation of products.

The first example investigated the effects of processing parameters on the acceptability of restructured steaks. Using a mobile sensory laboratory and the Mall Intercept Method, eight formulations of steaks were assessed for texture, saltiness, juiciness, taste, meatiness and overall liking by consumers in the North and South of England. Analysis of variance revealed that consumers were able to perceive differences in saltiness and juiciness, but there was no significant difference in overall liking. Internal preference mapping revealed that salt and fat content were influential in determining acceptability.

In the second example, consumer acceptability of a perfumed household product was mapped into a sensory space derived from a laboratory panel. The regression of acceptability data onto the first two principal components did not provide an obvious explanation of consumer preference. However, regression onto the second and third principal components revealed a high proportion of explained preference, with consumers partitioned into two groups: those who preferred samples with 'light' odours and those who preferred more intense odours.

INTRODUCTION

In the development of new products, both sensory and consumer tests are carried out. However, there are difficulties in using consumer data to optimise perceived acceptability of products.

There may be substantial confusion over the exact definition of a descriptive profile. Indeed, with a trained sensory panel, Langron (1981) showed that some tasters confused the terms, 'bitter' and 'astringent', thus the likelihood of consumers having this problem will be high. Moskowitz (1985) stated that if sensory attributes and liking attributes are presented together in a consumer test, the liking attributes always predominated, with the sensory attributes in the middle and any negative attributes, e.g. 'bitterness' at the bottom in terms of relative importance to the consumer.

There may also be substantial segmentation among consumers not revealed by simple averaging by socio-demographic factors.

The solution to these problems is to ask consumers only like/dislike questions and to use preference mapping (Carroll & Chang, 1970). The key difference between conventional methods for handling preference/acceptability data and preference mapping is that individual differences are not averaged but are built into the model, and play an integral role in the fitting algorithm. There are two ways of dealing with this data: in what is known as 'internal analysis', the objective is to achieve a consensus configuration of the stimuli based solely on the preference data, whilst in 'external analysis' the aim is to relate acceptability to other measurements on the stimuli (i.e. sensory data) using as economical a model as possible to take account of individual differences in scoring pattern. An important aspect of this approach is that consumers are asked few questions, but must receive at least 6 products at the same time for the method to operate. The method is therefore usually far cheaper than conventional consumer trials since recruiting 1200 consumers to assess 1 sample is 6 times more expensive than recruiting 200 to assess 6.

This chapter demonstrates the use of both types of preference analysis using two very different examples, namely grill steaks and the fragrance of a particular household product.

MATERIALS AND METHODS

Restructured Steaks

Eight formulations of restructured steaks were prepared following the procedure outlined by Jolley & Rangeley (1986). Formulation details are shown in Table 1. All samples were frozen after preparation and stored at $-20°C$ until required for consumer testing.

Consumer Trial

Consumer trials were conducted in two regions of the United Kingdom. A mobile sensory testing unit (a vehicle that is effectively a taste-panel room with 5 booths, incorporating controlled testing conditions) was set up in shopping precincts. Consumers were approached by professional interviewers and invited to take part in the tests. They were questioned about the texture, saltiness, juiciness, taste, meatiness and overall liking of the steaks. Each question was presented as a 100 mm line scale with anchor points at each end and consumers were asked to mark the line according to the intensity of their response. Steaks were cooked from frozen on a continuous burger broiler and the whole steak presented hot (internal temperature 70°C) in randomised order one at a time until all 8 were assessed. Consumers had a short rest after assessing 4 steaks to avoid sensory fatigue.

Table 1
Experimental design for restructured steaks $\frac{1}{4}$ replicate of a 2^4 factional design

	Fat		Salt		Temper		Blend time	
Steaks	20%	12%	1%	0·5%	Long	Short	12 min	6 min
1	+	−	+	−	I	−	−	+
2	+	−	−	+	+	−	+	−
3	−	+	−	+	+	−	−	+
4	−	+	+	−	+	−	+	−
5	−	+	+	−	−	+	−	+
6	−	+	−	+	−	+	+	−
7	+	−	−	+	−	+	−	+
8	+	−	+	−	−	+	+	−

All samples were coarsely comminuted.
+ indicates the level used.

Household Product Fragrance

Sensory Panel

Descriptive sensory analysis was conducted on 17 fragrances by a panel of 12 assessors previously screened for their sensory ability. The panellists derived their own vocabulary for describing the product fragrances over 4 sessions in which the 17 fragrances were presented. The agreed profile consisted of 39 descriptors and was used to generate odour profiles for the products. The assessments were conducted in triplicate with sample presentation randomised over the panel and over replicates to reduce order effects. The data were simplified and reduced to fewer sensory dimensions using principal component analysis, from which a sub-set of 6 products were identified for use in the consumer tests.

Consumer Test

Female consumers were approached in 2 sites in the South East of England. After a preliminary interview to identify users of this type of household product, consumers were then asked to assess 6 products presented in different orders in a balanced design. A total of 194 consumers took part in the tests.

The tests were carried out in the mobile sensory testing unit equipped with an air extraction unit to avoid carry over of fragrance odour. Products were presented singly, in capped plastic beakers, and consumers asked to sniff each sample and indicate how much they liked the fragrance in the context of the particular product, by giving it a score between 0 and 10. After 2 min or longer, depending upon the consumer, the next sample was presented. Each sample was from the same batch of product and all testing was completed in 2 days.

Statistical Analyses

Analysis of variance was carried out on the attribute ratings using formulation and assessors as factors. Preference mapping on the overall liking data was obtained using a Genstat program written by one of the authors (MacFie). Principal component analysis was used in the fragrance trial to provide a sensory space derived from the profile. The principal component scores for the first 3 dimensions were used as the coordinates for the stimulus space into which the consumers were mapped using the Phase IV linear vector model of Schiffman *et al.* (1981).

RESULTS

Restructured Steaks

Seventy-two people in the North and 70 in the South tasted the steaks. In the North there was a significant effect ($p < 0.001$) due to salt content differences between the samples: the four 1% samples were rated 'about right' (50 mm along the line) with mean values ranging from 44·1 to 51·3, and the four 0·5% samples were rated consistently lower with mean values ranging from 32·1 to 41·8. A similar effect was shown in the South ($p < 0.05$) with the means ranging from 47·7 to 52·7 for the 1% salt and 42·3 to 45·6 for the 0·5% salt samples. No significant effect due to texture was found in the results from the North or South, with means ranging from 43·6 to 55·8 in the North and 48·6

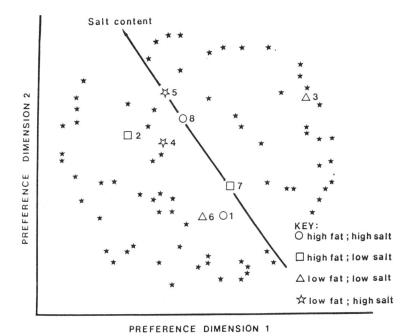

Figure 1. Internal preference map showing North consumers (★) mapped into the stimulus space. Different restructured steaks are designated by numbers corresponding with the formulations in Table 1. The position of the numbers represents preferences expressed by consumers as a whole. The salt vector is superimposed on the space by inspection.

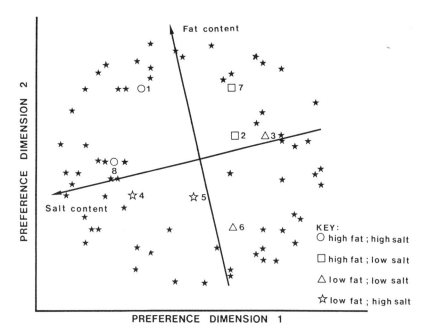

Figure 2. Internal preference map showing South consumers (★) mapped into the stimulus space. Different restructured steaks are designated by numbers corresponding with the formulations in Table 1. The position of the numbers represents preferences expressed by consumers as a whole. The 'fat' and 'salt' vectors are superimposed on the space by inspection.

to 56·8 in the South. For juiciness there was a significant effect ($p < 0·001$) in both the North and the South with means ranging from 51·1 to 68·2. Further analyses using formulation constituents as factors showed that fat, salt, temper and blend time were all significant effects. In the North but not in the South there were significant effects for taste ($p < 0·05$) and meatiness ($p < 0·05$). Despite these differences in the individual ratings, there were no significant differences in sample means for overall liking in either the North or South.

Internal preference mapping (Fig. 1) of the overall liking data for the North consumers revealed that only one vector, for salt, could be drawn. When individual consumers are placed in their region of highest preference, no single formulation suited all assessors, i.e. the consumers (stars) are scattered circularly over Fig. 1. In the South (Fig. 2), two preference vectors could be shown, fat (Dimension 2) and salt (Dimension 1). Again consumers were highly segmented, e.g. those in the top left of Fig. 2 preferred higher fat and higher salt; those in the bottom right preferred lower fat and lower salt.

Household Product Fragrance
Principal component analysis of the sensory data showed that the first 3 components accounted for 88% of the variation. The first component separated the products by contrasting 'natural' fragrance characters (florals, citrus fruits, lavender) with 'synthetic' fragrance characters (pear-drops, oily, chemical, medical); the second by contrasting sweet, fruity, floral notes, with green, spicy, medicinal notes, and the third by odour strength and the concept of light/heavy fragrances. Regression of the consumer scores onto the stimulus space defined by components 1 and 2 is shown in Fig. 3. The numerals indicate the position of the 6

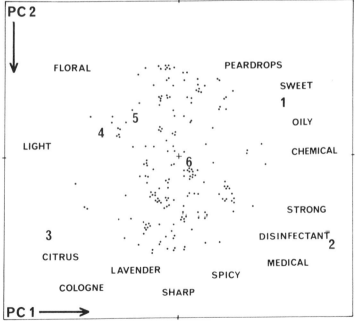

Figure 3. Regression of acceptability data on to the sensory space defined by Principal Components 1 and 2. (Each dot represents an individual consumer.)

products, the descriptive attributes, are shown in script and the individual (consumers) preference dimensions by dots. A line drawn between any dot and the centroid indicates the direction of the preference vector, and the distance from the centre an indication of the correlation between observed and fitted responses. Consumers were poorly fitted to the first 2 dimensions and the major sources of product variation are not apparent in determining consumer preference. When the consumer scores are regressed onto Dimensions 2 and 3, the majority of consumers fell into two groups (Fig. 4) along an axis describing odour strength and 'lightness' of the fragrance. This picture can be simplified if the frequency of respondents in any sector of the plot is shown as a radial bar chart, which shows the respondent count in each 10 degree sector (Fig. 5). The top left-hand corner contains 47% of consumers, who prefer stronger fragrances. The bottom right-hand side contains 26% of consumers, who prefer less

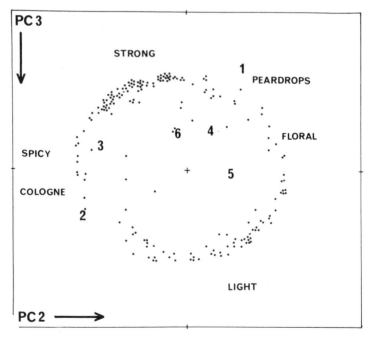

1. Regression of acceptability data on to the sensory space by Principal Components 3 and 4. (Each dot represents an individual consumer.)

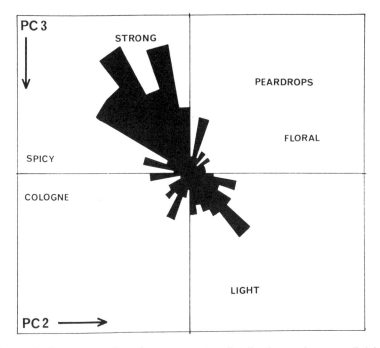

Figure 5. Summary of preference vector distribution using a radial bar chart.

strong fragrances and those described as 'light'. The remaining 27% of consumers are split into the two remaining quadrants. The major determinant of consumer acceptability in the fragrances is related to odour strength and the concept of light/heavy fragrances.

CONCLUSION

Preference mapping techniques provide useful means of revealing the underlying dimensions of perception and help to visualise individual opinions and segment the population into clusters grouped by similarity of preference. In the restructured steak trial, overall liking was linked to fat and salt, which were not revealed by conventional analysis of variance (ANOVA) techniques. Regional differences were also shown with consumers in the North who expressed no preference for higher or lower fat content, while in the South both salt and fat contributed to the preferred product.

The fragrance study revealed that consumer preference was best explained on a sensory dimension defined by odour strength and the concept of light/heavy fragrances. This dimension effectively split the population into 2 groups, the larger group preferring stronger, heavier fragrances in the product and the smaller group preferring weaker/lighter fragrances.

Demographic and product usage data were obtained in both studies, but examining the preference maps showed no obvious effects of any respondent variable.

These 2 studies have demonstrated that linking sensory and consumer liking data can yield useful data on acceptability and helps understand the importance of sensory attributes in determining consumer preference. It is therefore a useful aid in product development.

REFERENCES

Carroll, J. D. & Chang, J. J. (1970). Analysis of individual differences in multidimensional scaling via an N-way generalization of "Eckart-Young" decomposition. *Psychometrika,* **35,** 283–31.
Jolley, P. D. & Rangeley, W. R. D. (1986). Practical factors influencing the shape of a cooked, flaked and formed beef product. *Proceedings of 32nd European Meat Research Workers,* Vol. 2, Ghent, Belgium, pp. 353–6.
Langron, S. P. (1981). The statistical treatment of sensory analysis data. Ph.D thesis, University of Bath.
Moskowitz, H. R. (1985). Measuring the importance of attributes to consumers. In *New Directions for Product Testing and Sensory Analysis of Foods.* Food & Nutrition Press Inc., USA, pp. 17–52.
Schiffman, S. S., Reynolds, M. L. & Young, F. W. (1981). *Introduction to Multidimensional Scaling.* Academic Press, London.

Chapter 29

An Investigation of the Relationship Between Preference and the Sensory Characteristics of Nine Sweeteners

ANNE TUNALEY, DAVID M. H. THOMSON and
JEAN A. MCEWAN

Department of Food Science and Technology, University of Reading, Whiteknights, P.O. Box 226, Reading, RG6 2AP, UK

ABSTRACT

The acceptability of any product depends on a number of factors. One of these is preference for the sensory characteristics which the consumer perceives. To improve acceptability, sweeteners are added to numerous foods and drinks, plus certain pharmaceutical products. As sweeteners are not just sweet, detailed information about all their sensory characteristics is needed, and this can be achieved using profiling. It is very important to integrate such data with that on preference, as manufacturers can then apply the resultant information to optimise products.

For these reasons, a study was conducted with 17 assessors and 9 sweeteners, using consensus profiling, preference mapping and univariate statistical techniques. The sweeteners were sucrose, fructose, glucose, sorbitol, lactitol, aspartame, saccharine, acesulfame K and a mixed extract of the leaves of Stevia rebaudiana *Bertoni. The profiling data were analysed using generalised Procrustes analysis, and a perceptual space was obtained. Preference data were collected on the same 9 sweeteners, and then submitted to preference mapping*

(PREFMAP). Mean preference scores provided an overall indication of preference, but concealed individual differences. To obtain information on which characteristics were related to preference, correlation coefficients were calculated.

In summary, information about the relationship between preference and the sensory characteristics of these sweeteners, was obtained from PREFMAP, and univariate statistical techniques. This knowledge is useful to manufacturers who can use it to help improve the acceptability of products.

INTRODUCTION

Many factors influence the acceptability of food products (Thomson & McEwan, 1986), and one of these is preference for the sensory characteristics which the consumer perceives. This is often very important in determining acceptability (Pangborn, 1975; Williams, 1985).

Sweetness is one of the four basic tastes (Amerine *et al.*, 1965) and is usually regarded as a pleasant sensation, the preference for which appears to be present from birth (Desor *et al.*, 1973; Steiner, 1979; Rozin, 1982). Sweeteners are added to numerous foods and drinks, plus certain pharmaceutical products, to improve their acceptability. Manufacturers can choose from a range of nutritive and non-nutritive sweeteners, and choosing the most suitable becomes easier as more relevant knowledge is acquired. As one of the most important aspects of any product is how it is perceived by the senses, it is necessary to obtain detailed information on the sensory characteristics of sweeteners.

There are a number of techniques which can be applied to investigate these characteristics, and they include similarity/ dissimilarity scaling (Schiffman *et al.*, 1979; Thomson & Tunaley, 1987) or profiling methods (Williams, 1986; Tunaley *et al.*, 1988). Although the basic principles and concepts of these methods differ, there is evidence that they provide overall results and conclusions which are very similar (Chauhan *et al.*, 1983; Williams & Arnold, 1985). Each produces a perceptual space which enables determination of the relationship between the sensory characteristics, and the samples in which they are perceived. A multidimensional space also allows preference to be related to the perceptual dimensions using preference mapping (Schiffman *et al.*, 1981).

It is very important to integrate information on the sensory characteristics perceived in a product with preference data. For this reason, an investigation was conducted using consensus (conventional) profiling (Williams *et al.*, 1984) and preference mapping (PREFMAP), together with unidimensional statistical techniques. Manufacturers can apply such information to optimise products, and improve their acceptability.

MATERIALS

The sweeteners investigated were sucrose (Tate & Lyle, UK), fructose, glucose, sorbitol (BDH Chemicals, UK), lactitol (Express Dairies, UK), aspartame (Nutrasweet AG, CH.), saccharine (Sigma Chemical Co., UK), acesulfame K (Hoechst AG, FRG) and a mixed extract of the leaves of *Stevia rebaudiana* Bertoni (Terra Nova, Canada). Bottled still mineral water (Scottish Spring, J. Sainsbury, UK) was used to prepare the samples and as a palate cleanser.

METHODS

Samples
Equi-sweet aqueous solutions of all 9 sweeteners were prepared at concentrations which were perceived to be of equal sweetness to 5% sucrose, as determined in a previous study (Tunaley *et al.*, 1987). All solutions were prepared 24 h in advance and held at room temperature $(20 \pm 2°C)$.

Assessors
The panel comprised 17 volunteer assessors from the staff and postgraduate students in the Department. Their ages ranged from 19 to 58 years, and there were 9 females and 8 males. All the assessors were experienced and had participated in previous sensory experiments on sweeteners.

Consensus Profiling
Consensus or conventional profiling (Powers, 1984) was used to obtain qualitative and quantitative information on the sensory characteristics perceived in these 9 sweeteners. Assessors developed a consensus

Dislike   Like

Figure 1. Continuous line scale (150 mm) used to record preference responses.

vocabulary to describe all the characteristics, and then assessed their intensity. As with all consensus profiling, assessors were instructed to ignore the influence of preference when making their assessments. A detailed account of this experiment is to be published elsewhere (Tunaley *et al.*, 1988).

Preference Assessments
Assessments were performed in a controlled environment in individual partitioned booths (ASTM, 1973). 50 ml samples were presented in coded, glazed china cups. Assessors rinsed between each sweetener, and expectorated all samples and rinse water, to eliminate any influences which ingestion might have on their preference responses (Cabanac, 1971). The latter were recorded on a 150 mm continuous line scale (Fig. 1) anchored with 'dislike' on the left-hand extremity, and 'like' on the right (Thomson & McEwan, 1986). Assessors were familiarised with the scale and it was stressed that the preference for each sample should be assessed independently, and not as a comparison of the 3 samples presented at a session. An unbalanced block experimental design allocated a different trio of samples to each assessor, and helped to minimise order effects by ensuring that each sample appeared in every position an equal number of times. Three replicates of the experiment were conducted.

Data Analysis
Responses were converted to numerical scores between 0 and 150. Generalised Procrustes analysis (GPA) (Arnold & Williams, 1986) was performed on the profiling data, using the statistical package GENSTAT (General Statistics, 1983, NAG, Oxford, UK). A consensus perceptual space was obtained, and the characteristics which contributed most to each principal component were determined.

Although 3 replicates of the preference experiment were conducted, the means for each assessor were used, as there were no significant differences between the replicates. The computer program PREFMAP

(Davies & Coxon, 1983) fitted the preference data through the perceptual space obtained from the profiling experiment. The metric option was selected as it is more powerful statistically (Huber, 1975). Initially the preference data were fitted through the 3D solution, but the configuration matrix was singular, and hence non-invertible. As inversion is a necessary step to successfully conduct PREFMAP, the 2D solution was used.

Mean preference scores for each sweetener were obtained using SAS (Statistical Analysis Systems, 1982, SAS Institute Inc., Cary, NC, USA), and the corresponding least significant differences ($p < 0.05$) calculated. Also using SAS, correlation coefficients were calculated between preference and each sensory characteristic for every assessor.

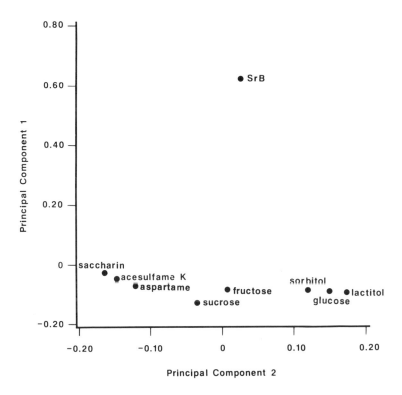

Figure 2. Consensus perceptual space: Principal Components 1 versus 2.

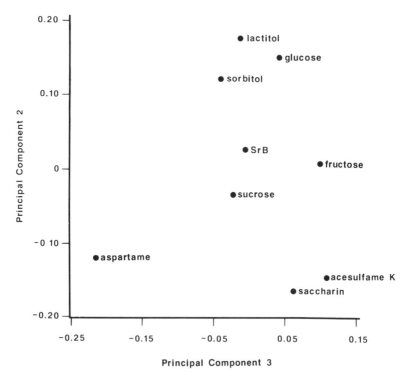

Figure 3. Consensus perceptual space: Principal Components 2 versus 3.

RESULTS

Figures 2 and 3 show the consensus perceptual space obtained using the profile data and GPA. The analysis was conducted at the individual level, but for clarity, only the means of the 3 replicates are shown. The first 3 principal components (PCs) explained 48%, 14% and 7% of the total variation in the data, respectively. GPA enabled formal interpretation of the results by indicating which characteristics and assessors contributed the most to each principal component (Table 1).

The PREFMAP models which the preference data fitted best, were the ideal point (Phase III) and vector (Phase IV) models (Fig. 4).

Table 2 shows the mean preference scores of the sweeteners together with their LSD's (Table 2). The number of times a sweetener

Table 1
Interpretation of the first three principal components

Principal Component	Important characteristics
1	Liquorice flavour (10+) Liquorice odour (6+) Liquorice aftertaste (5+) Persistent aftertaste (4+) Bitter aftertaste (3+) Fruity:non-citrus odour (3+)
2	Sweet flavour (6−) Bitter flavour (3−) Persistent aftertaste (3−) Syrupy/thick mouthfeel (3+)
3	Sweet aftertaste (5−) Sickly aftertaste (4−) Persistent aftertaste (3−)

Bracketed figures show the number of assessors who used that discriminatory characteristic.
+ or − refers to positive or negative loading of a characteristic.

was scored most and least preferred by assessors is shown in Table 3. Table 4 shows the frequency with which a characteristic was correlated with preference ($p < 0.05$).

DISCUSSION

Generalised Procrustes analysis enabled detailed interpretation of the profile data (Table 1), and revealed that each principal component was complex and comprised a number of sensory characteristics.

The PREFMAP results were complicated and therefore difficult to interpret. The models which best fitted the data were the ideal point (Phase III), and vector models (Phase IV). Five assessors (29%) fitted the ideal point model—these were 1, 2, 3, 6, 7, plus the 'Average Subject' (Fig. 4). Seven (41%) fitted the Phase IV vector model— Assessors 1, 2, 5, 6, 11, 14, and 15—but the 'Average Subject' did not fit this model (Fig. 4). Although Assessors 1, 2 and 6 fitted both

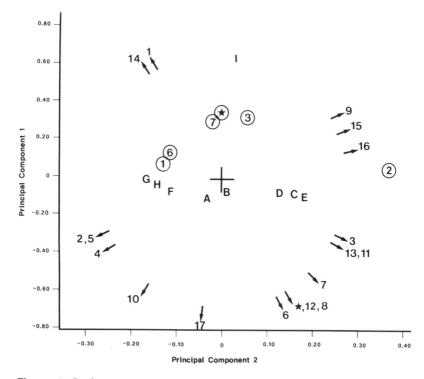

Figure 4. Preference mapping—Phase III and IV models. Arrows show preference vectors for individual subjects (Phase IV) and circled numbers show ideal points (Phase III). Key: A, sucrose; B, fructose; C, glucose; D, sorbitol; E, lactitol; F, aspartame; G, saccharin; H, acesulfame K: I, SrB; ★, average subject; ○, ideal point.

models, their between phase F-values indicated that no improvement in fit was achieved on moving from Phase IV to III.

There were several directions of preference, and examination of the Phase IV results for assessors who fitted that model, reveals that Assessors 1 and 14 are weighted in the positive direction of PC 1. They appeared to prefer the sensory characteristics associated with this principal component, which are liquorice flavour, odour and after-taste, persistent and bitter aftertaste and fruity:non-citrus odour (Table 1). These characteristics are primarily associated with Sample I and consultation of the raw preference data confirmed that their most preferred sweetener, was in fact SrB. This is also true of Assessor 15,

Table 2
Mean preference scores of the sweetoners

Sweetener	Mean preference score (mm)
Sucrose	74
Lactitol	70
Fructose	67
Sorbitol	62
Aspartame	55
Glucose	55
Saccharin	53
Acesulfame K	51
SrB	30

(Mean preference scores linked with a vertical bar are not significantly different—based on LSD.)

Table 3
Number of times a sweetener was scored most and least preferred

Sweetener	Most preferred	Least preferred
Sucrose	3	0
Lactitol	2	0
Fructose	4	1
Sorbitol	1	0
Aspartame	1	0
Glucose	0	2
Saccharin	1	2
Acesulfame K	2	4
SrB	3	8

Table 4
Frequency (No. of assessors) with which a characteristic was correlated with preference ($p < 0.05$).

Characteristic	Number of assessors
Bitter aftertaste	7 (−)
Persistent aftertaste	7 (−)
Clean flavour	6 (+)
Bitter flavour	4 (−)

+ positive correlation
− negative correlation

but his direction of preference is weighted towards the positive side of PC 2. This suggests that as well as liking some of the characteristics associated with SrB, Assessor 15 preferred sweeteners that are not too sweet, bitter or persistent, but are syrupy/thick. Assessor 11 is very similar in this respect, but is positioned in the negative quadrant of PC 1, and so probably liked SrB less than Assessor 15. This was again confirmed by looking at the raw data.

The direction of Assessor 6's preference vector suggests she disliked characteristics associated with SrB, but probably liked syrupy/thick samples such as lactitol and sorbitol. The 'Average Subject' is positioned very near Assessor 6, but the former does not fit this model, probably because of the diverse preferences across the assessors. Assessors 2 and 5 are weighted on the negative side of PC 2, which suggests they liked sweeteners which are not syrupy/thick, but are sweet, bitter and persistent, but not SrB. This assumption is supported by consulting the raw data, which showed that acesulfame K and saccharin were their most preferred sweeteners, respectively.

Of the 5 assessors who fitted the ideal point (Phase III) model, Assessor 2 is outside the stimulus space. It is very difficult to draw any conclusions from this result, but this assessor had commented that he did not like any of these sweeteners and had difficulty in using more than half of the hedonic scale. His data are probably better represented by the vector model. Both Assessors 2 and 6 had negative ideal points. These indicate that preference increases with the square of the distance from the point (Schiffman et al., 1981), and are really points of dislike. Assessor 1's ideal point indicates a preference for sweeteners perceptually similar to acesulfame K, saccharin and aspartame. However, as the vector model suggests a preference for the characteristics associated with PC 1, and SrB, this illustrates the different results and interpretations, when using different PREFMAP models. As Assessor 1's most preferred sweetener was SrB, the vector model appears to provide a better representation of her preference.

The ideal points for Assessors 3, 7, and the 'Average Subject' are very close. Their positions on the plot between SrB, and sucrose and fructose, indicate that their most preferred sweetener would comprise moderate amounts of the characteristics associated with these 3 sweeteners.

Interpreting the Phase III model, enables the sensory characteristics of a hypothetical ideal sweetener to be predicted, for individuals who fitted that model, and also for the 'Average Subject'. No one sweetener was ideal for any of these assessors. PREFMAP identifies differences in responses to preference, and in this case the results show wide individual differences in this respect. When interpreting these results, it must be remembered that Sample I (SrB) has considerable influence on PC 1.

To obtain additional information, the mean preference scores were examined (Table 2). Sucrose had the highest score and SrB the lowest, and it is of particular interest that the first 4 are sugars or sugar alcohols. However, the LSD's show that there are no significant differences between the means of some of the sweeteners. As with all mean values, individual differences within a group are hidden (Pangborn, 1981). This is highlighted in Table 3, by the fact that both SrB and sucrose were each the most preferred sweetener for three assessors.

Correlation coefficients were calculated to investigate which individual sensory characteristics were related to preference. Significant correlations ($p < 0.05$) were obtained for 4 characteristics (Table 4). Bitter and persistent aftertaste, and bitter flavour were negatively correlated with preference, while clean flavour, which was defined as a 'pure, fresh flavour which leaves no undesirable tastes in the mouth', was positively correlated. These results support the inferences made from the mean preference scores, as SrB, acesulfame K and saccharin, which were perceived as being bitter and persistent, are at the bottom of Table 3. Samples such as sucrose, lactitol and fructose, which were perceived to be clean, are in the top half of Table 3.

When interpreting these results, a number of important points should be taken into consideration. For example, it is possible that assessors may not have a well defined internal scale of preference for unfamiliar stimuli. This probably applies in this context as sweeteners are not usually consumed in plain aqueous solution. Assessors' preference dimensions may not have been represented in the sweetener space, obtained by profiling. Also, idiosyncratic use of the preference scale may have influenced the results (Giovanni & Pangborn, 1983). In this study, the number of samples, and therefore the degrees of freedom, were relatively small, especially in fitting the ideal point (Phase III) model. This may have contributed to the model not fitting some assessor's results, and to discrepancies between the 2 models.

It is only with the advent of GPA, PREFMAP and other appropriate multivariate mathematical and statistical techniques, that such detailed investigations and interpretations have been possible. However, univariate methods must not be ignored (Danzart, 1986). Using the PREFMAP vector and ideal point models, in combination with univariate methods, and by inspecting the raw data, increased understanding of the relationship between preference and the sensory characteristics of these sweeteners was obtained.

CONCLUSIONS

PREFMAP provided some information on the relationship between preference and the sensory characteristics of sweeteners. However, only a few assessors fitted any of the models and this limits interpretation.

Additional information was obtained from univariate statistical techniques.

As preference is often a predictor of consumption, this information, particularly regarding individual differences, is extremely useful to food manufacturers, who may use it to help improve the acceptability of products.

ACKNOWLEDGEMENTS

Grateful thanks are given to the staff and postgraduate students who volunteered as assessors.

The first author would like to thank the University of Reading, Department of Food Science and Technology, for a Departmental Studentship.

The third author acknowledges financial support from the Agricultural and Food Research Council (UK) and Cadbury Schweppes plc.

REFERENCES

Amerine, M. A., Pangborn, R. M. & Roessler, E. B. (1965). *Principles of Sensory Evaluation of Food.* Academic Press, New York.
Arnold, G. M. & Williams, A. A. (1986). The use of generalised Procrustes techniques in sensory analysis. In *Statistical Procedures in Food Research,* ed. J. R. Piggott. Elsevier Applied Science, London, pp. 233–53.

ASTM (1973). *Standard recommended practice for establishing conditions for laboratory sensory evaluation of foods and beverages.* Committee E-18, E480. American Society for Testing and Materials, Philadelphia, Pa.

Cabanac, M. (1971). Physiological role of pleasure. *Science*, **173**, 1103–7.

Chauhan, J., Harper, R. & Krzanowski, W. (1983). Comparison between direct similarity assessments and descriptive profiles for certain soft drinks. In *Sensory Quality of Foods and Beverages.* eds A. A. Williams & R. K. Atkin. Ellis Horwood, Chichester, pp. 297–309.

Danzart, M. (1986). Univariate procedures. In *Statistical Procedures in Food Research*, ed. J. R. Piggott. Elsevier Applied Science, London, pp. 19–59.

Davies, P. M. & Coxon, A. P. M. (1983). MDS(X) user manual: the MDS(X) series of multidimensional scaling programs. University of Edinburgh.

Desor, J. A., Maller, O. & Turner, R. E. (1973). Taste in acceptance of sugars by human infants. *Journal of Comparative and Physiological Psychology*, **84**(3), 495–501.

Giovanni, M. E. & Pangborn, R. M. (1983). Measurement of taste intensity and degree of liking of beverages by graphic scales and magnitude estimation. *Journal of Food Science*, **48**, 1175–82.

Huber, J. (1975). Predicting preferences on experimental bundles of attributes; a comparison of models. *Journal of Marketing Research*, **12**, 290–7.

Pangborn, R. M. (1975). Cross-cultural aspects of flavor preferences. *Food Technology (Chicago)*, **29**(6), 34–6.

Pangborn, R. M. (1981). Individuality in responses to sensory stimuli. In *Criteria of Food Acceptance*, eds J. Solms & R. L. Hall. Forster Verlag, A.G., Zurich, pp. 177–219.

Powers, J. J. (1984). Current practices and applications of descriptive methods. In *Sensory Analysis of Foods*, ed. J. R. Piggott. Elsevier Applied Science, London, pp. 179–242.

Rozin, P. (1982). Human food selection: the interaction of biology, culture and individual experience. In *The Psychobiology of Human Food Selection*, ed. L. M. Barker. Ellis Horwood Ltd, Chichester, pp. 225–54.

Schiffman, S. S., Reilly, D. A. & Clark, T. B. (1979). Qualitative differences amongst sweeteners. *Physiology and Behavior*, **23**, 1–9.

Schiffman, S. S., Reynolds, M. L. & Young, F. W. (1981). *Introduction to Multidimensional Scaling: Theory, Methods and Applications.* Academic Press, New York.

Steiner, J. E. (1979). Human facial expressions in response to taste and smell stimulation. In *Advances in Child Development, Vol. 13*, eds H. W. Reese & L. P. Lipsitt. Academic Press, New York, pp. 257–95.

Thomson, D. M. H. & McEwan, J. A. (1986). Predictive modelling and evaluation of food acceptability. In *Consumer Behavior Research and Marketing of Agricultural Products*, ed. J. E. R. Frijters. National Council for Agricultural Research, The Hague, pp. 63–82.

Thomson, D. M. H. & Tunaley, A. (1987). Examination of the sensory characteristics of sweeteners using multidimensional scaling. In *Flavour Science and Technology*, eds M. Martens, G. A. Dalen & H. Russwurm. John Wiley, Chichester, pp. 347–56.

Tunaley, A., Thomson, D. M. H. & McEwan, J. A. (1987). Determination of equi-sweet concentrations of nine sweeteners using a relative rating scale. *International Journal of Food Science and Technology*, **22**, 627–35.

Tunaley, A., Thomson, D. M. H. & McEwan, J. A. (1988). Investigation of the sensory characteristics of sweeteners using consensus profiling. Submitted to *Journal of Food Science*.

Williams, A. A. (1985). Recent developments in sensory analysis. *Food*, **7**(6), 28–31, 59.

Williams, A. A. (1986). The use of perceptual space approaches for determining the influence of intrinsic and extrinsic factors on food choice. In *Consumer Behavior Research and Marketing of Agricultural Products*, ed. J. E. R. Frijters. National Council for Agricultural Research, The Hague, pp. 29–38.

Williams, A. A. & Arnold, G. M. (1985). A comparison of the aromas of six coffees characterised by conventional profiling, free-choice profiling and similarity scaling methods. *Journal of the Science of Food and Agriculture*, **36**, 204–14.

Williams, A. A., Rogers, C. & Noble, A. C. (1984). Characterisation of flavour in alcoholic beverages. *Foundation for Biotechnical and Industrial Fermentation Research*, **3**, 235–53.

Chapter 30

A Comparison of Multivariate Approaches to Sensory Analysis and the Prediction of Acceptability

RICHARD D. POPPER

US Army Natick RD&E Center, Natick, MA 01760-5020, USA

EINAR RISVIK

Norwegian Food Research Institute, PO Box 50, N-1432 Aas/NLH, Norway

HARALD MARTENS and MAGNI MARTENS

Norwegian Computing Center, N-0314 Oslo 3, Norway

ABSTRACT

This chapter illustrates the use of partial least squares (PLS) regression for relating the results of sensory evaluation to the results of multi-dimensional scaling of dissimilarity. Data from a study of chocolates are used as an example. The prediction of acceptability from sensory data using PLS is also investigated.

The results suggest that PLS can be a useful tool for determining the extent to which sensory attributes capture the information contained in dissimilarity data and for developing predictive models of acceptability.

INTRODUCTION

Multivariate data are a fact of life in food research. In sensory analysis, for example, it is common to find 20 or 30 descriptive terms used to profile a product. A sensory evaluation of several products using multiple descriptors can quickly produce a sizeable data matrix. Some of the questions that the researcher is interested in answering are: What are the salient features that distinguish amongst products? Which of these features are important determinants of consumer acceptance?

Questions such as these reveal an important aspect of the mental model that commonly underlies these investigations. While measurements may be obtained on a multitude of variables, only a few dimensions are believed necessary for describing the important differences among products. The problem is to uncover these dimensions.

In multidimensional scaling (MDS) (Schiffman et al., 1981), these dimensions are usually derived from direct judgements of product dissimilarities (or similarities). Other approaches (Piggott & Sharman, 1986) derive these dimensions from sensory profiles. One advantage of the dissimilarity scaling approach is that it does not require specifying a set of attributes in advance of evaluating the differences among products. Instead, a judge is permitted to judge dissimilarity based on whatever combination of (unnamed) criteria he or she considers relevant. The product profile, on the other hand, may focus a judge's attention on some attributes at the expense of others or may be incomplete, lacking among its list of attributes those most relevant for describing differences.

Difficulties can arise for MDS in the interpretation of the dimensions spanning the product space, since it is often unclear what attributes or combination of attributes these dimensions represent. Several methods exist for relating information about product attributes, as obtained for example, from a profiling study or from a consumer acceptance study, to the dimensions derived by MDS (Hoffman & Young, 1983). The focus of this chapter is on the use of partial least squares (PLS) regression as a technique for relating results from MDS and profiling. A study of chocolates is used as an example. The prediction of acceptability from profile data using PLS is also investigated.

THE PLS METHOD

Consider the case where one wishes to predict a variable y from a number of x variables. Multiple regression is the familiar model for this case. However, when there are strong intercorrelations among the predictor variables, the application of multiple regression can yield unreliable results. More importantly, when the number of observations is less than the number of variables, multiple regression does not work at all.

In situations such as these, one is forced to reduce the number of x variables in some way. One method for doing this is principal component regression (PCR), which belongs to the class of latent variable regression methods (see Draper & Smith, 1981). In PCR, one first extracts the largest principal components of x and then uses these to predict y.

PLS can be considered an extension of PCR. The difference between PLS and PCR is that PLS, in looking to extract latent variables from x, chooses those directions in x which are *most relevant* for predicting y. In PCR, the principal component analysis proceeds without regard to y.

PLS can be extended to handle the case in which there is more than one y variable, thus relating a whole block of y variables to a block of x variables. The difference between PLS and canonical correlation, which also handles 2 blocks of variables, is analogous to the difference between PLS with one y variable and multiple regression. For example, canonical correlation requires that the number of observations be greater than the number of x and y variables. Martens & Martens (1986) contains a detailed discussion of PLS and the differences between PLS and other multivariate methods such as PCR and canonical correlation.

AN ILLUSTRATIVE EXAMPLE

Methods and Materials

A sensory panel (10 judges) completed an evaluation of 8 chocolate bars available commercially in Norway. Table 1 lists the chocolates by brand name and provides a brief description of each. In the first study, judges were presented once with each pairwise combination of the 8 samples and asked to rate the dissimilarity of the samples on a graphic line scale. In the second study, judges were presented twice with single samples and a list of attributes and asked to rate each sample on each attribute using a graphic line scale ranging from low to high intensity. Table 2 lists the 22 attributes that were used in this study. All responses were made using a SENSTEC registration system.

Table 1
Chocolate bars included in the study

Brand name	Description
CRISPO	Milk chocolate with rice crisps
STRATOS	Porous milk chocolate
TOPPRIS	Milk chocolate with rice crisps and toffee
DAJM	Milk chocolate with toffee
BOUNTY	Milk chocolate with coconut filling
SNICKERS	Milk chocolate with nuts and caramel
MELKESJOKOLADE	Milk chocolate
MINT	Dark chocolate with mint filling

Judges had no previous experience of evaluating chocolates or rating dissimilarity, but had extensive experience profiling other products and participated in a training session, using the attributes listed in Table 2, prior to the second study. Following the sensory profiling, judges were again presented with samples one at a time and were asked to rate the acceptability of each sample on a nine-point hedonic scale.

Results
Dissimilarity ratings were averaged across judges and were submitted to ALSCAL as implemented under SAS (Young et al., 1983). Figure 1 shows a two-dimensional solution based on an interval-level metric analysis, which accounted for 80% of the variance in the dissimilarity data. A one-dimensional solution accounted for only 55% of the variance, whereas a three-dimensional solution, which accounted for 95%, was not considered warranted with only 8 samples. A non-metric

Table 2
Attributes used in the profiling study

1. Colour saturation	9. Nutty	17. Brittle
2. Gloss	10. Dairy	18. Fatty
3. Cocoa	11. Burnt	19. Porous
4. Coconut	12. Rancid	20. Melting in
5. Caramel	13. Off-taste	the mouth
6. Sweet	14. Stale	21. Chewy
7. Mint	15. Bitter	22. Aftertaste
8. Vanilla	16. Hard	

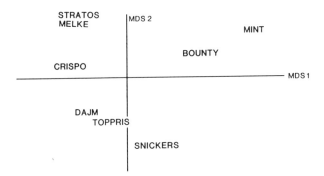

Figure 1. Two-dimensional solution found by ALSCAL for 8 chocolate bars. The horizontal axis is the first dimension (MDS 1).

two-dimensional analysis yielded essentially the same configuration of samples as the interval-level analysis.

In order to aid in the interpretation of the MDS space, a PLS analysis was performed, in which the coordinates of a two-dimensional ALSCAL solution were treated as y variables to be predicted by the 22 profile variables (x variables). The PLS analysis was conducted using the UNSCRAMBLER package (CAMO A/S, 1986) running on a personal computer. A two-factor PLS solution was chosen for interpretation of the MDS space, since this solution accounted for approximately 90% of the variation in the ALSCAL dimensions. A one-factor model explained only 40% of the variation; solutions with three or more factors improved predictive ability only marginally over the two-factor solution. Thus, the two-factor solution was best from the point of view of predictive ability and dimensional parsimony.

Figure 2 shows the loadings on the first and second PLS factors for the profile variables and for the ALSCAL dimensions. The loadings for the ALSCAL dimensions indicate that the ALSCAL and PLS dimensions are similar. The first ALSCAL dimension (MDS 1) loads on the first PLS factor, but not on the second; the opposite is true for the second ALSCAL dimension (MDS 2).

The ALSCAL dimensions can be interpreted with the aid of the attribute loadings. From the locations of these loadings in Fig. 2 one infers that the first ALSCAL dimension is positively associated with chewiness, for example, and negatively associated with hardness and brittleness. Certain flavour attributes also correlate with this dimension, for example 'dairy' (10) and 'mint' (7). In the second ALSCAL

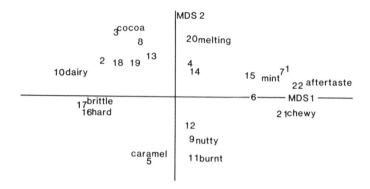

Figure 2. PLS loadings for the first (horizontal) and second (vertical) PLS factors. See Table 2 for the identity of the unlabelled attributes. MDS 1 and MDS 2 represent the loadings for the first and second ALSCAL dimensions respectively.

dimension, the negative direction corresponds to caramel, nutty and burnt flavours. The positive direction may represent the *absence* of a caramel or toffee flavour as well as the characteristic of melting in the mouth.

This interpretation of the MDS dimensions agrees with the placement of the samples in the MDS space in Fig. 1. For example, the samples with a caramel or toffee flavour are located at the bottom of the plot in Fig. 1; the chocolates with chewy fillings are located towards the right. Of course, the fact that certain attributes covary with the ALSCAL dimensions does not prove that these attributes were actually used by the judges when they made their dissimilarity judgements. Correlation is not causation.

A check on the appropriateness of using the PLS solution for interpretation of the ALSCAL space was provided by the PLS score plot (not shown), in which the products were configured almost as in the ALSCAL solution shown in Fig. 1. This is further evidence that PLS has recovered the MDS space.

For the purposes of interpretation, it can be desirable to plot samples and attributes together in the same space to portray more clearly which attributes and samples characterize a given factor. This is illustrated in Fig. 3, which is similar to Fig. 2, except that the samples are also plotted. The location of these points was determined in the following way. The original dissimilarity ratings (average data) were

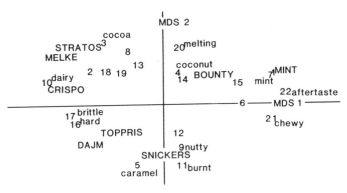

Figure 3. PLS loadings for the first (horizontal) and second (vertical) PLS factors showing the location of chocolates (capital letters) and attributes. Not all attributes are shown.

first converted to similarities so that large numbers represented highly similar instead of highly dissimilar samples. These similarities were then used to form 8 new attributes, where each attribute represented a measure of the similarity of a particular sample to itself and to each of the other samples. For example, one attribute represented the degree to which a chocolate was like SNICKERS. Since by definition SNICKERS is most similar to itself, this attribute was construed as representing the sample. These 8 attributes, 1 for each sample, were then fitted to the PLS scores by linear regression and the loadings plotted in Fig. 3.

Figure 3 shows that this procedure was able to reproduce the correspondence between dimensions, attributes and samples suggested by the previous figures. Note also that, in some cases, good agreement was achieved between samples and certain characteristic attributes. For example, SNICKERS is located near 'nutty', MINT near 'mint' and BOUNTY near 'coconut'. However, caution must be exercised in interpreting such plots. In a region with many attributes and samples, some attributes may be characteristic of some samples, but not of the others located there. Proximity in such a plot means that both sample and attribute correlate with the factor. They may correlate less with each other.

So far PLS has been used to reconstruct the ALSCAL space from the profiles. How does product acceptability relate to the PLS and MDS spaces?

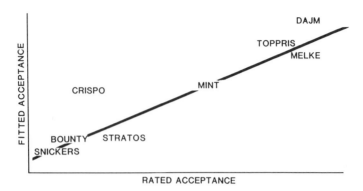

Figure 4. Rated acceptance of 8 chocolates plotted against the values fitted by a PLS regression on the sensory attributes (one-factor solution).

A simple regression indicated that acceptability was not related to either of the two PLS factors or MDS dimensions. Thus, acceptability appears not to have been a variable of importance in describing differences among the samples.

In order to predict acceptability from the profile data, a new PLS analysis was performed, where acceptability was the only y variable and the 22 attributes the x variables. A one-factor solution predicted close to 85% of the variance in the acceptability data. Additional factors did not markedly improve predictive ability. Positively related to acceptability were the attributes 'dairy', 'hard', and 'brittle', reflecting the high acceptability of MELKESJOKOLADE and DAJM; negatively related to acceptability were the attributes 'stale', 'off-taste' and 'rancid'.

In Fig. 4 is plotted the acceptability as predicted by the one-factor solution against the actual acceptability ratings. Prediction is indeed quite good, but the acceptability of CRISPO is overestimated. This could mean that attributes not included in the profile are needed to capture the acceptability of CRISPO or that additional factors should be included in the model.

DISCUSSION

Since a PLS model was able to account for nearly 90% of the variation in the MDS dimensions on the basis of the sensory attributes, it appears that the latter contain most of the information needed to describe the salient differences among the samples. This type of information may be important, if one desires, for example, to use the profile attributes in product development. Insofar as the attributes capture most of what is relevant to differentiating the products, one can have confidence that essential attributes have not been overlooked.

The results have also shown how PLS can be used to interpret MDS dimensions. Other models have been used for relating MDS solutions to attribute ratings. Schiffman *et al.* (1981) and Hoffman & Young (1983) use a series of multiple regressions to predict one sensory attribute at a time from the MDS dimensions. In the application of PLS reported here, the direction of prediction was in the opposite direction: the attributes were used to predict the MDS dimensions. This analysis yields a measure of how well the attributes, taken together, can account for the configuration of samples in the MDS space. Such information is not readily extracted from the results of the multiple regressions. On the other hand, the identification of MDS dimensions with particular attributes is probably accomplished equally well by both methods.

In a PLS analysis not reported here, the profile data were used to predict the dissimilarity ratings (instead of the ALSCAL dimensions), and a very similar configuration of products and attributes was obtained as in the analysis reported above. This suggests that it may also be possible to use PLS to relate dissimilarity and profile data without the intervening step of MDS.

The results of the PLS prediction of acceptability can be compared to a PCR analysis of the same data. In contrast to the one-factor PLS solution, a PCR analysis with three factors explained only 75% of the variance; additional factors did not markedly improve PCR's predictive ability compared to PLS. Thus, there seems to be some slight advantage in terms of dimensional parsimony and predictive ability of using PLS instead of PCR. Studies with a larger number of samples and employing cross-validation are needed to confirm this result.

REFERENCES

CAMO A/S, (1986). *UNSCRAMBLER*, Version 1.0. Trondheim, Norway.
Draper, N. R. & Smith, H. (1981). *Applied Regression Analysis*, 2nd ed. John Wiley, New York.

Hoffman, D. L. & Young, F. W. (1983). Quantitative analysis of qualitative data. In *Food Research and Data Analysis,* eds H. Martens & H. Russwurm Jr. Applied Science Publishers, London, pp. 69–93.

Martens, M. & Martens, H. (1986). Partial least squares regression. In *Statistical Procedures in Food Research,* ed. J. R. Piggott. Elsevier Applied Science Publishers, London, pp. 293–359.

Piggott, J. R. & Sharman, K. (1986). Methods to aid in the interpretation of multidimensional data. In *Statistical Procedures in Food Research,* ed. J. R. Piggott, Elsevier Applied Science, London, pp. 181–232.

Schiffman, S. S., Reynolds, M. L. & Young, F. W. (1981). *Introduction to Multidimensional Scaling.* Academic Press, New York.

Young, F. W., Lewyckyi, R. & Takane, I. (1983). The ALSCAL procedure. In *SUGI Supplemental Library User's Guide,* ed. S. P. Joyner. SAS Institute Inc., Cary, NC.

Topic 8

Applications and Innovations

Chapter 31

Sensory Attributes and Acceptance of Fat, Sugar, and Salt in Dairy Products

ROSE MARIE PANGBORN

Department of Food Science & Technology, University of California, Davis, CA 95616, USA

ABSTRACT

Degree of liking responses for vanilla- and chocolate-flavoured milk drinks varying in fat (0–36% fat) and sugar (0–36% sucrose) and for dill-flavoured sour cream dips varying in fat (3·5–28% milk fat) and salt (0–2·4% NaCl) were compared with corresponding perceived intensity of salient attributes. Similar sensory responses were measured in chocolate milk varying in fat and sweetened with equi-sweet concentrations of sucrose and aspartame. A separate study contrasted sensory attributes of chocolate milk with equi-weight concentrations of sucrose, fructose and glucose, tested at 5, 21 and 55°C.

Hedonic responses were stable across multiple exposures, with neither decrease due to monotony nor increase due to mere exposure. Hedonic optima were obtained for dips containing 14% fat and between 0·6 and 1·2% NaCl, and for vanilla drinks containing 20% fat and 9% sucrose. In chocolate milk, samples with 10% fat plus 10% sucrose had maximum liking; neither hedonic nor fattiness responses varied between samples sweetened with 10% sucrose and those with 0·137% aspartame, but sweetness of the latter was greatly reduced by fat.

Few differences in sweetness intensity were noted between sucrose and fructose in chocolate milk but equivalent levels of glucose were judged less sweet. Sweetness increased with increasing fat levels, with little effect of solution temperature. Perceived fattiness intensity increased with

413

increasing amounts of all sugars. The best-liked sample contained 10% fat and 16% sugar.

INTRODUCTION

Recent interest in the fat content of foods stems from two interrelated factors: (1) consumer concern with reducing intake of fat for health and vanity reasons, and (2) manufacturers' interest in providing low-fat products with functional properties, shelf-life, and acceptance comparable to the conventional fat level. Additionally, the use of low-calorie sweeteners and non-sodium salts in fat-containing foods raises the question of physical and chemical interaction effects which can alter sensory characteristics and potential acceptance. Fat contributes desirable qualities to many foods (Litman & Numrych, 1978; Drewnowski, 1987a). Creaminess, richness, smoothness, shortness and tenderness are among the many positive sensory characteristics of high-fat foods.

Most research on the interaction of fat with taste attributes has involved dairy products. Early studies (Pangborn & Dunkley, 1964) showed that visual differences contributed more than oral attributes to preferences for milk varying in fat (1–3·5%) and solids-not-fat (8·5–11%). This was confirmed by Tuorila (1986) who found that 3 visual attributes (transparency, bluish colour, and visual thickness) but only 1 oral attribute (greasy mouthfeel) were used by 20 judges to discriminate between non-fat, low-fat, and regular fat milks. Subsequently, Tuorila (1987) observed that 236 subjects had a strong preference for their usual milk (0, 1·9, or 3·5% fat), and that they were reluctant to shift, despite knowledge of nutritional recommendations. It was noted by Pangborn & Giovanni (1984) that neither dietary intake of fat nor of dairy products correlated significantly with preferences for fat in commercial milk (0, 2, 3·5%) nor with hedonic responses to experimental milks (0, 1, 2, 4, 8 and 16% fat). Discrimination, perceived intensity, paired preference and hedonic rating of 0–6% fat in milk and chocolate milk did not differ significantly with fat intake, type of milk normally consumed, nor body size (82–131% of ideal weight) of 186 women (Pangborn *et al.*, 1985).

Drewnowski & Greenwood (1983) and Drewnowski *et al.* (1985) were among the first investigators to record hedonic responses to milk varying in both fat (0–52%) and sugar (0–20% sucrose). Degree of liking depended on the level of both ingredients. For 15 normal-weight women, maximum hedonic response was obtained at 20·7% fat plus 7·7% sucrose while for 12 obese women, the optimum was at 35·1% fat plus 10% sucrose (Drewnowski, 1987b).

In the studies described herein, milk fat and sucrose were added to milks flavoured with vanilla and chocolate, which we believed to be more similar to conventional consumer products than unflavoured milk. In addition, data also were collected for a sour cream-yogurt dip varying in fat and salt.

MATERIALS AND METHODS

Vanilla Milk Drinks and Sour Cream Dips

Twenty samples of milk drink, containing 5 levels of milk fat (0, 3·5, 10, 20 and 36%) and 4 levels of sucrose (0, 9, 18 and 36%), flavoured with 0·4% vanilla extract were evaluated by 30 female volunteers of 21–34 years of age. The same subjects evaluated 16 samples of dip, containing 4 levels of milk fat (3·5, 7, 14 and 28%) and 4 levels of sodium chloride (0, 0·6, 1·2, 2·4%), flavoured with 0·5% dill weed. At separate sessions subjects tested, in randomized order, 16 × 10-ml samples of dip in 50-ml glass beakers or 20 × 20-ml samples of milk drink in 70-ml amber bottles. The amber bottles and use of straws to sip the milk minimized visual differences due to fat content. Samples were tested between 1400 h and 1700 h in individual booths under 'daylight' illumination. Subjects were instructed to taste and expectorate all samples, and to rinse orally with distilled water between samples. Hedonic value was recorded on a 10-cm visual analogue scale anchored at the ends with 'Dislike Extremely' and 'Like Extremely', and in the centre with 'Neither Like nor Dislike'. Intensities of selected product attributes were recorded on a similar 10-cm visual analogue scale anchored at the ends with 'Slightly' and 'Extremely'. To test the effect of repeated exposure on hedonic responses, the 10-day test period was structured as shown in Table 1. Full details are given by Kaye (1986) and summarized by Pangborn (1987b).

Chocolate Milk Drink

Nineteen female students of 18–30 years of age recorded hedonic responses and attribute intensities on scales similar to those described above. In Experiment I (Exp. I) 20 samples were tested: 5 levels of fat

Table 1
Details of 10-day test period

Dip	Milk drink
Session	Session
1 Hedonic	6 Hedonic
2 Saltiness, hedonic	7 Sweetness, hedonic
3 Sourness, hedonic	8 Fattiness, hedonic
4 Fattiness, hedonic	9 Creaminess, hedonic
5 Creaminess, hedonic	10 Viscosity, hedonic

(0, 3·5, 10, 20, 36%), and 4 levels of sucrose (0, 10, 20, 36%) at 0·2% cocoa (w/w). In Experiment II (Exp. II), ten samples were tested: five levels of fat (0, 3·5, 10, 20, 36%), 10% sucrose or 0·137% aspartame (equisweet to 10% sucrose in this product) at 0·2% cocoa. The test sequence was: (full details given by Wang, 1987)

Exp. I: Hedonic; Sweetness; Fattiness; Richness;
          Creaminess; Hedonic.
Exp. II: Hedonic; Sweetness; Fattiness; Hedonic.

Relative Sweetness
A subsequent study compared the relative sweetness of equi-weight concentrations of sucrose, fructose and glucose in chocolate milk served cold, hot and at room temperature. A total of 108 samples were tested, in replicate, 12 per session, by 10 males and 9 females of 15–44 years of age. The variables were 4 levels of milk fat (0, 3·5, 10·5, 36%), 3 levels and 3 types of sugar (8, 16, 32% sucrose, glucose or fructose) at 0·2% cocoa, served at 5, 21 or 55°C. At each test session, judges recorded degree of liking, took a 5-min rest, recorded sweetness intensity, took a 5-min rest, then recorded intensity of fattiness. The 12 samples per set varied in levels of fat and of sugar, within a temperature and within a sugar type.

RESULTS AND DISCUSSION

Vanilla Milk Drinks
As expected, sweetness intensity was rated proportionally to increasing sucrose content (Table 2). Generally, the levels of fat had minor

Table 2
Average responses to sensory attributes* of vanilla milk drink

Sucrose (%)	Added fat (%)				
	0	3·5	10	20	36
	Sweetness intensity[†] ($n = 30$)				
0	0·7^g	0·2^g	0·2^g	0·4^g	0·1^g
9	4·1^f	5·0^e	5·0^e	5·7^e	5·0^e
18	8·0^{bcd}	7·4^{cd}	8·1^{bc}	8·2^{bc}	7·1^d
36	9·2^a	9·1^a	9·1^a	9·1^a	8·6^{ab}
	Fat intensity[†] ($n = 30$)				
0	0·8^j	2·0^i	4·1^{fg}	6·3^{bc}	9·1^a
9	1·7^i	3·2^{gh}	4·6^{ef}	6·2^{bc}	9·0^a
18	2·6^{hi}	4·1^{fg}	5·1^{de}	6·7^{bc}	9·1^a
36	2·5^{hi}	4·8^{ef}	6·0^{cd}	7·1^b	9·4^a
	Creaminess intensity[†] ($n = 30$)				
0	0·7^k	2·3^{ij}	3·0^{ghi}	4·8^{ef}	9·2^a
9	1·7^j	3·2^{gh}	4·5^f	5·9^{cd}	9·3^a
18	2·3^{ij}	3·9^{fg}	4·6^{ef}	6·7^{bc}	9·4^a
36	2·9^{hi}	4·5^f	5·4^{de}	7·4^b	9·7^a
	Viscosity intensity[†] ($n = 30$)				
0	0·8^l	1·1^{kl}	2·1^{hij}	3·9^{de}	8·7^a
9	1·1^{kl}	2·0^{ij}	2·9^{fgh}	3·9^{de}	8·5^a
18	1·8^{jk}	2·6^{ghi}	3·1^{efg}	5·1^c	8·9^a
36	2·0^{ij}	3·7^{def}	4·5^{cd}	6·1^b	9·3^a
	Degree of liking[‡] ($n = 30 \times 5$ reps)				
0	2·1^i	2·7^h	3·0^{gh}	3·0^{gh}	2·2^i
9	3·1^g	4·9^d	5·9^b	6·4^a	5·3^{cd}
18	3·1^g	4·4^e	5·6^{bc}	5·9^b	5·2^d
36	2·2^i	3·8^f	4·2^e	4·4^e	4·3^e

* Within an attribute, means sharing superscripts do not differ at $p < 0.05$.
[†] Recorded on a 10-cm line anchored at ends with 'slightly' and 'extremely'.
[‡] Recorded on a 10-cm line anchored at ends with 'dislike extremely' and 'like extremely' and in the centre with 'neither like nor dislike'.

effects on perceived sweetness intensity, in concordance with results presented previously by Drewnowski *et al.* (1985). The degree to which additions of fat increased perception of fattiness is indicated in Table 2. In contrast to the Drewnowski results, perceived fattiness was augmented by increasing sugar levels for the 3 lower, but not for the 2 higher fat levels. Mean scores for fattiness and creaminess were almost identical throughout, while those for viscosity gave lower values, but a similar distribution as a function of fat or sugar, i.e. increasing sharply with fat content, and increasing moderately with sugar level but only for samples with lower fat contents. Drewnowski (1987c) also reported that judges ascribed increasing intensities of attributes called fat, creamy, buttery, rich, oily and greasy to increasing fat contents in unflavoured milk. However, the slopes of the response distributions were much lower for the two latter terms.

Hedonic responses were stable across the 5 replications ($F_{4, 116} = 1.46$, $p > 0.22$), with no change due to the quality attribute with which the set was paired in the presentation order, nor measurable influences of mere exposure or monotony. Therefore the 5 data sets were combined (Table 2). A distinct hedonic optimum was obtained for the milk drink with 9% sucrose and 20% fat followed by surrounding samples—9/10 and 18/20 (% sucrose/% fat). This contrasts with the observations of Drewnowski & Greenwood (1983) of a maximum response for unflavoured milk samples with 50% fat and 10% sucrose. The latter data showed a characteristic sucrose 'breakpoint' but no decline in fat preference, hence no fat 'breakpoint'. The data reported herein, however, show hedonic optima for both ingredients. Differences between the present results and Drewnowski's could be due to a combination of the testing of different subjects and of flavoured versus unflavoured milk drinks. This discrepancy warns us of the difficulty of extrapolating hedonic results from one medium to another and from one small population to another.

Sour Cream-Yogurt Dip

The first data set in Table 3 demonstrates the degree to which NaCl increased the saltiness of the dips. Fat significantly reduced apparent saltiness of all but the most highly-salted samples. Perceived sourness was significantly reduced by increasing fat levels mostly because fat replaced sour cream and yogurt in the formulation. Interestingly, sourness was enhanced by NaCl in the sample with maximum fat. Intensities of perceived fattiness and creaminess were, of course,

Table 3

Average responses to sensory attributes* of sour cream dip

NaCl(%)	Added fat (%)			
	3·5	7	14	28
	Saltiness intensity[†] (n = 30)			
0	4·4[f]	4·4[f]	3·3[g]	1·3[h]
0·6	5·7[de]	5·3[ef]	5·1[ef]	2·4[g]
1·2	7·0[bc]	6·4[cd]	6·1[cde]	5·9[de]
2·4	8·1[a]	7·8[ab]	8·3[a]	8·4[a]
	Sourness intensity[†] (n = 30)			
0	7·3[a]	6·6[abc]	5·5[cd]	0·7[f]
0·6	7·3[a]	6·1[bc]	5·5[cd]	1·6[ef]
1·2	7·7[a]	7·0[ab]	4·8[d]	2·3[e]
2·4	7·4[a]	7·1[ab]	5·6[cd]	2·5[e]
	Fat intensity[†] (n = 30)			
0	4·9[ef]	5·7[de]	6·4[cd]	7·9[ab]
0·6	5·1[ef]	5·9[de]	7·0[bc]	8·2[a]
1·2	5·9[de]	5·2[ef]	6·9[bc]	7·9[ab]
2·4	4·5[f]	5·0[ef]	6·9[bc]	7·9[ab]
	Creaminess intensity[†] (n = 30)			
0	6·2[efg]	6·0[fg]	6·9[def]	8·2[a]
0·6	6·3[defg]	6·3[defg]	7·9[abc]	8·7[a]
1·2	5·8[g]	6·6[defg]	7·0[cde]	8·8[a]
2·4	5·8[g]	6·4[defg]	7·2[bcd]	8·0[ab]
	Degree of liking[‡] (n = 30 × 5 reps)			
0	4·1[fg]	4·4[def]	4·8[cd]	2·9[h]
0·6	4·6[de]	5·2[bc]	6·0[a]	4·6[de]
1·2	4·6[de]	5·1[bc]	6·0[a]	5·4[b]
2·4	3·9[g]	4·0[g]	4·4[ef]	4·6[de]

* Same footnotes as Table 2.

directly proportional to fat content, with no significant alterations due to NaCl.

Hedonic response was stable across 5 exposures ($F_{4, 116} = 0.80$, $p < 0.53$). The final data set in Table 3 shows a hedonic 'breakpoint' for both fat and salt, with optima for samples with 0·6/14 and 1·2/14 (%NaCl/%fat). The unsalted sample with the highest fat content was disliked most.

Table 4
Average responses to sensory attributes* of chocolate milk drink

Sucrose(%)	0	3·5	10	20	36
	Sweetness intensity[†] (n = 19)				
0	0·2[g]	0·4[g]	0·3[g]	0·4[g]	0·2[g]
10	4·1[ef]	3·2[f]	4·1[ef]	4·3[e]	4·9[e]
20	6·5[d]	7·6[bc]	7·5[c]	7·6[c]	6·3[d]
36	8·6[a]	8·6[ab]	8·7[a]	8·8[a]	8·3[abc]
	Fat intensity[†] (n = 19)				
0	1·3[i]	1·5[hi]	2·1[hi]	4·0[def]	8·0[a]
10	1·5[hi]	2·5[gh]	3·3[fg]	4·8[cd]	8·0[a]
20	2·4[gh]	2·4[gh]	3·8[def]	4·5[cde]	8·0[a]
36	3·3[fg]	3·5[efg]	5·2[c]	6·7[b]	8·4[a]
	Creaminess intensity[†] (n = 19)				
0	1·0[j]	1·4[ij]	2·0[ghij]	3·4[de]	8·2[a]
10	1·7[hij]	2·1[fghi]	2·8[efg]	4·8[c]	8·2[a]
20	2·8[efg]	2·5[efgh]	4·0[cd]	4·9[c]	8·2[a]
36	3·1[def]	3·1[def]	4·9[c]	6·8[b]	8·7[a]
	Richness intensity[†] (n = 19)				
0	1·0[k]	1·8[jk]	1·9[ijk]	3·3[hi]	7·2[b]
10	3·5[gh]	2·8[h]	4·1[efgh]	4·8[def]	7·3[b]
20	3·9[fgh]	3·7[fgh]	4·6[defg]	5·5[de]	7·8[ab]
36	4·9[def]	4·7[defg]	5·7[cd]	6·9[bc]	8·9[a]
	Degree of liking[‡] (n = 19 × 2 reps)				
0	1·3[hi]	1·7[hi]	1·7[hi]	1·7[hi]	1·1[i]
10	3·9[bc]	4·4[ab]	4·9[a]	4·5[ab]	2·4[fg]
20	3·3[cd]	4·2[b]	4·0[b]	4·5[ab]	2·5[ef]
36	2·9[def]	3·3[cd]	3·2[cde]	2·9[def]	1·9[gh]

* Same footnotes as Table 2.

Chocolate Milk Drinks

Sweetness intensity responses in Table 4 resemble the corresponding data for vanilla milk in that sweetness was increased by sucrose but not by fat. Also, perceived fattiness and creaminess were closely associated and were significantly enhanced by sucrose, except in the sample with the highest fat content. Note that apparent richness increased significantly with both fat and sucrose across all levels.

Similar hedonic optima were obtained across several samples, i.e. 10–20% sucrose at 3·5–20% fat (Table 4). It is evident that the judges responded less favourably to the chocolate than to the vanilla milk with a pronounced dislike for the unsweetened chocolate samples, and for those with the highest level of fat. As with all scaling, the mean values represent a combination of the effects of averaging and of scale usage, as well as of product preference.

A comparison of sucrose versus aspartame-sweetened chocolate milk gave responses plotted in Fig. 1. Increasing fat content caused a pronounced decrease in perceived sweetness of the samples containing aspartame, probably due to the lesser lipid-solubility of this sweetener compared to sucrose. Recently, Redlinger & Setser (1987) reported that initial sweetness and maximum sweetness of all sweeteners, particularly fructose, aspartame, acesulfame K and cyclamate were lower in cream than in water. Figure 1 shows that perceived fattiness was the same for the 2 sweeteners, but degree of liking, also, was unchanged. One would anticipate that a change in sweetness would be reflected in altered hedonic response, an observation which merits further investigation. Intermediate concentrations of both ingredients were equally acceptable in these drinks.

Sucrose, Fructose and Glucose in Chocolate Milk at Three Temperatures

Relative Sweetness
Across the concentration and temperature variables of this experiment, equi-weight concentrations of sucrose and fructose were of equivalent sweetness, while corresponding weights of glucose were slightly less sweet. The data are given in Table 5, but can be appreciated better in Fig. 2. The separation of the lesser sweetness intensity of the glucose samples is more apparent at the two lower sugar concentrations.

That sweetness of all 3 sugars at all 3 solution temperatures was fairly independent of fat content is readily seen from the flatness of the response distributions in Fig. 2. Nonetheless, a slight enhancement of the sweetness of lower sugar levels by the highest fat level can be seen by reading down the columns in Table 5.

For a quick intercomparison of relative sweetness, the responses obtained for the non-fat chocolate milk were converted to the conventional 'if sucrose = 100' scale. The calculated relative values in Table 6 emphasize that in chocolate milk, the sweetness of fructose, ranging from 89 to 133 is lower than literature values calculated for

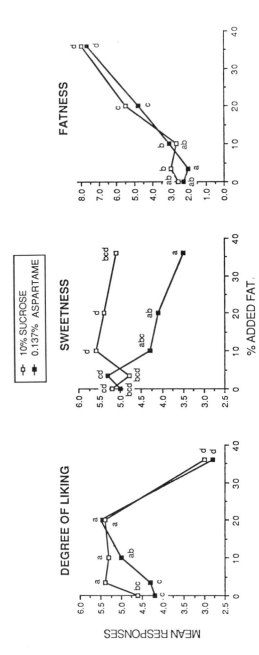

Figure 1. Influence of milk fat on responses to chocolate milk sweetened with 10% sucrose or 'equivalently sweet' 0·137% aspartame. Degree of liking was measured on a scale where 0 = dislike extremely, 5 = neither like nor dislike and 10 = like extremely. Intensity of fattiness and of sweetness were measured on a scale where 0 = slightly and 10 = extremely intense. Points sharing a letter do not differ at $p < 0.05$. ($n = 19$ judges × 2 replications).

Table 5
Relative sweetness of chocolate milk at three solution temperatures*

	Sucrose(%)			Fructose(%)			Glucose(%)		
	8	16	32	8	16	32	8	16	32
Fat(%)				5°C					
0	3·7[b]	6·0[c]	8·4[d]	3·3[a]	6·2[c]	8·5[d]	2·8[a]	5·7[b]	8·3[c]
3·5	3·9[b]	6·4[c]	8·4[d]	3·7[a]	6·1[c]	8·4[d]	2·5[a]	5·3[b]	7·7[c]
10	2·6[a]	6·3[c]	8·2[d]	3·7[a]	6·4[c]	8·4[d]	3·0[a]	5·9[b]	8·0[c]
36	3·9[b]	6·4[c]	8·1[d]	5·0[b]	6·3[c]	8·2[d]	2·8[a]	5·8[b]	8·0[c]
				21°C					
0	3·2[a]	6·2[d]	8·5[f]	3·7[bc]	6·4[d]	8·5[e]	2·5[a]	5·0[c]	8·0[f]
3·5	3·4[ab]	6·0[d]	8·2[f]	3·0[a]	6·6[d]	8·5[e]	2·2[a]	5·3[cd]	8·0[f]
10	4·0[bc]	6·0[d]	8·0[f]	3·5[ab]	6·5[d]	8·6[e]	2·6[a]	5·7[de]	7·8[f]
36	4·5[c]	7·0[e]	8·0[f]	4·3[c]	6·7[d]	8·9[e]	3·5[b]	6·3[e]	8·1[f]
				55°C					
0	4·0[a]	6·0[b]	8·2[d]	3·6[a]	6·3[c]	8·2[e]	2·9[a]	5·2[c]	7·6[d]
3·5	4·0[a]	6·6[bc]	8·6[d]	3·5[a]	6·2[c]	8·2[e]	2·5[a]	5·6[c]	8·0[d]
10	4·1[a]	6·3[b]	8·2[d]	3·4[a]	6·4[cd]	8·3[e]	3·1[a]	5·5[c]	7·7[d]
36	4·5[a]	7·1[c]	8·1[d]	5·2[b]	7·0[d]	8·6[e]	4·0[b]	5·2[c]	7·8[d]

* Average of 38 responses (19 judges × 2 reps), based on a scale where
0 = none and 10 = extremely intense. Within each set of twelve, means
sharing a superscript do not differ at $p < 0.05$.

aqueous solutions. Additionally, in chocolate milk, the sweetness of
glucose, ranging from 73 to 99, is considerably higher than calculations
in water media. Table 6 shows the virtual equality of sweetness of the
3 sugars at the highest concentration, consistent with previous results
(e.g. Cameron, 1947; MacBride, 1987) on the concentration-
dependent nature of relative sweetness. The latter phenomenon is
given as the reason why relative taste intensity at threshold cannot be
applied reliably to higher concentrations. The molar concentrations of
the 3 sugars are presented in Table 6 to intercept the suggestion that
equi-molar, rather than equi-weight concentrations should have been
compared.

These results amply demonstrate, at 3 solution temperatures and
across fat levels, the potential fallacy of extrapolating relative sweetness information from the International Critical Tables or from any
other water-derived calculation, to a complex food system.

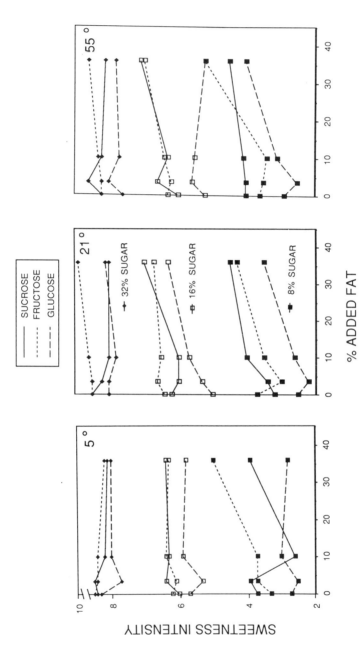

Figure 2. Influence of milk fat on relative sweetness of chocolate milk sweetened with equi-weight concentrations of sucrose, fructose and glucose, evaluated at three solution temperatures. Sweetness intensity was measured on a scale where 0 = not sweet and 10 = extremely sweet (n = 19 judges × 2 replications).

Table 6
Relative sweetness of fructose and glucose compared to sucrose in non-fat chocolate milk. This study versus literature values (sucrose = 100)

%	Molarity	Sugar	Serving temperature (°C)		
			5	21	55
8	0·23	Sucrose			
	0·44	Fructose	89	113	89
	0·44	Glucose	74	78	73
16	0·46	Sucrose			
	0·88	Fructose	104	102	104
	0·88	Glucose	95	80	87
32	0·92	Sucrose			
	1·76	Fructose	102	100	100
	1·76	Glucose	99	94	92

International Critical Tables (Walton, 1926); fructose: 100–150; glucose: 50–60.
Nieman (1958): at 10% sucrose; fructose: 114; glucose: 69.

Perceived Fattiness
In agreement with the previous experiments on vanilla and chocolate milks, apparent fattiness showed an increasing, near-linear relationship with fat content, as expected, and with sugar level, at all 3 solution temperatures. For the non-fat samples and for those with 3·5% and 10% fat, there was no separation of responses by type of sweetener. However, samples with 8% sugar generally were scaled lower in fattiness than those with 32%, with the 16% sugar samples falling between. Therefore, it was confirmed in three separate studies that increasing sugar level is translated into greater fattiness in all but the highest fat sample. The relationship is robust, appearing in both vanilla and chocolate milks, in cold, room-temperature, and hot samples, and in milk sweetened with sucrose, fructose, and glucose.

Hedonic Responses
Table 7 itemizes hedonic means for the 108 samples evaluated herein. Within each set of twelve, the optimum samples are enclosed. Overall, the best-liked samples were in mid-range for both ingredients, i.e. between 3·5 and 10% fat and between 8 and 16% sucrose or fructose.

Table 7
Hedonic response to chocolate milk at three solution temperatures*

Fat (%)	Sucrose(%)			Fructose(%)			Glucose(%)		
	8	16	32	8	16	32	8	16	32
5°C									
0	4·7^{cde}	5·1^e	4·6^{bcde}	5·4^c	5·3^c	4·0^b	4·4^b	5·1^{cd}	4·6^{bc}
3·5	5·9^f	5·8^f	4·3^{abcd}	5·8^c	5·8^c	4·2^b	4·6^{bc}	5·7^{de}	4·7^{bc}
10	4·9^{de}	5·8^f	4·4^{bcd}	5·9^c	5·9^c	4·2^b	5·4^d	6·1^e	5·1^{cd}
36	4·1^{abc}	4·0^{ab}	3·7^a	3·9^b	3·7^b	2·9^a	2·8^a	3·2^a	3·0^a
21°C									
0	4·9^c	4·8^c	3·8^b	5·1^{ef}	4·5^{de}	3·7^{bc}	4·0^b	5·1^{de}	4·0^b
3·5	5·0^c	5·3^{cd}	3·8^b	5·0^{ef}	4·8^{ef}	4·0^{cd}	4·2^{bc}	5·2^{de}	4·0^b
10	5·7^d	5·6^d	3·9^b	5·3^f	4·8^{ef}	3·6^{bc}	4·8^{cd}	5·5^e	4·0^b
36	2·5^a	2·9^a	2·6^a	3·4^{bc}	3·1^{ab}	2·6^a	3·1^a	3·0^a	2·6^a
55°C									
0	4·5^{de}	4·6^{de}	3·6^b	4·0^{bc}	4·6^{de}	3·3^a	4·4^b	5·1^{cd}	4·4^b
3·5	5·0^{efg}	4·8^{def}	4·3^{cd}	4·9^{ef}	5·1^{ef}	4·3^{bc}	4·7^{bc}	5·3^{de}	4·9^{bcd}
10	5·5^g	5·2^{fg}	3·8^{bc}	5·3^f	5·0^{ef}	4·0^{bc}	4·6^{bc}	5·8^e	4·4^b
36	3·0^a	2·8^a	2·9^a	4·1^{bcd}	3·6^{ab}	3·2^a	3·2^a	3·7^a	3·3^a

* Average of 38 responses (19 judges × 2 reps), based on a scale where 0 = dislike extremely, 5 = neither like nor dislike, and 10 = like extremely. Within each set of twelve, means sharing a superscript do not differ at $p < 0.05$.

For glucose, which was slightly less sweet, samples with 16% were clearly preferred.

At this juncture, cautionary comments are in order to avoid overinterpretation of the hedonic data: (1) The ingredient concentrations were selected to measure the test variables over a wide range, rather than to pin-point optimum levels, hence it is predictable that extremes would be disliked; (2) the absolute hedonic maxima of 5·3–6·1 are only slightly above the neutral point on the scale; on the average, the group was not ecstatic about any of the samples (typical of laboratory-generated hedonic data); (3) the judges were selected on the basis of availability, so their responses are not representative of any random consumer sample; (4) laboratory conditions, particularly the testing of 12 samples at a sitting, certainly do not duplicate any sane condition of consumption; (5) the 'sip-and-spit' procedure may result in preferences considerably at odds with those generated from actual consumption of consumer portions (see Mattes & Mela, 1986); (6) whereas many consumers may prefer the sensory characteristics of a milk drink with 10% fat, they may purchase milk drinks with lower fat levels for nutritional and/or price reasons; and finally (7) products like dips are seldom consumed alone, but in conjunction with other foods. Nonetheless, hedonic data such as those shown herein can be used to fine-tune concentration levels appropriate for market testing among a specific target population.

Temperature Effects

Only minor changes in perceived sweetness and fattiness were attributable to temperature. One might anticipate greater discrimination of attributes in solutions at room temperature, since very hot and very cold temperatures can interfere with taste perception (Cameron, 1947; Calviño, 1986; Pangborn, 1987a). The necessity of inter-comparing samples within a temperature no doubt contributed to the result, i.e. judges can discriminate much better in direct than in indirect comparison. Regarding hedonic responses, the cold samples were liked best, then the hot, and finally the room-temperature samples (overall means were 4·7, 4·3 and 4·2, respectively, on the 10-point scale).

CONCLUSIONS

The extent to which fat and sugar modify specific sensory attributes and the corresponding acceptance was demonstrated with excellent agreement between vanilla and chocolate milk drinks. Increasing sugar level was perceived as increasing fattiness, but not vice versa. The complexity of the milk system, particularly at the high fat levels, apparently masked differences in the relative sweetness of sucrose, fructose and glucose which are demonstrated in water solutions (e.g. Pangborn, 1963). The lesser sweetness of aspartame in milks with higher fat levels may be related to lipid solubility and merits more study. The effects of solution temperature and of fat on the relative sweetness of sucrose versus other high-intensity sweeteners remain to be investigated. Acceptance tests under normal conditions of consumption are needed to establish more precise preferences for fat and sugar in milk drinks as well as in other products, such as ice cream. In sour cream dips, optimum acceptance was attained at relatively high levels of both fat (14%) and NaCl (0·6–1·2% w/w). It would be informative to measure fat/salt preferences for dips eaten with crackers or crisps also differing in fat/salt as did Tuorila-Ollikainen *et al.* (1986) for NaCl in butter/bread combinations.

ACKNOWLEDGEMENT

The financial support of The Sugar Association, Inc., Washington, D.C. is gratefully acknowledged.

REFERENCES

Calviño, A. M. (1986). Perception of sweetness; The effects of concentration and temperature. *Physiol. Behav.*, **36**, 1021–28.

Cameron, A. T. (1947). *The Taste Sense and the Relative Sweetness of Sugars and Other Sweet Substances.* Sugar Research Foundation, New York, pp. 2–3.

Drewnowski, A. (1987a). Fats and food texture. Sensory and hedonic evaluations. In *Food Texture. Instrumental and Sensory Measurement*, ed. H. R. Moskowitz. Marcel Dekker, New York, pp. 251–72.

Drewnowski, A. (1987b). Sweetness and obesity. In *Sweetness*, ed. J. Dobbing. Springer-Verlag, London, pp. 177–92.

Drewnowski, A. (1987c). Fats and food acceptance: Sensory, hedonic and attitudinal aspects. In *Food Acceptance and Nutrition*, eds J. Solms, D. A. Booth, R. M. Pangborn & O. Raunhardt. Academic Press, London, pp. 189–204.

Drewnowski, A. & Greenwood, M. R. C. (1983). Cream and sugar: human preferences for high-fat foods. *Physiol. Behav.*, **30**, 629–33.

Drewnowski, A., Brunzell, J. D., Sande, K., Iverius, P. H. & Greenwood, M. R. C. (1985). Sweet tooth reconsidered: taste responsiveness in human obesity. *Physiol. Behav.*, **35**, 617–22.

Kaye, A. L. (1986). Relation of weight loss, food intake, and locus of control by obese and normal-weight women to degree of liking for fat, sucrose, and sodium chloride. M.S. thesis, University of California, Davis.

Litman, I. & Numrych, S. (1978). The role lipids play in the positive and negative flavors of foods. In *Lipids as a Source of Flavor*, ed. M. K. Supran. American Chemical Society, Washington, D.C., pp. 1–17.

MacBride, R. L. (1987). Taste psychophysics and the Beidler equation. *Chemical Senses*, **12**, 323–32.

Mattes, R. D. & Mela, D. J. (1986). Relationships between and among selected measures of sweet-taste preference and dietary intake. *Chemical Senses*, **11**, 523–39.

Nieman, C. (1958). Relative Süsskraft von Zuckerarten. *Zucker- u. Süsswarenwirtsch.*, **11**, 420–1089.

Pangborn, R. M. (1963). Relative taste intensities of selected sugars and organic acids. *J. Food Sci.*, **28**, 726–33.

Pangborn, R. M. (1987a). Factors influencing sensory perception of sweetness. In *Sweetness*, ed. J. Dobbing. Springer Verlag, London, pp. 49–66.

Pangborn, R. M. (1987b). Relationship of personal traits and attitudes to acceptance of food attributes. In *Food Acceptance and Nutrition*, eds J. Solms, D. A. Booth, R. M. Pangborn, & O. Raunhardt. Academic Press, London, 353–70.

Pangborn, R. M. & Dunkley, W. L. (1964). Difference-preference evaluation of milk by trained judges. *J. Dairy Sci.*, **47** (12), 1414–16.

Pangborn, R. M. & Giovanni, M. E. (1984). Dietary intake of sweet foods and of dairy fats and resultant gustatory responses to sugar in lemonade and to fat in milk. *Appetite*, **5**, 317–27.

Pangborn, R. M., Bos, K. E. O. & Stern, J. S. (1985). Dietary fat intake and taste responses to fat in milk by under-, normal-, and overweight women. *Appetite*, **6**, 25–40.

Redlinger, P. A. & Setser, C. S. (1987). Sensory quality of selected sweeteners: Aqueous and lipid model systems. *J. Food Sci.*, **52**, 451–4.

Tuorila, H. (1986). Sensory profiles of milks with varying fat contents. *Lebensm.-Wiss. u.-Technol.*, **19**, 344–5.

Tuorila, H. (1987). Selection of milks with varying fat contents and related overall liking, attitudes, norms and intentions. *Appetite*, **8**, 1–14.

Tuorila-Ollikainen, H., Salovaara, H. & Kurkela, R. (1986). Effect of saltiness on the liking and consumption of bread and butter. *Ecol. Food Nutrit.*, **18**, 99–106.

Walton, C. F. (1926). *International Critical Tables*, Vol. 1, McGraw-Hill, New York, p. 357.

Wang, C. T. (1987). Taste responses and caloric estimation of chocolate milk drink by American and Taiwanese students. M.S. thesis, University of California, Davis.

Chapter 32

The Consumer Acceptability of Some Underutilised Fish Species

PAULINE D. BAIRD, RODERICK BENNETT and
MORAG HAMILTON

*School of Home Economics, Robert Gordon's Institute of
Technology, Queen's Road, Aberdeen AB9 2PG, UK*

ABSTRACT

*Herring, mackerel and scad (horse mackerel) are underused fishery
resources with less than 20% of the potential UK catch being consumed
in the UK. Recently, the availability of herring to the domestic market
has fluctuated due to catching restrictions. This has led to an increase in
the consumption of mackerel to around 30 000 t/a which is still only a
fraction of the total catch of some 200 000 t/a. The potential catch of
oily fish is sufficient virtually to satisfy the UK demand for fish, yet at
least 350 000 t/a are imported into the UK. At the same time, the bulk of
oily fish species are sold cheaply to Eastern bloc vessels or are reduced
to fish meal and oil.*

*In the market place oily fish such as herring and mackerel are not
particularly popular in the fresh form and much of their sales are as
cured or smoked products, whilst scad has no firm market. In contrast
to this, two relatively oily fish, trout and salmon are apparently sought
after in the fresh form and command high prices.*

*The acceptability of the oily fish species in smoked, unsmoked and
product forms was investigated using sensory evaluation techniques and
untrained consumer type panels. Changes in acceptability during storage
were also investigated. In general the fresh fish were well liked and the*

liking declined linearly with storage time at 0°C. The liking for smoked and product forms was greater than for the fresh form and the decline in acceptability with storage time was slower. These data are presented in a form useful for making decisions on sell by dates of the chilled products.

An investigation of people's attitudes to oily fish was conducted by issuing questionnaires to customers at a number of fish retail outlets (i.e. fish buyers were deliberately selected). The questionnaires explored attitudes and attempted to clarify the factors which would induce increased consumption. The analysis revealed many strong and irrational negative reactions towards mackerel in particular, and mixed reactions, which were largely age-related, towards herring.

There is a striking contrast between the acceptability of the species, as presented to taste panels, and the reaction of the fish buying public towards them.

The changing place of fish in the UK diet and possible ways of improving consumption are discussed.

INTRODUCTION

At present the demand for oily fish species such as herring and mackerel is low in the UK and less than 10% of the potential UK catch is consumed here. Oily fish could virtually satisfy the total UK demand for fish, yet about 350 000 t of fish were imported into the UK in 1985 (MAFF, 1985), while the bulk of oily fish catches were sold cheaply to Eastern bloc vessels or reduced to fish meal and oil. Although consumption patterns seem to be slowly changing to include a wider variety of fish species, UK consumption for pelagic species of around 30 000 t/a is still only a fraction of the total catch of some 200 000 t. The availability of herring to the domestic market fluctuated due to recent catching restrictions, and it has failed to recapture its position in the consumer market now that supplies are more stable.

Considering the fact that the demand for fish amongst consumers remains high and exploitation of underutilised species represents a major means of ultimately reducing imports of fish, it was decided to explore consumer preferences for different fish species, in an effort to identify ways in which they could be changed or altered.

MATERIALS AND METHODS

Fish Samples

Supply

Herring and mackerel were caught by the research vessel G. A. Reay and frozen immediately after catching in polythene bags which were topped up with sea water to prevent oxidation and dehydration (Smith *et al.*, 1980; Hardy *et al.*, 1973). The 25 kg blocks were stored at −30°C on board and later at Torry Research Station, Aberdeen, until required for tasting (frozen storage deterioration does not occur to any significant extent at this temperature; Connell & Howgate, 1986).

Preparation

Blocks of fish were thawed overnight at ambient temperature before use in the following ways:

Raw samples were either block filleted, vacuum packed and used immediately in taste panel sessions, or stored, well iced in a chill room (2–4°C) for a specified period of time (at various intervals fish were removed, block filleted, vacuum packed and stored at −30°C until required).

Smoked samples

(a) Freshly thawed whole mackerel were block filleted, soaked in 60° brine solution (3 M) for 3 min, drained and held in the chillroom overnight before being hot smoked in the Torry mechanical smoking kiln for 1 h at 27°C, 1 h at 49°C and 45 min at 71°C.

(b) Freshly thawed whole herring were block filleted, brined and drained as above. The cutlets were smoked (kippered) for 2 h 20 min at 27°C.

   After cooling the hot smoked mackerel cutlets and kippered herring cutlets were stored as pairs, flesh to flesh, between thin polythene sheeting and were well iced. Melt water could not reach the samples and draining and icing were carried out every third day. Samples were removed at various intervals, vacuum packed and stored at −30°C until required.

(c) Freshly thawed whole herring were block filleted, brined and smoked as for hot smoked mackerel (hot smoked herring cutlets). After cooling they were vacuum packed and used immediately in taste panel sessions.

Preparation of Samples for Tasting

Fish samples were wrapped in aluminium foil and baked at 180°C for approx 15–20 min, depending on species and whether they were thawed or frozen cutlets. Hot smoked herring and mackerel cutlets were thawed to ambient temperature and presented to panellists without any further cooking. No condiments were used during cooking or provided at tasting sessions.

To assess acceptability of oily fish species in product form, two simple herring dishes (herring in oatmeal and fried, and baked herring with mustard sauce) were also presented to panellists.

Presentation of Samples

The tail end of each fillet was removed and the whole fillet presented on identical, coded, disposable, white polystyrene plates. Tasting was carried out in individual booths and tepid water was provided for rinsing the mouth.

Sensory Evaluation

The panels comprised academic, secretarial and ancillary staff and home economics students from Robert Gordon's Institute of Technology. The panels were 80% female and none of them had been trained in fish tasting. Samples were scored using a 9-point hedonic rating scale (9 = like extremely; 5 = neither like nor dislike; 1 = dislike extremely). Only unit marks were allowed and panellists rated the samples simultaneously for appearance, texture, flavour and overall acceptability. Samples were presented in random order and each panellist assessed up to 4 samples at a tasting session.

Chemical Analysis

The chemical composition, and in particular, the lipid content of oily fish like herring and mackerel varies considerably with the season of the year and the breeding cycle. A typical range of lipid content in mackerel throughout the year is 6–23% (Keay, Torry Note No. 66). These variations inevitably affect their performance in taste panel sessions and overall acceptability.

Total lipid content analyses were carried out by Torry Research Station on samples of fish used in taste panel sessions.

Statistical Analysis

The distribution of hedonic panel ratings usually showed a marked degree of skewness and so the calculated median values were used as a measure of the centre of the distribution. Percentage liking scores were calculated using the scores from panellists who expressed any degree of 'liking' for the sample, i.e. the number of scores 6–9 plus half the scores 5.

During the series of tests to examine the effects of chilled storage on acceptability, the medians of the distribution of acceptability ratings are plotted against chilled storage time with regression lines superimposed. As suggested by Smith (1984), lines of best fit were calculated by the method of least absolute deviations (Armstrong and King, 1978), which is the regression analogue of the median and is less influenced by outlying or aberrant values than the usual method of 'least squares'.

Survey Method

A questionnaire was distributed randomly to 200 consumers in 5 different Aberdeen retail outlets who were purchasing fresh wet fish (of any species), in an effort to assess purchasing behaviour and attitudes of fish consumers to oily fish species. Questions were designed to compare the position for oily fish species with that for white fish species and dealt specifically with haddock, herring and mackerel. There were also opportunities for respondents to express their own opinions on fish species in a number of 'open' questions provided. Respondents were requested to complete the questionnaire when they returned home and then post it using the pre-paid envelope provided.

RESULTS AND DISCUSSION

Chemical Analysis

The results of total lipid content analyses carried out on the herring and mackerel samples were: herring 7·9%, mackerel 19·6%. These values are typical of herring and mackerel caught during late summer and autumn.

Sensory Analysis

Acceptability of Oily Fish Species and Products
Table 1 shows the median panel scores and the percentage liking scores obtained in a hedonic rating test with 42 assessors and it can be

Table 1
Median scores using a 9-point hedonic rating scale and percentage of judges expressing liking for various fish species and products

	Median score	Expressing 'liking' (%)
Herring	5·7	62
Mackerel	6·3	84
Scad (horse mackerel)	5·6	61
Trout	5·6	57
Hot smoked mackerel	6·8	90
Hot smoked herring	6·9	84
Kippered herring	7·0	83
Herring in mustard sauce	6·0	74
Herring fried in oatmeal	7·5	92

seen clearly that more than 50% of assessors expressed a degree of liking for the overall acceptability of each fish species. Median scores for overall acceptability are also on the like side of neutrality for each of the 4 fish species. This would indicate that good quality fish, when presented to panels in simple baked form, are generally well liked. A comparison of acceptability scores for trout and herring, the more familiar species, with scores for mackerel and scad, shows that these underutilised and less familiar species are liked equally under taste panel conditions.

It was noted that the batch of herring used in this series of tests seemed to be of low intrinsic quality since the fillets developed blood stains in the belly wall area, especially during the subsequent storage experiment. A repeat experiment, carried out at a later date with better quality herring, showed that the increase in quality raised the level of liking and the overall acceptability of the fish samples.

By comparing the median scores for the acceptability of plain baked herring (Table 1), with those for the herring products, it can be observed that presenting the fish in a simple product form has increased its acceptability by approximately 1 unit mark. Smoking both the herring and mackerel raises their acceptability substantially and these products are liked by over 80% of the panellists. From previous analyses of data from plain baked samples, it seemed that negative features such as presence of bones and grey colour may have adversely affected the acceptability of herring and mackerel. These results show, that by presenting the fish in product form and thereby masking these features, consumer acceptability can be substantially increased.

The Effects of Chilled Storage on Acceptability

Figure 1 shows the medians of the distribution of acceptability ratings of smoked and unsmoked mackerel against chilled storage time and Fig. 2 shows the same for smoked and unsmoked herring.

Figure 3 shows the percentage of panellists expressing some degree of liking for smoked and unsmoked mackerel against storage time and

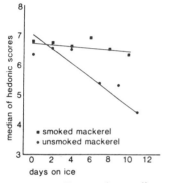

Figure 1. Change in median hedonic scores during iced storage of whole mackerel and hot smoked mackerel cutlets.

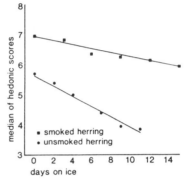

Figure 2. Change in median hedonic scores during iced storage of whole herring and 'kippered' herring cutlets.

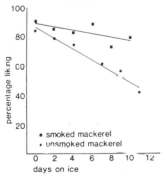

Figure 3. Change in percentage liking during iced storage of the mackerel samples shown in Fig. 1.

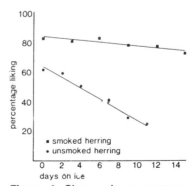

Figure 4. Change in percentage liking during iced storage of the herring samples shown in Fig. 2.

438   P. D. BAIRD, R. BENNETT AND M. HAMILTON

Fig. 4 shows the same for smoked and unsmoked herring. The data are plotted with the regression lines superimposed.

The acceptability of unsmoked herring and mackerel declined progressively with chilled storage, the decrease in acceptability being statistically significant after 4 days in both cases. Smoking mackerel raises its acceptability substantially and the decline in acceptability with time is at a reduced rate, being statistically significant after 8 days storage. In view of these findings, the storage trial period of smoked herring was extended to 15 days. Smoked herring was rated more highly than unsmoked and the decline in acceptability was again at a reduced rate and similar to that of the smoked mackerel. The decline in acceptability was significant after about 9 days. These results suggest that if consumer acceptability is to be assured, a short storage period of not more than 4 days at 0°C for unsmoked products and 10 days at 0°C for smoked products is recommended.

Manufacturers and retailers have to make recommendations and decisions regarding the chilled shelf-life of products since all prepackaged, chilled fish must now be date-stamped before sale (in the UK). This is clearly a complex matter which is of considerable commercial importance. Howgate (1983) advanced ideas for decision making in this area and Figs. 3 and 4 show, as he suggests, plots of the percentage of assessors who express some degree of liking for the product against storage time. One hundred per cent liking was never found even with the freshest product.

If 70% liking amongst all consumers is taken as the cut-off point, then the smoked products have a shelf-life at 0°C of more than 10 and possibly 15–16 days, unsmoked mackerel of about 4 days and the unsmoked herring would never be offered for sale.

Survey Results

A total of 124 completed questionnaires were returned with a similar response rate from each retail outlet. Results were analysed firstly in total for each question and secondly, for selected questions, by division into the different age groups.

The percentages do not always add up to 100 exactly due either to rounding or, that in reaction to some questions, respondents were required to give more than one reply.

Table 2 gives details of the respondents by sex and age showing that women are the main wet fish buyers. Purchase is highest amongst the

Table 2

The gender and age distribution of respondents to a survey amongst fish-buying consumers

Respondent	Total (%)		
Female	79·8		
Male	20·2		
Under 18	0		
18–24	3·2		
25–34	13·7		
35–44	16·9		
45–54	16·9		
55–65	23·4 ⎱		
Over 65	25·8 ⎰ 49·2		66·1

55+ age groups, with relatively few younger housewives buying fresh fish.

Table 3 shows the percentage of respondents who had bought haddock, herring and mackerel during the last month, with the majority of respondents claiming they had bought haddock. Just over half had purchased herring whilst few respondents had bought mackerel. Haddock is bought by consumers of all ages but the purchase of herring is biased towards the older respondents, i.e. 45 + age groups.

Table 3

An analysis of purchase of 3 fish species over the previous month

	No. of respondents	Haddock (%)	Herring (%)	Mackerel (%)
Yes	—	89·5	57·2	7·3
No	—	10·5	42·8	92·7
Under 18	0			
18–24	4	100	50	25
25–34	17	88·2	35·3	11·8
35–44	21	90·5	33·3	19·0
45–54	21	90·5	52·4	14·3
55–64	29	86·2	72·4	0
65 +	32	90·6	71·9	0

Table 4
An analysis of agreement with statements made about 3 fish species

Statement		No. of respondents	Agree (%)
Troublesome to eat because of the bones	Haddock	116	17·2
	Herring	119	63·0
	Mackerel	72	32·0
Unpleasant smell during cooking	Haddock	118	14·4
	Herring	113	51·3
	Mackerel	72	47·2
It looks nice	Haddock	114	94·7
	Herring	111	83·8
	Mackerel	72	68·1
Flavour is nice	Haddock	119	97·5
	Herring	117	88·0
	Mackerel	74	77·0
It's too oily	Haddock	—	—
	Herring	109	26·6
	Mackerel	74	51·4
It goes off quickly so you must buy it and use it the same day	Haddock	114	56·2
	Herring	107	67·3
	Mackerel	71	67·6

No response rate: haddock: 6% (average)
herring: 9·5% (average)
mackerel: 42% (average).

Respondents were asked to agree or disagree with a series of statements about haddock, herring and mackerel and the results are shown in Table 4. Respondents could also record any other comments about the three species in 'open questions'. Overall, respondents found haddock very acceptable, suitable for children, easy to digest and very versatile. There was a little concern expressed about the number of bones present and the quality of freshness of the fish during storage. Herring was generally acceptable and considered by respondents as good value for money. Although they liked its appearance and flavour, the presence of bones and unpleasant smells during cooking are definite negative features.

Table 5

The percentage of respondents indicating the three most important factors that would encourage them to buy more of three fish species

	Haddock (120) (%)	Herring (113) (%)	Mackerel (77) (%)
It was cheaper	65·0	43·4	26·0
It was boneless	45·8	59·3	31·2
It was boil-in-the-bag	0·8	6·2	10·4
It was easy to get	25·0	19·5	19·5
You had guaranteed freshness	62·5	51·3	42·8
It had better keeping qualities	25·0	19·5	24·7
You knew more ways of cooking it	30·0	24·8	42·8
Head/tail removed and fish filleted	—	47·8	33·8
Other	0	1·8	7·8

No response rate: haddock: 3·2%.
herring: 8·9%.
mackerel: 37·9%.

Response to the questions about mackerel was low, with about 42% of respondents failing to respond to each statement. There appear to be definite prejudices held against it, with many respondents commenting on their suspicions about its freshness, feeding areas and general inferiority.

Table 5 shows the percentage of respondents indicating the three most important factors influencing their purchasing behaviour of herring, mackerel and haddock. A lower price would be the main incentive to consumers to purchase more haddock, since it is already well liked by consumers. A boneless, filleted product, guaranteed freshness and more knowledge about cooking methods would be the most important reasons why respondents would increase their purchase of herring. Prejudices against mackerel persist, the large 'no response' rate indicating that nothing would encourage many respondents to buy more mackerel.

The responses indicate that the favourable reactions for oily fish species as presented during tasting sessions, are not reflected in consumer responses to questionnaire items. This suggests a need for education of consumers since it is likely that if they could be persuaded to buy herring and mackerel, enjoyable eating experiences would occur and repeat purchases made as a result. The current emphasis on 'healthy eating' makes this an ideal time for the fishing industry to promote the positive healthy aspects of oily fish species. The best way to increase the consumption of oily fish would appear to be by product innovation which could easily counteract the negative features perceived by consumers. It appears to be unlikely that younger consumers would acquire habits of purchasing them in the fresh form.

REFERENCES

Armstrong, R. D. & King, M. T. (1978). Algorithm AS 132: Least absolute value estimates for a Simple Linear Regression Problem. *Applied Statistics*, **27**, 363–9.

Connell, J. J. & Howgate, P. F. (1986). Fish and fish products. In *Quality Control in the Food Industry*, 2nd edn, Vol. 2, ed. S. M. Herschdoerfer. Academic Press, London, pp. 347–405.

Hardy, R., Smith, J. G. M. & Young, K. W. (1973). *Conferences in Conjunction with the 8th International Exhibition for the Food and Allied Industries*. BPS Exhibitions Ltd, London, pp. 1–5.

Howgate, P. (1983). Measuring the storage lives of chilled and frozen fish products. In *Proc. International Institute of Refrigeration, 16th Congress, Paris*. International Institute of Refrigeration, Paris.

MAFF (1985). *Sea Fisheries Statistical Tables*. HMSO, London.

Smith, G. L. (1984). Statistical analysis of sensory data. In *Sensory Analysis of Foods*, ed. J. R. Piggott. Elsevier Applied Science, London, pp. 305–49.

Smith, J. G. M., McGill, A. S., Thompson, A. B. & Hardy, R. (1980). In *Advances in Fish Science and Technology*, ed. J. J. Connell. Fishing News (Books) Ltd, London, p. 303.

Chapter 33

Influence of Flattering and Tri-band Illumination on Preferred Redness–Pinkness of Bacon

DOUGLAS B. MACDOUGALL and CLIVE B. MONCRIEFF

AFRC Institute of Food Research, Bristol Laboratory, Langford, Bristol BS18 7DY, U.K.

ABSTRACT

Most food displays are illuminated by fluorescent lamps with either broad band spectra and high or low colour fidelity, flattering red enhancement, or tri-band spectra coinciding with maximum visual response to red, green and blue. In this work the colour of bacon has been assessed in a specially constructed viewing room using six different types of lamps commonly used in shop displays and a reference lamp used for colour quality control. The changes in colour and acceptability were compared with the calculated colour shifts and related to the rendering and enhancing properties of the lamps.

INTRODUCTION

Acceptance of foodstuffs at retail is influenced by many factors. The necessity to buy particular food items, their price and anticipated value, the selection offered and the brand image, etc., all affect choice and decision to purchase. The layout and illumination of display in self-service areas are particularly important for sales appeal. The impact of attractive presentation, lasting impressions of cleanliness and

443

efficiency of store management each contribute to a customer's anticipation of product quality. Where these are realised consumer loyalty to particular stores is established. Product attractiveness, particularly colour, is affected by both type and level of illumination. Overhead and display cabinet lighting is predominantly by fluorescent lamps, although low voltage dichroic filtered quartz halogen lamps are sometimes used for fresh fruit and vegetable presentation. Some stores have adopted the policy of uniformity of lighting throughout whereas others favour a variety of tubes for different product emphases while others seem to rely on the type of lighting fitted in the display cases by the manufacturers.

Fluorescent lamps vary in their colour temperature and colour rendering properties. Lamps with different spectral power distributions but identical colour temperature are similar in colour when viewed directly. Colour temperature, however, is only a guide to the white/blueness (>4000 K; cool appearance) or to yellowness (<3000 K; warm appearance) of the lamp and gives no indication of a lamp's ability to render colours to their expected 'true' appearance (Halstead, 1978). A lamp's colour fidelity is measured by its colour rendering index Ra (CIE, 1974). This ranges from <60 for narrow band halophosphate lamps such as white and warm white, to >80 for broad band De Luxe phosphors with 'light red' augmentation, to >90 for specialist lamps such as artificial daylight used for colour appraisal and where faithful colour rendition is of prime importance, for example in art galleries. The high efficiency tri-band lamps with maximum emission near 450, 540 and 610 nm have $Ra > 80$.

The colour of fresh meat and cured meat products is usually considered attractive if red or pink and objectionable if brown to greenish-brown (MacDougall, 1982). Ferrous oxymyoglobin, the bright red pigment in fresh meat, and nitric oxide myoglobin, the cured pink pigment, are characterised by steep reflectance profiles between 560 and 610 nm. Pigment reflectances with steep profiles generate colours of bright chroma (McLaren, 1986). Metmyoglobin, the ferric pigment with its absorption band at 630 nm and increased green reflectance, has a much flatter profile. Hence the brown oxidised pigment appears dull and is the major reason for rejection of meat on display (Hood & Riordan, 1973).

Red enhanced flattering illuminants, augmented by phosphors with peak emission in the region of 610–630 nm, compensate for the loss of red reflectance by metmyoglobin. In a recent experiment fresh and oxidised beef and bacon were assessed in monadic presentation for degree of redness/brownness (MacDougall *et al.*, 1985). Red enhanced and tri-band lamps elicited greater colour changes in making brown appear red than making red appear redder. That experiment relied on the observer's memory because only one sample was presented at any session. This could be considered as a test of colour acceptability within the highly constrained limitation of the absence of coloured visual clues. The commercially more realistic situation, in which observers are confronted with the extremes of product colour under a variety of illuminants, is the basis of the experiment reported in this chapter.

METHODS

Material

Wiltshire bacon, purchased sliced in bulk pack, was trimmed to contain only the *M. longissimus dorsi,* with its subcutaneous fat and rind. The slices were arranged into stacks, 4 thick, vacuum packed in clear oxygen impermeable pouches and stored at 1°C. The approximately 1 cm thick stacks were optically infinitely thick. The top slice in each originated from near neighbouring slices in the muscle. Nitric oxide myoglobin, the pink cured pigment, developed fully under this anaerobic environment.

On the day prior to judging, two packs were opened, the slices placed singly on a white plastic tray and covered with oxygen permeable film to prevent desiccation. They were faded overnight by exposure to 1000 lux fluorescent light at 1°C. After oxidation to metmyoglobin was complete, the grey brown slices were repacked.

Viewing Laboratory

Packs of fresh and faded bacon were laid out on adjacent viewing booths in a specially constructed viewing room. Fourteen observers, in groups of 3 or 4, able to see both booths simultaneously, judged the samples under balanced illumination of 900 lux.

Illuminants

The lamps used were Thorn EMI Artificial Daylight (AD), Natural (NT), Deluxe Natural (DL) and White Pluslux 3500 (35), Philips Colour 83 (83) and Colour 84 (84) and Maurer NAFA-Light (NA).

Presentation

The 28 viewing sessions comprised 7 with identical lamps in both booths and 21 with different lamps in each booth. This was accomplished in 2 viewing sessions on each of 2 days for 7 weeks with 1 homogeneous (1 lamp) and 3 heterogeneous (2 lamps) presentations each week. Left and right booths were used equally often for each lamp.

Data Collection

The score form had 2 sets of questions. In the first, colour intensity was scored from nil to extreme on 10 cm line scales for 9 hue or hue related terms and 3 achromatic terms. The hue terms were red (RD), pink (PK), orange (OR), yellow (YL), cream (CR), brown (BR), green (GR), blue (BL) and purple (PL) and the achromatic terms were white (W), grey (G) and black (B). In the second set, three appearance ranges, dark to pale (pa), dull to bright (br), opaque to translucent (tr), and hedonic rating, dislike extremely to like extremely (HD), were similarly scored on 10 cm line scales.

Colour Measurement

Diffuse reflectance spectra of fresh and faded bacon, measured on a Pye Unicam SP100 spectrophotometer, were converted to CIELAB colour coordinates for each illuminant. CIELAB colour space has an adaptation correction which locates the illuminant at the origin of the a^*b^* chromaticness diagram (CIE, 1986).

RESULTS

Objective Colour

The reflectance spectra of the fresh and faded bacon (Fig. 1) show the characteristic reduction at >600 nm for the faded product which lowers the tristimulus value X (the 'red' response). Uniform lightness, L^*, of the fresh ranged from 52·4 to 54·7 depending on the emission spectrum of the lamp but was generally 1–2 L^* units less for the faded. CIELAB chromaticness is shown in Fig. 2. For the most red enhancing lamp (NA), fresh bacon had the largest value of a^* which gave it the highest chroma, C^*, that is its location in the a^*b^* diagram is farthest from the origin. For the lamp with the lowest Ra (35), faded bacon had the smallest a^* value, a low chroma and the largest hue angle ($h°$).

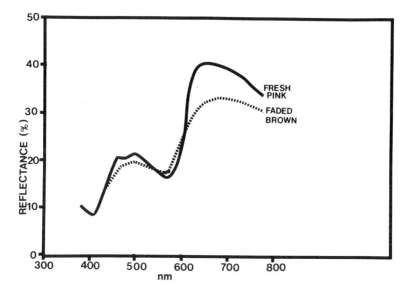

Figure 1. Reflectance spectra of fresh (—) and faded (••••) bacon.

Colour Assessment

Homogeneous Illumination
Panel data were analysed by analysis of variance (ANOVA). Table 1
lists the mean scores for the 7 'homogeneous' situations when identical
lamps were used in both booths. Overall, fresh bacon lean was

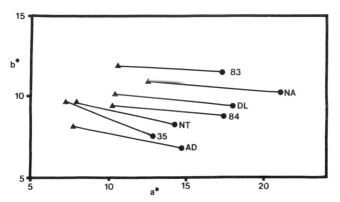

Figure 2. CIELAB diagram of fresh (●) and faded (▲) bacon.

Table 1

Mean response to hue and appearance terms and hedonic rating
(mm) for fresh and faded bacon

	AD	84	83	35	NT	DL	NA	sed
			Viewing lamp					
Response to:			*Fresh bacon lean*					
Red	26·6	31·8	27·4	32·7	36·9	36·9	29·9	0·84
Pink	40·1	41·6	39·4	43·6	39·6	40·0	43·6	0·87
Orange	2·7	3·1	2·4	4·6	4·3	1·3	4·8	0·46
Brown	0·9	2·4	2·3	4·5	1·0	2·6	1·7	0·56
Cream	4·1	3·1	3·4	7·6	1·6	1·6	1·7	0·31
Yellow	0·4	1·3	0·0	1·8	0·6	0·3	1·3	0·30
Green	0·3	0·3	0·0	1·1	0·0	0·0	0·0	0·12
Blue	1·5	3·1	1·9	1·6	3·2	0·8	3·1	0·42
Purple	12·4	13·6	9·5	23·0	20·3	15·4	11·7	1·33
White	0·8	1·0	2·0	2·2	0·1	0·3	0·3	0·17
Grey	0·6	0·7	0·0	2·1	0·3	0·0	0·8	0·21
Black	0·0	0·0	0·0	0·4	0·0	0·0	0·0	0·02
Paleness	48·5	40·4	52·8	37·3	39·7	44·7	48·1	1·32
Brightness	53·5	56·8	52·7	35·1	50·1	64·4	59·5	1·39
Translucence	63·6	57·2	63·8	61·5	61·1	68·9	63·6	1·00
Hedonic	56·8	55·3	53·5	50·1	57·9	52·6	54·9	1·18
			Faded bacon lean					
Red	3·3	3·3	4·0	3·3	2·4	8·9	3·1	0·49
Pink	1·2	3·5	2·5	5·6	1·4	2·0	3·5	0·83
Orange	3·7	8·1	6·6	7·6	8·3	5·4	5·5	1·25
Brown	44·5	45·1	44·0	40·8	55·1	50·0	44·6	1·18
Cream	15·4	12·0	13·4	20·5	13·2	7·1	11·2	1·22
Yellow	3·3	5·5	4·1	12·5	8·0	1·2	5·0	0·71
Green	5·0	3·9	3·9	9·1	4·1	1·6	4·2	0·36
Blue	1·1	0·8	1·1	0·1	0·9	1·6	0·2	0·18
Purple	2·7	1·3	5·9	2·4	3·5	5·4	2·2	0·36
White	0·5	1·0	0·0	2·1	0·1	0·2	1·7	0·32
Grey	14·3	12·9	11·5	11·4	12·5	6·3	8·6	0·66
Black	0·4	0·0	0·0	0·0	0·0	0·0	0·0	0·00
Paleness	55·2	54·6	58·4	55·8	56·0	46·0	53·8	2·21
Brightness	30·7	30·3	34·4	22·6	30·7	39·8	32·0	1·28
Translucence	63·8	65·7	64·0	59·8	58·9	65·1	68·9	1·74
Hedonic	21·4	23·5	25·6	26·0	21·0	31·1	27·4	0·77

described as approximately 40% brighter than the faded and the faded was 20% paler. Loss of brightness in the faded bacon was accompanied by an increase in greyness. For fresh bacon the colour terms with highest scores were pink, followed by red and purple, whereas for faded, the highest scores were for brown, cream and grey. Within the constraint of observer adaptation to only one light, irrespective of lamp, the magnitude of the differences in the most frequently used terms between lamps was small compared with the difference between fresh and faded samples.

Significant differences between lamps were found for the most used terms. Pink response progressively increased for fresh bacon and brown decreased for faded bacon with increase in the lamp's red enhancement from NT to DL to NA. In addition to the expected increases/decreases in pinkness/brownness, bacon colour changed in character under different lights as shown by the use of secondary colour terms. This is illustrated in Figs 3(a) and 3(b) for four of the lamps. Mean scores are presented on a colour diagram based on the Swedish NCS colour atlas. This locates the four unique hues, red, yellow, green and blue as the cardinal directions. The intermediate hues, orange and purple, are spaced according to language logic (Sivik, 1985). The hue related term cream has been located close to yellow because of its dilute yellow content and pink near to red but slightly orangewards. Brown was set between orange and yellow because it describes imprecisely a wide spread of desaturated colours whose hues range from greenish-yellow to red. For the fully adapted observer, there was little difference in bacon lean description between the most balanced broad band lamp (Artificial Daylight) with the highest *Ra* and the cooler of the tri-band lamps (Colour 84) (Fig. 3(a)). The moderate red enhancing lamp (DeLuxe Natural) increased the ratio of red to pink for the fresh and decreased the yellow content of the brown. Comparison of this lamp with that of the lowest *Ra* (Pluslux 3500) (Fig. 3(b)) shows that the poorer lamp distorted the colour of the fresh towards purple but, more importantly, it induced distinct greenness into the colour of the faded product.

Heterogeneous Illumination

A more complex task is presented to the observer when the booths are lit by different lights, especially if they induce contrast. In the observer's semi-adapted state the influence of white as the psychological reference is distorted and the grey/white background in the two

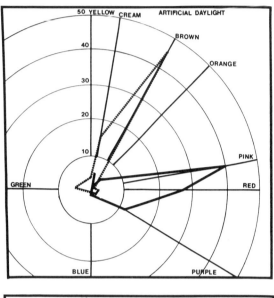

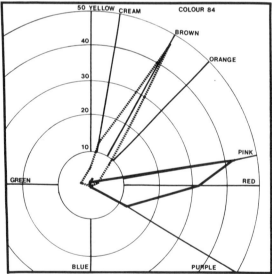

Figure 3. Mean colour term response for fresh (—) and faded (••••) bacon. (a) Under Artificial Daylight and Colour 84.

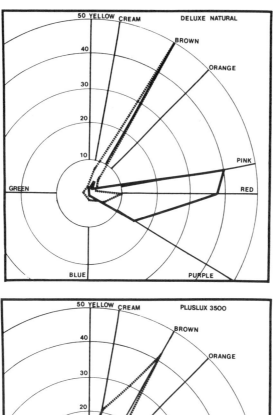

Fig. 3—contd. (b) Under De Luxe Natural and Pluslux 3500.

Table 2
Change in response to pink (+, −mm) as affected by light in adjacent booth

		AD	84	83	35	NT	DL	NA
				Fresh bacon lean				
Viewing	AD		−4·3	22·6	−0·4	4·9	6·6	−8·8
lamp	84	−5·4		1·2	4·2	3·4	−6·5	−6·8
	83	13·9	9·0		−1·3	5·8	0·0	−3·3
	35	−17·4	−11·1	−23·0		−13·7	−16·6	−12·6
	NT	7·5	5·3	2·7	−3·3		−9·6	−13·1
	DL	12·2	9·3	4·0	5·7	10·4		4·5
	NA	1·9	2·1	8·6	14·6	5·5	10·2	
				Faded bacon lean				
Viewing	AD		2·9	6·4	10·2	0·1	0·6	2·6
lamp	84	3·5		1·9	−0·6	−3·0	−1·3	−1·4
	83	5·3	2·3		4·3	−1·2	1·0	1·9
	35	−1·9	−5·6	−0·9		−3·9	−5·1	−4·5
	NT	−0·3	−0·7	5·9	3·1		0·5	−0·8
	DL	−0·8	0·5	1·0	0·0	5·6		7·0
	NA	2·5	9·6	5·5	6·5	6·8	12·3	

visual fields assumes different colours. A red enhancing light generates opponent greenness in the other booth if that lamp is deficient in red energy. The four bacon samples are now seen to possess four distinct colours. In some circumstances the faded sample under one lamp approaches the brightness of the fresh under the lamp in the adjacent booth. These induced changes in response from that in the homogeneous situation for the major hues, pink and brown, are listed in Tables 2 and 3. The low Ra lamp (35) elicited pinkness scores 40% lower than in the homogeneous situation and the red enhancing lamp (DL) decreased brownness.

Principal Component Analysis
An alternative to ANOVA as a means of describing complex changes in colour response is to use principal component analysis (PCA) as a map of visual directionality (MacDougall et al., 1985). The correlations of the first and second components (PC1, PC2) with the sensory terms are shown in Fig. 4. The first component is essentially pink-red versus brown-green and is highly correlated with the hedonic rating.

Table 3

Change in response to brown (+, −mm) as affected by light in adjacent booth

		Adjacent lamp					
		AD	84	83	35	NT	DL	NA
			Fresh bacon lean					
Viewing	AD		−0·9	4·6	0·5	−0·9	0·0	7·5
lamp	84	0·3		−0·7	−2·4	−2·4	−1·7	5·3
	83	1·4	−1·3		−1·2	−0·9	1·3	3·5
	35	2·9	−3·3	0·8		2·0	5·9	6·4
	NT	0·2	−1·0	1·1	0·6		5·0	5·1
	DL	−2·4	−2·6	−0·7	−2·3	−1·6		−1·4
	NA	−1·2	−0·6	−1·7	−0·9	−1·7	1·7	
			Faded bacon lean					
Viewing	AD		−10·2	11·8	−11·9	1·4	5·3	5·1
lamp	84	−10·0		3·3	1·4	4·0	4·2	8·4
	83	7·6	4·9		2·4	−3·4	11·9	2·4
	35	2·4	−2·4	5·0		8·8	9·6	7·8
	NT	−4·3	−7·1	−14·9	−8·9		−15·6	−13·1
	DL	22·9	4·5	9·7	0·2	−6·7		−16·5
	NA	5·8	−3·6	−12·6	−3·2	−7·9	−19·4	

The locations of the hue terms for the homogeneous situation are given in Fig. 5. The close packing of the fresh samples in the first component between +0·17 and +0·27 for all lamps endorses the ANOVA results. The wider spread of the faded samples between −0·09 and −0·38 shows the greater effects of differences in lamps spectra on the faded samples. The advantage of PCA in the heterogeneous situation is that it indicates direction and extent of visual change. The change in mean response for fresh bacon under AD (highest Ra) resulted in an increased PC1 when influenced by 35 (lowest Ra) (Fig. 6). The opposite effect is seen for 35 when influenced by AD. However, for faded bacon, both 35 and AD influenced by each other increased PC1. Similar opposite directional changes in PC1 occurred for fresh bacon under 83 and NA and the influence of 83 on NA for faded also increased PC1.

Hedonic Rating
The hedonic rating of faded bacon was generally half that of fresh bacon (Table 1). The hedonic ratings for the homogeneous situations

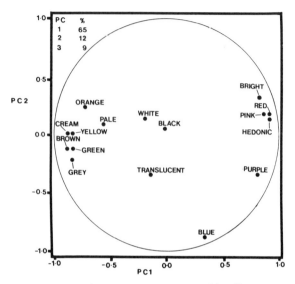

Figure 4. Correlations of sensory terms with first two principal components.

are compared with the monadic results from the previous experiment in Fig. 7. Bacon samples, presented as fresh and faded pairs, are clearly separated whereas in monadic presentation they are continuous. In both circumstances, the lamps with broad band spectra and moderate to high *Ra* (NT and AD) gave maximum differences in hedonic rating. Increasing the red enhancing properties of the lamps

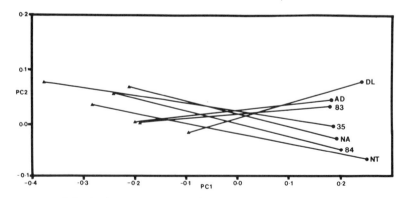

Figure 5. Principal components of colour response for fresh (●) and faded (▲) bacon for the seven homogeneous presentations.

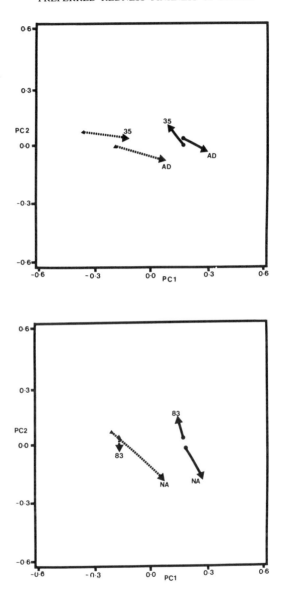

Figure 6. Change in principal components of colour response for fresh (—) and faded (▪▪▪▪) bacon influenced by another lamp for Artificial Daylight and Pluslux 3500 and for NAFA and Colour 83. Magnitude and direction of change indicated by arrow (→).

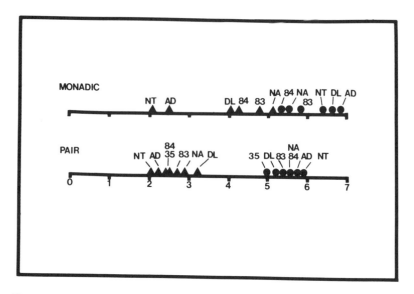

Figure 7. Mean hedonic scores for fresh (●) and faded (▲) bacon in monadic and pairwise presentation.

increased the hedonic rating for the faded samples but not for the fresh. The lamp with the poorest *Ra*, (35), produced the lowest rating for fresh bacon.

DISCUSSION AND CONCLUSIONS

Modern fluorescent lamps are usually classified into 3 groups. These are low cost broad band halophosphate lamps with good efficacy but only moderate colour rendering, special De Luxe lamps with excellent rendering but fairly low efficacy and tri-band lamps with high efficacy and good rendering. The optimum choice depends on the field of application (van Kemenade *et al.*, 1983). The preferred colour temperature for shop and department store lighting lies between 3000 and 4000 K where the primary objective is to help sell merchandise (Tate, 1972). However, colour rendering is probably more important than colour temperature (Thornton, 1982).

This experiment confirmed that colour rendering is more important than colour temperature for maximum discrimination between attractive pink-red bacon and faded grey-brown bacon. Red enhancement improved the faded product but did not make the fresh the most preferred, suggesting that the extra red energy may make the fresh product appear too pink. The contribution that overhead lighting makes to the adaptive state of the observer when assessing products lit by a different lamp is complex. If the general lighting is 'less red' or of a lower Ra than the lamp lighting the product then product colour may brighten.

Superior colour rendering for textiles and decorative materials is necessary to avoid colour distortion and metamorism; that is the mismatch of two colours under one lamp which match under a different lamp. In the food industry it would be useful to determine the consequences of lighting foods for maximum colour rendering rather than with red enhancement now that lamps are becoming available with $Ra > 90$ at preferred colour temperatures (Philips, 1987). Such lamps have lower output (lower lumens/watt) than tri-band lamps but, until now, this aspect of cost efficiency has not been a controlling factor in choice of lamp for food display.

ACKNOWLEDGEMENTS

The authors wish to thank the Institute's Panellists and Miss H. Poyser for her help in drawing the figures.

REFERENCES

CIE (1974). *Method of measuring and specifying colour rendering properties of light sources.* Publication No 13.2 (TC-3.2). Commission Internationale de l'Eclairage, Vienna.

CIE (1986). *Colorimetry*, 2nd edn, Publication No. 15.2 (TC-1.3). Commission Internationale de l'Eclairage, Vienna.

Halstead, M. B. (1978). Colour rendering: Past, present and future. In *AIC Colour 77*, Adam Hilger Ltd, London, pp. 97–127.

Hood, D. E. & Riordan, E. B. (1973). Discolouration in pre-packed beef: Measurement by reflectance spectrophotometry and shopper discrimination. *J. Food Technol.*, **8**, 333–43.

MacDougall, D. B. (1982). Changes in the colour and opacity of meat. *Food Chem.*, **9**, 75–88.

MacDougall, D. B., Francombe, M. & Whelehan, O. P. (1985). Visual descriptive profiling of meat under different illuminants. In *AIC Mondial Coleur 85*, **1**, 85. Association de la Couleur, Monte Carlo.

McLaren, K. (1986). *The Colour Science of Dyes and Pigments*, 2nd ed. Adam Hilger Ltd, Bristol.

Philips (1987). *Selection Guide Fluorescent Lighting*. Philips Lighting Division, Eindhoven, The Netherlands.

Sivik, L. (1985). Evaluations of colour combinations. In, *AIC Mondial Couleur 85*, **2**, 9. Association de la Couleur, Monte Carlo.

Tate, R. L. C. (1972). *Lamps and Lighting*. Edward Arnold, London, pp. 459–68.

Thornton, W. A. (1982). Customer acceptance of the colour rendering of illumination. *Lighting Design and Application*, **12**(3), 33.

Van Kemenade, J. I. C., Berns, E. G. & Peters, R. C. (1983). New special deluxe "TLD" fluorescent lamps. In *CIE 20th Session Amsterdam*, Commission Internationale de l'Eclairage, Vienna, D702/1–3.

Chapter 34

Electromyographic Evaluation of the Texture of Confectionery Products

ANITA EVES, MICHAEL M. BOYAR and DAVID KILCAST

*Leatherhead Food RA, Randalls Road, Leatherhead, Surrey
KT22 7RY, UK*

ABSTRACT

Texture is one of the main quality factors influencing the acceptability of foodstuffs. Texture profiling is the preferred method for quantifying those aspects of texture that are of greatest importance in determining consumer acceptability. Time and cost constraints, however, often result in the use of instrumental methods. Data from such techniques generally do not correlate well with subjective data, and yield only a very limited picture of textural characteristics.

Electromyography, a technique that measures the electrical potentials of muscles during chewing, encompasses the human advantages of sensory texture profiling and the time/cost advantages of instrumental techniques.

It has been proven that EMG integrated peak height data are highly correlated with biting forces and hence true force–time curves of food behaviour during the chewing are obtained.

Tests on confectionery gums have shown that reproducibility is good and that, in most cases, the choice of subject is not critical. Clear differences have been established between a variety of chocolate products.

459

INTRODUCTION

The acceptability of foods to the consumer is frequently determined by their textural characteristics. This is particularly true of confectionery products, in which their distinctive eating characteristics are achieved by careful control of texture. For example, use of different gelling agents can give textures ranging from tough and chewy to soft and short. Texture is no less important in chocolate confectionery, and new product introductions are increasingly being marketed on the basis of their textural novelty.

Successful design of texture relies on having a means of defining and quantifying the many distinct textural attributes that foods possess. The perception of texture is a psychological response to a tactile stimulus, and therefore a full description of texture can only be achieved through the use of people. A number of different subjective methods have been proposed and used. The first comprehensive attempt to define texture by subjective means was the Texture Profile Method (Szczesniak et al., 1963). Category scales were developed for a variety of textural descriptions such as hardness, chewiness and adhesiveness. Each category in each scale was defined by a reference food and the food identified by brand name and manufacturer. Intensive panel training in the use of these scales was required. Major problems were encountered, however, in the selection and availability of reference samples, especially outside the United States, and in the demands on time and cost for panel training and maintenance.

The method has now largely been replaced by the Quantitative Descriptive Analysis (QDA) method described by Stone et al. (1974). In this method textural (and non-textural) attributes are identified in discussion sessions at which panellists have available a range of products exemplifying attributes of interest. A consensus vocabulary is developed and panellists are trained in the use of the descriptors by scoring their intensity on unstructured line scales in replicate sessions. The data are analysed statistically, normally using analysis of variance and multiple comparison tests, but increasingly using multivariate methods such as principal components analysis.

Although the QDA method does have cost and time advantages over the Texture Profile Method, many food manufacturers have difficulties in justifying the resources necessary for the frequent running of panels over a long period. As a result, companies frequently rely on the use of instrumental measurements to give textural information.

The instrumental tests most commonly used rely on a measurement of force as a sample is deformed in some way, for example, by penetration or compression. The more sophisticated instruments, such as the Instron Universal Testing Machine and the Stevens CR Analyser, provide a continuous record of force against deformation, but many sectors of the industry rely on single-point measurements of force at a fixed, and often arbitrary, deformation. The value of such measurements for texture assessment is questionable. Although useful information can be obtained on the variation of relevant physical properties for quality control purposes, the use of such data in assessing texture demands a detailed understanding of the relationship between the physical parameter and relevant subjective textural parameters. This relationship is too often assumed rather than proven.

One notable attempt to improve on the use of objective measurements has been through acoustic emission studies. The importance of the sounds made by foods on biting is well appreciated in the snack foods industry, and sound can also be an important quality indicator for fruits and vegetables. Early work by Drake (1963) demonstrated that the sound spectrum produced on biting toasted bread was related to the degree of toasting. This work was extended by Vickers (1981), who investigated the auditory basis of crispness and crunchiness.

Although the practical applications of such ideas were limited strictly to those foods that emitted sounds, their importance lies in the concept of making quantitative instrumental measurement on human subjects as they eat. This concept, which may be described as *in vivo* texture measurement, has taken an important step forward at the Leatherhead Food RA through the development of the more widely applicable electromyography (EMG) technique (Boyar & Kilcast, 1986).

EMG measures the electrical activity of muscles that are used during chewing. The muscle most active during the chewing of solid foods is the masseter muscle. This is shallow-lying and the activity can readily be measured using surface electrodes, although the activity of deeper-lying muscles can also be recorded. This chapter considers the use of EMG for assessing the texture of confectionery products that are chewed using this muscle. Specific points considered are:

—measurement of biting force
—reproducibility of measurements on confectionery gums
—choice of sample dimensions
—applications to chocolate.

METHODS

Electromyography

Electromyographic patterns were recorded using a Grass Polygraph (Model 7D). The system has a regulated power supply, consisting of two DC driver amplifiers. One of these is connected to a pre-amplifier and displays the raw signal. The other is connected to the pre-amplifier and an integrator module and displays the integrated data. Both driver amplifiers include a 50 Hz filter rejecting interference from AC sources. All recordings were made with the amplifiers' frequency bands as wide as possible (10 Hz–40 kHz). This prevents the chart from undulating with the movement of the jaw and ensures a flat frequency response up to 200 Hz, this being the maximum response rate of the pens. The time base was set at 0·2 s at the recommendation of the manufacturer.

Surface electrodes were used to detect the electrical signals. The skin on the cheek and earlobe were cleansed with 95% (v/v) ethanol to remove traces of dust and perspiration, which may interfere with the signal. A position was located on the cheek at the maximum point of inflection of the masseter muscle and two electrodes were located above and below this point in line with the muscle and approximately 0·5 cm apart. A third electrode was placed on the earlobe, a point of no muscular activity, which acted as an earth. Electrode cream, a conductive paste, was applied to the electrode surface in all cases. The general arrangement of subject and instrument is shown in Fig. 1.

After the terminal ends of the electrodes had been located in the Polygraph, the subject was presented with a sample to chew. All samples were assessed in triplicate and all samples were of the same size and geometry. Data were recorded from the time the sample was put into the mouth to the time of swallowing. The form of the data is shown in Fig. 2.

The results presented in this chapter were all measured from the integrated data. These were collected, via an A/D convertor, on to a computer disc at a rate of 50 points per second. The stored data were analysed by a computer program calculating various trace parameters—peak height (PH), adjusted height (AH), pre-maximum gradient (PRG), post-maximum gradient (POG), and area under peak (A) (Fig. 3).

Gradients and area were calculated from minima rather than baseline, and all parameters were adjusted in relation to a pre-recorded baseline. Small inflections on the integrated trace were

Figure 1. General arrangement of subject and EMG.

eliminated by means of a rejection factor. The rejection was based on the ratio of the highest and smallest peaks required; in this case the factor used was 30%, so that any peak less than 30% of the height of the largest peak was rejected. Any of the trace parameters can be plotted against time, a line or curve being fitted to the data using the Genstat statistical package.

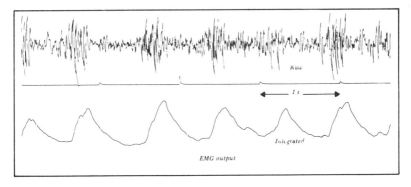

Figure 2. EMG output.

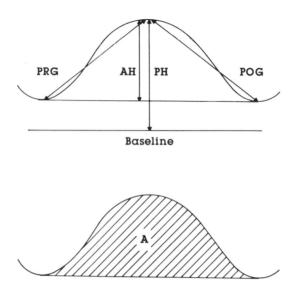

Figure 3. Integrated EMG trace parameters. (PH, Peak height; AH, Adjusted height; PRG, Pre-maximum gradient; POG, Post-maximum gradient; A, Area.)

Relationship between Peak Height and Biting Force

A strain gauge force transducer was constructed and calibrated under compression using a Stevens CR Analyser. A subject was linked to the Polygraph and asked to bite on the tip of the strain gauge using the molars. The voltage produced from the strain gauge was recorded, together with the integrated peak height.

Reproducibility

Between Occasions

A subject linked to the Polygraph was presented with 4-g samples of toffee. The procedure was repeated on a further 2 occasions and by a further 4 subjects, also over 3 days. Integrated peak height was evaluated for each subject on each day, a broken stick model being fitted to the data:

$$y = \{Ae^{-\alpha u} + Q(t - u)\} \quad \text{if} \quad t < U$$
$$y = Ae^{-\alpha t} \quad \text{if} \quad t \geq U$$

Between Subjects
A subject linked to the Polygraph was presented with fruit pastilles, each weighing 4·4 g. A further 29 subjects also carried out the test; approximately one-third of the subjects were male and two-thirds female. Integrated peak height was calculated and plotted against time for all subjects, the two-phase model previously described being fitted to the data.

Choice of Sample Dimension
On examining the textural differences of products with widely different densities, problems were encountered in determining whether to present equal weights or equal volumes of samples.

Samples of Cadbury's Dairy Milk Chocolate and Wispa were prepared to determine which criterion would be most discriminating in identifying textural differences. A 6·3-g sample (volume 4·6 cm^3) of Cadbury's Dairy Milk was compared with an equal weight of Wispa (volume 9·7 cm^3) and an equal volume of Wispa (weight 3 g). EMG recordings were made in triplicate as described previously, and an exponential curve fitted to all parameters.

$$y = Ae^{-\alpha t}$$

Assessment of Chocolate Products
Two separate experiments were carried out. In the first, a wide range of chocolate types was examined using an equal volume criterion on the basis of integrated peak height only. Samples examined were: Galaxy, Cadbury's Dairy Milk, Cadbury's Flake, Terry's Plain and Wispa. In the second experiment, samples of Cadbury's Dairy Milk and Bournville chocolate were examined on the basis of all measured parameters shown in Fig. 3.

EMG measurements were carried out as described previously and an exponential model was used for curve fitting. In addition, snap tests were carried out using a Stevens CR Analyser. A strip of 4 chocolate squares was placed across the supports with a 3·5-cm separation in a triple beam arrangement and force applied at 20 mm/min using a flat-ended blade. Six replicates were measured and the maximum force required to snap the bar recorded.

RESULTS AND DISCUSSION

Relationship between Peak Height and Biting Force
A plot of biting force against integrated EMG peak height is shown in Fig. 4. A good linear relationship can be seen, with a correlation coefficient of 0·96. The integrated peak height consequently provides a good measure of biting force in the mouth.

Reproducibility

Between Occasions
An example of the results obtained is shown in Fig. 5. The results apply to one subject only; similar results were, however, obtained for other subjects. Although differences were apparent in the initial phases of chewing, the breakdown rates of the samples over the 3 days remained the same. A slight shift is seen in the amplitude of the plot

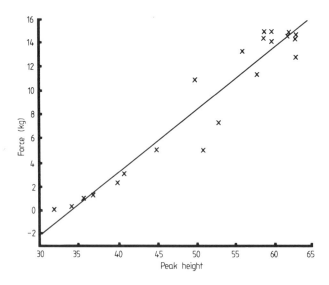

Figure 4. Plot of biting force against integrated peak height.

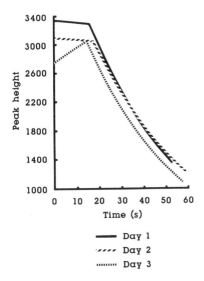

Figure 5. Between-occasion reproducibility.

on day three; this would probably be due to slightly inaccurate electrode placement. The initial upward phase of chewing is thought to arise through positioning of the food prior to chewing properly. Although research has concentrated predominantly on breakdown characteristics, useful information may be found in the upward phase of the curve regarding initial manipulation of foods.

Chew time on day one was slightly shorter than on the following 2 days.

From these results it would seem that from day to day, results do not vary considerably. Methods by which the amplitude of peaks can be maintained are under consideration, for instance the use of a standard material on which a subject would chew prior to any study

Between Subjects
Results showed 26 of the 30 subjects investigated to exhibit chewing patterns represented by a broken stick relationship (Group 1). Within this group, peak amplitudes and chew times varied considerably. The other 4 subjects fell into 2 groups; those who gave data best represented by a single exponential decay curve (Group 2) and those who produced steadily increasing forces during chewing (Group 3).

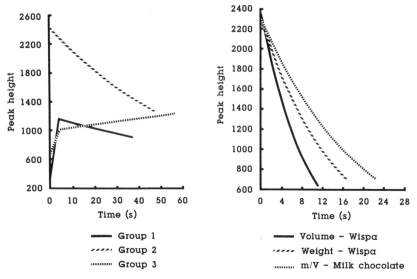

Figure 6. Between-subject reproducibility.

Figure 7. Selection of sample
weight or sample volume criterion.

Illustrative examples of the three curve types found are shown in Fig.
6.

Further work is required to determine the precise importance of
amplitude and time differences within Group 1.

Choice of Sample Dimensions

The results for peak height assessment are shown in Fig. 7. The rate of
breakdown of Wispa is greater than for the milk chocolate, but sample
size based on an equal volume criterion shows the greater discrimination. Initial peak heights (biting forces) are similar. Together with
giving improved discrimination between products, the use of a volume
criterion is probably better related to a practical consumer situation, in
which the bite size will be determined mainly by dimensions. The
volume criterion was used for subsequent studies.

Assessment of Chocolate Products

The peak height data for the 5 products is shown in Fig. 8. The Flake
and Wispa products show the fastest rate of breakdown and shortest
chewing times, although initial biting forces are, respectively, greatest
and smallest. Of the other 3 products, the plain chocolate requires the

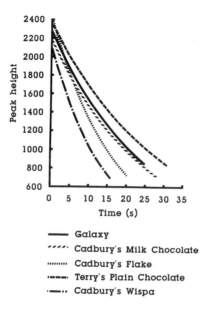

Figure 8. Peak height data on 5 chocolate products.

highest initial biting force, a slightly slower breakdown rate and the longest chewing time. The Galaxy and Cadbury's Dairy Milk chocolate samples are not easily discriminated by this data.

Results of the snap tests on the Cadbury's Dairy Milk and Bournville samples are shown in Table 1.

The mean force values were not statistically significantly different at the 5% level. Analysis of the EMG curves showed no statistically significant differences between samples for the height, area and pre-maximum gradient parameters. Statistically significant differences were found, however, in the post-maximum gradient data (Fig. 9). Informal subjective assessments indicated that the Bournville sample

Table 1
Force required to snap chocolate products

Product	Force (g)	Standard deviation
Cadbury's Dairy Milk	378·3	53·5
Bournville	357·5	57·9

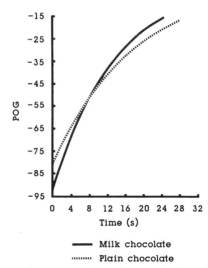

Figure 9. Post-maximum gradient data on 2 chocolate products.

was perceived as more sticky than the milk chocolate sample. Other observations made previously indicated that the post-maximum gradient data from toffees may be related to subjective stickiness (Eves, 1986). Typical integrated curve shapes are shown schematically in Fig. 10, in which the lower curve is typical of toffee.

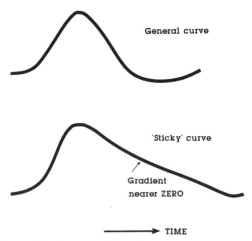

Figure 10. Schematic diagram showing distinction between sticky and non-sticky products.

GENERAL DISCUSSION

At the stage of development described in this chapter, EMG has been shown capable of discriminating between confectionery samples of known textural differences. In addition, informal subjective comments made by the subjects consuming the samples indicate that the differences reflect subjective experience.

A good correlation has been obtained between peak height and biting force. A fuller interpretation of the subjective relevance of EMG parameters requires correlation with attributes identified for specific products from sensory profile panels. Informal subjective assessments have, however, indicated that the post-maximum gradient may be related to subjective stickiness. It may also be hypothesised that the area under integrated curves may be related to the effort required to chew foods. Objective quantification of such parameters would be of great value to the confectionery industry and to other sectors of the food industry.

For practical application in the food industry, both for R&D and, perhaps ultimately quality control purposes, satisfactory reproducibility must be established. The data presented in this chapter show that most subjects show the same EMG patterns but that anomalous responses can be generated by a small proportion of subjects. These can, however, be screened for very quickly. Selection of subjects who show the normal response (Group 1) is not critical. As a result of the need to reposition electrodes between occasions, and possibly as a result of changes in skin condition, overall signal levels can vary between occasions, and work is currently being carried out to examine the use of a standard material for calibration purposes.

The data presented in this chapter were obtained from the masseter muscle only. Exploratory work has shown that monitoring the group of muscles controlling tongue movement can produce information related to viscosity characteristics (Dea et al., 1988). Such information would be of particular value in studying textural changes in foods such as ice cream, for which the melting characteristics are of great importance. Combining the information produced simultaneously from the 2 sets of muscles would provide a more complete picture of breakdown and melting characteristics.

EMG possesses the unique advantage of providing objective measurements which are closely related to a subjective process. Phenomena that are characteristic of the human chewing process, for example temperature changes and admixture of saliva, are an integral part of the measurements, which are made continuously throughout the chewing cycle. The technique is rapid and inexpensive in comparison with texture profiling and may be considered as an alternative for companies who do not possess the resources needed to train fully operational panels. EMG should, however, be seen in the wider context of a technique that provides information that is complementary to profile data and that gives a more complete picture of food texture than has been possible in the past.

REFERENCES

Boyar, M. M. & Kilcast, D. (1986). Electromyography as a novel technique for examining food texture. *J. Food Sci.*, **51**(3), 859–60.

Dea, I. C. M., Eves, A., Kilcast, D. & Morris, E. R. (1988). Relationship of electromyographic evaluation of semi-fluid model systems with dynamic shear viscosity. *Proceedings of the Fourth International Conference on Gums and Stabilisers for the Food Industry*, Wrexham 1987, Pergamon Press, Oxford, pp. 241–6.

Drake, B. K. (1963). Food crushing sounds. An introductory study. *J. Food Sci.*, **28**, 233–41.

Eves, A. (1986). Unpublished observations.

Szczesniak, A. S., Brandt, M. A. & Friedman, H. H. (1963). Development of standard rating scales for mechanical parameters of texture and correlation between the objective and sensory methods of texture evaluation. *J. Food Sci.*, **28**, 397–403.

Stone, H., Sidel, J., Oliver, S., Woolsey, A. & Singleton, R. C. (1974). Sensory evaluation by quantitative descriptive analysis. *Food Technol.*, **28** (11), 24, 26, 28, 29, 32, 34.

Vickers, Z. M. (1981). Relationships of chewing sounds to judgements of crispness, crunchiness and hardness. *J. Food Sci.*, **47**, 121–4.

Topic 9

Overview of Food Acceptability

Chapter 35

Negative Influences on Acceptability and Their Control

Taint Analysis & Sensory Quality Services, 8 High Bungay Rd, Loddon, Norwich NR14 6JT, UK

ABSTRACT

Reduced acceptability, which leads to rejection of food, can result from many different causes. These influence the interaction between consumers' expectations and their perception of the food; both may be innate, temporal, contextual or acquired. This scenario is discussed and illustrated with examples to show how these factors may interact to influence expected consumer behaviour. Some have to be accepted as factors influencing market segmentation, but others are amenable to control. The type of procedures which can be used to reduce the likelihood of food related factors unexpectedly appearing at the market place, and causing disruption and loss, are briefly given.

A high level of acceptability to the target population is an essential prerequisite for the success of any new product, at development, product launch and market consolidation stages. Reduced acceptability results in increasing rejection and a diminishing market; it can result from many causes To even understand, much less control those factors which influence acceptability, we must first have some insight into its development. This is a complex and rapidly developing field, and I shall not attempt to draw together current work and theories in the conventional referenced format, but I present some incomplete, speculative ideas as a working model which, I hope, will stimulate further discussion, dissent, and alternative testable hypotheses. I chose negative factors because it is much easier to reduce, than to increase, acceptability and I call the factors which reduce it, negative. Control of these factors is an obviously important part of quality assurance. I use the illustrative examples, not because they have more problems than other food products, but as a convenient group.

WHAT IS ACCEPTABILITY?

Two recent definitions of acceptance are:

an hedonic assessment of adequacy within a specified range (British Standard 5098); and

the act of a given individual or population of favourably consuming a product (International Standard 5492).

These definitions do not provide a basis for measurement; they describe *classification* into acceptable or not, which is hardly an adequate description of the observed range of acceptance behaviours. My rejection of these 'standards' illustrates the necessity for definition of terms, which are essential if we are to communicate and improve our understanding of any area. Despite the many hours spent discussing any definition, it is not until it is published and put into use that any deficiencies become apparent. These definitions are concepts, or ideas which develop into hypotheses; they can be tested most readily if they include a variable outcome which can be measured.

I propose the following definition, which does provide such a basis:

The acceptability of *a product* is the *level* of *continued purchase or consumption* by a *specified population.*

It is important to realise that this definition contains five essential elements which must be qualified:

1. The *product* is specific, not generic. It is only possible to draw conclusions about the acceptability (to a particular group) of, for example, yellow spreads (butter, margarines and the newer low-energy spreads) in general, by aggregating the results of tested samples of *specific* spreads. Only the *concept* of spreads (generic) can be tested. The definition is thus object-, not concept-based.

2. *Level* describes a degree within a range (high-low). This may

vary from avid desire, e.g. the specific cravings well-known in pregnancy, to total aversion, e.g. as induced by a previous simultaneous unpleasant experience, although most products tested will fall within a much narrower part of the possible response range.

3. *Continued* describes repeated, not single, momentary responses. Any response, despite any exhortations to the contrary, will be momentary, and a series of measures is necessary to obtain information of known properties, and with predictive value.

4. The *people* are specified. There are very large variations between people, and predictions of behaviour of a particular population are only valid if the test is on a specified sample, representative of that population.

5. The definition *implies purchase or consumption* for a particular *purpose or context*—use, time, or place. A yellow spread which is highly appropriate for baking will probably not be as acceptable on the table for a special occasion meal. Perhaps purpose should be explicit in the definition.

A CONCEPT MODEL

Each response from each person is the resultant of many factors, some tending to increase acceptability (*positive* influences), and some to decrease it (*negative* influences). These factors can be broadly divided into those which arise from the person, 'people factors', and those which arise from the product, 'product factors'. Table 1 lists some of these.

These factors may be more readily postulated, and subsequently experimentally tested within individuals, by means of that fashionable

Table 1
Factors influencing acceptability

People factors	Product factors
Experience, exposure, taboos—expectations	Breed, cultivar
Sensitivity	Environment
Physiological state	Maturity
Personality, security	Processing, packaging
Occasion/values	Storage
Finance	Preparation, cooking, adjuncts
Mood	Contamination
	Availability

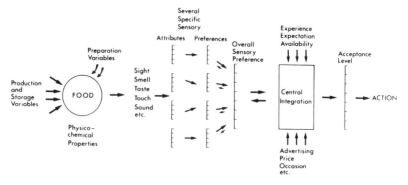

Figure 1. Schematic model of sensory and cognitive inputs resulting in food acceptance action. (From Land, D. G. (1983). What is sensory quality? In *Sensory Quality in Foods and Beverages: Definition, Measurement and Control,* eds A. A. Williams & R. K. Atkin. Ellis Horwood, Chichester. Reprinted by permission.)

device, a model. Figure 1 is only one of several possible variants, some given in other chapters in this symposium, but it illustrates some of the concepts involved. Its purpose is primarily to aid identification of operationally testable elements of the concept.

The factors involved may occur at many points along this sequence of events leading to a particular momentary response. All involve various levels of feedback from prior experience, for the key element is the comparison of the information coming in from the senses, with that which is expected from prior information and experience, and the consequences (pay-off) resulting from any differences. All deviations from expectation will be registered. Some might be scrutinised more closely, and weighted in terms of pay-off to influence the expressed acceptability level, whether at points of purchase or of consumption. At the point of consumption physiological feedback, not explicitly shown in the model, will also contribute. Most deviations are likely to be negative, because expectations are usually set high. Many of these processes are not conscious or externalised, and are possibly conditioned; the most obvious exception is price.

SOME EXAMPLES

Some of these factors can also be illustrated with examples from yellow spreads. If a batch of margarine turns green during cold storage, it would never reach the consumer because it is immediately recognised as not being within the accepted range of yellow spread colour. However, suppose it just becomes paler, and is distributed? Pale butter used to be accepted as quite normal in winter, increasing to a much stronger yellow for the rest of the year, although as most butter is now blended, probably only older consumers now know this. However, in a manufactured product much less variation (i.e. more control) is expected than in a 'natural' product, and the margarine would be scrutinised more carefully, and probably drop below the acceptability threshold (tolerance level) for a number of people.

The acceptability of yellow spreads is now influenced by promotion-induced factors, e.g. spreadability from the 'fridge'. If a new spread is advertised as having this attribute, and the consumer finds that it is not easily spread on freshly store-baked bread, or fresh home-part-baked rolls, the product will not match up to expectation, and acceptability will be reduced, with its consequent effect on future purchase behaviour. Another example is the low calorie factor, usually motivated by health or cosmetic concern. The advertisement-generated expectation is for a spread with all the attributes of a yellow spread, but with substantially less energy content. If, on opening the pack after purchase, it looks different, e.g. with either more or less gloss than expected for yellow spreads, the consumer is alerted to look for other differences, e.g. texture on spreading, mouthfeel, flavour and satisfaction after eating. All of these, if different, may reduce acceptability. However, they will be weighted against the benefit of either reducing calorie intake, or being able to increase food intake without increasing calorie intake. Much depends on the motivation of the individual. The low-fat spreads are a good example of new, but related to existing, products which expand the acceptable range of acquired expectations for those for whom the pay-off is sufficiently great.

THE ROLE OF STANDARDS

The presence of these expectations, or internal reference standards, is an essential feature of acceptability. The absence of such standards may, to some degree, explain neophobia, which is not confined to the very young. Standards give stability, and also confidence to try what is new. It is well known that those people who have had least opportunity to try new foods under 'secure' conditions, are the least willing to try new ones. 'Everyone Needs Standards' is an advertising slogan of some years ago which certainly applies to acceptability of novel food products.

NEGATIVE FACTORS

The factors which have the most profound negative effects on acceptability are those which are totally unexpected, particularly if they are not perceived until after the food has been chewed. For example, if you buy your usual yellow spread, and, on chewing the bread or biscuit on which it is spread, you find it is rancid, bitter, or worst of all, disinfectant or putrid, the reaction is likely to be swift and strong. You would either spit it out, or even find involuntary forces causing you to vomit. Such is the power of our innate protection against ingestion of noxious materials. The experience will have a powerful effect on the acceptability of that product for you, sometimes for a long time afterwards. The classical example is a boiled egg which smells bad when opened—few people ask for a replacement, and often will not risk repeating the experience for some time.

PEOPLE ARE NOT INTERCHANGEABLE

One complicating factor with taint negative factors is the great variation in sensitivity amongst people. Very often a taint, which is a contaminant which is smelt or tasted, is only present at a level which is detectable by a small proportion of consumers; they reject the food, whilst others happily accept it as normal. This is caused by the very wide range in sensitivity amongst people. It also has consequences for likes and dislikes of particular foods by different people, for what may be liked by one person for its flavour may be rejected as too strongly flavoured by someone more sensitive to the main flavour components, and as uninterestingly flavourless by someone less sensitive. These variations in response to a product by individuals are one of the contributory elements which produce market segments of products for particular groups of consumers.

A combination of what is probably variations in sensitivity and variations in expectations is illustrated in the sequence of three cartoons (Figs. 2(a), (b) and (c)). In Fig. 2(a) the person on the left

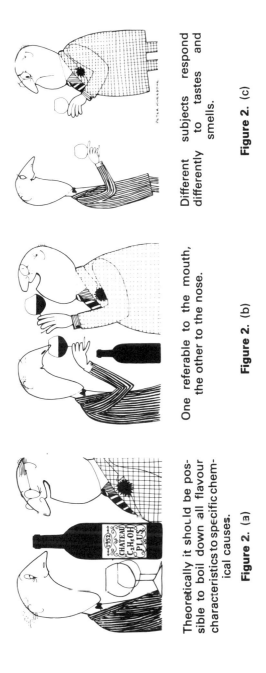

Theoretically it should be possible to boil down all flavour characteristics to specific chemical causes.

Figure 2. (a)

One referable to the mouth, the other to the nose.

Figure 2. (b)

Different subjects respond differently to tastes and smells.

Figure 2. (c)

does not know the particular wine, but is interested to try it; the one on the right does know it and is clearly anticipating the pleasure of consuming it. In Fig. 2(b), unlike the man on the left, he does not bother to explore its bouquet before drinking, but in Fig. 2(c) he is clearly disappointed, for it does not fulfil his expectations. The man on the left, however, after testing the bouquet and tasting the wine, is well-pleased with his new experience. Their reactions to the same wine are very different, and their expectations on the next occasion that wine is offered to each will also be very different. The same stimulus has had opposite effects on acceptability for each man.

SURROUNDINGS AND TIME

Acceptability is meaningless without context, and contextual incongruity can have a marked negative effect. Perhaps the best known example is that of the dinner, happily being consumed under very carefully selected low light; when bright white light was switched on it revealed blue peas, green meat and other incongruent colours. Half the party were immediately nauseated, despite their evident enjoyment seconds previously. Similar, but less extreme reactions occur with unfamiliar combinations, e.g. cheddar cheese served with strawberry jam, quite acceptable in some areas, but not in most. It is also seen in terms of what is appropriate for the occasion or situation. A hot chunky soup would be much more acceptable as the starter for a winter lunch in Aberdeen than for a summer lunch in Majorca, and for someone conscious of the need for body-weight control, a yoghurt, or even no dessert, would be more acceptable than a large portion of steamed pudding.

CHANGING ACCEPTABILITY FACTORS

Some negative influences are amenable to change, as illustrated by acquired tastes, e.g. to the bitterness of coffee or beer. In young children, there is an innate, neonatal aversion to bitterness which is gradually overcome by exposure and social pressures. Much of this behaviour is caused by the absence of a standard, although in some cases, e.g. taboos, there may be a counter-standard which prevents acceptance.

A major influence on manipulable acceptability factors is of course the basis of the marketing industry. They are concerned with the generation of new 'internal standards', which supplement, compete with, and they hope, supplant existing standards.

CONTROL

I have now illustrated just a few of the many ways in which various factors can and do interact to reduce acceptability. How then can they be controlled?

The first point which must be made is that many of the people factors cannot be controlled, but may be influenced to find their own level in terms of food choice and individual preferences. These result in market segments, where there is demand for a range of broadly similar, but different products catering for a whole range of individual needs.

One people factor which can be influenced is that of expectation, particularly that generated by advertising. Products which do not fulfil these expectations, especially those which are implicit rather than explicit, will produce negative effects on acceptability.

The broad area which can be largely controlled is in product factors. Some of these are listed in Table 1. Most require detailed knowledge from which critical specifications can be designed. Their application will not totally eliminate the occasional occurrence of unforeseen, or previously unknown, factors which reduce acceptability, but they will certainly greatly reduce the chances of them first being found by the consumers. Furthermore the application of such designed systems sharpen the systems used by all suppliers of inputs, and, if a problem caused by an input does occur, it greatly speeds up rectification and greatly increases the likelihood of adequate recompense being obtained from the supplier.

Chapter 36

Food Acceptability, Past, Present and Future

ROLAND HARPER*

29, Harrow Court, Bath Road, Reading RG1 6JF, UK

ABSTRACT

Relevant questions about food acceptability may be raised at all or any times, but the specific issues and answers will vary with circumstances. In practice, even the boundaries between past, present and future are diffuse. The questions posed and the answers given will vary according to national, geographical, socio-economic and individual circumstances. Many different disciplines are involved and a high priority must be given to communication and mutual understanding by all concerned.

More specifically, the following topics are considered:
Some early literature—The impact of the agricultural depression of the late 1920s and early 1930s—Early examples of food grading—The UK National Mark Scheme—The effects of World War II—The end of food rationing The re-emergence of interest in the neglected senses—Food acceptability and choice become a matter of practical significance again—The importance of RELIABILITY and VALIDITY in indirect predictions of sensory quality and acceptability—Some early Symposia—Hints about the future.
Selected references.

* Formerly Reader in Food Science, University of Reading, UK.

485

'No point of view has absolute, permanent validity. Each has importance only for a given end'.

Mach, E. (1914)

'Has it ever occurred to you that nothing is ever done until everyone is convinced that it ought to be done, and has been convinced for so long that it is now time to do something else'.

Cornford, F. M. (1908)

INTRODUCTION

The two previous quotations are highly relevant and reflect the range of topics listed in the abstract, though not necessarily their proper sequence. Even that selection is far from complete, but it admirably illustrates the range of disciplines involved.

The multidisciplinary nature of food acceptability is now well recognised, but it emphasises the increasing need for us to promote understanding by using non-technical language. This is a challenge to us all, since the technical or scientific terms we would commonly use may be essential for precise understanding and personal progress within our own professional groups. Without such a compromise, practical achievements may be limited to the lowest common denominator. There was a time when one almost had to apologise for having multi-disciplinary interests. Although this stage has now passed, even working together with experts in subjects other than our own may take an appreciable time before understanding and collaboration is effective. Derek Land (Chapter 1) has already made this point in outlining some of our own collaboration between 1964 and 1967.

The precise boundaries between past, present and future, particularly in terms of detail will differ from one country to another. Most of the observations which follow refer to the United Kingdom, except where what has happened in one country (possibly at a different stage) has had a direct impact here. The earliest reference which has been selected (Anon., 1753) is taken from a section entitled 'Directions for marketting' [sic] in *The Lady's Companion,* intended to guide the lady of the house, in her 18th Century mansion, in the purchase of food. Altogether, some 24 sets of detailed descriptions of the desirable qualities that should be met are mentioned. These include meat, various dairy products, eggs and 10 varieties of fish.

DEVELOPMENTS IN FOOD GRADING

The preceding example might be regarded as early illustrations of the practices of food grading. These were eventually developed in the context of the needs of the export trade. One of the first examples of grading dairy products occurred in New Zealand as early as 1894 (see Thomson, 1925). The only examples to be discussed in detail here concern cheese grading. Grading has direct implications for acceptability, since it increases confidence in what is available and establishes distinct categories involving different prices. The introduction of grading systems in the United Kingdom was intended originally to help to bring to an end the agricultural depression of the late 1920s and early 1930s. The first example was a scheme for Cheshire cheese introduced about 1927. It was followed in 1933 by a National Mark Scheme. This was voluntary and covered a number of classes of food including eggs, fruits and vegetables (fresh and canned) as well as beef and a range of dairy products. A National Mark Calendar of Cooking was published by the Ministry of Agriculture, the first issue in 1934 and the second in 1936. The second issue provided a series of monthly recipes, for use throughout the year, based on the products having the National Mark. However, the National Mark Scheme was itself abandoned in 1940 when the Ministry of Food became the sole bulk purchaser of nationally produced food in the United Kingdom during World War II.

During this period a modified inspection scheme was introduced, consisting of three categories, consistent with war-time needs. Translating these into their practical consequences for cheese they were:

Grade I	fit for keeping
Grade II	fit for immediate use
Grade III	fit for processing

This scheme was also abandoned when bulk buying ceased to be necessary and a new voluntary scheme introduced for specified varieties of cheeses. This took place in 1955 in the form of the NACEPE scheme. It was based upon the judgements of experienced graders, who gave 'points' for Flavour and Aroma (45), Body and Texture (40), Finish (10) and Colour (5). Comprehensive instructions were given of what the various terms signified. The points were added together and rules provided to define the categories EXTRA SELECTED, SELECTED, GRADED and NO GRADE. These in turn, were accompanied by a distinctive mark or label which would determine expectations and price. This scheme continued until about 1975, when it was discontinued partly on account of the large number of cheeses then being manufactured and available for grading on a single visit from the grader. (For a fuller account of cheesemaking and cheesegrading, see Scott, 1981, 1986).

SOME NUTRITIONAL CONSIDERATIONS

Perhaps nutritional matters have received more emphasis in surveys and research in the United Kingdom than many of the broader aspects of food acceptability, especially its sensory bases. During World War II, in spite of all the restrictions on quality and variety for the population in general, the standard of nutrition was satisfactory. The National Food Survey was initiated in 1940 as an instrument of war-time planning. The real 'age of austerity' occurred during the period 1945–51 and its relevant aspects have been described by Susan Cooper (1964) in a chapter entitled 'Snoek piquante: The trials and tribulations of the British Housewife'. The post-war food situation was aggravated by the severe winter of 1946–47 and was affected by the need for food and economic assistance for most of Europe and many other parts of the world. During the war, apart from more general shortages, most tropical fruits previously available disappeared from the market and such novel products as snoek, whale meat, were added to what was available. Reference should also be made to dried egg, which, although its general appeal has been criticised, played an important part in war-time nutrition and was generally most acceptable. In the immediately post-war period, this imported product ceased to be available for a time and even the bread ration had to be cut.

THE NEGLECTED SENSES AND THEIR STUDY

The neglected senses consist primarily of taste and smell, and a complex of touch and kinaesthesis. The sense of touch involves a range of sensory qualities, but its meaning needs no special explanation. Kinaesthesis is a technical term referring to a range of sensations resulting from the response of sensitive receptors in the muscles and joints. This technical term was first used about the middle of the last century. It has direct bearing on the perception of texture and consistency, quite apart from the effects of associated visual or auditory stimulation. Apart from sight and hearing the other senses have received very limited attention, although since the end of World War II this unbalance has been partly rectified. Even so, what is perceived and its relationship to the physico-chemical stimuli and the pattern of activities in the nerves remains complex. Many of the explanatory principles lie within the area of Gestalt psychology, an essentially European viewpoint of the 1930s. The word itself, 'Gestalt' is the German word for 'a pattern'. The essential characteristics of many distinctive foods fall under this heading, the 'elements' being the separate sensations generated through the separate senses.

Progress in understanding the senses proceeds in many different directions, often by studying the response to simple systems such as varying concentrations or intensities of the chemical or physical stimuli. This approach is largely analytical rather than synthetic, or concerned with an overall pattern. The analytical approach is characteristic of the development of much of science in the past. Since the major studies in the late 19th century were based on physical stimuli, this sub-division of investigation came to be known as 'psychophysics'—a term still used today. Had the order of development been different the term 'psychochemistry' might equally well have arisen to classify studies involving chemical stimuli, like those of taste and smell. The main quantitative aspects concern the measurement of thresholds and the formulation of simple scales, usually numerical, capable of quantifying clearly distinguishable 'levels of sensation'. The thresholds provide a measure of what is *just detectable* in one context, or *just detectably different* in a situation involving comparisons. Traditionally, our knowledge of the senses began with intensive studies of a small number of individuals; later attention was turned to representative averages. Gradually more and more attention has been given to individual (and group) differences. These may be important in understanding differences in response to foods. One critical requirement here is that at least two responses, and possibly more, are required from the same individual, under the same circumstances, to establish the existence of these individual differences. (For a comprehensive review of the senses and their uses, see Harper, 1972.)

RELIABILITY AND VALIDITY OF ALTERNATIVE TESTS

The use of quantitative tests, especially as means of predicting some, more complex human response, is common, especially since direct information about human subjects and their responses is usually costly to obtain. In terms of food acceptability the subjects are usually consumers, unless the information is to be used simply as part of food research or product development, prior to testing the consumer's response. The concept of *reliability* applies to all forms of quantitative measurement which are subject to error. It is usually measured by a particular index of the extent to which two separate measurements of the same thing agree. A commonly used procedure is the statistical correlation between the two sets of measurements of the same thing, taken in pairs. In the ideal case the correlation will be high, approaching 1·00. In other cases, especially those involved in the measurement of complex properties which may be altered by the process of testing, the reliability will be very much less that 1·00. The concept of validity is even more complex, for it represents the extent to which a particular test correlates with another, qualitatively different from the first. In our case, the second test will involve some form of human response. If the instrumental test and the assessment are very similar in what they probe, the validity of the test as a predictor of the assessment can approach its reliability.

The correct conclusion can usually only be evaluated by examining both reliability and validity in an actual investigation. The results will also depend upon the circumstances, including the range of variation included in the test data or the assessments concerned. There are many instances in which instrumental tests have been surprisingly useful as an indication of some form of human response, for example the firmness of a Cheddar cheese and its hardness, as measured with a special instrument simulating the pressure of the thumb. Since the correspondence between the two operations in this example is very close, correlations approaching 1·00 may be obtained. In contrast, an attempt to develop an instrument to measure the crumbliness of a Cheshire cheese, using a simple fracture test, analogous to the methods used in physical studies of the properties of materials, not only provided a measure low in reliability but, in the research context, this also had low validity. It did not measure the right thing. This example from the distant past has been selected deliberately to illustrate the point. Modern instrumentation and recording can provide much more subtle and sensitive information, but whether or not an instrumental test, or a physical or a chemical measure, is a valid predictor of a human response must be demonstrated. There is an extensive psychological literature on reliability and validity. The importance of the subject was examined critically in the context of food and nutrition by Talmage & Rashter (1981).

LIKES, DISLIKES AND PREFERENCES

Likes, dislikes and preferences, including their consequences on purchasing behaviour and consumption, represent further critical aspects of food acceptability. The background literature on this important aspect of human behaviour is substantial. It ranges from theoretical speculation, with practical consequences, to the study of individual reactions to carefully specified stimuli, including different concentrations of substances responsible for taste and flavour. All possible sensory qualities come within the scope of experimental investigation, including sight and hearing, any one of which may be important in recognising and choosing a particular food or product. One of the earliest detailed texts on *Pleasantness and Unpleasantness,* including many aspects associated with food, is that of Beebe-Center (1932). At this point in time, he was establishing himself as one of many distinguished psychologists at Harvard. He used the term 'hedonic', or 'hedonic tone', to designate important aspects of the distinction between what is pleasant and what is unpleasant and its consequences. He includes one reference as early as 1871, to Fechner, one of the pioneers of 'psychophysics', but in this case dealing with hedonic matters.

Reverting to more contemporary contributions, the importance of more general types of survey of likes and dislikes, and preferences is obvious. Many of these go back to the late 1920s and early 1930s, particularly in the United States. Originally very limited attention was given to foods. One of the earliest studies of food preferences and how to change them was that of Hollinger & Roberts (1929). This dealt with reactions to evaporated milk; at that time a novel commercial product. With time, examples could be multiplied. The anthropologist Margaret Mead became actively involved in the wider subject as the invited chairman of the (US) Committee on Food Habits (1943). This was set up before America entered the war, with a view to identifying and providing understanding and assistance in solving the post-war needs for food in parts of the world devastated by the war. Later (Mead, 1964) the problems of food habits research in the 1960s were examined in a report of the National Academy of Sciences—National Research Council. (This includes over 300 references.)

Among the most extensive surveys, using the now familiar nine-point hedonic scale, are the whole series carried out by the Food Acceptance Branch of the US Quartermaster Food and Container Institute for the Armed Forces, in Chicago between 1943 and 1963. These surveys, and many other aspects of the subject, were continued after an interval of time at the Natick Laboratories. My own interests in the use of the nine-point hedonic scale were stimulated by these earlier studies. A survey of attitudes to certain vegetables, as included in a market research survey by Mass Observation Ltd is reported by Harper (1963).

THE FUTURE

The PRESENT has been amply covered by contributions presented earlier in this Symposium. Changes and developments in studies of food acceptability and its sensory background have been considerable and rapid in the last 20–25 years, with a small number of pioneers going back even longer than this. However, referring to the United Kingdom (where my experience of the subject—however intermittently—goes back to demobilisation in 1946) the acceleration in interest and activity has been particularly rapid during the last 7 years. The reasons for this are no doubt numerous. Computerised methods of data handling, following the development of micro-processors has played its part. I am well aware of this through prolonged analyses carried out between 1946 and 1950 in which all the calculations were done personally on a bulky electrical calculating machine. The whole process would now take a few hundred microseconds—but that is a skill that I have not acquired personally. The fact remains that data analyses, no matter how complicated or efficiently processed, are no better than the quality of the original data. Much care and skill in formulating the right questions will always be relevant in ensuring that quality.

At one stage, a critical requirement which had to be satisfied before undertaking applied investigations involving sensory analysis or food acceptability was that of management support. Can we assume now that this support is forthcoming? However, the nature of the task, particularly that of applied studies, is undergoing changes. Although sensory aspects will continue to be important in the product itself, even in identifying it, other variables have come into play more and more since the days of rationing. The progressively increasing number and variety of prepared meals introduce a new complexity into the subject. Advertising promotion including that on television also introduces new variables. So too, does the increasing interest in gourmet foods for a limited section of the population, including future participants in space flight! The scope is unlimited, but the fundamental questions are likely to remain much the same.

REFERENCES

Anon. (1753). *The Lady's Companion: Or an infallible guide to the fair sex.* 6th edn, Vol. 2. Printed for J. Hodges and R. Baldwin, London, pp. 405–10.

Beebe-Center, J. G. (1932). *Pleasantness and Unpleasantness.* D. van Nostrand, New York.

Cooper, S. (1964). Snoek Piquante. In *Age of Austerity, 1945–1951,* eds M. Sissons & P. French. Penguin Books, Harmondsworth, pp. 36–57.

Cornford, F. M. (1908). *Microcosmographia Academica: Being a Guide for the Young in Academic Politics,* Reprinted, 5th edition 1953. Bowes and Bowes, Cambridge.

Harper, R. (1963). Some attitudes to vegetables and their implications. *Nature, Lond.,* **200,** 14–18.

Harper, R. (1972). *Human Senses in Action.* Churchill Livingstone, London.

Harper, R. (1977). A short history of sensory analysis in the United Kingdom. In *Sensory Properties of Foods,* eds G. G. Birch, J. G. Brennan & K. J. Parker. Applied Science Publishers, London, pp. 167–86.

Hollinger, M. & Roberts, L. H. (1929). Overcoming food dislikes: A study with evaporated milk. *J. Home Econ.,* **21,** 923–32.

Mach, E. (1914). *The Analysis of Sensations,* 4th edn, English Trans. Open Court Pub. Co., Chicago, p. 37.

Mead, M. (1964) *Food Habits Research Problems of the 1960's.* National Academy of Sciences—National Research Council, Washington, D.C.

NACEPE (undated) *Scheme for grading of butter and cheese: Provisions relating to manufacture, packaging and grading.* The National Association of Creamery Proprietors and Wholesale Dairymen (Inc.). (Scheme operative from 1955 to 1975 approx.)

Scott, R. (1981, 1986, 2 Vols.) *Cheese Making Practices.* Elsevier Applied Science, London.

Talmage, H. & Rashter, S. P. (1981). Validity and reliability issues in measurement instrumentation. *J. Nutr. Educ.,* **13,** 17–19.

Thomson, G. S. (1925). *Grading Dairy Produce.* C. Lockwood, London.

Index